QUMRAN HEBREW

Society of Biblical Literature

Resources for Biblical Study

Marvin A. Sweeney,
Hebrew Bible/Old Testament Editor

Number 76

QUMRAN HEBREW

AN OVERVIEW OF ORTHOGRAPHY, PHONOLOGY, AND MORPHOLOGY

Eric D. Reymond

Society of Biblical Literature
Atlanta

Library of Congress Cataloging-in-Publication Data

Reymond, Eric D.
Qumran Hebrew : an overview of orthography, phonology, and morphology / Eric D. Reymond.
p. cm. — (Society of Biblical Literature resources for biblical study ; number 76)
Includes bibliographical references and index.
ISBN 978-1-58983-931-1 (paper binding : alk. paper) — ISBN 978-1-58983-932-8 (electronic format) — ISBN 978-1-58983-933-5 (hardcover binding : alk. paper)
1. Hebrew language—Orthography and spelling. 2. Hebrew language—Phonology. 3. Hebrew language—Morphology. 4. Dead Sea scrolls. I. Title.
PJ4583.R49 2013
492.4'82421—dc23 2013035944

Printed on acid-free, recycled paper conforming to
ANSI/NISO Z39.48-1992 (R1997) and ISO 9706:1994
standards for paper permanence.

To Robin, Lucy, and Oliver

אשרי איש שמח באחריתו

ἐμακάρισα … ἄνωθρωπος εὐφραινόμενος ἐπὶ τέκνοις

Happy is the person who rejoices in his children. (Sirach 25:7)

Contents

Acknowledgments ix

Abbreviations xi

A Note on Transliteration, Etymological Bases, and Manuscript Identification xv

Introduction 1

1. Corpus 5

2. General Remarks 13

3. Orthography 23
   3.1. Scribal Mistakes 23
   3.2. *Plene* Orthography 35
   3.3. *Aleph* as Internal *Mater* 43
   3.4. Etymological Short /u/ Marked with *Waw* 47
   3.5. Digraphs 51
   3.6. Two *Yodh*s for a Consonantal *Yodh* and Two *Waw*s for a Consonantal *Waw* 61

4. Phonetics and Phonology 65
   4.1. Phonemic Inventory 65
   4.2. Spirantization 70
   4.3. Weakening of Gutturals 71
   4.4. *Aleph* < *Yodh* and *Yodh* < *Aleph* 114
   4.5. *Aleph* < *Waw* and *Waw* < *Aleph* 131
   4.6. *Waw* < *Yodh* 134

4.7. Accent or Stress 135
4.8. Vowel Reduction 137
4.9. /å/ < /ā/ < Proto-Semitic /a/ 138
4.10. Diphthongs and Triphthongs 140

5. Morphology 151
5.1. Prothetic *Aleph* 151
5.2. Pronouns and Particles 153
5.3. Nouns 164
5.4. *Waw* Marking /u/ Class Vowel in Nouns Where MT Has No /u/ Class Vowel 170
5.5. **quṭl* Nouns 181
5.6. Verbs 188
5.7. *Qal* Imperfect+Suffix 209
5.8. *Qal* Imperative+Suffix 221
5.9. Adverbial *Heh* 223

Conclusions 225

Bibliography 235

Sources Index 257

Word Index 293

Author Index 307

Acknowledgments

Although often written by a single individual, a book also represents a collaborative effort between many people, some of whom (I am thinking of my young children) are just beginning to comprehend the challenges involved in sitting at a desk for hours at a time, typing, deleting, typing more. For the past three years, I have had the good fortune to teach Biblical Hebrew to students at Yale Divinity School, students whose goals range from ministry to doctoral study. I have enjoyed and continue to enjoy the intellectual stimulus afforded by the daily interactions with these students. The book, as explained below, has its original impetus in my attempt at teaching some of these students post-Biblical Hebrew. Also at YDS, I have enjoyed the warm collegiality of the entire faculty and have benefited from numerous conversations on matters relating to the Hebrew language and the scrolls with my Bible colleagues. I am also grateful to my friends outside YDS who have read and commented on different aspects of this work. In addition, the staff of the YDS library has been an essential aid in finding and obtaining books; I have made much work for them and am thankful for their earnest assistance.

My thanks go out, in particular, to James Nati, a doctoral candidate at Yale, who read through my manuscript several times, identifying errors of argument, logic, and spurious reference; Joel Baden, who has generously shared his store of articles and books on grammatical matters that I might have otherwise missed; Jeremy Hultin, who drew my attention to articles that have informed my study of the Hebrew guttural consonants.

I also want to thank the editors and staff at SBL for helping me work through the manuscript. I have appreciated their attention especially in the pointing of so many words and forms throughout the book. Furthermore, they have been patient at my slow pace and have spotted many errors that I missed.

Finally, my deepest and most profound appreciation belongs with my wife and children. They have been an ever-present source of encouragement and inspiration, not only in the patience they have shown at my frequent absences but also in the concerted efforts they have made to afford me more time to bring this project to its completion.

Abbreviations

AB	Anchor Bible
BASOR	*Bulletin of the American Schools of Oriental Research*
BDB	Brown, F., S. R. Driver, and C. A. Briggs. *Hebrew Lexicon of the Old Testament*. Oxford: Oxford University Press, 1906.
BHS[3]	*Biblia Hebraica Stuttgartensia*. Edited by K. Elliger and W. Rudolph. 3rd ed. Stuttgart: Deutsche Bibelgesellschaft, 1987.
Bib	*Biblica*
BSOAS	Bulletin of the School of Oriental and African Studies
BZAW	Beiheft zur Zeitschrift für die alttestamentliche Wissenschaft
CBQ	*Catholic Biblical Quarterly*
DCH	*The Dictionary of Classical Hebrew*. Edited by David J. A. Clines. 8 vols. Sheffield: Sheffield Phoenix, 1993–2007.
DJD	Discoveries in the Judaean Desert
DNWSI	Hoftijzer, J., and K. Jongeling. *Dictionary of North-West Semitic Inscriptions*. 2 vols. Leiden: Brill, 1995.
DSD	*Dead Sea Discoveries*
DSS	Dead Sea Scrolls
DSSEL	*Dead Sea Scrolls Electronic Library*. Edited by E. Tov. Provo, Utah: Brigham Young University, 2006.
DSSSE	*The Dead Sea Scrolls Study Edition*. Edited by Florentino García Martínez and Eibert J. C. Tigchelaar. 2 vols. Leiden: Brill; Grand Rapids: Eerdmans, 1997–1998.
GKC	*Gesenius' Hebrew Grammar*. Edited by E. Kautzsch. Translated by A. E. Cowley. 2nd ed. Oxford: Oxford University Press, 1910.

GQA	T. Muraoka. *A Grammar of Qumran Aramaic*. ANES Supp 38. Leuven: Peeters, 2011.
HALOT	Koehler, Ludwig, and Walter Baumgartner. *The Hebrew and Aramaic Lexicon of the Old Testament*. Translated by M. E. J. Richardson. 5 vols. Leiden: Brill, 1994–2000.
HAR	*Hebrew Annual Review*
HGhS	Bauer, Hans, and Pontus Leander. *Historische Grammatik der hebräischen Sprache des Alten Testamentes*. 2 vols. Halle: Niemeyer, 1922.
HSS	Harvard Semitic Studies
HUCA	*Hebrew Union College Annual*
IPA	International Phonetic Alphabet
JAOS	*Journal of the American Oriental Society*
JBL	*Journal of Biblical Literature*
JJS	*Journal of Jewish Studies*
JNES	*Journal of Near Eastern Studies*
JNSL	*Journal of Northwest Semitic Languages*
Joüon-Muraoka	Paul Joüon and T. Muraoka. *A Grammar of Biblical Hebrew*. 2 vols. Rome: Pontifical Biblical Institute, 1991.
JSJ	*Journal for the Study of Judaism*
JSPSup	Journal for the Study of the Pseudepigrapha Supplement Series
LBH	Late Biblical Hebrew
LSAWS	Linguistic Studies in Ancient West Semitic
LSJ	Liddell, H. G., R. Scott, and H. S. Jones. *A Greek-English Lexicon*. Rev. ed. Oxford: Clarendon, 1968.
MT	Masoretic Text, specifically the Leningrad Codex, as represented in *BHS*[3]
RB	*Revue Biblique*
RevQ	*Revue de Qumran*
RH	Rabbinic Hebrew
RH1	Rabbinic Hebrew of the Mishnah, Tosefta, etc.
RH2	Rabbinic Hebrew of the Talmuds, etc.
SBH	Standard Biblical Hebrew
SBL	Studies in Biblical Literature
Sem	*Semitica*
STDJ	Studies on the Texts of the Desert of Judah

TAD	Porten, Bezalel, and Ada Yardeni. *Textbook of Aramaic Documents from Ancient Egypt*. Jerusalem: Hebrew University, 1986–1999.
ThWQ	*Theologisches Wörterbuch zu den Qumrantexten*. Edited by H.-J. Fabry and U. Dahmen. Stuttgart: Kohlhammer, 2011–.
VT	*Vetus Testamentum*
VTSup	Vetus Testamentum Supplement Series
ZAH	*Zeitschrift für die Althebraistik*
ZAW	*Zeitschrift für die alttestamentliche Wissenschaft*

3ms	third masculine singular
3fs	third feminine singular
2ms	second masculine singular
2fs	second feminine singular
1cs	first common singular

3mp	third masculine plural
3fp	third feminine plural
2mp	second masculine plural
2fp	second feminine plural
1cp	first common plural

A Note on Transliteration, Etymological Bases, and Manuscript Identification

In the following pages I will generally transliterate the letters of the scrolls into the Hebrew/Aramaic block script (e.g., נביא "prophet"). The hypothetical pronunciation of these words is rendered in Roman letters in italics, as is the pronunciation of words presumed by the Tiberian vocalization tradition. The indication of pronunciation differs in several ways from the standard transliteration of Biblical Hebrew. For example, due to the quiescence of *aleph* at syllable end, I will not represent *aleph* in a word such as נָבִיא "prophet"; this word is represented as *nābī*. Also, due to the fact that the etymological lateral fricative phoneme (often transliterated as ś and represented in the Tiberian text as שׂ) had merged with the sound of etymological *samekh*, I will render etymological /ś/ as *s*. Thus מַשָּׂא "utterance" is represented as *massā*. When referring to individual phonemes, I indicate the respective symbol between slashes (e.g., /o/ and /s/).

Etymological forms and bases are, as is customary, preceded by an asterisk and are put in italics (e.g., **qul*, **quṭl*). These forms may reflect different stages in the development of a given word or form; for example, the form preceded by an asterisk may reflect a stage of the language from circa 2000 B.C.E. or 1000 B.C.E. or 600 B.C.E. The precise dating is not crucial to the arguments presented below, so the hypothetical datings for specific forms are not given. The corresponding vocalizations of these forms in the Tiberian tradition are generally clear from the context and are sometimes explained by parenthetical comments. Nevertheless, to make clearer my presentation in the pages that follow, I wish to note three of the more common references to etymological forms and their realizations in Tiberian Hebrew. More complete explanations of such bases and their realizations in Tiberian Hebrew can be found in Joüon-Muraoka and *HGhS*.

III-*yodh* roots are realized in the *qal* perfect as in the examples of בָּנָה "to build," חָזָה "to see," עָשָׂה "to do." The *heh* in these forms is simply a *mater* for the preceding vowel; the etymological *yodh* has disappeared. In the same way, the *heh* at the end of שָׂדֶה "field" is a *mater*; the root is III-*yodh*. Words from III-*waw* roots are comparatively less common; where these roots are attested and distinct morphologically from III-*yodh* roots, the *waw* consonant has often shifted to /ū/, as in בֹּהוּ "emptiness"; תֹּהוּ "formlessness."

"Geminate" nouns or adjectives are those that etymologically had three root consonants the second and third of which were identical (**qall*, **qill*, **qull*). The paradigm words for these in many Biblical Hebrew grammars are, respectively, עַם "people," חֵץ "arrow," חֹק "statute." These generally show the gemination of the second and third root consonants and the emergence of the etymological vowel when any suffix is added to the lexical form: עַמִּי "my people," חִצִּי "my arrow," חֻקִּי "my statute." Feminine geminate nouns (**qallat*, **qillat*, **qullat*) generally show the same features: אַמָּה "cubit," פִּנָּה "corner," חֻקָּה "statute." Both masculine and feminine plural forms also show gemination and the emergence of the etymological vowel (e.g., עַמִּים, חִצִּים, חֻקִּים, אַמּוֹת, פִּנּוֹת, חֻקּוֹת).

"Segholate" nouns or adjectives are those that etymologically had three distinct root consonants and only one vowel in their singular form (**qaṭl*, **qiṭl*, **quṭl*). The paradigm words for these in many Biblical Hebrew grammars are, respectively, מֶלֶךְ "king," סֵפֶר "book," קֹדֶשׁ "holiness." Sometimes, despite their name, these nouns do not attest a *seghol*, as in בַּעַל "master." When suffixes are added to the lexical form, the etymological vowel (or /o/ in the case of **quṭl* nouns) reemerges: מַלְכִּי "my king," סִפְרִי "my book," קָדְשִׁי "my holiness." Feminine segholate nouns (**qaṭlat*, **qiṭlat*, **quṭlat*) generally show the etymological vowel (or /o/ in the case of **quṭlat* nouns) in their first syllable: מַלְכָּה "queen," גִּבְעָה "hill," חָרְבָּה "desolation." Most segholate nouns from II-*waw/yodh* roots have different vowel patterns in Tiberian Hebrew (**qaṭl*—מָוֶת "death" and בַּיִת "house"), as do III-*yodh* roots (**qaṭl* or **qiṭl*—פֶּתִי "simple," **quṭl*—חֳלִי "sickness"). Segholate nouns/adjectives usually have two vowels in their plural absolute bases, both masculine (**qaṭalīm*—מְלָכִים and פְּתָיִים, **qiṭalīm*—סְפָרִים, **quṭalīm*—חֳדָשִׁים and חֳלָיִים) and feminine (**qaṭalōt*—מְלָכוֹת, **qiṭalōt*—גְּבָעוֹת, **quṭalōt*—חֳרָבוֹת).

Specific passages from the nonbiblical DSS are identified in the standard fashion, with the cave number (1Q, 2Q, 3Q, etc.) followed by the manuscript number (1, 2, 3, etc.), followed by fragment number and/or column number, then line number. The exceptions are texts commonly indicated with an abbreviation, such as 1QS, $1QH^a$, and 1QpHab. In order to make the references to passages less cumbersome and the pages below less cluttered, I have not used the alternative designations for manuscripts such as 4QD^{a} or 4QDamascus Document^{a} but have restricted myself to the numerical titles, 4Q266. This means that individuals unfamiliar with the numeral designations may sometimes not recognize the text that is being referred to. For the sake of clarity, I present below the most commonly cited texts that might occasion confusion. The list is not comprehensive but points to the most commonly cited texts (e.g., Jubilees is also attested in other scrolls, but 4Q216–228 are the ones most frequently cited).

Jubilees and texts related to Jubilees: 4Q216–228
Damascus Document: 4Q266–273
4QMMT: 4Q394–399
Songs of the Sabbath Sacrifice: 4Q400–407
Instruction of the Maven (4QInstruction): 4Q415–418
Temple Scroll: 11Q19–20

In order to highlight the biblical DSS and to indicate the texts to which they correspond, the simple numerical title as well as their nonnumerical title are given together (e.g., 4Q88 [4QPs^{f}]). Specific passages in these texts are indicated by reference to scriptural passage; this succinctly provides reference to a location in a scroll (since almost all editions of DSS biblical texts indicate scripture verses along with column and line numbers), as well as to a location in the Bible.

Introduction

The following pages began as a handout on the grammar of the Dead Sea Scrolls (= DSS). While preparing to teach a class on Post-Biblical Hebrew, I found that the descriptions of the Hebrew of the DSS in Qimron's *Hebrew of the Dead Sea Scrolls* (= *HDSS*) and Kutscher's *The Language and Linguistic Background of the Complete Isaiah Scroll* did not suit the needs of students.[1] Although Kutscher's treatment is thorough, careful, and nuanced, it treats a text that exhibits numerous idiosyncrasies not shared by other texts; as such it cannot easily be used to introduce students to the language of the DSS as a whole. Qimron's book, on the other hand, does assess the (non-biblical) scrolls as a whole; nevertheless, it too has some shortcomings. What I find problematic about Qimron's *HDSS* are the following: (1) The book presumes that many linguistic idiosyncrasies witnessed in the scrolls reflect a single vernacular dialect.[2] (2) The book proposes dramatic

1. Elisha Qimron, *The Hebrew of the Dead Sea Scrolls* (Atlanta: Scholars Press, 1986); this work is in some ways an expansion of, while also being a summary of Qimron's dissertation: *Grammar of the Hebrew Language of the Scrolls of the Judean Desert* (Hebrew; Jerusalem: Hebrew University, 1976). E. Y. Kutscher, *The Language and Linguistic Background of the Complete Isaiah Scroll* (STDJ 6; Leiden: Brill, 1974), originally published in Hebrew as *Ha-Lashon ve-ha-Reqa' ha-Leshoni shel Megillat Yesha'yahu ha-Selema mi-Megillot Yam ha-Melaḥ* (Jerusalem: Magnes, 1959).

2. Qimron refers throughout the book to the language of the DSS as though the texts (with few exceptions) reflect a common dialect. That the idiosyncrasies of the scrolls' language are, in part, attributable to a spoken idiom is suggested by Qimron in the final paragraph of his concluding chapter, where he refers to (among other things) the pronouns הואה and היאה and *yqwṭl* + suffix verb forms: "These unique features show that DSS Hebrew is not merely a mixture of BH, MH and Aramaic, but also draws on a distinct spoken dialect" (*HDSS*, 117–18). More recently Qimron writes: "It is my contention that the grammar of the DSS reflects the Hebrew of the period spoken in Jerusalem or its vicinity" (Elisha Qimron, "The Nature of the DSS Hebrew and Its Relation to BH and MH," in *Diggers at the Well: Proceedings of a Third International Symposium on the Hebrew of the Dead Sea Scrolls and Ben Sira* [ed. T.

differences between the language of the DSS and the Hebrew as evidenced in the MT, though the evidence for these differences is sometimes tenuous (based on a single example) and often ambiguous.[3] (3) The book does not sufficiently discuss the ambiguities inherent in many of its examples and sometimes does not entertain other possible explanations. (4) The book is sometimes imprecise in its description; for example, it refers to the "weakening" of gutturals without a more precise description of where and when specific phonemes "weaken." (5) The book, although it has recently been reprinted in 2008, contains no references to recently published texts or secondary literature (including Qimron's own numerous publications).

Of course, the study of the Hebrew of the DSS is not limited to these two books. There are a plethora of studies and sketches on the languages of the scrolls. Nevertheless, these other sketches often give only an overview of the main features of the languages and do not present the background necessary for a student to understand the respective phenomena in Hebrew. For these reasons, I felt compelled to create my own descriptions and explanations, commenting especially where I disagreed with Qimron's *HDSS*.

In reference to the above-listed criticisms, I should explain briefly my approach. (1) I have taken a broader view of the linguistic phenomena and assume that the linguistic peculiarities found in the scrolls are potentially due to a wide spectrum of causes, only one of which is the underlying spoken idiom of the sectarian writers and scribes. Moreover, I am not concerned with isolating the vernacular idiom of the writers; it

---

Muraoka and John F. Elwolde; STDJ 36; Leiden: Brill, 2000], 232). For criticisms of Qimron's assumptions, see Avi Hurvitz, "Was QH a 'Spoken' Language? On Some Recent Views and Positions: Comments," in *Diggers at the Well*, 110–114. See, also, Florentino García Martínez, "Review of E. Qimron, *Hebrew of the Dead Sea Scrolls*," *JSJ* 19 (1988): 115–17.

3. For example, Qimron notes that the single spelling of "Sheol" with a prothetic *aleph* (אשאול), combined with the fact that the word is always spelled with a *waw* after the *aleph* is evidence that the word was always pronounced "*eš'ol*"; he also calls attention to the tendency in Samaritan Hebrew for the prothetic *aleph* to appear in the oral tradition but not in the written tradition (*HDSS*, 39). For more on this, see §5.1 below, "Prothetic *Aleph*." In a similar way, he claims "For the contraction $\bar{o}y \rightarrow \bar{o}$, I was able to find only one instance הוה (= הוי)" from 1QIsa[a] at Isa 1:24 (*HDSS*, 35). He also suggests that the word מבואי in 4Q405 23 i, 9 is further evidence of this (or a similar) shift, though a far more pedestrian explanation is also available (see §4.10, "Diphthongs and Triphthongs").

is more important, it seems to me, for students to understand the reading and writing register(s) of those copying the scrolls and composing their texts. (2) I attempt, wherever relevant, to point to examples of phenomena from the MT that are similar to the phenomena found in the DSS. It is assumed that the MT is made up of texts that reflect numerous dialects and registers of Hebrew; I assume a similar diversity in the DSS. Nevertheless, I also assume that the writers of the DSS were (at least at times) attempting to write in a register that approximated the writing/reading register reflected in the MT.[4] (3) I try to explore the ambiguities inherent in the examples cited by Qimron, Kutscher, and others, in order to illustrate different possible explanations and to question some underlying assumptions. (4) I attempt to be as precise as possible in identifying the parameters of certain phonological shifts; for example, each guttural consonant is described separately and its specific "weakness" explored. (5) I provide further examples of the same phenomena described by Qimron and others from my own readings as well as from consulting Accordance software and the *Dead Sea Scrolls Concordance*; and I incorporate more recent insights from linguistics and philology of the DSS into my descriptions.[5] Despite my best efforts at analyzing the following phenomena, I recognize that my observations do not represent the final word on these matters and in many ways remain preliminary.

It should be added that, although I disagree with Qimron's book in many ways, it is also an incredibly rich source of information. Further, I do not entirely disagree with it. Many of the observations in it seem well-founded. The general approach of assessing the vernacular dialect(s) from

---

4. One indication that at least some writers of the DSS were familiar with the form of the MT as we know it is suggested by the close correspondence in spelling between some biblical scrolls and the MT: e.g., ותהינה (4Q70 [4QJer[a]] at Jer 18:21) for MT וְתִהְיֶנָה; יכבדנני "he will honor me" (4Q85 [4QPs[c]] at Ps 50:23) for MT יְכַבְּדָנְנִי vs. *יְכַבְּדַנִי, which is what we would expect based on forms like תְּבָרֲכַנִי "you will bless me" (Gen 27:19); also the defective orthography in ירגמהו "they will stone him" (4Q26a [4QLev[e]] at Lev 20:2) for MT יִרְגְּמֻהוּ; בנו "his children" (4Q35 [4QDeut[h]] at Deut 33:9) for MT בָּנָו; כדרכו "according to his ways" (4Q70 [4QJer[a]] at Jer 17:10) for MT כִּדְרָכָו.

5. Martin G. Abegg, "Qumran Text and Tagging," in Accordance 9.5 (Altamonte Springs, Florida: OakTree Software, 1999–2009); Martin G. Abegg et al., "Grammatical Tagging of Dead Sea Scrolls Biblical Corpus," in Accordance 9.5 (Altamonte Springs, Florida: OakTree Software, 2009); Martin G. Abegg et al., *The Dead Sea Scrolls Concordance* (3 vols.; Leiden: Brill, 2003–).

the written sources is also profitable and well worth considering. It seems likely that many aspects of the language he outlines were, in fact, features of a dialect spoken by some writers and readers of the texts.

Two other very helpful resources that students should consult are the synopses of the Hebrew language offered by Martin Abegg in *The Dead Sea Scrolls after Fifty Years* and in *Qumran Cave 1, II: The Isaiah Scrolls, Part 2: Introductions, Commentary, and Textual Variants*.[6] Although for the first synopsis he could not draw on all the texts now available, and does not draw on the biblical scrolls, his statistics are still useful in getting a general idea for the frequency of certain forms and the basic outline of the language. The second synopsis offers observations not only on the Isaiah scrolls, but on all the scrolls in general. A third synopsis, that of Antoon Schoors, catalogs many forms and vocabulary, but only treats the texts considered part of the Wisdom tradition.[7]

I have chosen to describe around twenty-five topics. These, in my estimation, are not addressed sufficiently in Abegg's synopses (or in other synopses) and have not been treated adequately in Qimron's *HDSS*. Some items that are covered sufficiently in Qimron's *Grammar* and in his *HDSS* have not been addressed again here.[8] This means, of course, that the following pages are not intended as a comprehensive grammar of DSS Hebrew.

As might already be obvious, the orthography, phonology, and morphology of the DSS are often intimately linked. Thus, I have tried not to repeat myself by addressing the same topic from the perspective of orthography, phonology, morphology, but have, instead, addressed topics where they are most relevant in the description of the language. Discussing the same features in three different sections would be needlessly repetitive and would obscure the explanations offered.

---

6. Martin G. Abegg, "The Hebrew of the Dead Sea Scrolls," in *The Dead Sea Scrolls after Fifty Years: A Comprehensive Assessment* (ed. Peter W. Flint and James C. VanderKam; 2 vols.; Leiden: Brill, 1998–1999), 1:325–58 and idem, "Linguistic Profile of the Isaiah Scrolls," in *Qumran Cave 1, II: The Isaiah Scrolls, Part 2: Introductions, Commentary, and Textual Variants* (ed. Eugene Ulrich and Peter W. Flint; DJD 32; Oxford: Clarendon, 2010), 25–41.

7. Antoon Schoors, "The Language of the Qumran Sapiential Works," in *The Wisdom Texts from Qumran* (ed. C. Hempel et al.; BETL 159; Leuven: Peeters, 2002), 61–95.

8. For example, I have not provided a list of words found in the DSS according to their bases, as Qimron has done.

1
Corpus

The corpus of the Dead Sea scrolls preserves texts mostly in Hebrew, though some are in Aramaic and Greek. The texts are often associated with the Essenes, though in its broadest sense, the Dead Sea scrolls—that is, the texts found around the Dead Sea—are from a number of groups, including the followers of Bar Kokhba, the Masada Zealots, as well as other groups. Nevertheless, the term Dead Sea Scrolls typically refers to those texts discovered in caves near or adjacent to Wadi Qumran and an ancient group of structures called collectively Qumran. (Some believe the structures were home to the writers of the scrolls, others think it might have been a garrison, or served some other purpose.) Those texts discovered around Wadi Qumran are often subdivided into those that seem to be from the "Essenes" or the "Qumran Community" and those that are not; in other words, those that imply the theological ideas of the "sect" (like dualism) as well as their vocabulary, and those that do not reflect these specific notions or vocabulary. Often it is difficult to determine whether a partially preserved text should fit into one or the other category since such a text could have contained expressions of "Essene theology" in the portions that have been lost. Another common way of dividing the texts is between biblical manuscripts and nonbiblical manuscripts (in other words, manuscripts that contain texts that would later become part of the Bible and those that did not). Here, too, categorizing texts is not always as unambiguous as one might initially think. First, the very concept is anachronistic since what the ancients felt to be scripture and what moderns think of as scripture are not coterminous. Second, some scrolls are made up of only portions of what we identify as scripture; the other material does not belong to any modern canon. For the sake of simplicity, "biblical" in relation to the scrolls will refer to those nonpesher, nonreworked scrolls that contain texts that are currently part of the Jewish canon, though portions of them may have no parallel in the contemporary Tanakh. The phylactery texts, although of a different character than the biblical texts, will here be labeled "biblical" based on the similar labeling in the *Dead Sea Scrolls Concordance* and in Accordance software. "Nonbiblical" will refer to everything else. In all, much of the nonbiblical material seems to bear "sectarian" ideas. These texts also contain certain peculiarities in spelling that may (or may not) reflect peculiarities of pronunciation and morphology. In the analyses below, both biblical and nonbiblical Dead Sea Scrolls are considered; the abbreviation DSS will refer to all texts found in the caves around Wadi Qumran.

As just described, there are various ways of dividing up the DSS. When discussing especially the linguistic features of the scrolls, most scholars follow a model something like that presented by Morag in which the texts that exhibit distinctive linguistic features (such as 1QS and 1QM with the long form of the 3ms independent pronoun הואה) are set in one group and characterized as reflecting General Qumran Hebrew (= GQH); 4QMMT is set in another group and its language is characterized as closer to Mishnaic Hebrew than most other texts (perhaps reflecting the spoken idiom of the sect, as Qimron suggests); the Copper Scroll (3Q15) is set in a third group as its language bears the strongest affinities to Mishnaic Hebrew.[1] Despite this rather common-sense approach, which we will also partially follow, there is a problem with it: a significant minority of the texts do not actually exhibit the most distinctive linguistic traits. These texts might be understood as reflecting only a more conservative orthography, their orthography not representing how the words were really pronounced. For example, one might assume that the 3ms independent pronoun was always pronounced as *hūʾā*, not only when it is spelled in a distinctive manner with final *heh*, הואה, but also when it is spelled in a more conventional way, as הוא.

In addition, we will attempt to determine whether the linguistic traits investigated are peculiar to the texts that exhibit a special scribal practice, as described by Tov.[2] Since we will concentrate on attempting to under-

1. Shelomo Morag, "Qumran Hebrew: Some Typological Observations," *VT* 38 (1988): 149; Elisha Qimron, "The Language," in *Qumran Cave 4.V: Miqsat Maʿase ha-Torah* (ed. Elisha Qimron and John Strugnell; DJD 10; Oxford: Clarendon, 1994), 108.

2. See Emanuel Tov, *Scribal Practices and Approaches Reflected in the Texts Found in the Judean Desert* (STDJ 54; Leiden: Brill, 2004). By contrast, some view the existence of a scribal practice associated specifically with the sectarians as dubious (see,

stand the peculiar linguistic traits that distinguish the scrolls from texts that would become part of the Hebrew Bible, it might be expected that we will find these traits concentrated in texts that exhibit the scribal practice associated with the authors of the sectarian scrolls. If not, then the linguistic traits may be part of a widespread linguistic phenomenon.

The abbreviation DSS-SP9 will refer to those texts identified by Tov in the ninth appendix of his book *Scribal Practices and Approaches Reflected in the Texts Found in the Judean Desert*; most of these texts evidence one or more of the following morphological traits whose explicit indication through orthography Tov believes is part of "Qumran scribal practice." In other words, the scribal practice of those who, he believes, lived at Qumran and wrote many of the sectarian scrolls. These traits are: long 3ms, 3fs, and 2mp independent pronouns: הואה, היאה, אתמה, respectively; long 3m/fp and 2m/fp pronominal suffixes on nouns and prepositions: מה- and כמה- (for nouns), המה- and כמה- (for prepositions); long 2mp suffix conjugation forms in *qal* and other stems: for example, קטלתמה; forms of the *qal* prefix conjugation with object suffix that attest a *waw* between the first and second root consonants, that is, *yqwṭl* + suffix (יקוטלני); long forms of adverbs like מואדה; the writing of the word כי as כיא.[3] The presence of one or more of these traits does not exclude the occurrence of the more regular forms known from the MT.[4] The texts included in this category are listed below.[5]

Biblical Texts: 1Q4 (1QDeut^{a}); 1QIsa^{a}; 2Q3 (2QExod^{b}); 2Q7 (2QNum^{b}); 2Q12 (2QDeut^{c}); 2Q13 (2QJer); 4Q13 (4Q[Gen–]Exod^{b}); 4Q27 (4QNum^{b}); 4Q37 (4QDeut^{j}); 4Q38 (4Q Deut^{k1}); 4Q38a (4QDeut^{k2});

---

e.g., P. Alexander and G. Vermes, *Qumran Cave 4.XIX: 4QSerekh Ha-Yaḥad and Two Related Texts* [DJD 26; Oxford: Clarendon, 1998], 8).

3. Tov, *Scribal Practices*, 337–38.

4. It might be mentioned that some traits that are sometimes said to be characteristic of the DSS are not listed in the above list, including so-called "pausal" verbal forms occurring where one would not expect a pausal form to occur, the spellings of זאת as זות, of כה as כוה, of משה as מושה, of לא as לוא, of כל as כול, and the long form of the 2ms suffix conjugation קטלתה. These traits occur in the texts listed above, though they also occur in other texts too.

5. The list is based on "Appendix 9" in Tov's *Scribal Practices*, 339–43. The biblical texts 2Q3, 11Q7 and the nonbiblical 1QH^{b}, 1Q36, 4Q433a, 4Q435, 4Q440, 4Q505 do not exhibit the above-listed traits that occupy columns 1–3, 5–6, 8–10, 16 in Tov's appendix but are nonetheless considered by Tov to exhibit Qumran Scribal Practice due to the presence of other diagnostic features.

4Q40 (4QDeut^{m}); 4Q53 (4QSam^{c}); 4Q57 (4QIsa^{c}); 4Q78 (4QXII^{c}); 4Q80 (4QXII^{e}); 4Q82 (4QXII^{g}); 4Q96 (4QPs^{o}); 4Q109 (4QQoh^{a}); 4Q111 (4QLam); 11Q5 (11QPs^{a}); 11Q6 (11QPs^{b}); 11Q7 (11QPs^{c}); 11Q8 (11QPs^{d}). And Phylactery Texts: 4Q128 (4QPhyl A); 4Q129 (4QPhyl B); 4Q134–136 (4QPhyl G–I); 4Q137–138 (4QPhyl J–K); 4Q139–141 (4QPhyl L–N); 4Q142 (4QPhyl O); 4Q143 (4QPhyl P); 4Q144 (4QPhyl Q).[6]

Nonbiblical Texts: 1Q14 (1QpMic); 1QpHab; 1Q22 (1QDibreMoshe); 1Q26 (1QInstr); 1Q27 (1QMyst); 1QS (= 1Q28); 1QSa (= 1Q28a); 1QSb (= 1Q28b); 1QM (= 1Q33); 1QH^{a} (= 1Q34); 1QH^{b} (= 1Q35); 1Q36 (1QHymns); 4Q158 (4QRP^{a}); 4Q159 (4QOrdin); 4Q160 (4QVisSam); 4Q161 (4QpIsa^{a}); 4Q163 (4Qpap pIsa^{c}); 4Q165 (4QpIsa^{e}); 4Q166 (4QpHos^{a}); 4Q171 (4QpPs^{a}); 4Q174 (4QFlor); 4Q175 (4QTest); 4Q176 (4QTanḥ); 4Q177 (Catena A); 4Q180 (AgesCreat A); 4Q181 (AgesCreat B); 4Q184 (4QWiles); 4Q186 (4QHorosc); 4Q200 (4QTobit^{e}); 4Q215 (4QTNaph); 4Q215a (4QTimes); 4Q219 (4QJub^{d}); 4Q221 (4QJub^{f}); 4Q222 (4QJub^{g}); 4Q223–224 (4QpapJub^{h}); 4Q225 (4QpsJub^{a}); 4Q227 (4QpsJub^{c}); 4Q251 (Halakha A); 4Q254 (ComGen C); 4Q256 (4QS^{b}); 4Q257 (4QpapS^{c}); 4Q259 (4QS^{e}); 4Q260 (4QS^{f}); 4Q265 (Misc Rules); 4Q266 (4QDamascus Document^{a}); 4Q267 (4QDamascus Document^{b}); 4Q268 (4QDamascus Document^{c}); 4Q269 (4QDamascus Document^{d}); 4Q271 (4QDamascus Document^{f}); 4Q273 (4QpapDamascus Document^{h}); 4Q274 (4QToh A); 4Q277 (4QToh B); 4Q280 (4QCurses); 4Q285 (4QSefer ha-Milḥamah); 4Q286 (4QBer^{a}); 4Q287 (4QBer^{b}); 4Q289 (4QBer^{d}); 4Q292 (4QWork Cont. Prayers B); 4Q299 (4QMyst^{a}); 4Q301 (4QMyst^{c}?); 4Q303 (4QMeditation on Creation A); 4Q364 (4QRP^{b}); 4Q365 (4QRP^{c}); 4Q365a (4QT^{a}?); 4Q369 (4QPrayer Enosh); 4Q375 (4QapocrMos^{a}); 4Q377 (4QapocPent B); 4Q382 (4Qpap paraKgs); 4Q384 (4Qpap apocr Jer B?); 4Q393 (4QComConf); 4Q394 (4QMMT^{a}); 4Q396 (4QMMT^{c}); 4Q397 (4QMMT^{d}); 4Q398 (4QpapMMT^{e}); 4Q400 (4QShirShabb^{a}); 4Q401 (4QShirShabb^{b}); 4Q402 (4QShirShabb^{c}); 4Q403 (4QShirShabb^{d}); 4Q405 (4QShirShabb^{f}); 4Q410 (4QVison Int); 4Q414 (RiPur A); 4Q415 (4QInstr^{a}); 4Q416 (4QInstr^{b}); 4Q417 (4QInstr^{c}); 4Q418 (4QInstr^{d}); 4Q418a (4QInstr^{e}); 4Q419 (4QInstr-like Composition A); 4Q420 (4QWays^{a}); 4Q421 (4QWays^{b}); 4Q422 (4Q

6. The listings of 4Q134–136 (4QPhyl G–I); 4Q137–138 (4QPhyl J–K); 4Q139–141 (4QPhyl L–N) follow the DJD numbers in Emanuel Tov, *Revised Lists of the Texts from the Judaean Desert* (Leiden: Brill, 2010), 32, not those of Tov, *Scribal Practices*, 340, which lists them as 4Q137 (4QPhyl G–I); 4Q138 (4QPhyl J–K); 4Q139 (4QPhyl L–N).

4QParaGen–Exod); 4Q423 (4QInstr^{g}); 4Q426 (4QSapiential Hymn Work A); 4Q427 (4QH^{a}); 4Q428 (4QH^{b}); 4Q429 (4QH^{c}); 4Q432 (4QpapH^{f}); 4Q433a (4QpapHodayot-like text); 4Q435 (4QBarki Nafshi^{b}); 4Q436 (4QBarki Nafshi^{c}); 4Q437 (4QBarki Nafshi^{d}); 4Q438 (4QBarki Nafshi^{e}); 4Q440 (4QHodayot-like text C); 4Q443 (4QPersonal Prayer); 4Q460 (4QNarrartive Work); 4Q462 (4QNarrative C); 4Q464 (4QExposition on the Patriarchs); 4Q471 (4QWar Scroll-like text B); 4Q473 (4QTwo Ways); 4Q474 (4QText Concerning Rachel and Joseph); 4Q477 (4QRebukes Reported by Overseer); 4Q491 (4QM^{a}); 4Q496 (4QpapM^{f}); 4Q501 (4QapocrLam B); 4Q502 (4QpapRitMar); 4Q503 (4QpapPrQuot); 4Q504 (4QDibHam^{a}); 4Q505 (4QpapDibHam^{b}?); 4Q506 (4QpapDibHam^{c}); 4Q509 (4QpapPrFêtes^{c}); 4Q511 (4QShir^{b}); 4Q512 (4QpapRitPur B); 4Q513 (4QOrd^{b}); 4Q522 (4QProph Josh); 4Q524 (4QT^{b}); 4Q525 (4QBeatitudes); 5Q13 (5QRule); 6Q18 (6QpapHymn); 11Q11 (11QapocPs); 11Q12 (11QJub + XQText A); 11Q13 (11QMelch); 11Q14 (11QSefer ha-Milḥamah); 11Q16 (11QHymns^{b}); 11Q19 (11QT^{a}); 11Q20 (11QT^{b}); 11Q27 (11QUnidentified C); Mas 1k (MasShirShabb); Mas 1n (MasUnidentified Qumran-Type Frag.).

Additional texts, labeled in what follows as DSS-SP1c, are listed in “Appendix 1c” in Tov’s *Scribal Practices.*[7] These texts contain few if any of the above-listed traits associated with the “Qumran Scribal Practice,” though they are sometimes associated with the sectarians and/or are alternative versions of texts in DSS-SP9: 1Q16 (1QpPs); 1Q29 (1QTongues Fire); 1Q30 (1QLit Text? A); 1Q31 (1QLit Text? B); 3Q4 (3QpIsa); 3Q5 (3QJub); 3Q6 (3QHymn); 3Q9 (3QSectarian Text); 4Q162 (4QpIsa^{b}); 4Q164 (4QIsa^{d}); 4Q167 (4QpHos^{b}); 4Q168 (4QpMic?); 4Q169 (4QpNah); 4Q172 (4QpUnidentified); 4Q182 (4QCatena B); 4Q185 (4QSap Work); 4Q255 (4QpapS^{a}); 4Q261 (4QS^{g}); 4Q262 (4QS^{h}); 4Q263 (4QS^{i}); 4Q264 (4QS^{j}); 4Q270 (4QDamascus Document^{e}); 4Q272 (4QDamascus Document^{g}); 4Q290 (4QBer^{e}); 4Q304 (4QMeditation on Creation B); 4Q305 (4QMeditation on Creation C); 4Q306 (4QMen of People who Err); 4Q317 (4QCryptA Lunisolar Cal); 4Q320 (4QCal Doc/Mish A); 4Q321 (4QCal Doc/Mish B); 4Q322 (4QMish A); 4Q323 (4QMish B); 4Q324 (4QMish C); 4Q324a (4QMish D); 4Q324b (4QpapCal Doc A?); 4Q324c (4QMish E); 4Q325 (4QCal Doc/Mish D); 4Q328 (4QMish F); 4Q329 (4QMish G); 4Q329a (4QMish H); 4Q330 (4QMish I); 4Q337 (4QCal Doc E?); 4Q371

7. Tov, *Scribal Practices*, 285–87.

(4QNarr and Poet Comp); 4Q390 (4QapcroJer C[e]); 4Q392 (4QWorks); 4Q399 (4QMMT[f]); 4Q404 (4QShirShabb[e]); 4Q407 (4QShirShabb[h]); 4Q409 (4QLiturgical Work A); 4Q412 (4QSap-Didactic Work A); 4Q418c (4QInstr[f]); 4Q424 (4QInsruction-like Comp B); 4Q425 (4QSap-Didactic Work B); 4Q430 (4QH[d]); 4Q431 (4QH[e]); 4Q434 (4QBarki Nafshi[a]); 4Q439 (4QLament); 4Q442 (4QIndiv Thanksgiving B); 4Q444 (4QIncant); 4Q457b (4QEschat H); 4Q461 (4QNarr B); 4Q463 (4QNarr D); 4Q464a (4QNarr E); 4Q471a (4QPol Text); 4Q471b (4QSelf-Glorifying Hymn); 4Q475 (4QRenewEarth); 4Q487 (4QpapSapB?); 4Q492 (4QM[b]); 4Q493 (4QM[c]); 4Q494 (4QM[d]); 4Q495 (4QM[e]); 4Q498 (4QpapSap/Hymn); 4Q499 (4QpapHymn/Prayer); 4Q500 (4QpapBenediction); 4Q507 (4QPr Fêtes[b]); 4Q508 (4QpapPr Fêtes[b]); 4Q510 (4QShir[a]); 5Q10 (5QapocrMal [5QpMal?]); 5Q11 (5QS); 5Q12 (5QDamascus Document); 6Q9 (6Qpap apocrSamKgs); 6Q12 (6Qapocr Proph); 11Q15 (11QHymns[a]); 11Q17 (11QShirShabb); 11Q29 (11QFrg Rrelated to S).

Tov does not include the Copper Scroll (3Q15) in the lists from which the above categories are drawn. It is best to think of this text as in its own category. However, as we will see, many idiosyncrasies found in the DSS-SP9 are also found in 3Q15. For ease of reference, where summaries are offered of how many times a given feature occurs in the DSS, the instances from 3Q15 will be included with those from DSS-SP9 texts, though the number of occurrences in 3Q15 will also be singled out.

The rest of the scrolls do not evidence the "Qumran scribal practice"; they are labeled hereafter as DSS-NSP. These are also sometimes related to the texts of DSS-SP9, like 4Q300 (4QMyst[b]).

Several things will be immediately apparent upon glancing at these groupings. First, DSS-SP9 includes texts that many would not label as "sectarian." As Joosten remarks, however, those nonbiblical scrolls whose attribution to the sect is disputed "such as Jubilees, 4QInstruction, or the Temple Scroll—evince a linguistic profile that is rather close to that of the sectarian scrolls."[8] Second, the DSS-SP9 list groups 4QMMT together with the other sectarian writings (1QS, 1QM, and so on) and nonsectarian ones (Jubilees, and so on), despite the fact that 4QMMT exhibits palpable differences from all the other texts. The distinctive character of 4QMMT will be addressed when relevant and necessary; examples drawn from this

8. Jan Joosten, "Hebrew, Aramaic, and Greek in the Qumran Scrolls," in *The Oxford Handbook of the Dead Sea Scrolls* (ed. Timothy H. Lim and John J. Collins; Oxford: Oxford University, 2010), 355.

work will always be identified explicitly. And, even excluding 4QMMT, it should be recognized that there is not necessarily consistency within the DSS-SP9 texts. For example, 1QIsa^{a} exhibits characteristics that are not shared with many of the other scrolls. Again, where necessary, specific traits of this scroll will be mentioned.

It will become apparent fairly quickly that, in addition to the texts mentioned immediately above like 1QIsa^{a}, 3Q15, and 4QMMT, certain texts exhibit concentrations of particular scribal/linguistic traits. For example, 4Q175, although relatively short, exhibits at least six misspellings related to *aleph*, reflecting the letter's quiescence. Another relatively short text, 4Q491c, exhibits at least twenty examples of the digraph יא- to mark word-final /ī/. A relatively short biblical text, 4Q107 (4QCant^{b}), exhibits numerous features attributable to Aramaic influence. Such concentrations will be remarked on in the appropriate places.

In addition to the texts listed above, the following notes will draw on other scrolls from surrounding sites (e.g., Masada), where such texts contain examples of phenomena also attested in the DSS.

2
General Remarks

The language of the scrolls bears traits that connect it, on the one hand, with Standard Biblical Hebrew (SBH) as found in the Masoretic Text (MT), with Late Biblical Hebrew (LBH) as also found in the MT, with Mishnaic Hebrew (MH), even in some instances with Samaritan Hebrew, and the Hebrew of the Babylonian tradition.[1] And yet, the Hebrew of the scrolls also represents features that have no parallel in other traditions. Although these basic ideas are affirmed by almost everyone, there is still much that remains unsettled. Scholars differ, for example, in how they describe the language of the scrolls, whether they emphasize the aspects that reflect a naturally developed and developing spoken dialect or emphasize the aspects that reflect a literary heritage with earlier Hebrew. Kutscher, Morag, and Qimron, for instance, describe the language of the scrolls especially in light of what it reveals about the natural speech of their writers.[2] A slightly different approach, but one not entirely incompatible with this, is to describe the language of the DSS as a literary idiom based in LBH, as Blau does.[3] On the other hand, Schniedewind, Rendsburg, and

1. See, e.g., Kutscher, *Isaiah*, passim; Kutscher, *A History of the Hebrew Language* (ed. R. Kutscher; Jerusalem: Magnes, 1982), 93. See also Joosten, "Hebrew, Aramaic, Greek," 357: "In diachronic perspective, Qumran Hebrew represents a phase that neatly fits between Biblical Hebrew on the one hand and Mishnaic Hebrew on the other." For a summary of the proposed characteristics shared between DSS Hebrew and Babylonian and Samaritan traditions, see Qimron, *Grammar*, 28–30.

2. Kutscher, *Isaiah*, 3; Shelomo Morag, "Qumran Hebrew: Some Typological Observations," 148–64; Qimron, "Observations on the History of Early Hebrew (1000BCE—200CE)," in *Dead Sea Scrolls: Forty Years of Research*, 349–61; and Qimron "The Nature of DSS Hebrew and Its Relation to BH and MH," 232–44. See also Rudolf Meyer, "Das Problem der Dialektmischung in den hebräischen Texten von Chirbet Qumran," *VT* 7 (1957): 139–48.

3. See Blau, "A Conservative View of the Language of the Dead Sea Scrolls," in

Charlesworth emphasize (following the lead of Rabin) that the language of the scrolls should be thought of as an artificial and archaizing language, generated in opposition to the language spoken by the writers' religious rivals; they refer to the Hebrew of the scrolls as an "anti-language."[4] In all these cases, however, the assumption seems to be that some aspects of the pronunciation and morphology in the scrolls are unique among other Hebrew traditions.

Some scholars see in the idiosyncrasies of the scrolls' orthography two basic dialects, one spoken and one literary, a situation sometimes described as diglossia.[5] Recently, however, Naudé has argued that such a twofold view is too simplistic, pointing to the variety of factors that contribute to linguistic variation ("time, society, and the individual") and the fact that even individuals "have multiple grammars, for example, to

---

Diggers at the Well, 22. Morag states: "It is not the spoken language of Qumran which emerges in the literature of the Scrolls…the texts themselves, as we have them, are literary" (Morag, *Studies on Biblical Hebrew*, 114–15, as quoted by Hurvitz, "Was QH a 'Spoken' Language," 114; see also Shelomo Morag, "Language and Style in *Miqṣat Maʿaśe ha-Torah*: Did *Moreh ha-Ṣedeq* Write This Document?" [Hebrew], *Tarbiz* 65 [1996]: 209–23). It might be mentioned that the dichotomy between spoken and literary languages can, itself, become complicated when considering whether the sectarians would have *spoken* to each other in a *literary* dialect—for this idea one may consult William M. Schniedewind, "Linguistic Ideology in Qumran Hebrew," in *Diggers at the Well*, 246. For a concise summary of the different ways that the scrolls have been approached, see Jacobus A. Naudé, "The Transitions of Biblical Hebrew in the Perspective of Language Change and Diffusion," in *Biblical Hebrew: Studies in Chronology and Typology* (ed. Ian Young; London: T&T Clark, 2003), 195–96. He notes that Kutscher viewed the language of the scrolls as heavily influenced by Aramaic (*Isaiah*, 8–9); he also notes that Joseph A. Fitzmyer saw it as an imitation of Biblical Hebrew (*A Wandering Aramean: Collected Aramaic Essays* [Missoula, Mont.: Scholars, 1979], 44–45)

4. Chaim Rabin, "Historical Background of Qumran Hebrew," in *Aspects of the Dead Sea Scrolls* (ed. Chaim Rabin and Yigael Yadin; ScrHier 4; Jerusalem: Magnes, 1958), 144–61; William M. Schniedewind, "Qumran Hebrew as an Anti-language," *JBL* 118 (1999): 235–52; idem, "Linguistic Ideology in Qumran Hebrew," 245–55; Gary A. Rendsburg, "Qumran Hebrew (with a Trial Cut [1QS])," in *Dead Sea Scrolls at Sixty: Scholarly Contributions of New York University Faculty and Alumni* (ed. Lawrence H. Schiffman and Shani Tzoref; STDJ 89; Leiden: Brill, 2010), 217–46; James H. Charlesworth, *The Pesharim and Qumran History: Chaos or Consensus* (Grand Rapids: Eerdmans, 2002), 20.

5. See Naudé, "Transitions of Biblical Hebrew," 196, who cites J. C. Kesterson, "Tense Usage and Verbal Syntax in Selected Qumran Documents" (Ph.D. diss.; Washington, D.C.: Catholic University of America, 1984), 172.

generate different linguistic styles or registers, idiolects, local dialects and standard speech."[6]

More basic than questions of dialect, subdialect, and idiolect is the question concerning what the marks on the scrolls indicate. Do they accurately reflect their writers' pronunciation or are the words written one way and intended to be pronounced in an entirely different way? For example, where the 3ms independent pronoun is written הוא in a text that predominantly spells the word with a final *heh mater*, הואה, are we to assume that the shorter form was pronounced like the longer (that is, *hūʾā*)?[7] A similar problem pertains to even short words like כי. This word is often spelled כיא in the DSS-SP9. Does the spelling with *aleph* reflect a different pronunciation (as Ben-Ḥayyim argues) or is it simply an orthographic peculiarity that does not reflect a special pronunciation (as Kutscher and others presume)?[8] This problem pertains to almost every phonological and morphological question. It is compounded by the fact that to an even greater degree than in the MT spelling varies from text to text, even from line to line.

Another good example of these problems is the question of the pronunciation of the gutturals, especially *ʿayin*. Does the occasional spelling of words without an internal *ʿayin*, which ended a historically closed syllable (e.g., וישה *wayyase* in 1QIsa[a] at Isa 5:4 [reflecting etymological *ויעשה **wayyaʿăse*] for what MT preserves as וַיַּעַשׂ) suggest that the voiced pharyngeal fricative (/ʿ/) was never pronounced in this environment and that when we find יעשה in this text (e.g., in both 1QIsa[a] and in the MT at Isa 56:2) the same pronunciation is implied, *wayyase*? Or, should we assume that the phoneme was only occasionally dropped from the end or middle

6. Naudé, "Transitions of Biblical Hebrew," 213, 207. He notes that such an explanation as diglossia "excludes the possibility of more than two grammars and complicates the explanation of inter-relation between innovation and diffusion in QH" (ibid., 207). See also J. J. Ohala, "Sound Change," in *Encyclopedia of Language and Linguistics* (ed. Keith Brown; 14 vols.; 2nd ed.; Oxford: Elsevier, 2006), 11:522 and Douglas Biber, *Dimensions of Register Variation: A Cross-Linguistic Comparison* (Cambridge: Cambridge University, 1995), 1–2.

7. E. L. Sukenik, e.g., argued that the full and defective spellings reflected the same pronunciation so that, in relation to 1Q8 (1QIsa[b]), הוא reflects the same pronunciation implied in the form הואה (*The Dead Sea Scrolls of the Hebrew University* [Jerusalem: Magnes, 1955], 31).

8. Ze'ev Ben-Ḥayyim, *Studies in the Traditions of the Hebrew Language* (Madrid: Instituo Arias Montana, 1954), 82–85; Kutscher, *Isaiah*, 178–79.

of a word, due, for example, to a hurried pronunciation and that the spelling ויֹשה reflects *wayyase* and the spelling יעשה reflects *ya'ăse*?[9] Or, was the phoneme always dropped in the spoken vernacular of some scribes and writers but normally retained in the writing/reading register of the same scribes (or of some subset of the Qumran scribes)?

Yet another axis of debate concerns the question of Aramaic's influence; some linguistic traits may derive from the writers' or scribes' knowledge of Aramaic or they could be the result of common linguistic developments shared between Aramaic and Hebrew. For example, does the 3mp possessive suffix הום- derive from Aramaic הם- or from the etymological form of the suffixed pronoun, common to both Aramaic and Hebrew, *-humu*?[10]

One also wonders to what degree a given morpheme, word, or syntax is due to the influence of Biblical Hebrew.[11] Since the writers of the DSS revered earlier scriptural writings so much, it is not surprising to find they imitate its words and phrases, even when not directly alluding to a specific passage. A similar influence of Biblical Hebrew is felt on Mishnaic Hebrew.

The variables and uncertainties do not stop here. Blau mentions many of the factors that contribute to making DSS Hebrew and its description so opaque.

---

9. A similar elision of the glottal stop due to rushed pronunciation is also commented on by scholars. See G. Bergsträsser, *Hebräische Grammatik* (2 vols.; Leipzig: Vogel 1918 [vol. 1 phonology and morphology]; Leipzig: Hinrichs, 1926–1929 [vol. 2 verb]), 1:92, as well as the discussion below in the section titled "Weakening of Gutturals" (§4.3).

10. For the forms of the pronominal suffix with this apparent Aramaic form, see Qimron, *HDSS*, 39. The example of this suffix is found in עליהום (4Q176 20, 3). Although the morphology of one language is less likely to be influenced by that of another, the Hebrew of the DSS does evidence some influence from Aramaic in this regard, e.g., the 3ms suffix on plural nouns והי-. For cross-linguistic evidence, see Bloomfield, *Language*, 406–7, cited by Qimron, "History of Early Hebrew," 353 n. 10, and, for a summary of Aramaic influences on morphology, Joosten, "Hebrew, Aramaic, Greek," 359, and the section below "Conclusions" (§6).

11. Joosten writes: "It is undoubtedly correct to view Qumran Hebrew as a continuation of Biblical Hebrew, but it is not true that the two languages are identical. To an important extent, the similarity between the two is artificial. It is due to the conscious effort of the sectarian authors to imitate the style of the older corpus" ("Hebrew, Aramaic, Greek," 359).

> [T]he simplest explanation of all the linguistic facts known to us remains that Qumran Hebrew reflects basically the latest stage of artificial (literary) biblical language, exposed, to some extent, to the influence of the spoken vernaculars, viz. Aramaic and some sort of Middle Hebrew, which later crystallized as Mishnaic Hebrew, but also representing various traditions, genres, fashions, scribal schools, and personal inclinations, which introduced changes into the language of the Dead Sea Scrolls, just as they modified Middle Arabic by using, e.g., an artificial literary feature like accusatival *faʿalilan*.[12]

This, to my mind, concisely touches on many of the variables that affect languages in general, and in particular the language of the DSS.[13]

In fact, most scholars addressing the language, whether they view it as artificial or natural, as reflecting a spoken idiom or a literary one, try to nuance their position in a way that recognizes the many dimensions of language use. For example, Kutscher, when summarizing the dialect of the scribes of 1QIsa[a], writes: "the component linguistic factors normally differ from locality to locality, from class to class and from individual to individual."[14] Morag, while investigating the grammar in view of finding traits of a specific spoken dialect, recognizes the possible existence within the language of "boundaries of Hebrew dialects and speech-types" which were most likely due to separate geography, but which "may, of course, have marked social or sectarian groupings as well."[15] He further recog-

12. Blau, "Conservative View," 22. Blau emphasizes that just because a language is not spoken does not mean it does not change. A similar thesis is argued by John C. Poirier ("The Linguistic Situation in Jewish Palestine in Late Antiquity," *Journal of Greco-Roman Christianity and Judaism* 4 [2007]: 86), who cites Yohanan Breuer's list of sixteen linguistic features that distinguish Amoraic Hebrew from Tannaitic (see Breuer, "On the Hebrew Dialect of the *ʾĀmōrāʾīm* in the Babylonian Talmud," in *Studies in Mishnaic Hebrew* [ed. Moshe Bar-Asher; ScrHier 37; Jerusalem: Magnes, 1998], 149).

13. Other scholars also remark on different variables; see Moshe H. Goshen-Gottstein, "Linguistic Structure and Tradition in the Qumran Documents," in *Aspects of the Dead Sea Scrolls*, 101–37 and Joosten, "Hebrew, Aramaic, Greek," 354. Moshe Bar-Asher, in referring to orthography, writes: "To sum up: the orthography of every ancient text is unique, due to the personal habits of scribes, the varieties of practices taught in scribal schools, and features which accrue through copying" ("On the Language of '*The Vision of Gabriel*,'" *RevQ* 23 [2008]: 498).

14. Kutscher, *Isaiah*, 61–62.

15. Morag, "Qumran Hebrew," 150.

nizes that the scrolls are literary in nature, writing: "It would be superfluous to say that the texts do not precisely represent the language spoken by the scribes who were bound, in their orthography, grammar and lexicon, to a certain literary tradition."[16] Qimron, in describing the language of 4QMMT, writes: "In dealing with Hebrew as a living language, we must recall that we are dealing with sporadic representations of the language, from different places and times, as transmitted to us in different traditions of pronunciation."[17] Joosten, referring to the linguistic diversity revealed among the scrolls, writes: "Partly, such diversity may reflect the stylistic predilections of individual authors, and partly the orthographic idiosyncrasies of scribes."[18] He also remarks "[T]he different registers of the language interpenetrated one another in several ways."[19] Given these many variables, it is helpful to outline some of the assumptions I hold in what follows.

From a theoretical standpoint, I assume that the DSS reflect a combination of idioms and registers, each text containing an idiosyncratic blending of literary idioms (stylized not *in accord with* LBH, but reflecting in part a development of the literary tradition found in LBH, as well as other genre-specific expectations); influence of the writers' or scribes' spoken dialects; Aramaicizing tendencies (perhaps due to the individual writers'/scribes' spoken dialects); archaizing tendencies; a desire to mimic SBH orthography, vocabulary, and style; a desire to deviate from the same SBH categories; and different scribal traditions of orthography. Some of these phenomena must have changed over time and some variations within and between texts may be due to the different periods in which the texts were written or copied. In theoretical terms we do not need to limit ourselves to the dichotomy of spoken versus written expression; rather, we can recognize that the way in which individuals listened was different from the way

16. Ibid. In relation to Biblical Hebrew, Morag has also called attention to the lack of homogeneity in a single individual's language ("Historical Validity," 307–8). Another scholar, Steve Weitzman, exploring why the sectarians used Hebrew, recognizes genre as a possible determining factor in language ("Why Did the Qumran Community Write in Hebrew," *JAOS* 119 [1999]: 37). Weitzman also suggests comparing the status of Aramaic and its use within specific genres (ibid., n. 17).

17. Qimron, "Language," 106. See also Elisha Qimron, "The Language and Linguistic Background of the Qumran Compositions," in *The Qumran Scrolls and Their World* (ed. Menahem Kister; Jersualem: Yad Ben-Zvi, 2009), 2:553.

18. Joosten, "Hebrew, Aramaic, Greek," 354.

19. Ibid., 353.

in which they spoke or wrote. I imagine the way they perceived writing could admit of various different registers, depending on what they were hearing (scripture, liturgy, instruction), where they were hearing it (in an assembly, in a smaller group, from another individual), and why they were hearing it (for worship, contemplation, the purpose of copying out a text). Such variables might have resulted in different pronunciations and different perceptions of pronunciation. Perhaps due to this, slightly different morphologies emerged. For example, it is conceivable that slower pronunciation (e.g., in an austere ritual context) would have affected the form of certain verbs, creating what are sometimes called "pausal forms" (e.g., the *qal* imperfect: יִקְטֹלוּ).[20] Such pronunciations could have been perceived as "more correct" by an audience of scribes who remembered these and later used these forms in their writing.

In general, I attempt to describe the salient features of the writing/reading register(s) of the scrolls. When possible, I try to identify features of the language that are more likely to be characteristic of a vernacular spoken idiom and/or features that might be part of a particular writer's or scribe's subdialect or idiolect. In essence, I assume that the pronunciation of the writing/reading register will more closely match the spelling of words (e.g., אביהו = *ʾābīhū* "his father"), while the spoken idiom may not (e.g., אביהו = *ʾābīyū*).[21] I often (but not always) interpret varying orthography as a reflection of different phonetic realizations in the writing/reading register, where the literary dialect(s), vernaculars, and idiolects are mixing and coming together (in other words, אביהו = *ʾābīhū* and אביו = *ʾābīyū*). That the Masoretes could preserve various and divergent morphologies in

20. Kutscher makes a similar argument to explain different pronunciations of the word נְאֻם in 1QIsa[a] as *nūm* versus *nəūm*; he writes: "It is probable that in the Jewish pronunciation, since they took pains to insure correct liturgical reading of the Bible, this difference was manifest in quick speech opposed to slower speech. When speaking quickly they would say *nu:m*...but in slow reading were careful to pronounce the *shwa*" (*Isaiah*, 499). Similarly, Blau writes in relation to II-*aleph* nouns in Biblical Hebrew (*Phonology and Morphology of Biblical Hebrew: An Introduction* [LSAWS 2; Winona Lake, Ind.: Eisenbrauns, 2010], 55). See also Bergsträsser, *Hebräische Grammatik*, 1:92.

21. Compare Muraoka's comments on the writing of the suffixed pronouns in DSS Aramaic: "[W]e are assuming that the orthography in Q[umran] A[ramaic], as far as the representation of word-final vowels is concerned, reflects a certain phonetic reality. In other words, the spelling -C implies that the consonant was not followed by a full vowel, whereas -Cה or -Cא indicates a full vowel following the -C-" (*GQA*, 43).

their literary tradition (e.g., פִּיהוּ and פִּיו "his mouth" in Exod 4:15) suggests that previous scribes probably could too—something suggested in the orthography of the scrolls themselves (e.g., פיהו and פיו in 1QIsa[a] at Isa 34:16 and 29:13, respectively; אביהו and אביו in 4Q416 2 iii, 16 and 2 iv, 1, respectively).[22] Based on what linguists have observed concerning the variety of ways language is used by single individuals, such variations would not be surprising.

Furthermore, since at the time of the DSS the biblical texts held numerous variations in orthography, phonology, and morphology, I assume that the writers and scribes connected with the DSS were at least partially familiar with these variations. In choosing forms to write, the scribes might have drawn from their knowledge of a standard orthography (reflected in the MT) or might have chosen a rare form.[23] I assume that the scribes felt a degree of freedom in this process due, in part, to the literary tradition that included orthographic variation.

This approach to the Hebrew of the scrolls leads to the impression that some linguistic phenomena were the outcome of natural processes that presumably reflect one or more spoken idioms, while others are secondary or artificial. One senses that some linguistic developments as well as many orthographic practices helped to preserve the etymological contours of words, while other linguistic developments tended to obscure them. In general, these conflicting trends suggest a context where scribes and writers were speaking and composing in Hebrew as well as Aramaic; a context where scribes and writers were inventing new genres and literary idioms while engaging intensively with former genres and idioms; a

22. The fact that אביו may be part of an allusion to Gen 2:24 is tangential to this point (see John Strugnell and Daniel J. Harrington, *Qumran Cave 4.XXIV: Sapiential Texts, Part 2, 4QInstruction (Mûsār Lĕ Mēvīn), 4Q415 ff.* [DJD 34; Oxford: Clarendon, 1999], 126). In commenting on the different dialects reflected in the DSS, Meyer writes: "Man wird also mit Fug und Recht sagen dürfen, dass in Qumran ein ausgesprochenes Dialektgemisch vorliegt, wobei nicht übersehen werden darf, dieses Gemisch auch im masoretischen Konsonantentext noch nachklingt und zugleich von hier aus bestätigt wird" ("Problem der Dialektmischung," 144).

23. Compare James Barr's ideas on spelling variation in the Hebrew Bible (*The Variable Spellings of the Hebrew Bible: The Schweich Lectures of the British Academy, 1986* [Oxford: Oxford University Press, 1989], 194), as well as the critique of this view offered by Tov, "Review of James Barr, *The Variable Spellings of the Hebrew Bible*," in *Hebrew Bible, Greek Bible, and Qumran: Collected Essays* [TSAJ 121; Tübingen: Mohr Siebeck, 2008], 15–16, originally published in *JSS* 35 (1990): 303–16.

context in which the boundaries between spoken and written registers, vernacular and literary idioms, local and distant dialects were constantly mixing and interacting.

3
Orthography

3.1. Scribal Mistakes

Everything discussed below depends on understanding the orthographic representation of words as intentional in some sense. By intentional I mean that the scribes intended to write a particular word according to a specific orthographic style (for example, יעשה "[who] will do" in 1QIsa[a] at Isa 56:2), or, when diverging from this style (even unintentionally), they wrote letters with the assumption that they indicated specific sounds (for example, ויशה *wayyase* "it made" in 1QIsa[a] at Isa 5:4 for what is in the MT וַיַּעַשׂ).[1] Despite this, there are many cases where scribes have simply made gaffs or errors in their spelling—errors that are only graphic and that do not (presumably) reflect the pronunciation of a word or phoneme.[2] These are attested in all text groups (DSS-SP9, DSS-SP1c, and DSS-NSP).

The purpose of the following lists is not to present a complete index of mistakes, but to emphasize the frequency and nature of mistakes. Recognition of these matters can help inform our interpretation of certain word forms where the spelling may or may not reflect something significant about the phonology and/or morphology of the language. For example, the metathesis of *mater*s between nonguttural letters suggests that a similar metathesis between guttural letters may not necessarily reflect the elision of the guttural phonemes; they may simply be visual mistakes. Similarly, the fact that various sibilant consonants are confused, and that various velar/uvular consonants are confused suggests

1. On the transliteration of *śin* with *s*, see above, "A Note on Transliteration, Etymological Bases, and Manuscript Identification," and §4.1, "Phonemic Inventory." Conceivably, the word in 1QIsa[a] was realized as *wayyāse* due to compensatory lengthening.

2. See Tov, *Textual Criticism of the Hebrew Bible* (3rd ed.; Minneapolis: Fortress, 2012), 221–39; idem, *Scribal Practices*, 221–30.

that where pharyngeal consonants (that is, *ʿayin* and *ḥeth*) are confused this may be due to the common place of their articulation, not to the loss of all distinction between them.

The well-known mistakes of dittography, haplography, and metathesis are attested throughout the scrolls. Examples of dittography include repetitions of individual letters, sequences of letters, words, and phrases: מאלוהוהים (4Q400 2, 3) corrected to מאלוהים "from God";[3] בבבץ(1QH[a] XV, 5) for *בבוץ "in the mire";[4] נכונה העצת היחד (1QS VIII, 5) corrected to נכונה עצת היחד "the council of the community is founded"; ולצצפון (11Q19 XXXVIII, 14) for *ולצפון "and to the north"; זהב טהוב (4Q365a 2 ii, 7) for *זהב טהור "pure gold";[5] שפתי שפתי "lips of, lips of" (1QH[a] XV, 14–15);[6] העם העם (11Q19 LVIII, 5) corrected to העם "the people"; כיא הואה כיא הואה (4Q417 2 i, 5) corrected to just כיא הואה "because he." Cases of two *yodh*s or *waw*s written together to represent one (or two juxtaposed) consonantal *yodh* or *waw* are possible examples of dittography, though at least some of these probably represent an alternative orthographic practice (see §3.6, "Two *Yodh*s for a Consonantal *Yodh* and Two *Waw*s for a Consonantal *Waw*").

Examples of haplography (including those subsequently corrected) include: אל[והי]ם מברכים "[they] bless God" (4Q405 19, 7); ואלה המשפטים "and these (are) the judgments" (1QS VI, 24); אנש שחת "man of the pit" (1QS X, 19); בליעל על "Belial, over" (1QH[a] XI, 30); וידבר אל אל "God said to" (1QpHab VII, 1); בכלו אתו (4Q381 33a–b + 35, 8) for *בכלוא אתו "when (he) restrained him"; לאנוש עם עם רוח "to Enosh with a people of spirit" (4Q417 1 i, 16); טוה רוחות (4Q405 20 ii - 22, 11) for *טוהר רוחות

---

3. See Carol Newsom, "Shirot ʿOlat HaShabbat," in *Qumran Cave 4.VI: Poetical and Liturgical Texts, Part 1* (ed. E. Eshel et al; DJD 11; Oxford: Clarendon, 1998), 188.

4. See Hartmut Stegemann, Eileen Schuller, and Carol Newsom, *Qumran Cave 1.III: 1QHodayot[a] with Incorporation of 4QHodayot[a-f] and 1QHodayot[b]* (DJD 40; Oxford: Clarendon, 2009), 201.

5. See E. Tov and S. White "Reworked Pentateuch," in *Qumran Cave 4.VIII: Parabiblical Texts, Part 1* (ed. H. Attridge et al.; DJD 13; Oxford: Clarendon, 1994), 328. Note that although Accordance and *DSSEL* parse טהוב as from טוב, the word טוב preceded by זהב only occurs once in the scrolls (זהב טוב 11Q19 XXXVI, 11), while there are nine examples of what I interpret (following *DSSSE*) as the intended phrase, זהב טהור, in the nonbiblical DSS (e.g., 1QM V, 10 and 12).

6. See Stegemann, Schuller, Newsom, DJD 40:203, for other, less likely interpretations.

"…purely, spirits." The simple dropping of a letter is found too: [מ]ל^{ש}מע "[better] to hear" (4Q109 [4QQoh^{a}] at Qoh 7:5) for MT שְׁמֹעַ.[7]

Examples of metathesis include: אכשיל (1QH^{a} XVIII, 8) for *אשכיל "I will consider";[8] החיד (1QS VI, 3) for *היחד "the community," שרי (1QSa I, 16) corrected to ר^{ש}י "heads of";[9] דכרכיו (4Q425 1 + 3, 6) for *דרכיו "his paths"; [י]אצאו "they will go forth" (4Q491 1–3, 9 = MT יֵצְאוּ);[10] כער (4Q27 [4QNum^{b}] at Num 24:9) for MT כָּרַע "he bowed down"; ולרקרוב (4Q58 [4QIsa^{d}] at Isa 57:19) for MT וְלַקָּרוֹב "to the one near"; מבדבר (4Q62 [4QIsa^{h}] at Isa 42:11) corrected to מדבר, for MT מִדְבָּר "wilderness"; בשקתי (4Q107 [4QCant^{b}] at Song 3:1) for MT בִּקַּשְׁתִּי "I sought"; and perhaps also הנא יאנה (11Q19 LIII, 20) for what would be in the MT הָנֵא יְנִיאֶהָ "he will surely forbid her."[11]

A special variety of dittography and metathesis involves *maters*: וביחרי (1QS VIII, 6) corrected to ובח׳רי "and the chosen ones of"; קיראי (1QSa II, 2) for *קריאי "those called of";[12] עיצה (1QpHab X, 1) for *עציה

7. Some examples are ambiguous: אביה (11Q19 LXVI, 13) for *אביהו; it is conceivable (albeit less likely I think) that אביה reflects the Aramaic pronoun (see Yigael Yadin, *The Temple Scroll* [3 vols.; Jerusalem: Israel Exploration Society, 1983], 2:299).

8. See Stegemann, Schuller, Newsom, DJD 40:237. They note that a scribe noted the *kaph* as an error with marks above and below the letter, but he did not add further corrections.

9. See James H. Charlesworth and Loren Stuckenbruck, "Rule of the Congregation," in *The Dead Sea Scrolls, Hebrew, Aramaic, and Greek Texts with English Translations, Volume 1: Rule of the Community and Related Documents* (ed. James H. Charlesworth; Princeton Theological Seminary Dead Sea Scrolls Project 1; Tübingen: Mohr Siebeck, 1994), 112 n. 12.

10. This is a case of uncorrected metathesis or a case of *aleph* as a *mater* for /ē/ (cf. עואר 1QIsa^{a} at Isa 42:19 [twice] and 43:8 and see §3.3, "*Aleph* as Internal *Mater*").

11. The 11Q19 text alludes to or paraphrases Num 30:6, which has just the perfect form הֵנִיא. Understanding the verb in 11Q19 to mean "he will lament" or "he will offend" (i.e., from one of the verbs associated with אנה) does not make good sense, especially with what looks to be the preceding *hiphil* infinitive absolute of נוא.

12. Note that this is the reading of J. T. Milik "Textes Non Bibliques," in *Qumran Cave 1* (ed. D. Barthélemy and J. T. Milik; DJD 1; Oxford: Clarendon, 1955), 110. Later editions have read this as קוראי (e.g., *DSSSE*, 102 and Charlesworth and Stuckenbruck "Rule of the Congregation," 114), i.e., as the *qal* passive participle with metathesis of the *resh* and *waw mater* or with the displacement of the /u/ vowel to the first syllable. The biblical parallels are not terribly helpful in disambiguating: the similar phrase in Num 16:2 (קְרִאֵי מוֹעֵד) implies reading the second letter of the DSS word as a misplaced *yodh*, as does the *kethib* of the similar phrase in Num 1:16 and the *qere* in Num 26:9, though the *qere* to Num 1:16 and the *kethib* to 26:9 imply the

"its wood";[13] מבכריה (1QHª XI, 8) for *מבכירה "one bearing a child";[14] וגזעו (1QHª XVI, 8) for *גוזעו "its stock";[15] מתוך (1QHª XXI, 25) corrected to מתך reflecting what would be in the MT מֻתָּךְ (a *hophal* participle of נתך) in the absolute "poured out";[16] נושיאי[ם] "those bearing" (4Q364 11, 3 at Gen 45:23) for MT נֹשְׂאִים;[17] ואתועדדה "I will stand up" (4Q382 23, 1) for *ואתעודדה;[18] מרישיעי (4Q387 3, 6) for *מרשיעי "those doing wrong";[19] יקופץ (4Q418 88, 5) corrected to יקפוץ "it will shut"; איוב

---

qal passive participle. Milik implies that the mistake is due to the uvular nature of the *resh* ("Textes Non Bibliques," 116).

13. Unless the *yodh* is representing the /ē/ that follows the *ʿayin*, as seems to be the case in עיצים (4Q176 24, 2).

14. Most scholars understand this as a *hiphil* participle, though *DSSEL* reads it as a *min* preposition plus the word "firstborn," reflecting the interpretation of earlier scholars.

15. Unless, the first *waw* should be read as a *yodh* (as in Stegemann, Schuller, Newsom, DJD 40:216 [יגזעו for *גיזעו]), though this seems less likely based, in part, on the *plene* writing in other passages, where it is more common for a word-internal /u/ or /o/ vowel to be marked with a *mater* than for an /i/ vowel to be so marked.

16. See the interpretation of this word in Stegemann, Schuller, Newsom, DJD 40:266. It is likeliest that this is a simple case of metathesis of the *mater*, with the expected *mater* (for the initial /u/ vowel) left out, the mistake perhaps being caused in part by the commonness of the sequence מתוך. The possibility that this represents the words "from the midst of" (= MT מִתּוֹךְ) seems unlikely since the scribe would likely not have erased the *waw mater* in this case; all the other examples of תוך "midst" in 1QHª (and the scrolls in general) carry the *waw mater*. Alternatively, it is possible (though less likely) that, as Stegemann and Schuller suggest, the scribe first wrote a nominal form (i.e., a **maqṭul* or **maqṭāl* base noun) and then corrected it to a *hophal* participle; the absence of such a *mem*-preformative noun in Biblical Hebrew and in RH suggests that this is less likely than a simple scribal slip.

17. Perhaps this spelling reflects the quiescence of *aleph*, the scribe hearing *nōsīm* and then remembering the more conservative form with *aleph*/glottal stop: *nōsəʾīm*. Certainly, the metathesis evidenced in התנאה (4Q107 [4QCant[b]] at Song 2:13) for MT הַתְּאֵנָה is most likely due to the quiescence of *aleph* and subsequent misplacement of the letter, as Tov suggests (Emanuel Tov, "Canticles," in *Qumran Cave 4.XI: Psalms to Chronicles* [ed. Eugene Ulrich et al.; DJD 16; Oxford: Clarendon, 2000], 212). Note also מלכאה "work" (4Q263 3) for *מלאכה.

18. See Saul Olyan, "ParaKings et al.," in DJD 13:375. This is perhaps also influenced by the weakness in pronunciation of the *ʿayin*; see §4.3, "Weakening of Gutturals."

19. D. Dimant writes confusingly that the *yodh* after the *resh* in this word "may stand for the *i*-sound of *reš* which was pronounced as the *i*-sound of the following *šin*" (*Qumran Cave 4.XX: Parabiblical Texts, Part 4, Pseudo-Prophetic Texts* [DJD 30; Oxford: Clarendon, 2001], 193).

(4Q44 [4QDeut^q] at Deut 32:42) for MT אֹיֵב "enemy."[20] A similar phenomenon of metathesized *maters* is found in the MT, as reflected in the *kethib* to Job 26:12: וּבִתְוּבָנָתוֹ "and in his understanding."[21] The fact that dittography and metathesis occur among nonguttural letters like *gimmel*, *peh*, and *shin* is one piece of evidence that suggests that mistakes like וביחרי are not attributable simply to the weakness of gutturals (and *resh*), as has been previously implied.[22] The inherent weakness of the gutturals is only one factor.

In some instances two *maters* are written next to each other for one vowel: מעשייכה "your deeds" (1QSb III, 27); כויל "all" (1QH^a IX, 10) corrected to כול;[23] קצוות "to cut off" (1QpHab IX, 14) for what would be in the MT קְצוֹת;[24] בתווך עממי "in the midst of my peoples" (4Q216 VII, 10); העדוות "the testimony" with correction dots above and below the second *waw* (4Q364 17, 3); זיות "this" (1QIsa^a at Isa 9:11).[25] Note the similar mistake in the MT, דְּבָרוֹו (Ps 105:28). On the one hand, it seems best to inter-

20. This interpretation seems easier than positing a **qiṭṭūl* noun otherwise unattested in Hebrew (except in some manuscripts of the Samaritan Pentateuch). In other cases metathesis produces a reading that is plausible in its context, as in והוי "and O, …" (1QIsa^a at Isa 49:23) for MT וְהָיוּ "and they will be." Similarly for dittography: כהתמכך "when you are humbled (מכך)" (1QIsa^a at Isa 33:1) for MT כַּהֲתִמְךָ "when you are finished (תמם)."

21. For this and other possible examples, see Friedrich Delitzsch, *Die Lese- und Schreibfehler im Alten Testament* (Berlin: de Gruyter, 1920), 52–53. Note especially נָטָוּיֵ (Ps 73:2), the *qere* implying *נָטָיוּ; and the name מְוּמֻכָן (Esth 1:16), which is spelled correctly, מְמוּכָן, in Esth 1:14 and 21.

22. See Milik's analysis of קיראי in the above footnote 12 and Qimron, *Grammar*, 95.

23. Note also כויל (4Q376 1 iii, 2); כוול corrected to כול in 4Q504 1–2R iv, 11.

24. This understanding assumes that the letters represent the *qal* infinitive construct "cutting off," which appears in the MT at Hab 2:10 as קְצוֹת. In a following line of this manuscript, in X, 2, the text of Hab 2:10 is quoted again, this time where the relevant word has just one *mater*: קצות. Alternatively, it may be that both words should be translated "ends of," which also makes sense in the context: "you have counseled shame for your house and (the) ends of many peoples." If this is right, then קצוות may represent the plural construct of קצת (= MT קְצָת, pl. cstr. *קְצוֹת) and קצות in 1QpHab X, 2 may represent the plural construct of קצה (= MT קָצָה, pl. cstr. קְצוֹת). For more on these words, see §3.3, "*Aleph* as Internal *Mater*."

25. More uncertain is כעו]נתיינו] in 4Q84 (4QPs^b) at Ps 103:10 (for MT כַעֲוֹנֹתֵינוּ) since the two *yodhs* are heavily damaged according to the transliteration in Eugene Ulrich et al., eds., *The Biblical Qumran Scrolls* (VTSup 134; Leiden: Brill, 2010), 665; Accordance reconstructs the entire word.

pret these as cases of dittographic error (especially since some of them were actually corrected). On the other hand, this does not explain cases, as in זוית, where a second *mater* was actually added to the word. One is left to wonder about the reason for such interlinear additions; was it perhaps a way for a later scribe to confirm that a possibly ambiguous mark was a *waw* and not a *yodh* or vice versa? In a few cases, the *mater* is left off a word, as in בתול (11Q19 LXV, 10) for *בתולי "virginity of"; and יור (4Q35 [4QDeut^h] at Deut 33:10) for MT יוֹרוּ "they will teach."

In some rare examples, it seems that the sounds of a preceding word have affected the spelling of a following word. For instance, שלום עולום "perpetual peace" (1QH^a XIX, 30 for what would be in the MT *שְׁלוֹם עוֹלָם).[26] A similar phenomenon is evidenced in the MT: וּמוֹצָאָיו וּמוֹבָאָיו "its exits and entrances" (Ezek 43:11) for *וּמוֹצָאָיו וּמְבוֹאָיו and similarly אֶת־מוֹצָאֲךָ וְאֶת־מֹבָואֶךָ (2 Sam 3:25).[27]

Sometimes a mistake is also due to confusion of similar sounding consonants; especially common are confusions between the sibilants and between velar/uvular consonants.[28] Such confusions do not imply that the respective letters were pronounced in an identical manner, rather, it merely reflects the common place of their articulation.[29] Note especially עשים (4Q365 23, 5) corrected to עצים "trees"; אפץ (4Q418 7b, 11) for אפס "nothing" (4Q416 2 i, 20); החרוש (4Q491 8–10 ii, 13) for *החרוץ "the

26. It seems very unlikely that this would be the aberrant form of the word attested in 2 Chr 33:7, עֵילוֹם. The tentative suggestion Qimron (*HDSS*, 39) makes that the same spelling for "eternity" (עולום) is found in 1QSb V, 23 is not followed by more recent editions of that text in James H. Charlesworth and Loren Stuckenbruck's edition ("Blessings," in *Dead Sea Scrolls…Rule of the Community and Related Documents*, 128), in *DSSSE*, or in Accordance, all of whom read עולם.

27. See Delitzsch, *Lese- und Schreibfehler*, 52.

28. For similar confusions in the MT, see Delitzsch, *Lese- und Schreibfehler*, 123–129. For the confusion between *sadeh* and *śin/shin*, note first the parallel verbs צָחַק and שָׂחַק "to laugh" and the two versions of Isaac: יִשְׂחָק/יִצְחָק; note also the different verbs in the parallel accounts in 2 Sam 8:3 (לְהָשִׁיב) and 1 Chr 18:3 (לְהַצִּיב) and the presumed mistake in Hos 5:11: צָו for *שָׁו (ibid., 125). For confusion of velar consonants, consider the possible error in 2 Sam 15:24: וַיַּצִּקוּ "they poured" for *וַיַּצִּגוּ "they set" (ibid., 125).

29. Assuming that the following mistakes reflect an identical pronunciation for the respective sets of letters would imply that the language had lost distinction between *samekh*, *sade*, *śin*, and *shin*, as well as between *gimmel*, *kaph*, and *qoph* and between *daleth*, *tet*, and *taw*. Such a simplification of the phonemic inventory seems wholly unjustified.

appointed";[30] רוכנים (1QS XI, 1) for *רוגנים "(those) murmuring";[31] תנכח (1QSb V, 27) for *תנגח "may you gore"; אגזרי (1QIsa[a] at Isa 13:9) for MT אַכְזָרִי "cruel"; יקדילו (4Q403 1 i, 31) for *יגדילו "they magnify";[32] דקלי (4Q503 51–55, 8) for *דגלי "divisions of"; עמלך (4Q14 [4QExod[c]] at Exod 17:8) for MT עֲמָלֵק "Amalek."[33] A confusion between dentals is presumably the cause of different readings: הנפתר (1QS VII, 10) corrected to הנפטר "the one separated"; ישפטתו (4Q73 [4QEzek[a]] at Ezek 23:45) for MT יִשְׁפְּטוּ;[34] טמוט (11Q5 [11QPs[a]] at Ps 93:1) for MT תִּמּוֹט "it will (not) be shaken."[35] On the other hand, confusion in the spelling of words containing *śin* and *samekh* is due to the identical pronunciation of the letters (for examples and explanation, see §4.1, "Phonemic Inventory").

Guttural consonants are prone to be confused in the DSS-SP9 texts, as illustrated in "Weakening of Gutturals" (§4.3). For perhaps similar reasons, *resh* was also frequently elided in spelling (see §4.1, "Phonemic Inventory"). Qimron notes that *resh* "is omitted far more often than any other nonguttural root consonant."[36] He also observes that such misspellings typically occur next to gutturals; he counts thirty-five total instances of "spelling irregularities" related to *resh* among all the scrolls, twenty specifically among the Hebrew nonbiblical scrolls.[37] His examples suggest this phenomenon occurred especially with certain words in certain texts: המערכות "battle formation" (1QM V, 3; VI, 5); מערכת (1QM VI, 10); משע "from the gate of" (11Q19 XL, 15) for *משער; משער (11Q19 XLIV, 15); אבחר "I will choose" (11Q19 LII, 16).[38] Other examples include תקצר

30. See Maurice Baillet, *Qumran Grotte 4.III (4Q482–4Q520)* (DJD 7; Oxford: Clarendon, 1982), 25, who notes the complexities of the reading.

31. See Ze'ev Ben-Ḥayyim, "Traditions in the Hebrew Language, with Reference to the Dead Sea Scrolls," in *Aspects of the Dead Sea Scrolls*, 202. There is no need to propose a new verb (as done in *DCH*); such a verb would be easily confused with the homophonous Aramaic root רכן "to incline," which is clearly not a possible derivation for the word in 1QS XI, 1.

32. See Newsom, DJD 11:270 and references there.

33. For some of these examples, see Qimron, *HDSS*, 27.

34. See Judith E. Sanderson, "Ezekiel" in *Qumran Cave 4.XI: Psalms to Chronicles* (ed. Eugene Ulrich et al.; DJD 15; Oxford: Clarendon, 2000), 210.

35. Note also לעת (1QIsa[a] at Isa 64:8) for MT לָעַד "forever" (though LXX has ἐν καιρῷ) (see Ulrich et al., *Biblical Qumran Scrolls*, 457).

36. Qimron, *HDSS*, 26.

37. Ibid., 26–27; idem, *Grammar*, 94–96.

38. Kutscher (*Isaiah*, 531) notes אשו (1QIsa[a] at Isa 36:2) for *אשור "Assur," and

"it will (not) be short" (4Q504 7, 6); יואמר "he will say" (4Q129 [4QPhyl B] at Deut 5:27); אבעים (11Q5 [11QPs[a]] XXVII, 9) for *ארבעים "forty." The examples derive from all text groups, including DSS-NSP (e.g., וספרנו "we recounted" 1Q36 25 ii, 3 and הסרפד "the nettle" 1Q8 [1QIsa[b]] at Isa 55:13).[39]

In other cases, similarly shaped letters will lead to confusion: מבוד (1QpHab XI, 9) for *מכבוד "more than glory"; באש (1QH[a] X, 28) corrected to כאש "like fire";[40] הנכבד "the one honored" (4Q403 1 i, 4); ונכבדות "and those honored" (4Q521 2 ii + 4, 11); ויכבס "it will be washed" (11Q2 [11QLev[b]] at Lev 13:58); בקודעו (4Q403 1 i, 31) for *בקודשו "in its holiness";[41] אכס (1QIsa[a] at Isa 54:15) for MT אֶפֶס "nothing."[42] Especially frequent is the confusion of *daleth* and *resh*: גדי (1QH[a] XV, 15) for *גרי "those attacking me";[43] ויתעבד (4Q31 [4QDeut[d]] at Deut 3:26) for MT וַיִּתְעַבֵּר "he was angry"; אבידי (4Q111 [4QLam] at Lam 1:15) for MT אַבִּירַי "my mighty ones."[44] In some cases, a mistake was engendered by the graphic similarity of whole words: ורחץ במים "he will wash in water" (11Q19 L, 14) corrected to ורחץ בים "he will wash in the day of," the former phrase appearing in the same text a few lines later (in 11Q19 LI, 5). Note also the confusion of *heh* and *ḥeth* due to their graphic similarity, discussed below in §4.3, "Weakening of Gutturals."

It seems that the fatigue of writing the same word over and over again has sometimes contributed to a mistake, as in וחצוצרות "trumpets of" (1QM III, 2); [ש]בעה בשבעה "seven, with seven…" (Mas 1k ii, 23), and the similar mistakes of בקד הקדשים (4Q364 17, 3) and בקוד קודשים (4Q503 15–16, 5) for *בק(ו)דש ק(ו)דשים "in the holiest sanctuary." In other cases,

---

חמ (at Isa 29:16) for *חמר "clay," as well as וחרבו "they will be dry" (at Isa 19:6); תלשישה corrected to תרשישה "toward Tarshish" (at Isa 23:6); ויואמר "he said" (at Isa 39:8 and 63:8); and מעוצר "from oppression" (at Isa 53:8).

39. For more examples, see Qimron, *Grammar*, 94–95.

40. See Stegemann, Schuller, Newsom, DJD 40:139.

41. See Newsom, DJD 11:270 and references.

42. Similar confusions appear in the MT, see Delitzsch, *Lese- und Schreibfehler*, 103–123. Note especially the confusion of *beth* and *kaph* in וַיַּבוּ (2 Kgs 3:24), the *qere* reflecting *וַיַּכּוּ which occurs earlier in the verse (ibid., 110); confusion of *ʿayin* and *shin* in וַיֹּדַע (Judg 8:16) for a presumed *וַיָּדָשׁ (ibid., 119).

43. See Stegemann, Schuller, Newsom, DJD 40:203.

44. For parallels in the MT, see Delitzsch, *Lese- und Schreibfehler*, 105–107. Note especially וַיֵּדֶא (Ps 18:11) versus וַיֵּרָא (2 Sam 22:11) (ibid., 105); and the confusion of names: רִיפַת in Gen 10:3 and דִיפַת in 1Chr 1:6 (ibid., 107).

the scribe seems simply to have been confused by the multiple meanings of words and/or by the multiple words with the same general meaning, as in למכאובנו "for our pain" (4Q179 1 i, 14) corrected to למכתינו "for our blows"; כאב "like a father" (4Q416 2 iii, 16) for *כאל "like a God";[45] שועתם "their cry" (4Q434 1 i, 3) corrected to זעקתם "their cry";[46] -ישרא "Isra-" (4Q462 1, 19) corrected to ירושלם "Jerusalem"; אברהרם (4Q464 3 i, 6, for אברם) corrected to אברהם "Abraham"; תורישון "you will dispossess" (4Q140 [4QPhyl M] at Deut 5:33) for MT תִּירָשׁוּן "you will possess."

Another kind of mistake is the incorrect division of words. For example, in 4Q259 III, 17–18 one finds ואם תיתם דרך סוד / היחד לה[לך].[47] The text should perhaps be read, however,... ואמת יתם "of truth and [he will] give them" (*DSSSE*) or ... ואמת ותם "truth, and the perfection" (Qimron and Charlesworth).[48] In either case, the reading above seems to imply that the scribe thought the text should be a circumstantial clause, "if the behavior of the council of the community is perfect, going...," an understanding engendered by similar phrases like אם תתם דרכו "if his behavior is perfect" (in 1QS VIII, 25).[49]

Sometimes these mistakes were combined, as in the simultaneous confusion of *daleth* and *resh* in מוסדרות[ימו] (11Q7 [11QPs^c] at Ps 2:3) for MT מוֹסְרוֹתֵימוֹ "their bonds," the spelling in 11Q7 reflecting a confusion of the words מוסדה "foundation" and מוסר "bond." In still other cases, it is hard to understand the mistake: כנחה (11Q1 [11QpaleoLev^a] at Lev 26:19) for MT כַּנְּחֻשָׁה "like copper"; אלמושה (4Q27 [4QNum^b] at Num 19:1) for MT אֶל־מֹשֶׁה "to Moses"; ויכה "he struck" (1Q7 [1QSam] at 2 Sam 23:12). These cases suggest that the loss of a letter is not always triggered by clearly discernible phonetic or visual causes.

45. See Strugnell and Harrington, DJD 34:120.

46. See Emanuel Tov, "Correction Procedures in the Texts from the Judean Desert," in *The Provo International Conference on the Dead Sea Scrolls: Technological Innovations, New Texts, and Reformulated Issues* (ed. Donald W. Parry and Eugene Ulrich; STDJ 30; Leiden: Brill, 1999), 257.

47. This follows the reading in Alexander and Vermes, DJD 26:145. Elisha Qimron and James H. Charlesworth read תותם ("Cave IV Fragments," in *Dead Sea Scrolls ... Rule of the Community and Related Documents*, 88).

48. The correct reading is based on a partially parallel text in 1QS IX, 18–19 and 4Q258 VIII, 3, where both have ואמת בתוך אנשי היחד.

49. The *plene* writing of the verb is unusual, but has a precedent in אֵיתָם (Ps 19:14). See Alexander and Vermes, DJD 26:149.

The frequency with which the gutturals and *resh* are elided has already been noted. Note also the frequency with which *daleth* and *lamedh* seem to disappear (before being inserted above the line). Most examples derive from DSS-SP9 texts, though not all (for example, 4Q74 is DSS-NSP).

Daleth is dropped (at least initially) in מוסדי "foundations of" (4Q286 1 ii, 3); למקדש "to the sanctuary" (4Q394 [4QMMT] 3–7 i, 8); צדק "righteousness" (4Q403 1 i, 27); עדת "the congregation of" (4Q403 1 ii, 24); אבדינים "Abaddons" (4Q491 8–10 i, 15); קדשא[י]ם "holy ones" (4Q509 7, 6); ליהודה "for Judah" (4Q51 [4QSam^{a}] at 2 Sam 6:2); מדבר "desert" (1QIsa^{a} at Isa 63:13); יעמדו "they stood" (4Q74 [4QEzek^{b}] at Ezek 1:21); ויאב (4Q77 [4QXII^{b}] at Zeph 2:13 for MT וְיאַבֵּד "then he will destroy); ועבדכה "your slave" (11Q5 [11QPs^{a}] at Ps 119:140). Presumably, *daleth*'s graphic similarity to other letters like *beth*, *kaph*, and *resh* is partially attributable for its elision.

Lamedh is dropped initially and then written above the line in וינחילם "he caused them to inherit" (1QS XI, 7); ולא "and not" (4Q381 69, 8); נפלאותיו "his wonders" (4Q403 1 i, 19); לאלפים "to thousands" (4Q491 1–3, 10); שאול "Sheol" (4Q491 8–10 ii, 17); הפלה "to do a wonder" (4Q491c 11 i, 8); וכולעצביכם "all your laborers" (1QIsa^{a} at Isa 58:3); קול "voice" (4Q56 [4QIsa^{b}] at Isa 13:4); מעלליו "his works" (4Q70 [4QJer^{a}] at Jer 17:10); יכלכלנו "(who) will sustain it?" (4Q78 [4QXII^{c}] at Joel 2:11) for MT יְכִילֶנּוּ; קול "voice" (4Q135 [4QPhyl H] at Deut 5:28).[50] The letter is dropped entirely in חקקא (1QS X, 1) for *חקק אל "God inscribed."

Nun is also sometimes elided: שים (4Q216 VII, 15) for *שנים "two"; ולנמוגי "and to those melting at" (4Q491 8–10 i, 4); לנגוע "to touch" (4Q53 [4QSam^{c}] at 2 Sam 14:10); פניך "your face" (4Q70 [4QJer^{a}] at Jer 17:16); [אנח]נ[ו] "we" (11Q5 [11QPs^{a}] at Ps 124:7).

There is sometimes confusion in the spelling of III-*waw/yodh* roots such that they are spelled with a final *aleph mater* instead of a *heh mater* (for example, התורא in 1QSa I, 11 for *התורה "the law"; בזא 4Q434 1 i, 2 for *בזה "he despised"); sometimes the reverse also happens (וירה 4Q381 50, 4 for *וירא "he feared"). Some texts show a concentration of this kind of error (for example, 4Q381 shows eight examples of *aleph* written for

50. I have not included instances where the erasure or secondary inclusion of *lamedh* is due to confusion over the *lamedh* preposition, as seems to be the case in some passages like[ד]למוע (1QH^{a} XVII, 23); בצרלהם (4Q380 2, 4); לשבט corrected to שבט (4Q491 1–3, 8); ולמאיות (4Q491 1–3, 10); לכחצ (1QIsa^{a} at Isa 49:2); לעולם (1QIsa^{a} at Isa 51:6); and ולקדוש (1QIsa^{a} at Isa 55:5).

heh, as in מא for *מה).[51] A similar confusion is more common in Aramaic and is due to the merging of III-*waw/yodh* roots with III-*aleph* roots.[52] The same merger does not appear to happen regularly in the Hebrew of the DSS, where (to judge from the orthography) the two root types are almost always distinguished (for more on this, see the subsection "Lack of Confusion between III-*Waw/Yodh* and III-*Aleph* Verbs" in §5.6, "Verbs").

It should also be pointed out that, as Tov comments, sometimes errors were only partially corrected, even when they were recognized.[53] He cites, as an example, איש ל לפי "each person according to" (4Q266 5 i, 13), where the first *lamedh* is not erased or marked by any cancellation marks. Other examples include אכשיל (1QHª XVIII, 8) for *אשכיל "I will consider" (quoted above), where the *kaph* is marked with cancellation marks, but another *kaph* is not written between the *shin* and *yodh*; ורחץ במים "he will wash in water" (11Q19 L, 14) corrected to ורחץ בים "he will wash in the day of" (quoted above), where the scribe has not included a *waw mater* in the word "day" though the overwhelming consistency in the spelling of this word in the nonbiblical scrolls (יום) would seem to have demanded it;[54] עשו "they made" (1QIsaª at Isa 40:24) for MT נָשַׁף "he blows," corrected to נעשף, where the final *waw* was reshaped into a final *peh*, an interlinear *nun* was added, but the *ʿayin* was not erased or marked with cancellation marks.[55] Another case is עליו (4Q53 [4QSamᶜ] at 2 Sam 15:3) corrected to אליו by attempting to reshape the *ʿayin* into an *aleph*; this resulted in a messily written letter, so the scribe wrote a second, interlinear *aleph* to indicate the intended letter, but did not erase the initial *ʿayin/aleph* or mark it with cancellation marks.[56] Such examples suggest that other spellings may reflect recognized but uncorrected errors. Thus, it is conceivable that יושור "uprightness of" (1QHª XIV, 13) reflects the correction of ישור to יושר, though the scribe did not place cancellation marks around the second *waw* nor did he erase it. Similarly, יעיבורנה "he will not cross it"

51. See Eileen Schuller, "Non-Canonical Psalms," DJD 11:90.

52. See Muraoka, *GQA*, 23–24.

53. Tov, *Scribal Practices*, 221.

54. Out of the hundreds of attestations, the word is spelled defectively in only three other instances in the nonbiblical scrolls, according to my search of Accordance.

55. See Ulrich et al., *Biblical Qumran Scrolls*, 408; Kutscher, *Isaiah*, 507. For other examples, see Tov, *Scribal Practices*, 28–29.

56. See Frank Moore Cross et al., *Qumran Cave 4.XII: 1–2 Samuel* (DJD 17; Oxford: Clarendon, 2005), 261.

(1QIsa[a] at Isa 35:8) may reflect the correction of יעוברנה to יעיברנה. In such cases, the spelling of similar forms should be taken into account. For example, given the spelling of other **quṭl* nouns with two *waw maters* in similar positions, it seems less likely that יישור represents an uncorrected mistake (see §5.5, "**quṭl* Nouns"). On the other hand, since no other *qal* imperfect verbs carry two *waw maters* before and after the second root consonant, it is likeliest that יעיבורנה does represent a correction for an intended spelling of יעיברנה (see §5.7, "*Qal* Imperfect + Suffix").

It is also important to note that, even when spelling was corrected through interlinear additions, the correct letter was sometimes added just to the left or right of the space where it should go. This was sometimes due to the spacing of the other letters and sometimes, presumably, due to the cramped writing space. In the majority of cases, therefore, one should not assume that these reflect peculiar pronunciations. For example ההיגי "the meditation" (4Q267 9 v, 12) for *ההגוי;[57] המל איחז "the king Ahaz (1QIsa[a] at Isa 14:28) for MT הַמֶּלֶךְ אָחָז; יימי (1QIsa[a] at Isa 38:10) for an intended יימי (akin to ביימי "in days of" in 1QIsa[a] at Isa 1:1 and יומי "days of" in 1QS II, 19 and III, 5) for MT יָמַי "my days";[58] תשיא "do (not) bear" (4Q70 [4QJer[a]] at Jer 17:21) for MT תִּשְׂאוּ.[59]

Finally, we should note here that sometimes what is a word-initial/medial letter appears in final position and what is a word-final letter appears at the beginning or in the middle of the word. Tov attributes some of these mistakes to the development of final forms of letters and the gradual adoption of these forms by scribes.[60] Note, for example, המלכ "the king" (4Q448 II, 2); עמכ "your people" (II, 3); ממלכתכ "your kingdom" (II, 8). In other cases, initial/medial-letters are found frequently at the end of short words like גמ "also" and אמ "if"; word-final letters are often found as the penultimate letter of a word, suggesting that in these

57. This assumes that the interlinear *waw* is not intended to replace the *yodh* (see Joseph M. Baumgarten, "Damascus Document," in *The Dead Sea Scrolls, Hebrew, Aramaic, and Greek Texts with English Translations, Volume 3: Damascus Document II, Some Works of the Torah, and Related Documents* [ed. James H. Charlesworth; Princeton Theological Seminary Dead Sea Scrolls Project 3; Tübingen: Mohr Siebeck, 2006], 100). Note the spelling הגוי in 4Q417 1 i, 17 (see Strugnell and Harrington, DJD 34:165 on the occurrence of the same spelling in 4Q417 1 i, 16).

58. See Kutscher, *Isaiah*, 531. The spelling of "days" sometimes occurs with a *waw* in 1QIsa[a] and 1QS, as it does in Aramaic.

59. See Emanuel Tov, "Jeremiah," in DJD 15:165.

60. Tov, *Scribal Practices*, 230.

cases, as Tov puts it, "the scribe must have thought that he had finished the word."[61] Some texts show the final form of the letter in all positions, like the final form of *mem* in at least eight separate words in 4Q68 (4QIsa°). For example, םשרש "from the root of" (at Isa 14:29); נםוג "melt" (at Isa 14:31); וםה "what" (at Isa 14:32). The same phenomenon is attested twice in 4Q116 (4QDan^e) (for example, [ם]השםי "the heavens" at Dan 9:12).

3.2. *Plene* Orthography

The orthography of the scrolls varies from text to text, version to version. In some ways it follows a model more-or-less similar to that of the MT and in other ways it seems to follow a model like that found in Mishnaic Hebrew and later forms of Rabbinic Hebrew, with a tendency for *plene* or full spellings. Despite such tendencies, it bears mentioning that, just as in the MT, there is never consistency in spelling. As Qimron illustrates, in 1QH^a כול "all" appears at least 208 times and כל at least thirteen times.[62] Further, certain forms are attested in different distributions in different texts. For instance, the spelling of the 2ms perfect with a final *heh* marker (קטלתה) is found almost uniformly in most texts of the DSS-SP9 category (for example, 1QS and 1QH^a), as indicated in the ninth appendix to Tov's *Scribal Practices*.[63] All the same, some texts, like 1QIsa^a, show a greater tendency to oscillate, from verse to verse, between the defective and *plene* spellings (קטלתה/קטלת). Texts of the DSS-NSP category (for example, 4Q381), on the other hand, often do not attest the *plene* spelling of the 2ms perfect verb, though rarely they do. Sometimes there is a clear distinction within a single scroll; in 1QH^a, the first eight columns are dominated

---

61. Ibid., 232.

62. Qimron, *HDSS*, 18. The analysis of the same word through Accordance produces similar, but slightly different numbers; for example, there are twelve examples of the spelling כל according to Accordance, not thirteen. See also Qimron's lists of defectively spelled words according to their etymologies (*Grammar*, 39–52 for *waw* and 55–56, 60–61 for *yodh*).

63. Tov, *Scribal Practices*, 339–343. All the same, note that the exceptions are more widespread than Tov's lists would lead one to believe. For example, although Tov's list labels as "all" the number of occurrences of the 2ms perfect verb in 1QH^a spelled with final תה-, there are actually two forms of the 2ms perfect that are defective, יצרת "you formed" 1QH^a IX, 17 and סתרת "you hid" 1QH^a XIII, 28 (Stegemann, Schuller, Newsom, DJD 40:125). Tov comments that the label "all" indicates simply five or more occurrences of a given feature (Tov, *Scribal Practices*, 337).

by defective spelling of the 2ms suffixed pronoun (ךְ-), while the following columns are dominated by the *plene* form (כה-); despite this, the 2ms perfect verbs are still spelled *plene* throughout 1QH[a]. For certain forms, defective orthography is not uncommon and is encountered with approximately equal frequency in the biblical and nonbiblical texts among the DSS-SP9 and DSS-NSP texts. For example, defective spelling is routinely encountered (at least fifty times) in the 3ms pronominal suffix on plural nouns (for example, אבותו "his fathers" 4Q365 26a–b, 8) and prepositions (for example, עלו 1QpHab VIII, 7).[64] However, defective spelling for other pronominal suffixes on plural nouns and prepositions is not found nearly as often (for example, for the 2ms suffix, perhaps as many as three times in the nonbiblical texts, all in 4QInstruction, and as many as six times in the biblical scrolls, where the defective orthography often matches the orthography in the MT).[65]

Note also the following peculiar distributions of defective spelling. The 3mp imperfect plus suffix is spelled defectively (without a *waw* to mark the masculine plural /ū/) six times in 1QS (where there are no *plene* forms, for example, יכתובהו "they will write him" 1QS VI, 22) but very rarely outside this text among the nonbiblical scrolls.[66] Word-internal /ē/

64. See "Diphthongs and Triphthongs" (§4.10).

65. See נעוות֯כ֯ה "your perversities (4Q417 2 i, 13); חטאותכה "your sins" (4Q417 2 i, 15), where the last three letters are heavily damaged; גבורותכה "your great deeds" (4Q418a 14, 1), which mirrors the spelling of this word in the plural with suffix in Deut 3:24 and Isa 63:15. The examples from biblical scrolls are וכגבורתכה (4Q27 [4QNum[b]] at Num 20:13 in an addition, found in the Samaritan version spelled *plene* וכגבורותיך); עבדך "your servant" (4Q53 [4QSam[c]] at 2 Sam 14:31) for MT עֲבָדֶךָ; וגבורתכה (1QIsa[a] at Isa 63:15) for MT וּגְבוּרֹתֶךָ; [מ]צותך (1Q10 [1QPs[a]] at Ps 119:32) for MT מִצְוֹתֶיךָ; בדרכך (4Q89 [4QPs[g]] at Ps 119:37) for MT בִּדְרָכֶךָ; למשפטך 4Q89 [4QPs[g]] at Ps 119:43) for MT לְמִשְׁפָּטֶךָ. There are perhaps only five cases of the 2mp suffix on plural nouns and prepositions being spelled defectively: נפשתכמה "yourselves" (11Q5 [11QPs[a]] XVIII, 1) מקנכם "your possessions" (4Q31 [4QDeut[d]] at Deut 3:19) for MT מִקְנֵכֶם; לאבותכמה (4Q138 [4QPhyl K] at Deut 11:9) for MT לַאֲבֹתֵיכֶם; idem (4Q130 [4QPhyl C] at Deut 11:21) for MT לַאֲבֹתֵיכֶם; אלוההכמה (1QIsa[a] at Isa 40:9) for MT אֱלֹהֵיכֶם.

66. See Qimron, *HDSS*, 18 n. 4 and the literature there. More predictably, in the biblical scrolls, the defective writing often parallels the defective writing in the MT, almost exclusively among the DSS-NSP texts (e.g., ירגמהו "they will stone him" 4Q26a [4QLev[e]] at Lev 20:2 for MT יִרְגְּמֻהוּ; [י]שתהו "they will drink it" 1Q8 [1QIsa[b]] at Isa 62:9 for MT יִשְׁתֻּהוּ), while DSS-SP9 texts exhibit *plene* forms (e.g., ישתוהו 1QIsa[a] at Isa 62:9).

vowels are sometimes not represented in the orthography, though they are in the MT: תטיב *tēṭīb* "you will do good" (4Q525 10, 6) and יטיב "he will do good" (4Q525 10, 6) for what would be in the MT תֵּיטִיב and יֵיטִיב.[67] The defective spelling of *qal* passive participles appears rarely among non-biblical scrolls (primarily in DSS-NSP texts, for example, בחרים "those chosen" 4Q381 46a + b, 5), while in the biblical scrolls they are found more commonly (again primarily among DSS-NSP texts), both where this parallels the MT spelling (פקדיהם "those accounted for" 4Q23 [4QLev–Num^{a}] at Num 4:40 for MT פְּקֻדֵיהֶם), but also where the MT spelling is *plene* (שדפות "scorched by" 4Q5 [4QGen^{e}] at Gen 41:6 for MT שְׁדוּפֹת; חלצים "warriors" 4Q31 [4QDeut^{d}] at Deut 3:18 for MT חֲלוּצִים; רצצים "those oppressed" 1Q8 [1QIsa^{b}] at Isa 58:6 for MT רְצוּצִים). This kind of minor disparity between the orthography of the biblical scrolls and that of the MT is seen in a number of ways among the DSS-NSP texts. For example, the text 4Q107 (4QCant^{b}) attests defective spelling where the MT has *plene* forms (קל "voice," מר "myrrh" הראני "show me" versus קוֹל, מוֹר, הַרְאִינִי) and *plene* forms where the MT has defective spelling (הרועה "the one shepherding," סוב "turn," שפתותיך "your lips" versus הָרֹעֶה, סֹב, שִׂפְתֹתַיִךְ); in many other cases it parallels the spelling of the MT.[68] Peculiarly, sometimes the biblical scrolls attest a defective spelling that occurs only once in the MT. For example, in the MT, the spelling of the 3/2fp imperfect and *waw*-consecutive imperfect of היה is usually written with two *yodhs*, (וַ)תִּהְיֶינָה or (וַ)תִּהְיֶיןָ, but it is once written with a single *yodh*: וְתִהְיֶנָה (Jer 18:21); by contrast, in the biblical scrolls, the form with just one *yodh* appears three times, both in a DSS-NSP text (4Q70 [4QJer^{a}] at Jer 18:21) and in a DSS-SP9 text (1QIsa^{a} at Isa 16:2 and 17:2), while the form with two *yodhs* appears just twice (1Q8 [1QIsa^{b}] at Isa 16:2 and 4Q22 [4QpaleoExod^{m}] at Exod 25:27).[69]

Despite the peculiarities just mentioned, the increased use of *maters* in the DSS is part of a tendency evidenced throughout the first millennium; initially consonant letters are used to indicate vowels at the ends of words, then they are used for the same purpose within words. The development is

---

67. Note that the majority of the spellings of this word in the DSS use a *plene* orthography, parallel to the one found in the MT (i.e., ייטיב). Cf. יליל *yēlīl* "he will wail" (1QIsa^{a} at Isa 15:2) for MT יְיֵלִיל and ילילו (4Q82 [4QXII^{g}] at Hos 7:14) for MT יְיֵלִילוּ, where the sequence *yəyē-* has collapsed to *yē-*.

68. See the list of disparities between this text and the MT in Tov, DJD 16:208.

69. See Tov, DJD 15:150.

also attested in the Bible itself, in the spelling of words like David, spelled without a *yodh mater* in the earlier texts (דָּוִד) and often (but not always) with a *yodh mater* in later writings (דָּוִיד). The spelling of words among the DSS witnesses to the general continuation of this trend.[70]

One nuance to the use of *maters* in the MT is that frequently when one might expect to see two *maters* in a single word, as in the plural form of "voice" קוֹל, one often finds only one *mater* or none at all: *קוֹלוֹת (never), קֹלוֹת (six times), קוֹלֹת (once), and קֹלֹת (five times).[71] In the DSS, by contrast, one often finds two *maters*: קולות (four times in the nonbiblical scrolls and once in the biblical scrolls), קלות (four times in the biblical scrolls), קולת (never), and קלת (never). Compare also the regular defective writing of "generations" in the MT (דֹּרוֹת and with suffixes often -דֹּרֹת), but the consistent *plene* spelling in the nonbiblical DSS (דורות [with and without suffixes], at least thirty-five times in nonbiblical texts and five times in biblical texts). Where a *waw* appears as a consonant before an /o/ vowel or when a *yodh* appears before an /i/ vowel, *plene* spelling is found in the DSS more often than in the MT. However, the most frequent spelling in the DSS is still that of the MT (that is, a defective spelling). For example, looking at the form of the words without suffixes, in the MT גּוֹיִם "peoples" appears hundreds of times and גּוֹיִים only twice; in the nonbiblical DSS, גוים occurs at least sixty times and גויים thirteen times; similarly, מִצְוֹת "commandments" occurs around thirty times in the MT and מִצְווֹת only once, while in the nonbiblical scrolls מצות occurs around nine times and מצוות twice. It also bears mentioning that the *plene* spellings of these or similar nouns are attested in all text groups (DSS-SP9, DSS-SP1c, DSS-NSP).

In the DSS, final *maters* presumably represent the same types of vowels that they represent in the MT. That is, the *heh* is used to mark /ā/, /ē/, /e/, what would be in the MT *qamets-gadol*, *sere*, *seghol* (= /å/ [IPA ɔ], /ē/, /e/ [IPA ɛ]).[72] The use of word-final *aleph* in the DSS to mark the vowels /ā/,

70. Of course, the use of *maters* does not develop in a straight line. Alexander and Vermes note in their introduction to the *Serekh* texts from Cave 4 that "Predominantly full spelling seems to be found throughout the S tradition, but predominantly defective spelling occurs only in later manuscripts" (DJD 26:8).

71. See GKC §8k–l.

72. The possibility of word-final *heh* representing /ō/ in the DSS depends on how one understands the *heh* suffix representing the 3ms pronoun (see §5.2, "Pronouns and Particles").

/ē/, /e/ is rare.[73] Similarly, word-final *waw* typically represents /o/ and /u/ class vowels; word-final *yodh* represents /ī/ and /ē/ vowels. Word-internal *maters* also represent the same kinds of vowels as they do in the MT.

In general, the DSS witness to a greater use of the *heh maters* to represent /ā/ and *waw maters* to represent /o/ and /u/ class vowels. The use of *heh* is primarily found at the ends of words (for example, on the 2ms perfect קטלתה and 2ms possessive suffix כה-) while the *waw* is found word-internally and in word-final position. The way that the *waw* is used to represent all manner of /o/ or /u/ vowel (what would be, if found in the MT, *hatef-qamets, qamets-hatuf, holem, holem-waw, qibbutz, shuruq*) is certainly one of the obvious ways that the orthography of the scrolls differs from that of the MT; for more on this, see §3.4 below, "Etymological Short /u/ Marked with *Waw*." In addition, word internal /a/ and /ā/ vowels are sometimes indicated with *aleph*, as explained below in §3.3, "*Aleph* as Internal *Mater*." Instances of /e/ or /ē/ represented by word-internal *aleph* are rare.

Occasionally two different *maters* are used to mark a single word-final vowel; these examples are illustrated in "Digraphs" (§3.5). The doubling of *waw* and *yodh* to mark word-internal vowels are best construed as errors (see §3.1, "Scribal Mistakes," for some examples), while the same doubling at the end of a word is usually indicative of a phonetic shift (see §§4.4–5, "*Aleph* < *Yodh* and *Yodh* < *Aleph*" and "*Aleph* < *Waw* and *Waw* < *Aleph*").

Yodh as marking short /i/ is uncommon but seems to be found, for example, with תישאום "you [mp] will lift them" (1QIsa^{a} at Isa 15:7) for MT יִשָּׂאוּם "they will…"; היגד "he declared" (1QIsa^{a} at Isa 21:2) for MT הֻגַּד "it was declared"; ייזל "let it flow" (1QIsa^{a} at Isa 45:8) for MT יִזְּלוּ "let them…";[74] פיתאום "suddenly" (1QH^{a} XVI, 19);[75] היראתי "I showed" (4Q158 4, 6) for

73. See Qimron, *HDSS*, 23 and Abegg, "Hebrew of the Dead Sea Scrolls," 327–328. Note that the relative pronoun ש is spelled אש in 4QMMT (4Q394 3–7 i, 5, 29; 3–7 ii, 14; 4Q396 1–2 i, 3).

74. For a summary of examples, see Qimron, *Grammar*, 53–54. Kutscher reads the last example as ויזל (*Isaiah*, 400). Alternatively, the reading ייזל might be interpreted as an example of a consonantal *yodh* written twice (see §3.6, "Two *Yodhs* for a Consonantal *Yodh* and Two *Waws* for a Consonantal *Waw*").

75. Stegemann and Schuller (DJD 40:221) note that the reading, פותאים, proposed by Carmignac ("Compléments au texte des hymes de Qumrân," *RevQ* 2 [1959–1960]: 552) and preferred by Qimron ("The Distinction between Waw and Yod in the Qumran Scrolls" [in Hebrew], *Beth Mikra* 52 [1972]," 110–11) does not fit the context.

what would be in the MT הִרְאִיתִי;[76] וכיבשו[ה] "they subdued it" (4Q483 1) for what would be in the MT וְכִבְשֻׁהָ, though the scroll is extremely fragmentary and the *yodh* damaged.[77] Many of the other possible examples are debated: לניכנעים (1QS X, 26; for what would be in the MT לְנִכְנָעִים "to those humbled") is also read לנוכנעים as a *nuphal* stem (see the subsection "Conjugations" in §5.6, "Verbs"); similarly וניקפו "they were struck down" (4Q161 8–10, 6; in a quotation of Isa 10:34, which has in the MT וְנִקַּף) is also read ונוקפו, as a *nuphal*. Other possible examples are listed and discussed by Qimron.[78] The practice of marking a short /i/ with a *yodh mater* is far more common in the Aramaic scrolls.[79]

Yodh as a marker for /ī/ is used in a way analogous to how it appears in the MT.[80] Unfortunately, as in the MT, its application is inconsistent and in some cases this creates difficulty in determining the parsing of a given word. A good example of this is seen in the *hiphil* infinitives. Although the infinitive construct is usually marked in the DSS with a *yodh mater*, it is not in several instances.[81] This makes the words look like infinitives

---

Another possible example of the same spelling, פיתאום, occurs at 4Q178 5, 2, though the text is very fragmentary.

76. Although Accordance reads here הראתי, the photograph in the *DSSEL* shows a clear *yodh* after the *heh* (the photograph in the DJD edition contains a shadow due to a fold in the leather).

77. See Baillet, DJD 7:2 and Elisha Qimron, "Waw and Yod," 104. The text is so fragmentary that its identity is ambiguous, as reflected in its descriptive title: "4QpapGen or papJub?" The reading כובשי[ם], as Baillet comments, is also possible. The reading וכיבשו[ה] could reflect the *piel* (as Accordance parses); another possibility is to read וכובשו[ה] (similar to the *qal* imperative plus suffix presupposed in the reconstruction דורש[והו] in 1QSa II, 10).

78. See his *Grammar*, 53–54 and the various discussions in Qimron, "Waw and Yod." Certainly, it seems preferable in some cases to follow Qimron's readings (e.g., גוזעו 1QH[a] XVI, 9 instead of גיזעו as in Stegemann, Schuller, Newsom, DJD 40:216). In other cases, it is hard to decide. The word מחיתה in 4Q438 4 ii, 5 is read as מחותה "terror" by Qimron (see *HDSS*, 66 and "Waw and Yod," 111–112), מחיתה "terror" by M. Weinfeld and D. Seely, "Barkhi Nafshi," in *Qumran Cave 4.XX: Poetical and Liturgical Texts, Part 2* (ed. E. Chazon et al.; DJD 29; Oxford: Clarendon, 1999), 330, and מחיתה "you have wiped out" by *DSSSE*. See also the discussion of forms like כובוד or כיבוד in "**quṭl* Nouns" (§5.5).

79. See Muraoka, *GQA*, 26.

80. See Qimron, *HDSS*, 19.

81. Among just the nonbiblical scrolls (as parsed by Accordance): להברך (1QS VI, 5 and 6); להשב (1QS VIII, 6); להקם (1QS VIII, 10); לוסף (1Q14 8–10, 7); להמטר (1Q22 1 ii, 10); להוכח (4Q302 3 ii, 7); להשב (4Q368 10 ii, 5). These are from both

absolute. Abegg notes that the defective forms of the *hiphil* infinitive occur primarily after the negative particle אין and after the *lamedh* preposition.[82] In the MT, by contrast, defective spellings of the *hiphil* infinitive construct are most often (though not exclusively) when the infinitive has a suffix.[83] A similar tendency affects the orthography of Ben Sira manuscripts from Masada and the Genizah; in the case of these manuscripts, other parts of the *hiphil* paradigm are also written defectively (participle, perfect, imperfect).[84] One may also note the rarity of the *yodh mater* in *hiphil* forms in epigraphic Hebrew.[85]

The use of *yodh* in association with /ē/ (either as a historical spelling or as a *mater*) is also somewhat inconsistent and diverges from the model found in the MT. Qimron stresses that we sometimes find no *yodh* where we might expect one from the MT, and find a *yodh* where we would not expect one in the MT.[86] Thus, the *qal* 3mp imperfect of ישב is spelled יישבו "they will dwell" (4Q158 14 i, 8; compare MT יֵשְׁבוּ); the imperative שׁיבנא (4Q382 9, 6, reflecting 2 Kgs 2:4 שֵׁב־נָא);[87] the *niphal* 1cs imperfect of חלל is איחל "(why) should I be profaned" (1QIsa[a] and 4Q57 [4QIsa[c]] at Isa

DSS-SP9 and DSS-NSP text categories. Qimron sees these as infinitives construct (*HDSS*, 47).

82. Abegg, "Hebrew of the Dead Sea Scrolls," 341. See the subsection "Infinitives" in §5.6, "Verbs."

83. E.g., הַקְרִב (Num 9:7); הַשְׁמִדְךָ (Deut 7:24); הוֹדִעֲךָ (Deut 8:3). James Barr considers the defective spellings of the *hiphil* in the MT as reflective of an earlier short vowel (*The Variable Spellings of the Hebrew Bible: The Schweich Lectures of the British Academy, 1986* [Oxford: Oxford University Press, 1989] 84–85).

84. See Wido Th. van Peursen, *The Verbal System in the Hebrew Text of Ben Sira* (SSLL 41; Leiden: Brill, 2004), 44–46. He considers the possible cases of the infinitive construct written defectively to be examples of the infinitive absolute, used in a manner akin to the infinitive construct.

85. See S. L. Gogel, *A Grammar of Epigraphic Hebrew* (SBLRBS 23; Atlanta: Scholars, 1998), 138–149. Other examples of defective writing for /ī/ from the DSS are found in some attestations of historical I-*yodh* roots in the *qal* imperfect, as in ויראו *wəyīrəʾū* "and they will fear" (11Q19 LVI, 11; 1QIsa[a] at Isa 41:5; and passim); יטב *yīṭab* "it will be good" (4Q137 [4QPhyl J] at Deut 5:16 for MT יִיטַב and passim in the phylactery texts); see the subsection "Explanation of DSS Forms" in §4.4, "*Aleph* < *Yodh* and *Yodh* < *Aleph*."

86. Qimron writes "The use of *yod* as a vowel letter to represent the sound *e* shows considerable inconsistency, and a tendency to deviate from the largely etymological spelling found in the Bible" (*HDSS*, 19–20).

87. See Olyan, DJD 13:369.

48:11) for MT יֵחָל "(why) should it be profaned"; the *piel* is written תשויע *təšawwēʿ* "you will cry out" (1Q8 [1QIsa[b]] at Isa 58:9) for MT תְּשַׁוַּע;[88] the *hiphil* 2ms perfect + 1cp suffix [הו]ציאתנ[ו] (4Q364 26c–d, 2 at Deut 9:28) for MT הוֹצֵאתָנוּ.[89] These examples do not represent the typical spellings of these forms; that is, there are no other examples of I-*yodh* verbs like ישב that take a *yodh mater* in the imperfect prefix. We should also remember that the MT contains numerous examples of defective writings and even inconsistent uses of the *yodh mater*, as in תֵּישַׁבְנָה "they will dwell" (Ezek 35:9, *kethib*) and אֵיתָם "I will be complete" (Ps 19:14). The *yodh* in the DSS can also mark word-internal /ē/ in nouns and adjectives, as in ושיש "and linen" (4Q365 12a i, 4 at Exod 36:35 for MT וְשֵׁשׁ); ריעיכה "your friend" (11Q19 LIV, 20 for what is more commonly רעיכה; compare רֵיעֲכֶם in Job 6:27); ביבישה "in dry ground" (1QH[a] IV, 16).

Another idiosyncrasy of DSS orthography is the use of *yodh* to mark /ē/ at the end of singular III-*waw*/*yodh* words that are in construct: מעני לשון "answer of tongue" (4Q171 3–10 iv, 27) for what would be in the MT and elsewhere in the DSS מענה* לשון (for example, 1QH[a] X, 9 and passim). This happens repeatedly in some scrolls, even those that are DSS-NSP, עטי "one wrapping oneself" (4Q86 [4QPs[d]] at Ps 104:2) for MT עֹטֶה and עשי "one making" (4Q86 [4QPs[d]] and 4Q93 [4QPs[l]] at Ps 104:4) for MT עֹשֶׂה.[90] More rarely a similar thing occurs at the end of III-*aleph* words: וחוטי נפשכה "incurring the penalty of your life" (1QpHab X, 2) quoting Hab 2:10: וְחוֹטֵא נַפְשֶׁךָ.[91] In 1QIsa[a], *aleph* is sometimes replaced by a *yodh* that seems to function as a *mater* for what would be a *sere* in the MT (for example, וטמיתם "you defiled" at Isa 30:22 for MT וְטִמֵּאתֶם); this does not represent a loss of distinction between III-*aleph* and III-*waw*/

---

88. The pronunciation *təšawwēʿ* reflects what would be in the MT a pausal form: תְּשַׁוֵּעַ (see Job 24:12). Alternatively, תשויע could be read תשווע, where two consecutive consonantal *waws* are represented with two separate *waws*; see §3.6, "Two *Yodhs* for a Consonantal *Yodh* and Two *Waws* for a Consonantal *Waw*."

89. Also, note the form משריתכה (1QH[a] XIII, 23) that is corrected to משרתיכה "those serving you," the initial form reflecting the metathesis of the *mater* or the scribe's *plene* writing of the *piel* participle without suffix (משרית* *məšārēt*).

90. It is rare to see what would be a *seghol* in the MT marked with a word-internal *yodh mater*: [ו]תצינה "they went forth" (4Q365 6b, 6 at Exod 15:20) for MT וַתֵּצֶאןָ.

91. Qimron, *Grammar*, 61–63. In the case of this example, the participle is not necessarily in construct with the following noun.

yodh roots, as in Aramaic, but rather the *plene* marking of /ē/ and the quiescence of the glottal stop.[92]

Note also that in some cases the inconsistent use of the *yodh mater* is due to confusion over the spelling and/or etymology of the word. For example, Qimron lists the inconsistent spellings of "rams" and "divine beings."[93] In the DSS, the plural "rams" (אילים = MT אֵילִים) is sometimes spelled like the plural "angels" or "divine beings" (אלים = MT אֵלִים) and vice versa.[94] Perhaps, due to the metaphorical meaning of "ram" as "ruler," speakers became confused as to whether or not "ram" and "divine being" were etymologically related and, therefore, should be spelled the same.[95]

3.3. *Aleph* as Internal *Mater*

In the minds of those writing, copying, or reading the scrolls, it might have appeared that *aleph* could function as a *mater* for /ā/ and perhaps also for /ō/ word-internally. As explained below in "*Aleph* < *Waw* and *Waw* < *Aleph*" (§4.5), verbal forms like באוו "they came" (4Q398 [4QMMT] 11–13, 2 and 3), for what would be in the MT בָּאוּ, presume the pronunciation *bāwū*, where the *aleph* assimilates to the following /u/ vowel and becomes /w/. It is difficult to know if the *aleph* in the spelling באוו and similar words was construed as a historical spelling, as an indication of the preceding vowel, or both.[96] In other cases, where the *aleph* is clearly not etymological, it often seems to be a *mater* for /ā/: דאוה "unwell" (4Q223–224 2 i, 45) for what would be in the MT דָּוָה; עישאו "Esau" (4Q223–224 2 ii, 4, 12; 2 iii, 12; 2 iv, 18; 4Q364 3 ii, 7) for what would be in the MT עֵשָׂו; יאבואו "they will come" (4Q277 1 ii, 8) for *יבואו (unless this is a case of metathesis); ראש and ראשו "possess" (4Q364 24a–c, 4 and 26a ii, 3, respectively, at Deut 2:31 and 9:23 for MT רֵשׁ and רְשׁוּ); שביא[ם] "their captivity" (4Q385a 18 i a–b, 7), which echoes the phrase from Jer 30:10 and 46:27 אֶרֶץ שִׁבְיָם; as well as

92. See Kutscher, *Isaiah*, 505, and the subsection "Lack of Confusion between III-*Waw*/*Yodh* and III-*Aleph* Verbs" in §5.6 below, "Verbs."

93. Qimron, *HDSS*, 19.

94. Qimron, *HDSS*, 19. E.g., אלים "rams" (11Q19 XVII, 15 and passim) and אילים and אילי "angels" (4Q381 15, 6; 4Q403 1 i, 38; 4Q418 69 ii, 15; 4Q511 10, 11). Note that "rams" is spelled without a *yodh* in Exod 36:19, Ezek 32:21, and 2 Chr 29:22 and "angels" is spelled with a *yodh* in various medieval biblical manuscripts. See BDB and *HALOT*.

95. See Strugnell and Harrington, DJD 34:291; Newsom, DJD 11:308.

96. See also: ראוו (1QIsa^a at Isa 66:19) for MT רָאוּ.

the many cases from 1QIsa[a]; יאתום "orphan" (at Isa 1:17, 23) for MT יָתוֹם; הבאימות "the high places" (at Isa 15:2) for MT הַבָּמוֹת; איאל "deer" (at Isa 35:6) for MT אַיָּל; גמלאם "he rewarded them" (at Isa 63:7) for MT גְּמָלָם; פריאם "their fruit" (at Isa 65:21) for MT פִּרְיָם; יואן "Javan" (at Isa 66:19) for MT יָוָן; and עאון "iniquity" (at Isa 1:15, though the word is not found in the MT version) for what would be in the MT עָוֹן.[97]

In some cases, it seems likely that a scribal confusion has led to the *aleph* and it is not due to a scribal convention of marking a preceding /a/ vowel: תאמר (4Q418 8, 6) reflects either *tammēr* "do (not) embitter (מרר)," *temer* "do (not) reject" (compare Ps 106:33 מרה + רוח), or *tāmēr* "do (not) exchange (מור)." The writing with *aleph* likely reflects a scribe's confusion at seeing תמר in the manuscript he was copying from and thinking this a defective spelling for the verb "to say," as found, for example, in יומר a few lines later in the same text, 4Q418 8, 11; and תמרו "you said" (4Q129 [4QPhyl B] at Deut 5:24) for MT וַתֹּאמְרוּ.[98] A similar situation likely relates to ויאמרו "they showed disobedience (*hiphil* of מרה)" (4Q370 1 i, 2).[99]

In the case of עאון (1QIsa[a] at Isa 1:15), it is possible that here the *aleph* is marking a glottal stop, reflecting the shift /w/ > /ʾ/: *ʿāʾōn* (see §4.5, "*Aleph* < *Waw* and *Waw* < *Aleph*"). The same explanation is not likely for קצאוות *qəṣāwōt* "ends of" (1QIsa[a] at Isa 41:5) for MT קְצוֹת "ends of"; the *aleph* in the scroll's word appears to be a *mater* for a preceding /ā/ vowel. The word קצאוות appears to be the plural construct of קצת (MT קְצָת, plural abs. קְצָוֹת) while the word in the MT version of Isa 41:5 is the plural construct of קָצָה, both words meaning "end."[100] The word קצת is an Aramaic-like

97. The examples from 1QIsa[a] are drawn from Kutscher, *Isaiah*, 160–161. Qimron also lists examples from 1QIsa[a] and elsewhere ("Initial *Alef* as a Vowel in Hebrew and Aramean Documents from Qumran Compared to Later Hebrew and Aramaic Sources" [in Hebrew], *Leshonenu* 39 [1975]: 134–35; this is the title provided in the English summary section, but "Medial Alef…" seems intended). Some other examples are somewhat more conjectural. For example, הנא יאנה in 11Q19 LIII, 20 (for what would be in the MT הָנֵא יְנִיאֶהָ "he will surely forbid her") might be conceived of as representing *hānē yānīhā*, presupposing the quiescence of the *aleph* root consonant and the contraction of the *hiriq* and *seghol* vowels, though a scribal slip reversing *aleph* and *nun* seems more likely.

98. See Strugnell and Harrington, DJD 34:98.

99. See Carol Newsom, "Admonition on the Flood," in *Qumran Cave 4.XIV: Para-Biblical Texts, Part 2* (ed. M. Broshi et al.; DJD 19; Oxford: Clarendon, 1998), 93.

100. Kutscher (*Isaiah*, 207) explains קצאוות as an Aramaized plural construct (קְצָאוֹת < קְצָאוֹוּת).

noun (in which the /ā/ vowel does not reduce, even in construct), while קצה is Hebrew.[101] In two other places where the MT vocalization reflects the word קָצָה (קְצוֹת at Isa 40:28 and 41:9) 1QIsa[a] has a form reflecting קְצָת (קצוות); similarly note קצוות *qəṣāwōt* "ends of" (4Q365 13, 1 at Exod 39:17) for MT קְצוֹת. It might also be mentioned that the *aleph* of קצאוות cannot be part of a digraph for /ō/ since the first of the two *waws* is consonantal.[102] Furthermore, if one were to argue that the *aleph* represented a shift from *waw* (analogous to the *aleph* resulting from the shift /y/ > /ʾ/ in מְנָאוֹת), then one would have to suppose that the two *waws* were a double *mater*. Since the repetition of the *mater* is relatively uncommon (though note the apparent spelling of the etymologically similar *qal* infinitive construct קצוות in 1QpHab IX, 14), and since the representation of word internal /ā/ with *aleph* is relatively common in 1QIsa[a], it seems best to interpret קצאוות as using an *aleph mater* to help represent *qəṣāwōt*.[103]

The word כלאיות "kidneys of" (1QIsa[a] at Isa 34:6) for MT כִּלְיוֹת bears an *aleph*, perhaps, for the same reason (to mark preceding /ā/), as though from *כְּלָת, though such a noun is not attested in Hebrew or even in Aramaic. Alternatively, the scribe perhaps wrote the absolute form of the word (= MT כְּלָיוֹת), with a word-internal *aleph mater*, though the context demands a construct form.[104]

A similar graphic convention to mark word-internal /ā/ with an *aleph* is found in the MT: דָּאג "fish" (Neh 13:16), though normally דָּג; as well as with *qal* II-*waw*/*yodh* roots: לָאט "secrecy" (Judg 4:21), though normally

---

101. See *HGhS*, 463x''. For a morphological parallel to קצת, note מְנָת "portion" and the construct forms: מְנָיוֹת "portions of" (Neh 12:47) and מְנָאוֹת (Neh 12:44). For this word, *yodh* is the etymological third root consonant and it shifts to *aleph* in the second attestation in Nehemiah (see §4.4, "*Aleph* < *Yodh* and *Yodh* < *Aleph*"). In the MT, מְנָת appears only in construct, always with a *qamets* (Jer 13:25, passim). Note also that the singular קְצָת is found four times in the MT Hebrew sections of Daniel and three times in the Aramaic sections. On this word, see also Moshe Bar-Asher, "Some Unusual Spellings in the Qumran Scrolls" [Hebrew], *Meghillot* 3 [2005]: 173–74).

102. See "Digraphs" (§3.5).

103. For קצוות in 1QpHab, see §3.1, "Scribal Mistakes." The pronunciation *qəṣāwōt* would be the same for the other examples of the word spelled with two *waws*: קצוות cited above, as well as in 1QM I, 8 and 4Q511 63 i, 4. Presumably, the spellings without the double *waw* reflect *qəṣōt* as in 4Q181 2, 9.

104. Contrast this explanation with Kutscher's tentative suggestion that the spelling of this word suggests that the shewa was pronounced as /a/ (*Isaiah*, 501–2).

לָט; רָאשׁ "poor" (2 Sam 12:1), though normally רָשׁ.[105] It is also found in the Aramaic of the DSS. Muraoka comments that this convention is "rather common" in the Aramaic of the scrolls.[106] The fact that 1QIsa[a] contains the most examples of this phenomenon is, thus, not surprising; it seems simply another trait in which Aramaic influence can be found in this scroll.[107] All the same, note that in all the examples (with the exception of ראשו/ראש, גמלאם, הבאימות) the *aleph mater* comes before a consonantal *yodh* or *waw* (כלאיות, קצאוות, עאון, עישאו, דאוה) or after a consonantal *yodh* or *waw* (יואן, פריאם, איאל, יאתום, שביא[ם], יאבואו).[108] At least for Hebrew, then, although the internal *aleph mater* does not explicitly mark the following or preceding *waw/yodh* as consonantal, it does help to disambiguate the value of these two consonants in relation to a preceding or following /ā/. Such usage is not typical in DSS Aramaic.[109] Thus, if the practice of using *aleph* to mark /ā/ was adopted from Aramaic, it seems to have been used especially where useful in producing a more explicit orthography in relation to *waw* and *yodh*.

In addition, the short /a/ seems to be marked with an *aleph* in למעאן "so that" (4Q175 4) for what would be in the MT לְמַעַן, as well as in יאכה "he will strike" (1QIsa[a] at Isa 30:31) for MT יַכֶּה and האזורה "the crushed one" (1QIsa[a] at Isa 59:5) for MT הַזּוּרֶה.[110] The *aleph* in תתיאמרו (1QIsa[a] at Isa 61:6) for MT תִּתְיַמָּרוּ "you will boast" (*hithpael* of אמר) could be a *mater* and/or a historical writing. The *aleph* in לאשו "vainly" (4Q129 [4QPhyl B], 4Q137 [4QPhyl J], 4Q139 [4QPhyl L] at Deut 5:11) for MT לַשָּׁוְא may reflect a use of the letter as a *mater*, if not also a repeated scribal confusion. The *aleph* marking a short /a/ seems also to be attested, though rarely, in DSS Aramaic, as in איתאי "there is" (4Q542 3 ii, 13).[111]

Kutscher suggests that *aleph* is also used as a *mater* for /ē/ where the *aleph* is not part of the etymology of the word. This occurs primarily with

---

105. See GKC §9b and 72p.

106. Muraoka, *GQA*, 28.

107. The few other texts where it is attested are DSS-SP9 (4Q175, 4Q227, 4Q223–224, including perhaps 4QMMT [4Q398]). Only one DSS-NSP text attests this practice: 4Q385a.

108. See Qimron "Initial *Alef*," 136. The examples above suggest that for Hebrew this distribution was more-or-less equal, the *aleph* just as likely to come before *waw/yodh* as after.

109. Muraoka, *GQA*, 28 n. 194.

110. Kutscher, *Isaiah*, 160–161.

111. See Muraoka, *GQA*, 29 for more possible examples.

the word עואר "blind" (1QIsaª at Isa 42:19 [twice] and 43:8), but also ונאלכה "we may go" (1QIsaª at Isa 2:3).[112] In addition, note נאכר "foreign" (4Q372 1, 11 and 15 and 4Q387 3, 6) for what is usually נכר (= MT נֵכָר);[113] and perhaps [י]אצאו "they will go forth" (4Q491 1–3, 9) for what would be in the MT יֵצְאוּ (if this is not a scribal mistake; see §3.1, "Scribal Mistakes"). Note as well the cases of the digraph -יא- for /ē/, noted below in "Digraphs" (§3.5): תיאמינו *tēmīnū* "you turn to the right" (1QIsaª at Isa 30:21 for MT תַאֲמִינוּ < *tēmīnū* [compare וְאֵימְנָה in Gen 13:9] or < *taymīnū* [compare מַיְמִינִים in 1 Chr 12:2]), כסיא *kissē* "throne" (4Q57 [4QIsaᶜ] at Isa 9:6 for MT כִּסֵּא). Conceivably the forms in which *aleph* functions as a *mater* for /ē/ were derived by analogy from spellings like דניאל "Daniel" (in the DSS and MT passim), which was pronounced in the writing/reading register of the DSS as it is in the MT דָּנִיֵּאל = *dānīyēl* (see §4.4, "*Aleph* < *Yodh* and *Yodh* < *Aleph*"). Kutscher's hypothesis that *aleph* marks /ē/ is encouraged by the use of *aleph* to mark word-internal /ē/ in DSS Aramaic words, like פותאהון "their width" (5Q15 1 ii, 7); גאפה "its bank" (11Q10 XXXV, 2); ראסין "stadia" (4Q554 1 i, 15).[114]

For the use of *aleph* as part of a digraph with *waw* or *yodh* to mark /o/ and /u/ class vowels, see "Digraphs" (§3.5).

3.4. Etymological Short /u/ Marked with *Waw*

One of the most obvious orthographic differences between the DSS and the MT is that etymological short /u/ is often marked in the DSS with a *waw*.[115] This is the case in most classes of words, like those with the bases **qul* (for example, תור "dove"), **qull* (for example, חוק "statute"), **quṭl* (קודש "holiness"), **qaṭul* (עמוק "deep"), **quṭul* (בכור "firstborn" and the *qal* imperative קטול and infinitive קטול),[116] **quṭulat* (אחוזה "possession"),

---

112. Kutscher, *Isaiah*, 162. Ben-Ḥayyim, on the other hand, argues that נאלכה should reflect the *piel* form of הלך ("The Tradition of the Samaritans and its Relationship to the Linguistic Tradition of the Dead Sea Scrolls and Rabbinic Language" [Hebrew], *Leshonenu* 22 [1958]: 236–237).

113. See Matthew Morgenstern, "Notes on the Language of the Qumran Scrolls" (Hebrew), *Meghillot* 2 (2004): 161–162.

114. See Muraoka, *GQA*, 29.

115. See, e.g., Qimron, *HDSS*, 17.

116. Alternatively, the infinitive construct derives from the same base as the infinitive absolute, **qaṭāl*; see Yoo-Ki Kim, "The Origin of the Biblical Hebrew Infinitive Construct," *JSS* 57 (2012): 25–35.

**quṭṭal* (and related *pual* forms: קוטל, יקוטל, מקוטל), **huqṭal* (and related *hophal* forms: הוקטל, יוקטל, מוקטל), **yaqṭul(u)* (that is, the *qal* imperfect and *waw*-consecutive imperfect of strong roots יקטול and ויקטול), **way-yaqul* (that is, the *waw*-consecutive imperfect of II-*waw* roots: ויקול).

However, it is not the case for all historic /u/ vowels. Note the absence of an initial *waw mater* in the typical *qal* imperative and infinitive just cited from the base **quṭul*, as well as in the bases **quṭulat*, **quṭāl* (אנוש "person"), **quṭūl* (כרוב "cherub")—all presumably for the same reason, that is, the initial /u/ shifted to /i/ and then to /ə/ before the DSS were written.[117] For other words, it seems that it is a secondary vowel that is given a *waw mater* while the etymological /u/ vowel does not get a *mater*, as in some construct forms of **quṭl* nouns like קדוש *qŏdoš* "holiness of" (4Q418 81 + 81a, 4) and in צהורים "noon" (1QIsa[a] at Isa 58:10 and 59:10) for MT צָהֳרַיִם.

Furthermore, it bears mentioning that marking short /u/ with a *waw* is common, but not universal. Many forms that would take a *waw* do not receive one. Note, for example, that approximately half the **quṭl* nouns and *pual* forms in 1QIsa[a] do not bear a *waw* in the appropriate place; as Kutscher remarks, it seems very unlikely that the *plene* and defective spellings reflect different pronunciations.[118] The *plene* spellings among nonbib-

---

117. There are exceptions, apparently, as suggested by עווז in 1QIsa[a] at Isa 42:25 and perhaps לאוכולה (*qal* infinitive + suffix or noun) in 4Q176a 19–20, 3 (see below, footnote 121). In the case of some nouns of the **quṭulat* base the first historical /u/ was lost, but then another /u/ class vowel emerged due to assimilation: אוחזת (1QS XI, 7); כוהונו[ת] (4Q400 1 ii, 19); כוהנתנו (4Q400 2, 6); פועלתי (1QIsa[a] at Isa 49:4); פועלתמה (1QIsa[a] at Isa 65:7) (see Elisha Qimron, "A Work Concerning Divine Providence," in *Solving Riddles and Untying Knots: Biblical, Epigraphic, and Semitic Studies in Honor of Jonas C. Greenfield* [ed. S. Gitin et al; Winona Lake, Ind.: Eisenbrauns, 1995], 199; and the sections below titled "Digraphs" [§3.5] and "*Waw* Marking /u/ Class Vowel in Nouns Where MT Has No /u/ Class Vowel" [§5.4]). In the case of these words, it is the second /u/ that is not represented by a *waw mater*. Notice, also, that the *qal* infinitive construct when followed by suffix and the imperative when followed by suffix do often evidence a *waw mater* after the first root consonant but not after the second; inf. const.: שופטם in 1QH[a] XII, 19 and impv.: עובדם in 4Q416 2 iii, 17; this is in keeping with the developments also evidenced in the Tiberian tradition where these verbal forms look like they derive from a **quṭl* base.

118. Kutscher, *Isaiah*, 138–141. For the ninety-five examples of *plene* writing of short /u/ and /o/ in the MT, see Francis I. Andersen and A. Dean Forbes, *Spelling in the Hebrew Bible: Dahood Memorial Lecture* (BO 14; Rome: Pontifical Biblical Institute, 1986), 95–100.

lical texts are found in all three corpora (DSS-SP9, DSS-SP1c, and DSS-NSP). The defective spelling, without a *waw*, may be found in all corpora too, but is less common overall. Thus, one finds the word "holiness" (= MT קֹדֶשׁ) written with a *waw mater*, קודש, in DSS-SP9 (1QH[a] XV, 13), DSS-SP1c (4Q185 4 i, 3), and DSS-NSP (4Q179 1 i, 7) texts; the spelling without a *waw* appears rarely in all three corpora as well. A similar pattern holds for the *pual* forms. A greater discrepancy is found, however, among the biblical scrolls; the biblical scrolls that are part of the DSS-SP9 texts often have forms with a *waw*, while the biblical scrolls that are part of the DSS-NSP texts have words that lack a *waw* and which are closer to the forms one finds more commonly in the MT. Such a distribution presumably reflects the conservative nature of copying biblical texts among the scribes associated with DSS-NSP texts and the corresponding freedom of the scribes associated with DSS-SP9 texts.

Conceivably, as Qimron suggests, **quṭlat* nouns like חכמה are really of another base, like **qaṭlat*, and a word like "wisdom," when written defectively, represents the pronunciation *ḥekmā* (with Tiberian vowels: *חֶכְמָה).[119] This seems less likely now since there are more examples of חָכְמָה written with *waw mater*.[120] There are also additional examples: עורמת "shrewdness of" (4Q299 3a ii - b, 5); אוכלה "food" (4Q378 3 i, 5 [interlinear *waw*] and 11Q19 LIX, 7);[121] חורבה "ruin" (4Q462 1, 14 and

119. Qimron, *HDSS*, 17. Qimron implies a kind of uniformity in relation to these nouns when he writes: "עָרְמָה is always written defectively (7 times) and ... the word חָכְמָה is written 10 times without *waw* and only once with *waw*."

120. In a more recent study, Qimron counts thirteen examples of חָכְמָה spelled *plene* versus twenty-six without a *waw* ("Work Concerning Divine Providence," 192). According to Accordance, the absolute form of the word חָכְמָה with *waw mater* is found in 1QH[a] V, 20; 4Q299 17 i, 2; 4Q413 1–2, 1; 4Q487 2, 8 (partially preserved); 4Q525 1, 1 and 2; 23, 6; 11Q5 (11QPs[a]) XVIII, 3; 11Q5 (11QPs[a]) at Ps 104:24; PAM43686 9,1. Schoors also lists 1Q27 1 i, 3, though the reading of the word is significantly damaged ("Language of the Qumran Sapiential Works," 64). In addition, the word חָכְמָה is found with a *waw mater* in the construct and with suffixes numerous times: 1QH[a] IX, 16; XVIII, 4 (partially preserved); 4Q299 3a ii - b, 5; 4Q300 1a ii - b, 4; 3, 3; 4Q418 126 ii, 5; 139, 2; 4Q432 5, 2; 4Q88 (4QPs[f]) at Ps 107:27; 11Q5 (11QPs[a]) XXVIII, 14. The cumulative count, including the passage from 1Q27 and others that are partially preserved is twenty-one instances of the word with a *waw mater* out of a total of sixty-five (biblical scrolls: 10; nonbiblical scrolls: 55). Thus, the *plene* spelling of חכמה is found in a third of the word's occurrences.

121. Devorah Dimant notes that the occurrence in 4Q378 might also be construed as the infinitive construct of the verb אכל, though it seems more likely to be the

11Q19 LIX, 4). It also seems significant that the instances of חוכמה occur primarily among the DSS-SP9 texts, where we might have expected to see the best evidence for the alternative form *חָכְמָה.[122] Thus, it seems more likely that nouns of the *quṭlat pattern did not get a *mater* as regularly as nouns of other patterns. On the other hand, some words like טהרה "purity" may really be from a different base; this word occurs over sixty times where at least the first two root consonants are preserved and only three times is it written with a *waw mater* טוהרה (1QS VI, 22; 4Q266 6 ii, 11; 4Q525 5, 5).

That *quṭlat nouns are not consistently represented with a *waw mater* (חכמה, ערמה), though the etymologically similar vowel in *quṭl nouns with suffixes (for example, *quṭlō, *quṭlāh, *quṭlām) is almost always represented with a *mater* in the DSS-SP9 and DSS-SP1c texts (קודשו in 1QSb V, 28 and קודשך in 1QH^a V, 25; קודשם in 4Q405 23 ii, 8) suggests that the inclusion of a *waw mater* may not have been exclusively determined by phonetics, but also partially conditioned by the common spelling of the singular absolute form.[123] Exceptions to this rule are rare; note the com-

---

noun "food," based on the ancient translations (LXX, Peshitta, Targum Neophyti) of Deut 31:17 (on which verse the text of 4Q378 and 11Q19 is based) ("Two Discourses from the Apocryphon of Joshua and Their Context (4Q378 3i–ii)," *RevQ* 23 [2007]: 49). She also notes that Ezek 34:8 has a similar expression with "food." By contrast, Deut 31:17 in the MT has the infinitive construct. Note also לאוכולה (4Q176a 19–20, 3; based on the reading by Menahem Kister, "Newly-Identified Fragments of the Book of Jubilees: Jub. 23:21–23, 30–31," *RevQ* 12 [1985–1987], 531–534); *DSSSE* and Accordance read לאוכולהו, which seems unlikely based on the photographs. The spelling seems to be a conflation of the infinitive and nominal forms, perhaps precipitated by the kind of alternative readings evidenced in the MT and versions of Deut 31:17.

122. The word חכמה with *waw mater* occurs four times in the DSS-NSP texts (4Q88, 4Q300, 4Q413) and once in a DSS-SP1c text (4Q487). Qimron writes "It is less likely that all the cases of חכמה (without *waw*) are defective spellings, since some of them occur in manuscripts that consistently mark any *u*/*o* vowel with a *waw*" ("Work Concerning Divine Providence," 193). While this might be the case, the word occurs both with and without a *waw* in at least four texts: 1QH^a; 4Q299; 4Q300; 4Q418. As Kutscher observes for *quṭl nouns and *pual* forms in 1QIsa^a, it seems unlikely that the *plene* and defective forms reflect different pronunciations (*Isaiah*, 138–141).

123. The few examples of *quṭl nouns with suffixes attested in DSS-NSP texts suggest that they occurred without the *waw mater*. The tendency to write *quṭlat nouns without a *waw* may be to avoid confusion between "her cleverness" (*עורמה) and "cleverness" (ערמה). The singular *quṭl nouns that always or almost always see a *waw mater* in their first syllable when followed by a suffix include אזן (9 out of 13 times),

monly occurring word רוקמה "embroidered work," spelled some twenty times with a *waw* (though early editions of 1QM usually read the occurrences in this scroll as ריקמה).[124]

As is well recognized, the orthography of the DSS often does not represent the etymological origin of the /u/ and /o/ vowels in the same way that the orthography in the MT does. For example, in the MT an /ō/ from an etymological /u/ in a monosyllabic noun often is not marked with a *waw mater* (for example, כֹּל), though an /ō/ from an etymological /ā/ often is (for example, טוֹב); in the DSS both are marked with a *mater* (כול, טוב). Although this is the case, there is at least one group of nouns where the *plene* spelling in the DSS actually seems to reflect the etymology of the vowel more clearly than the orthography in the MT. The plural form of the word שֹׁרֶשׁ "root" appears with suffixes most commonly in the MT with a *qamets* under the initial *shin*, שָׁרָשָׁיו (Hos 14:6), in contrast to the etymologically expected form with shewa or *hateph-qamets* *שְׁרָשָׁיו or *שֳׁרָשָׁיו. The plural for קֹדֶשׁ "holiness" appears in the MT after the definite article in the expected manner הַקֳּדָשִׁים but without the article as קֳדָשִׁים. In the DSS, by contrast, the plural forms of the words are regularly given a *waw mater* after the first root consonant, indicating clearly the quality of the vowel: קודשים (4Q274 2 i, 9 [with definite article], 1QS VIII, 8 [without definite article]); משורשיו (4Q433a 2, 9), even where the MT has a form with *qamets* משורשיו (1QIsa[a] at Isa 11:1) for MT מִשָּׁרָשָׁיו.

3.5. Digraphs

As indicated in "*Aleph* as Internal *Mater*" (§3.3), the *aleph* might have been construed in some forms as a *mater* for /a/ class vowels. In addition, it seems to have been used to mark /i/, /o/, and /u/ vowels at the end of words, often when accompanied by a *waw* or *yodh mater*. A similar orthographic

אכל (3/3), ארך (5/7), גבה (9/9), גדל (4/4), גרן (1/1), חזק (0/1), טהר (2/3), כפר (2/2), נגה (2/3), סלת (1/1), עצם (1/1), ערף (8/8), קדש (84/87), רבע (1/1), רחב (7/8), שרש (1/1), תאר (2/5). Where they do not, the text is usually a DSS-NSP.

124. For more on this word and its orthography, see John Elwolde, "*RWQMH* in the Damascus Document and Ps 139:15," in *Diggers at the Well*, 77–79. That the word is רוקמה and not ריקמה is based, in part, on the rarity of internal *yodh* marking short /i/ and the frequency of *waw* marking short /o/ and /u/. Another word where one sees some variation is in the feminine plural עושרות (e.g., 1QM II, 17) for what is in the MT עֲשָׂרֹת, though the singular in the DSS regularly does not contain the *waw*.

practice is evidenced within words where the presence of an *aleph* is due to the etymology of the word: ראוש/רואש "head" (for MT רֹאשׁ) and ריאשון/ ראישון "first" (for MT רִאשׁוֹן).[125] These and similar words are also addressed in this section, though technically these are best construed not as containing digraphs per se, but rather cases of *aleph* being preserved as a historical spelling and accompanied by a *waw*/*yodh mater*.

At first blush, the place of the *waw* or *yodh* in relation to the *aleph* does not seem to matter, the variation being a result of the *aleph*'s quiescence.[126] That is, it seems one could write either וא- (as would be expected from the MT) or או- in any environment. Thus, לקראו "to call" in 1QIsa[a] at Isa 8:4 appears for MT קְרֹא; ויבאו "so that he may enter" in 1Q8 (1QIsa[b]) at Isa 26:2 appears for MT וְיָבֹא; likewise ויבאו "he entered" in 4Q73 (4QEzek[a]) at Ezek 23:44 for MT וַיָּבוֹא;[127] and יבאו "he will come" in 4Q76 (4QXII[a]) at Mal 3:1 for MT יָבוֹא.[128] But, it is not true that the *mater* could exchange places with the *aleph* in any circumstance. This variation is not found regularly in words where the *aleph* separates two syllables; in these cases, the *aleph* consistently precedes the *mater*. Thus, we find מאור *māʾōr* "light"

125. Of the fifty times the word ראש is spelled with *aleph* in the nonbiblical texts, it is spelled ראוש in around ten passages from 1QM, 4Q186, 4Q364, 4Q403, 4Q416, 4Q418, 11Q19 (DSS-SP9 texts) and רואש in around fifteen passages from 1QS, 1QSa, 1QSb, 1QM, 4Q160, 4Q163, 4Q267, 4Q289, 4Q365, 4Q405, 4Q494, 11Q19 (DSS-SP9, with one exception: 4Q494 is among the DSS-SP1c texts). The common MT spelling ראש is found in all manner of texts, including some of those listed above, like 1QM, 4Q416, 4Q418, as well as from some DSS-NSP texts like 4Q216, 4Q381, and 4Q385. For more on this noun, see the subsection "Quiescence of Aleph" in §4.3, "Weakening of Gutturals." As a comparison, note the spelling of the common word "flock" in the MT at Ps 144:13: צאוֹנֵנוּ.

126. See Abegg, who writes "the weakened *ʾalep* often (30x) changes position with the following *o* or *u* vowel, acting then as a digraph rather than a consonant" ("Linguistic Profile," 29).

127. Conceivably, ויבאו in 4Q73 represents the 3mp; in the MT the verb ויבא is in the singular but later in the verse one finds באו "they came." In the preceding verse in the MT, the *qere* to יִזְנֶה implies the plural "they prostitute themselves." The scroll is fragmentary and contains none of these other verbs.

128. A similar alternation appears in the DSS and the MT with infinitives construct from III-*aleph* roots, like מלואת (1QS VII, 20, 22) versus מלאות (4Q258 VII, 2; 4Q259 II, 3, 5; 4Q367 1a–b, 6, 8; 11Q1 [11QpaleoLev[a]] at Lev 25:30) in the DSS and מְלֹאת (Jer 25:12 and passim) versus מְלֹאות (Est 1:5). See GKC §74h. Note also שמאול "left" (1QIsa[a] at Isa 9:19) for MT שְׂמֹאול versus שמואל (1QIsa[a] at Isa 54:3) for MT שְׂמֹאול.

occurring around thirty-five times where relevant letters are preserved, always with *aleph* and with the *mater*, where it occurs, after the *aleph*. In at least fifteen of its occurrences מאור would have, according to the Tiberian tradition, a shewa after the *mem* (in the plural absolute and construct forms), an environment where we might expect the quiescence of the *aleph* and/or the misplacement of the *waw* (*מואר). This never occurs. Similarly, the plural form נפלאות *niflā'ōt* "wonders" occurs around sixty-five times always with an *aleph* and with the *mater*, where it occurs, after the *aleph* (with one exception in a broken context where the letters are damaged, and, thus, the reading less certain: [נפל]ואתיכ[ה] in 1QH[a] II, 12).[129] This word occurs in at least fifty passages in the construct or with a suffix, where the *aleph* is preceded by a shewa according to the Tiberian vocalization (*niflə'ōt*). The name שאול *šə'ōl* "Sheol" occurs around seventy times (twenty times in nonbiblical scrolls, fifty in biblical) always with *aleph* and the *mater* after it; צבאות *ṣəbā'ōt* "hosts" occurs around twenty times in the nonbiblical scrolls and 120 times in the biblical scrolls, where the relevant letters are preserved, and only once (11Q19 LXII, 5) is the *waw* initially written before the *aleph* (צבואת) and even here it was corrected to the proper spelling;[130] the forms of חטאת "sin" (= MT חַטָּאת) that exhibit quiescence of the *aleph* in the MT (that is, the plural construct and plural form with suffixes [= MT חַטֹּאת< * *ḥaṭṭə'ōt*]) are spelled with and without an *aleph* (חטאות and חטות), though where they are spelled with an *aleph* and *waw*, the *aleph* always comes first (seven times in the nonbiblical scrolls and eight times in the biblical scrolls); גאון "majesty" (= MT גָּאוֹן) is spelled consistently two times in the nonbiblical scrolls and twenty-one times in the biblical scrolls (in all but one case where the word is in construct or followed by a suffix); גאות "majesty" (= MT גֵּאוּת) is spelled consistently four times in the nonbiblical scrolls and six times in the biblical scrolls (at least three times in construct or with suffix); שאון

129. In the case of this misspelling, it is important to note that the form (if read correctly) would presumably have a shewa in the syllable preceding *aleph* (according to the MT model) and, thus, the *aleph* might have quiesced resulting in the pronunciation *niflōtekā*, or, conceivably, the *aleph* shifted to *waw*, *nifləwōt*.

130. Note also הטמואת (11Q19 LI, 6) corrected to הטמא'ות. Presumably, the misspellings reflect the respective pronunciations *ṣəbāwōt* and *haṭṭŏmāwōt* and the shift *aleph* > *waw* due to the *aleph*'s assimilation to the following /o/ vowel. See Elisha Qimron, "Diphthongs and Glides in the Dead Sea Scrolls" (in Hebrew), *Meḥqarim* 2–3 (1987): 271; and §4.5 below, "*Aleph* < *Waw* and *Waw* < *Aleph*."

"roar" (= MT שָׁאוֹן) is spelled consistently twice in the nonbiblical scrolls and at least eleven times in the biblical scrolls; הביאותה "you brought" and other *hiphil* perfect forms of בוא with the /ō/ connecting vowel occur about twelve times in the nonbiblical scrolls, never with the *mater* before the *aleph*. Note also words like לאומים "peoples" (at least fifteen times in the biblical and nonbiblical texts; never without *aleph*; never with *waw* before the *aleph*); ראובן "Reuben" (twenty times; three times spelled without *aleph* but never with *waw* before *aleph*); and the *qal* infinitive ראות "to see" (spelled consistently in every occurrence, around fifty times in biblical and nonbiblical scrolls).[131] Although the word "utterance" (= MT נְאֻם) seems to defy this pattern, occurring often as נואם instead of נאם or נאום, it seems likely that the word was understood (and pronounced) as a **quṭl* noun (see §5.5, "**quṭl* Nouns"). The same applies for מאד "much" and תאר "form."

The same consistency holds for combinations of prefixal particles and words that begin *aleph* + *waw mater*. For example, באור "with light" appears consistently seventeen times in the nonbiblical scrolls and three times in the biblical scrolls; לאור "for light" and כאור "like light" attest the order *aleph-waw* in all their occurrences (לאור seven times among the nonbiblical scrolls and twenty-one times among biblical scrolls; כאור once in the nonbiblical scrolls and four times in the biblical scrolls). In many of these cases the noun "light" is in construct with a following noun and, according to the Tiberian system, the preceding preposition would take a shewa. Similar consistency is found with all nouns that begin in this way: אהל "tent," אוב "necromancer," אופיר "Ophir," אופן "wheel," אוצר "storehouse," אור "fire," אורה "light,"אורים "Urim," אות "sign," אזן "ear," איב "enemy," אכל "food," אכלה "food," אניה "ship," ארך "length." Only one exception emerges from these many examples: בוארים בארם כבוד[ו] (4Q57 [4QIsa[c]] at Isa 24:15) for MT בָּאֻרִים כַּבְּדוּ "in the east, honor…" Conceivably, here the scribe of 4Q57 was representing *bōrīm*, in other words, the preposition ב followed by the word אוּרִים "lights" in the absolute; the passage from 4Q57 might be translated: "with lights in Aram (is) [his] glory" (for a parallel, see 4Q503 21–22, 1: באור כבודו "his glory is in

131. I have not found exceptions among other, less frequently occurring common nouns/adjectives, like מאומה or תוצאות. I have found only one exception among proper nouns: יואר in 4Q55 (4QIsa[a]) at Isa 23:3 for MT יְאוֹר. Note, by contrast, the name "Saul" שאול is spelled the same way thirty times.

the light" and 4Q403 1 i, 45: [הכ]בוד באור אורותם "the glory is in the light of their lights").[132]

In a similar way, there is consistency among III-*aleph* verbs in the 3cp perfect and in the 3mp and 2mp imperfect (and *waw*-consecutive imperfect), in other words, the forms that end in *-ū*. The sequence *aleph* + *waw mater* is consistently present in over three hundred clearly legible examples in biblical and nonbiblical texts (according to Accordance). I could find only two exceptions where the *waw* precedes the *aleph*, both in 1QIsa[a] (ימחוא "they will clap" 1QIsa[a] at Isa 55:12 for MT יִמְחֲאוּ and תקרוא "you (mp) will be called" at Isa 61:6 for MT תִּקָּרֵאוּ); the first perhaps could be explained as a case of the *aleph*'s quiescence after a muttered vowel and the second as an example of *aleph* assimilating to a following /u/ (as in ראוו *rāwū* "they saw" 1QIsa[a] at Isa 66:19 for MT רָאוּ).[133]

The preceding examples (found in DSS-SP9, DSS-SP1c, and DSS-NSP texts) demonstrate that the combination of *aleph* + *waw mater* is almost always preserved when a vowel (often even shewa) immediately precedes the *aleph*, when the *aleph* separates two syllables. When the vowel that would have preceded *aleph* is a shewa (at least according to the MT tradition) then the *aleph* will rarely be lost, but, where the *aleph* is preserved, the *waw mater* almost always follows the *aleph* (for example, מאור *mā'ōr*). Where the *waw mater* frequently alternates with *aleph*, it is always where the *aleph* comes at the end of a syllable and/or is no longer pronounced: ראוש/רואש "head," יאומר/יואמר "he will say," יבוא/יבאו "he will enter," לקרוא/לקראו "to call," מלאות/מלואת "to fill, fulfill," זאות/זואת "this."[134] The cases where *aleph* should separate syllables but is found, instead, after the *waw mater*, can be explained as examples where the glottal stop has quiesced due to a preceding muttered vowel, the *aleph* being preserved as a historical writing (for example, [נפל]ואתיכ[ה], בוארים, יואר, ימחוא)

132. Or, בוארים might represent *bāwūrīm* "in the east" (see §4.5, "*Aleph* < *Waw* and *Waw* < *Aleph*"). If this explanation is right, then בארם "in Aram" is a gloss. The text of 4Q503 is from a broken context and might also be translated "in the light of his glory" (see *DSSSE*).

133. It is less likely the spellings are due to confusion between III-*aleph* and III-*waw*/*yodh* verb types, since even in 1QIsa[a] the confusion of III-*aleph* and III-*waw*/*yodh* verbs is not common. See the subsection "Lack of Confusion between III-*Waw*/*Yodh* and III-*Aleph* Verbs" in §5.6, "Verbs."

134. See the discussion of מלאות/מלואת in the subsection "Infinitives" in §5.6, "Verbs." For more examples of words where the *waw* alternates with *aleph* and there is no preceding vowel, see Qimron, *Grammar*, 72.

or as examples where the glottal stop has assimilated to a neighboring vowel, the *aleph* again being preserved as a historical writing (for example, צבואת, הטמואת, תקרוא).[135] These observations help encourage the view that etymological *aleph* was usually pronounced as a consonantal glottal stop at the beginning of syllables.[136] For a full explanation, see the subsection "Quiescence of *Aleph*" in §4.3, "Weakening of Gutturals.".

The preservation of the *yodh mater* within a word after an etymological *aleph* shows a similar distribution (even when the *aleph* is preceded by a silent shewa), though there are far fewer examples. Thus, the relevant *hiphil* forms for II-*aleph* roots evidence the sequence *aleph* + *yodh mater* (תדאיגי "do [not] be anxious" 4Q223–224 2 ii, 11), as do examples of verbs like אור "to light" where the *aleph* is preceded by a muttered vowel in the Tiberian tradition (for example, האירותה "you give light" 1QH[a] XVII, 27 and מאירי[ם] "they give light" 4Q405 19, 5). By contrast, in words in which we find the sequence consonant + /i/ + *aleph* + consonant (that is, -Ci'C-), the sequence of the *aleph* and *yodh mater* will vary, just as the *aleph* and *waw mater* vary in words like יאומר/יואמר; thus we find ראישון *rīšōn* "first" (1QM VI, 1 and passim, = MT רִאשׁוֹן) as well as ריאשון *rīšōn* (4Q252 I, 22; 11Q12 3, 2).

The sequences וא-, או-, יא-, אי- are sometimes used to mark word-final vowels; these are cases where two *maters* represent a single vowel. In almost every case, where such digraphs appear at the end of words, the

---

135. That the spellings צבואת, הטמואת reflect assimilation is suggested by other cases of assimilation, where the phonetic shift is more explicit due to two *waws* being written together: בוו, באוו, יבאוו (see "*Aleph* < *Waw* and *Waw* < *Aleph*" [§4.5]). A similar spelling where the *aleph* is not part of the etymology of the word is עדואתיך *ʿēdəwōtekā* "your decrees" (4Q90 [4QPs[h]] at Ps 119:14) for MT עֵדְוֹתֶיךָ; and תעואת *taʿăwōt* "errors" (4Q381 79, 5) for *תעוות (sing. תעות *taʿūt*). In these cases, presumably, the *waw* is consonantal, as well as part of the digraph indicating /ō/. Perhaps the *aleph mater* helps to indicate not only the /ō/ vowel, but also the consonantal value of the preceding *waw*, as the *aleph* seems to do in association with /ā/ vowels; see §3.3, "*Aleph* as Internal *Mater*." In other cases, a spelling with *aleph* is due to analogy to another word, as in לנואם in 1QIsa[a] at Isa 56:10 for MT לָנוּם "to slumber," where the form in the DSS is (presumably) influenced by the word "utterance" a few verses earlier at the beginning of 56:8 (נואם in 1QIsa[a] for MT נְאֻם).

136. In addition, these observations suggest for nouns like פועלה "work" the development **puʿulā* > **pəʿulā* > **pəʿullā* > *puʿullā* (see §5.4, "*Waw* Marking /u/ Class Vowel in Nouns Where MT Has No /u/ Class Vowel"), and for the noun/adverb מאד/מואדה/מאודה "much" the pronunciation *mōd* (see §5.5, "**quṭl* Nouns").

waw or *yodh* appears first and the *aleph* second. Qimron lists two cases where *waw* + *aleph* marks a final long /ō/ vowel: in the preposition *beth* followed by the 3ms suffix, בוא "in it," in 4Q174 I, 6, and the *kaph* plus *-mō* affix, כמוא "like," in 1QH^a XIV, 24 (= MT כְּמוֹ).[137] It bears mentioning that this kind of supplementation of a final long vowel (*ō*, *ū*) with a following *aleph* is also found in the MT with several different particles (for example, אֵפוֹא for אֵפוֹ, and לוּא for לוֹ).[138] The word אפו appears in one DSS spelled with a final *aleph*, אפוא (4Q423 6, 3), while in other cases a word has no *aleph*, even where the MT does, as in לו (4Q51 [4QSam^a] at 2 Sam 19:7) for MT לֹא.[139] Spelling word-final /o/ or /u/ vowels with וא-, although rare, seems to be attested in all groups of texts (DSS-SP9, DSS-SP1c, and DSS-NSP). Although it might be based on analogy to words like ראוש/רואש, it seems more likely that it was influenced by the negative particle, which is spelled לוא in LBH and in the DSS.

The digraph יא- in final position often marks /ī/, usually on short words, specifically the conjunction כי as כיא and the interrogative pronoun מי as מיא, but also occasionally on other words.[140] In 4Q491c 11 i, the digraph appears associated not only with the particles כי and מי, but with many words and particles ending in /ī/, like הגיא "meditation" (4Q491c 11 i, 21), even the 1cs pronominal suffix: ביא "in me" (4Q491c 11 i, 13); יגידניא "they will attack me" (11 i, 17); אניא "I" (11 i, 18); כבודיא "my glory" (11 i, 18). Word-internal use of the digraph is also sometimes found, as in יאר[ש] "he will [not] inherit" (4Q365 1, 2), though this case might be attributable to a scribe who initially thought the verse should read: "the son of this handmaid will not marry (יארש)"; he recognized his mistake and added an interlinear *yodh* but then failed to erase the *aleph* or mark it with cancellation dots. Kutscher suggests that the DSS forms like כיא and

137. Qimron, *HDSS*, 21. Note also cases like יאמינוא (1QpHab II, 6) (see Qimron, *Grammar*, 100).

138. GKC §23i.

139. It should also be noted that the inclusion of a final *aleph* is, according to Muraoka, also found in Aramaic, once in an inscription from the Sheikh Fadl Cave Inscription (twice written נכוא for "Necho," elsewhere in the same text נכו, as in the MT of Jeremiah and 2 Chronicles) and once in Ezra 6:15 (שֵׁיצִיא). See T. Muraoka, "Hebrew," in *Encyclopedia of the Dead Sea Scrolls* (ed. Lawrence H. Schiffman and James C. VanderKam; 2 vols.; New York: Oxford University Press, 2000), 1:341.

140. A supplementation of word final /ī/ by a following *aleph* is also found in the MT with נָקִיא for נָקִי "innocent" (GKC §23i).

מיא are based on analogy to such words as נביא "prophet."[141] The fact that this word (and similar words) is spelled in 1QIsa[a] with and without the final *aleph* (נבי at Isa 28:7), while כי is also spelled with and without the final *aleph* perhaps reinforces this thesis. On the one hand, such variation in spelling may reflect confusion as to which words should be written with an etymological *aleph* (נביא) and which do not (כי), or may reflect the fact that scribes simply liked to vary their spelling.[142] James Barr has argued a similar preference for variation in spelling in the MT, writing that spelling varied simply "because the scribes liked it to vary."[143]

Although Kutscher's suggestion of analogy to words like נביא is quite possible, one wonders if the spelling of כיא was encouraged by other forms too, like the spelling of the more common 3fs independent pronoun היא, which, no doubt, would be considered to reflect an old, prestigious spelling tradition.[144] Due to its frequency and similar shortness, it might have offered a better model for spelling word-final /ī/ with an *aleph* in words like כיא, not to mention a good pedigree for this spelling.[145]

---

141. Kutscher, *Isaiah*, 21. Compare the similar lack of *aleph* in forms from the MT: יַשִּׁי for *יַשִּׁיא in Ps 55:16; יָנִי for *יָנִיא in Ps 141:5. For many other examples, see GKC §74k.

142. Note the frequent variation in the spelling of short words like כי within the same text, sometimes from one line to the next (e.g., 1QH[a] VII, 34 has כי, line 35 has כיא, line 36 has כי, and line 37 has כיא).

143. Barr, *Variable Spellings*, 194. He continues: "Their approach to spelling was not systematic or consistent but occasional, opportunistic and at times exceptional: they did something, but they did not do it all the time; either they did it occasionally, or they did it most of the time, but if they did it most of the time they also made exceptions some of the time. If they liked variation, they could also equally well prefer consistency for a time and produce a block spelling of a word over a long series of instances." Tov writes in relation to this idea: "Simple 'inconsistency' is another way of formulating the combination of block spellings and rapid alternation" ("Review of Barr, *The Variable Spellings*," 15–16).

144. Blau considers the spelling of היא, along with words like בריא, as the possible origin of mistaken writings like נקיא in the MT (*On Pseudo-Corrections in Some Semitic Languages* [Jerusalem: Israel Academy of Sciences and Humanities, 1970], 31).

145. Notice, in relation to this pronoun, that even though it often has a final *heh* (היאה), the form familiar to us from the MT is also found, even in texts that attest היאה (e.g., 1QH[a] V, 30; XII, 14 versus היאה in XII, 19 and XX, 12; see also 4Q266 where the short form occurs in frag. 6 i, 3 and the long form in 6 i, 5, and similarly passim). And, whether or not it is spelled with a final *heh*, the combination of *yodh-aleph* is always present in the word. Most examples of this phenomenon are among the DSS-SP9 texts.

The sequence -יא- rarely seems to mark word-internal or word-final /ē/ or /ī/; when it does, one or the other letter can usually be construed as a historical writing. For example, the *aleph* can be construed as a historical writing in כסיא *kissē* "throne" (4Q57 [4QIsa^c] at Isa 9:6 for MT כִּסֵּא).[146] The second *yodh* in יארׁ[ש] "he will [not] inherit" (4Q365 1, 2) can be construed as a historical writing (though see above for the complexities of the word). An apparent exception is רציאן (1QIsa^a at Isa 9:10) for MT רְצִין.[147]

Similarly, the *yodh* could be construed as a historical writing in תיאמינו *tēmīnū* "you turn to the right" (1QIsa^a at Isa 30:21) for MT תַאֲמִינוּ, though a better understanding is probably Aramaic influence, as suggested by Kutscher, since in Aramaic I-*aleph* verbs appear as I-*yodh* in the *haphel*.[148] Such an origin also explains האיריכי (1QIsa^a at Isa 54:2) corrected to האריכי.

The sequence -אי- is found rarely: שדאים *šēdīm* "demons" (4Q510 1, 5; elsewhere שדים);[149] נכאי "stricken" (1QIsa^a at Isa 66:2 for MT נְכֵה).[150] The correction reflected in א^יחל "(why) should I be profaned?" (4Q58 [4QIsa^d] at Isa 48:11) for what would be in the MT *אֵחַל perhaps reflects how -אי- could represent /ē/, though it is perhaps more likely the correction reflects the scribe's intention to write אחל, in line with the MT orthography.[151]

Another, less common digraph, is the sequence -הא to mark word-final /ā/: דעהא "knowledge" (1QS VII, 4, = MT דֵּעָה); עתהא "now" (4Q175 11, quoting Num 24:17) for MT עַתָּה; חופהא "canopy" (4Q321a V, 7 = MT חֻפָּה); היהא (1QIsa^a at Isa 5:1, 12:2) for MT הָיָה and וַיְהִי.[152] The

146. Note also ויוציא "he brought forth" in 11Q5 (11QPs^a) at Ps 136:11 for MT וַיּוֹצֵא.

147. However, note the complex etymology of the name (Kutscher, *Isaiah*, 119).

148. Kutscher, *Isaiah*, 200.

149. Perhaps also קדשא[י]ם (4Q509 7, 6) for *קדשים.

150. The writing might be occasioned by the preceding word עניא "humble" (= MT עָנִי), or to indicate a synonymous root with *aleph* root consonant (נכא "to strike"), while also indicating explicitly the preceding /ē/ vowel (similarly with ראיש "head" in DSS Aramaic, e.g., 1Q20 XIV, 9; see Muraoka, *GQA*, 29).

151. If this is correct, then the scribe did not bother to erase the mistaken אי. It is also conceivable, though unlikely, that the *niphal* of יחל was intended (vocalized according to Tiberian Hebrew *אֵיָחֵל). The MT has יֵחָל, which seems like a mistake itself, or, following the LXX, the verse is missing its intended subject שְׁמִי.

152. See Kutscher, *Isaiah*, 185. הי^אה (1QIsa^a at Isa 65:10) and היאה (2Q13 [2QJer] at Jer 48:27), in each case for MT הָיָה, perhaps represent the 3fs independent pronoun.

origin of this digraph is unclear. Perhaps, this marking is on analogy to the 3fs possessive suffix on plural nouns, as in חטותיהא "her sins" (4Q176 1–2 i, 6, quoting Isa 40:2) for MT חַטֹּאותֶיהָ. Note also that הא-is a rare spelling for the 3fs suffix on singular nouns in 1QIsa[a] where the MT has ה- (= *-āh*), as in כותבהא "write it" (1QIsa[a] at Isa 30:8) for MT כָּתְבָהּ and בהא "in it" (at Isa 34:10, 11; 62:4; 66:10) for MT בָּהּ.[153]

Scholars have proposed various explanations for these digraphs. Qimron believes they make explicit that the preceding vowel is /o/, /i/, or /e/, not /ā/ or /ɛ/.[154] Kutscher believes their primary function is to insure a Hebrew pronunciation over against an Aramaic one, while Ben- Ḥayyim thinks they indicate a particular pronunciation, for example, מיא *miyya* "who?" (= TH מִי).[155] Kutscher also suggested that these spellings derived from a wish to archaize; he wrote: "Even if—as I think really was the case—this spelling developed thanks to a vogue for archaism…" and "the more complicated a spelling, the more archaic and erudite it appears."[156]

To my mind, both Kutscher's and Qimron's ideas contribute something to the explanation of this orthography. The inclusion of *waw* and *yodh maters* in general were attractive to the DSS writers due to the fact that they clearly indicate the vowel (for example, the case of וא- and או- in words like רואש and its variant ראוש, as well as in יואמר, לוא). The *maters* would have facilitated pronunciation of the words, even encouraged quicker acquisition of reading, not to mention they would have made the words distinctly Hebrew in form (as opposed to Aramaic רֵאשׁ, יֵאמַר, לָא). But, word-final digraphs are not essential in discriminating between different vowels. In the case of these digraphs, it would seem that Kutscher's explanation is more likely; they are due to a mimicking of what was perceived to be archaic spelling.

For a discussion of the use of *aleph* in place of a *yodh* and *waw* in words like כתאים "Kittim" and מצאותי "my commandments," see the respective

153. See §5.2, "Pronouns and Particles." The reverse sequence (אה-) also occurs where it is precipitated by the quiescence of the *aleph* and the incorrect insertion of the letter: מלכאה "work" (4Q263 3) for *מלאכה; התנאה "the fig" (4Q107 [4QCant[b]] at Song 2:13) for MT הַתְּאֵנָה (see Tov, DJD 16:212).

154. Qimron, *HDSS*, 22.

155. Qimron, *HDSS*, 21–22. Kutscher, *Isaiah*, 21. Ben-Ḥayyim, *Studies in the Traditions*, 82–85.

156. Kutscher, *Isaiah*, 21.

discussions in §§4.4–5, "*Aleph* < *Yodh* and *Yodh* < *Aleph*" and "*Aleph* < *Waw* and *Waw* < *Aleph*."

3.6. Two *Yodhs* for a Consonantal *Yodh* and Two *Waws* for a Consonantal *Waw*

Two *yodh*s are sometimes written when comparable MT forms have a single consonantal *yodh*. The numerous examples suggest that these are not simply cases of dittography. Two *yodh*s for a single consonantal *yodh* occur with the verb היה "to be," as well as with a few nouns. The examples include those instances from 1QIsa[a], cited by Kutscher: *qal* perfect 3ms: הייה (at Isa 19:20); 3fs: הייתה (1:21, 6:13, 11:16 [twice], 17:9, 28:4, 29:2 [twice], 34:9, 34:13, 50:11, 64:9); היית (17:1, 19:17); and infinitive הייותך (60:15).[157] Additional examples include the *qal* perfect 3ms הייה (4Q219 II, 21); *qal* imperfect 3ms: יהייה (4Q252 II, 6); *niphal* perfect 3ms נהייה (1QS III, 15).[158] Note too ישייכה *yaššīyəkā* "may he (not) deceive you" (1QIsa[a] at Isa 37:10) for MT יַשִּׁאֲךָ, the *hiphil* imperfect 3ms + 2ms suffix; here the spelling in the scroll reflects the shift /ʾ/ to /y/, which is found especially where the preceding vowel is /ī/.[159] Alternatively, the second *yodh* could be a *mater* and the word pronounced *yaššīyekā*, analogous to the pausal form of the imperfect + 2ms suffix יַשְׁחִיתֶךָ "he will (not) destroy you" (Deut 4:31). Among the nouns that Kutscher lists as having an extra *yodh*, the most important to note is: בעיים "with the heat/strength of" (1QIsa[a] at Isa 11:15) for MT בַּעְיָם.[160] Other examples of verbs and nouns may be ייזל "it will flow" (1QIsa[a] at Isa 45:8) for MT יִזְּלוּ;[161] יידי "two hands of" (1QM XVII, 11); בייד "in the hand/power of" (4Q219 II, 26); רעייתו "his companion" (4Q502 1, 7).[162] The same phenomenon is found in Qumran Ara-

157. Kutscher, *Isaiah*, 159–160. Kutscher also lists הייא (16:2) which is now read as היא corrected from הי (see Ulrich, *Biblical Qumran Scrolls*, 361).

158. Note also the *niphal* participle נהיית (in CD II, 10). The spelling ייוכל (4Q266 5 ii, 7) is another possible example, though perhaps this spelling is due to an attempted correction of *waw* in place of *yodh*.

159. See Kutscher, *Isaiah*, 516; §4.4, "*Aleph* < *Yodh* and *Yodh* < *Aleph*."

160. Kutscher, *Isaiah*, 159.

161. This is the reading of Accordance and Ulrich et al., *Biblical Qumran Scrolls*, 420. Kutscher reads this as וייזל (*Isaiah*, 400). Conceivably the second *yodh* marks the short /i/ vowel; see §3.2, "*Plene* Orthography."

162. The word רעייתו is parsed by Accordance and the *Dead Sea Scrolls Concordance* as the noun רעיה (= MT רַעְיָה) "companion." Accordance identifies it as singu-

maic with the participle כוייה "burn," in 4Q204 1 i, 26. Comparable nouns + suffixes occur in Hebrew inscriptions from the Common Era, as noted by Kutscher, as well as in texts of the Mishnah, as in the spelling of the *qal* feminine singular passive participle רְאוּיָיה in *m. Pe'ah* 5:1 and *m. Soṭ.* 4:3 in the Kaufmann manuscript (versus רְאוּיָה in *m. Sanh.* 1:6 and 8:4).[163]

More rarely, two *yodhs* are written for two adjacent consonantal *yodhs*, as inענייה "afflicted one" (1QIsa[a] at Isa 54:11) for MT עֲנִיָּה; היים "the sea" (1QpHab XI, 2); היימים "the days" (4Q219 II, 31); צ״י[ה] "dry" (4Q286 5a–c, 2).[164] This too is evidenced in later Hebrew, as in הַיְירָקוֹת "the green vegetables" from *m. Ber.* 6:1.

A similar phenomenon appears to take place with *waw*. The MT שָׁוְא "nothingness" is written שוו (1QpHab X, 10 and 11), similar to its spelling שָׁוְוא in the Kaufmann manuscript of *m. Šebu.* 3:11.[165] The MT עָוֶל "injustice" is written עוול in 11Q13 II, 11 in quoting Ps 82:2. Note also הוות "destructions of" (1QH[a] XI, 39) for what would be (presumably) in the MT *הוֹת, though הוות might also be construed as one consonantal *waw* surrounded by two *mater waws*.

Two separate *waws* written for two adjacent consonantal *waws* may be evidenced in the 3ms *piel waw*-consecutive imperfect form of צוה "to command," ויצווהו "he commanded him" in 4Q219 I, 12.[166] Conceivably, תשויע "you will cry out" in 1Q8 (1QIsa[b]) at Isa 58:9 for MT תְּשַׁוַּע is another example of this and should be read תשווע.[167] The spelling עווה

---

lar, though one wonders if it should not be read as plural רעיותו. The text is extremely fragmentary. Examples like תענייות "humiliations" (4Q511 8, 5 and 121, 2 [with interlinear second *yodh*]) are probably due to analogy to other gentilic words like כתיים (see §4.4, "*Aleph* < *Yodh* and *Yodh* < *Aleph*").

163. Kutscher, *Isaiah*, 160. M. H. Segal, *A Grammar of Mishnaic Hebrew* (Oxford: Clarendon, 1927), 35. Similarly, note שְׁיֵיר in, e.g., *m. Pe'ah* 3:8 (Kaufmann manuscript).

164. More conjectural is וייכ[תבו] (4Q269 10 ii, 10).

165. See Kutscher, *Isaiah*, 148 for this example. Another example Kutscher cites from 1QpHab (IX, 9), ב[א]וון, is now read as בעוון by Accordance and *DSSSE*.

166. The fact that ויצווהו is a singular verb is based on the fact that this passage from *Jubilees* has Abraham speaking to Isaac. The superficially similar תצוום "you (mp) will command them" (4Q364 30, 5) uses an initial *waw* to mark the consonant and a second to mark the /ū/ vowel, cf. MT תְּצַוֻּם (in Deut 32:46); see Tov and White, DJD 13:243. The possibly similar ישתחווה from 1QIsa[a] at Isa 45:14 is probably a spelling mistake since the MT form is plural ישתחוו (see Kutscher, *Isaiah*, 148).

167. See §3.2, "*Plene* Orthography."

"ruin" in 11Q5 (11QPs[a]) XIX, 15 for what would be in the MT עַוָּה may be another example of this orthographic practice, though I prefer reading the word as עויה "iniquity."[168]

Although Qimron writes that the "occasional instances of the spellings יו ,וו are mostly misreadings by modern editors," there are a sufficient number of cases to suggest that this was a rare reflex of the orthography, particularly when the preceding consonant is a guttural or *waw*.[169] All the texts cited above are from the DSS-SP9 texts, except 4Q252 and 1Q8 (1QIsa[b]), which are DSS-NSP.

---

168. See Eric D. Reymond, *New Idioms within Old: Poetry and Parallelism in the Non-Masoretic Poems of 11Q5 (= 11QPsa)* (SBLEJL 31; Atlanta: Society of Biblical Literature, 2011), 154, 160.

169. Qimron, *HDSS*, 24. He also cites his earlier article "The Language of the Temple Scroll" (Hebrew), *Leshonenu* 39 (1975):144. In his *Grammar* (65), he lists only three cases of *yodh* written twice to indicate a consonant outside 1QIsa[a].

4
Phonetics and Phonology

4.1. Phonemic Inventory

The phonemic inventory of the Hebrew attested in the DSS is unknown, but it seems quite possible that it was similar to that found in Tiberian Hebrew. The following list of Tiberian Hebrew consonants gives the phoneme between slashes and the approximate phonetic realization in brackets (using the IPA system of phonetic notation). Labials /b/ [b], [v]; /m/ [m]; /p/ [p], [f]; /w/ [w], [v]; dentals/alveolars: /t/ [t], [θ]; /d/ [d], [ð]; /ṭ/ [ṭ]; /s/ [s]; /z/ [z]; /ṣ/ [ṣ]; /š/ [ʃ]; /n/ [n]; /l/ [l]; palatals: /y/ [j]; velars and uvulars: /k/ [k], [χ]; /g/ [g], [ʁ]; /q/ [q]; /r/ [ʀ]; laryngeals/pharyngeals: /h/ [h]; /ʾ/ [ʔ]; /ḥ/ [ħ]; /ʿ/ [ʕ].[1] The assumption that the *begadkephat* letters were spirantized in the Hebrew of the DSS is addressed below in §4.2, "Spirantization."

As explained below in detail, the gutturals (/ʾ/, /h/, /ḥ/, /ʿ/) certainly seem to be confused in particular texts, suggesting that there was less distinction between them than in earlier Hebrew and less than that reflected in the Tiberian tradition. Nevertheless, this is not a universal phenomenon; not all texts reveal such confusion and not all gutturals were equally indistinguishable.

I assume that the /y/ sound was preserved in the writing/reading register of most DSS, both in intervocalic position and at the beginning of a word, though sometimes it did shift to a glottal stop (as explained in §4.4, "*Aleph* < *Yodh* and *Yodh* < *Aleph*"). I also assume it forms a diphthong where it appears at the end of a word (e.g., גוי = *gōy*). Nevertheless, in some

1. See Geoffrey Khan, "The Tiberian Pronunciation Tradition of Biblical Hebrew," *ZAH* 9 (1996): 3–13. The above list is a simplification of Khan's more subtle and nuanced description.

texts and dialects it is conceivable that /y/ was not pronounced. Qimron asserts that the earlier syllable-initial *yi-* shifted to *i-* and that this is evidenced in the misspelling of a single personal name: ישמעאל "Ishmael" (1QM II, 13) being written as אשמעל in 4Q496 13, 1.[2] A similar shift is asserted for Biblical Hebrew, where יִשַׁי "Jesse" (1 Sam 16:1 and passim) is spelled אִישַׁי once (1 Chr 2:13).[3] Another biblical example may be אִשׁ "there is" (2 Sam 14:19) for יֵשׁ.[4] If such a shift is prevalent in the Hebrew of the DSS, it is strange that there is just one example of it. One wonders if this is best understood in the MT as well as in the DSS as a rare expression of a different (sub-)dialect of Hebrew. Muraoka is cautious as to the existence of this phenomenon in DSS Aramaic.[5] In the Hebrew of the scrolls, *yodh* may also rarely be lost at the end of syllables and words (for examples, see §4.10, "Diphthongs and Triphthongs").

Mem and *nun* are distinguished, I assume, in the writing/reading register. Where *mem* appears for *nun* and vice versa, one can often attribute such a shift to Aramaic influence or hypercorrection due to a perceived Aramaic influence. Cases where *nun* appears for a *mem* in the masculine plural morpheme are probably due to Aramaic influence (פחין "traps" 4Q184 1, 2; ימין 11Q20 XII, 5 corrected to ימים "days"; בשמין 4Q107 [4QCant[b]] at Song 4:10 for MT בְּשָׂמִים "spices") as are the forms of the 3mp suffix with a *nun* (ובשוכן 4Q405 20 ii–22, 12, for what would be in the MT וּבְשָׁכְבָם "and in their descent [from שכב]"; אביהן 4Q17 [4QExod–Lev[f]] at Exod 40:15 for MT אֲבִיהֶם "their father").[6] Cases of hypercorrec-

2. Qimron, *HDSS*, 32 n. 31 and "Diphthongs and Glides," 264 n. 24.

3. Joüon-Muraoka §26e. They note that initial *yi-* was pronounced *i-* "at least in certain schools." See also Bergsträsser, *Hebräische Grammatik*, 1:104–5 and Gumpertz, *Mivṭaʾe Śefatenu*, 55–65. The same shift is evidenced in Modern Israeli Hebrew (Dorit Diskin Ravid, *Spelling Morphology: The Psycholinguistics of Hebrew Spelling* [Literacy Studies 3; New York: Springer, 2012], 92).

4. C. D. Isbell, "Initial ʾ*Alef-Yod* Interchange and Selected Biblical Passages," *JNES* 37 (1978): 228.

5. Muraoka, *GQA*, 21.

6. The word פחין (see John Strugnell, "Notes en marge du volume V des 'Discoveries in the Judaean Desert of Jordan,'" *RevQ* 7 [1970: 264) is read as פחוז "wantonness" (a noun or infinitive) by John M. Allegro (*Qumran Cave 4.I (4Q158–186)* [DJD 5; Oxford: Clarendon, 1968], 83) and Qimron (*HDSS*, 112). Note the concentration of apparent Aramaisms in 4Q107, noted by Tov, DJD 16:209. Notice also that the Hebrew words that have a *nun* in the plural are words that also occur in DSS Aramaic. Others (e.g., *DSSSE* and Accordance) derive ובשוכן from שכן "to dwell." On the similar shifts

tion may include מדים (1QIsa[a] at Isa 9:3 and 60:6) for MT מִדְיָן "Midian"; ולבנימים נתן "to Benjamin he gave" (4Q364 11, 2); ובנימים "and Benjamin" (4Q385a 18 ii, 7); אתנם "wages" (4Q166 II, 18), for what would be אֶתְנָן in the MT, in a quotation of Hos 2:14 for MT אֶתְנָה.[7] All the same, there might also have been a confusion of the two phonemes in some dialects. According to Kutscher, the final *mem* of some words was pronounced as a *nun*, though still written with a *mem* in dialects of Hebrew from the region of Jerusalem south.[8] Qimron, on the other hand, believes there is no distinction between the two consonants at the end of words.[9]

In some cases, where one would expect a *nun* to assimilate to a following consonant, it does not. Qimron lists numerous cases where this occurs with the preposition *min* (e.g., מן טהרת "from the purity of" 1QS VII, 3, instead of *מטהרת).[10] He notes that this tendency also appears in the MT and that Kutscher observed the same phenomenon in 1QIsa[a] and attributed it to influence from Aramaic (in Aramaic, the *nun* on the corresponding preposition does not typically assimilate). If this is so, then it is ironic, since the Aramaic of the DSS seems to show the influence of Hebrew in this respect, as Muraoka observes: the assimilation of /n/ of the preposition *min* is "fairly common in Q[umran] A[ramaic]."[11] Other apparent cases of nonassimilation include וינתן (4Q17 [4QExod-Lev[f]] at Exod 40:18, 20, 22) for MT וַיִּתֵּן "he set"; this may reflect dissimilation of gemination through nasalization, as in Aramaic (though note the possible assimilation of the *nun* in other attestations of the same verb in this same manuscript, e.g., נתת at Exod 40:8). In other cases, the nonassimilation may be part of the idiosyncracies of the scroll and its scribes, as in ינתן "he will give" and ינצר "he will guard" in 4Q175 3 and 17, respectively,

---

in Aramaic, see Muraoka, *GQA*, 19. Note too the ין- ending on all m.p. nouns in the Copper Scroll (3Q15).

7. On מדים, see Kutscher, *Isaiah*, 61. On the spelling of Benjamin with a *mem*, see Kutscher, *Galilean Aramaic*, 62 n. 82. Sometimes the replacement of *nun* with *mem* is due to the generic use of the 3mp suffix, as in קולם (4Q104 [4QRuth[a]] at Ruth 1:9) for MT קוֹלָן (cf. עֲשִׂיתֶם in the MT Ruth 1:8 and לָכֶם Ruth 1:9, in each case with Naomi's daughters-in-law as antecedent).

8. Kutscher, *Isaiah*, 61. Kutscher bases his conclusion on various misspellings from inscriptions and the LXX, especially where a place name that should end with a *mem* ends with a *nun* or Greek *nu*.

9. Qimron, *HDSS*, 27.

10. Qimron, *HDSS*, 30–31.

11. Muraoka, *GQA*, 7.

together with the numerous other oddities of this scroll (e.g., למעאן "so that" in line 4 for what should be *למען).[12] Another possible explanation is the preference for pausal forms (in the MT, I-*nun* verbs in pause sometimes do not evidence assimilation).[13]

The pronunciation of *resh* in the MT depends on certain variables, according to Khan.[14] Alone, it would be pronounced either as a voiced uvular role or as a uvular frictionless consonant, a pronunciation close to that of the spirantized version of *gimmel* (which was articulated as a voiced uvular fricative similar to the pronunciation of French ar and Arabic *ġayin*).[15] Near an alveolar consonant (/d/, /z/, /ṣ/, /s/, /t/, /ṭ/, /l/, /n/), however, *resh* would be articulated as a velarized or uvularized "linguo-alveolar roll."[16] The uvular articulation of this letter means that it was (at least sometimes) made in the mouth close to where the gutturals are made. It would seem that the pronunciation of *resh* was similar in the time of the DSS.[17] Thus, it is no wonder that, like the gutturals, the *resh* was sometimes dropped from the spelling of some words, though often reintroduced as a correction (see §3.1, "Scribal Mistakes"). Such mistakes should be distinguished (to the extent possible) from the confusions that derive from *resh*'s graphic similarity with *daleth* (אבידי [4Q111 (4QLam) at Lam 1:15] for MT אַבִּירַי); that derive from metathesis (תברנו "you created us" [4Q504 1–2R iii, 7] corrected to תרבנו "you made us numerous"); and from haplography (טוה רוחות [4Q405 20 ii–22, 11] for *טוהר רוחות "...purely, spirits").

As in Tiberian Hebrew, the pronunciation of *samekh* and etymological *śin* is identical: /s/. In early Hebrew, the single symbol ש represented two separate phonemes, one a lateral fricative (/ś/) and the other an unvoiced postalveolar fricative (/š/).[18] In exilic and postexilic books of the Bible,

---

12. Abegg, "Hebrew of the Dead Sea Scrolls," 342.

13. See Joüon-Muraoka §72b and Muraoka, *GQA*, 8, 10–11.

14. Khan, "Tiberian Pronunciation Tradition," 11.

15. Ibid., 4, 11.

16. Ibid., 11.

17. Kutscher together with other scholars concluded that *resh* in the DSS "was not firm." See Kutscher, *Isaiah*, 531 and the references there.

18. See Richard C. Steiner, *The Case for Fricative-Laterals in Proto-Semitic* (AOS 59; New Haven: American Oriental Society, 1977); idem, "Addenda to *The Case for Fricative-Laterals in Proto-Semitic*," in *Semitic Studies in Honor of Wolf Leslau* (ed. A. S. Kaye; Wiesbaden: Harrassowitz, 1991), 1499–1513; idem, "Ancient Hebrew," in *The Semitic Languages* (ed. R. Hetzron; London: Routledge, 1997), 148; and Khan, "Tibe-

the lateral fricative phoneme appears to have merged with the phoneme represented by ס, an unvoiced alveolar sibilant (/s/).[19] Most words that had the earlier lateral fricative phoneme, nevertheless, continued to be written with the ש symbol. By the time of the Masoretes, a diacritic dot was placed above the letter ש to distinguish those instances in which it was representing /s/ and those instances in which it was representing /š/. Since the scribes of the DSS era did not have such a diacritic mark, it is not surprising that one sometimes finds words with an etymological lateral fricative (/ś/) spelled with ס and words with an etymological unvoiced alveolar sibilant (/s/) spelled with a ש.

The cases where etymological /ś/ is spelled with *samekh* are generally considered spelling errors which reflect the merging of the respective phonemes. Examples are relatively common and listed by Abegg.[20] For the sake of clarification, I give two: בסר "flesh" (1QHª XXIV, 26) for *בשר and תסיג "it will (not) reach" (4Q418 126 ii, 13) corrected to תשיג. Most of the examples that Abegg cites come from DSS-SP9 texts, though examples can also be found in DSS-NSP texts: יסטמוני "they accuse me" in 4Q88 (4QPs^f^) at Ps 109:4 for MT יִשְׂטְנוּנִי. The reverse mistake (of writing a *śin*/*shin* [ש] for etymological *samekh* /s/) is also evidenced: פשח (4Q136 [4QPhyl I] at Exod 12:48) for the expected *פסח "Passover"; כשפו (4Q136 [4QPhyl I] at Exod 12:44) for MT כָּסֶף "silver"; מאשו (1QpHab I, 11) for *מאסו "they rejected"; משיגי (4Q271 1, 2 or 4Q280 3, 2) corrected to מ^ס^יגי "one who moves back"; שכות (4Q522 9 i–10, 14) for *סכות "Sukkoth."[21] Again, most examples are from DSS-SP9 texts, though this kind of misspelling is also found in DSS-NSP texts: [מ]שה (4Q14 [4QExod^c] at Exod 17:7) for MT מַסָּה "Massah"; שפרתי (4Q90 [4QPs^h] at Ps 119:13) for MT סִפַּרְתִּי "I recount"; ישד (4Q93 [4QPs^l] at Ps 104:5) for MT יָסַד "he founded." Although Qimron suggests that the latter kind of misspellings can only be explained as hypercorrections, or as reflecting the collapse of the two separate phonemes, /s/ and /š/, it seems far likelier that scribes had simply

rian Pronunciation Tradition," 12. The transliteration of the lateral fricative in the IPA is /ɬ/ and that of the postalveolar fricative is /ʃ/.

19. Gary A. Rendsburg, "Ancient Hebrew Phonology," in *Phonologies of Asia and Africa* (ed. A. S. Kaye; Winona Lake, Ind.: Eisenbrauns, 1997), 73.

20. Abegg, "Hebrew of the Dead Sea Scrolls," 327.

21. On 4Q280, B. Nitzan writes: "This little fragment was ascribed by the first generation of editors to two different compositions" ("Curses," in DJD 29:8).

become confused as to the etymology of the words and sometimes wrote a ש when the etymology presumed ס and vice versa.[22]

The vowels for DSS Hebrew also are not known, but conceivably correspond to the vowels of Hebrew in the early part of the first millennium C.E.: /a/ [a]; /e/ [ɛ]; /o/ [o]; /u/ [u]; /i/ [i]. I assume that there was still a distinction in vowel length at this time, something reflected in various sources, including the Secunda.[23] For the discussion of the supposed shift of Proto-Semitic /a/ to /å/, see §4.9 below, "/å/ < /ā/ < Proto-Semitic /a/."

4.2. Spirantization

The development of spirant versions of /b/, /g/, /d/, /k/, /p/, /t/ is posited for Aramaic based on readings like אחוית "I was informed" (a passive A-stem, 4Q196 2, 1), which was interpreted as אחבית "I hid myself" (from an earlier אתחבית) by the LXX translators.[24] Muraoka cites Fitzmyer, who believes spirantization is evidenced for Hebrew in וגויתם "(in?) their body" (4Q169 3–4 ii, 4 in a quotation of Nah 3:3 which has in the MT בִּגְוִיָּתָם).[25]

22. Qimron, *HDSS*, 28–30. If the phonemes /s/ and /ś/ had really collapsed, we would expect to see more examples of etymological /ś/ written with a *samekh*, but Qimron lists only one well-accepted example, יכחס (1QS VII, 3) for what should be *יכחש "he will deceive." Furthermore, confusion of *samekh* for the etymological /ś/ does not necessarily presume hypercorrection, as though the scribe thought that the root actually contained an etymological /ś/. See also Steiner, "Addenda," 1501–3.

23. For the hypothetical correspondences between the vowels presumed by the Secunda and those of the Hebrew text, see G. Janssens, *Studies in Hebrew Historical Linguistics Based on Origen's Secunda* (Orientalia Gandensia 9; Leuven: Peeters, 1982), 111–33 and passim. On the complexities of studying the Secunda and what era of Greek it represents, consult ibid., 20–23; Einar Brønno, "Zu den Theorien Paul Kahles," *ZDMG* 100 (1951): 532–33; Geoffrey Khan, "The Historical Background of the Vowel Ṣere," *BSOAS* 57 (1994): 133–44.

24. Muraoka, *GQA*, 13. Klaus Beyer, on the other hand, dates the development of spirantized allophones in Aramaic from the first century B.C.E. to the third century C.E., though the aspiration of /k/, /p/, /t/ occurs around 250 B.C.E. (*Die Aramäischen Texte vom Toten Meer, samt den Inschriften aus Palästina, dem Testament Levis aus der Kairoer Genisa, der Fastenrolle und den alten talmudischen Zitaten* [Göttingen: Vandenhoeck & Ruprecht, 1984], 125–28). For the evidence from Greek sources, see Janssens, *Studies in Hebrew*, 45–50.

25. See Joseph A. Fitzmyer, "Tobit," in DJD 19:10. Despite the *daghesh* in the *beth*, the preceding word ends in a vowel, thus making the spirantization of the *beth* in the DSS version possible

Allegro mentions a similar kind of mistake in 4Q171 3-10 iv, 7, where an erased *waw* stands before בהשפטו "in his being judged"; he assumes that the *waw* is due to confusion with a spirantized *beth* (the preceding word ends with a vowel).[26] Other possible examples also exist. The phrase יורו לחתוף (4Q429 2, 10) is similar to לחתף יורבו "they lie in wait (ארב) for prey" (1QH[a] XIII, 12).[27] If the verb ארב was intended in 4Q429, then the writing יורו may imply a pronunciation where the second *waw* represents the spirantized *beth* (*yōrəbū*), though it seems more likely that the scribe simply forgot to write the *beth* or that the verb ירה was intended.[28] Another possible example is צפה *ṣāfā* "he watches" (4Q111 [4QLam] at Lam 1:17) for MT צִוָּה "he commanded."[29] I assume that spirantization in Hebrew derives from Aramaic influence and that it was a feature of the writing/reading register of most scribes and writers.

4.3. Weakening of Gutturals

Alexey (Eliyahu) Yuditsky makes the following straightforward statement: "There is a consensus among Hebraists that the gutturals underwent weakening in the idiom of the DSS."[30] The statement seems characteristic of brief descriptions of DSS Hebrew phonology.[31] He, like most scholars who

26. Allegro, DJD 5:41, 49.

27. See Eileen Schuller, "Hodayot" in DJD 29:186. Note also that the 1QH[a] passage had לחתוף initially, though the *waw* was erased.

28. For more on this line, see Schuller, DJD 29:187 and the literature cited there and Menahem Kister, "Three Unknown Hebrew Words in Newly-Published Texts from Qumran" (Hebrew), *Leshonenu* 63 (2000–2001): 38–39.

29. Cross ("Lamentations," in DJD 16:237) thinks that the original text must be that of the scroll; note also that the vowels of the two verbs are not close.

30. Yuditsky, "Weak Consonants," 236.

31. From the early era of DSS studies is the example of Goshen-Gottstein who writes: "It will not come as unexpected news that the system of four separate laryngal and pharyngal phonemes has collapsed in [the] Q[umran] S[crolls]" ("Linguistic Structure," 107). Angel Sáenz-Badillos, recognizing the possibility of multiple dialects, writes in relation to the phonology in the scrolls "Weakening, merger, and loss of laryngeals and pharyngeals is typical" (*A History of the Hebrew Language* [trans. J. Elwolde; Cambridge: Cambridge University, 1993], 137). More recently, Muraoka writes: "The frequent deletion of guttural letters … and their indiscriminate interchange … attest to the general weakening of these consonants" ("Hebrew," 1:341). Frequently, however, in-depth sketches, including those just quoted, often try to nuance this weakening in one way or another. For example, after the sentence just quoted from page 107,

make similar statements, is, I think, referring to a spectrum of guttural weakening in the "living substratum" of Qumran Hebrew.[32] Nevertheless, the statement (and others like it) is problematic due to its vagueness. First, one is left to wonder whether the "weakening" applies to all gutturals equally, primarily the laryngeals, or some other grouping. Second, one wonders what is implied by "underwent weakening." Did the respective phonemes disappear from the language all together, were they usually unarticulated, or only occasionally unarticulated?

Compounding the confusion is that Yuditsky, like almost all others who comment on the phenomenon, cites, in a footnote, references to Kutscher's work on Isaiah and then to Qimron's *HDSS*. In the relevant passage, Kutscher states that "the laryngeals and pharyngeals were indistinguishable in the dialect of the scribe of the [Isaiah] Scr[oll]. This feature, with some variations, is true of the other writings of the sect as well, but this is not the place for a detailed discussion."[33]

This suggests to my mind that all the gutturals were equally indistinguishable from all the other gutturals and that this was a feature not only of 1QIsa[a], but of all the DSS generally. But, this is not exactly what Kutscher means. He writes more precisely in an earlier part of his book:

> Apparently they [the laryngeals and pharyngeals] had become so weak that no differentiation was made between ח-ה, א-ע and quite likely very little was made even between the two groups. The "א" was not pronounced.... The "ע" seems to have been like the "א" in this respect.... The "ח" was apparently pronounced very nearly like a "ה".[34]

Goshen-Gottstein remarks: "whereas in some places the 'original' sounds could be still realized correctly, at least under certain circumstances, inhabitants of other localities were completely incapable of the 'correct' pronunciation" ("Linguistic Structure," 107). Muraoka too notes that such weakening does not imply the weakening of the consonants in all dialects throughout Palestine ("Hebrew," 1:341). When Rendsburg mentions guttural weakening, he refers specifically to 1QIsa[a] ("Qumran Hebrew," 221). Abegg qualifies it in the following way: "Although there is some confusion in the representation of gutturals which points to the lack of distinction or weakening of their pronunciation (*HDSS* §200.11), the vast majority of the misspellings concerns the confusion of א and ה or the elision of א" ("Hebrew of the Dead Sea Scrolls," 327).

32. For the term "living substratum" see Joosten, "Hebrew, Aramaic, Greek," 355.

33. Kutscher, *Isaiah*, 508. Note that Yuditsky cites Kutscher's work in Hebrew, 398–403; the above quoted text occurs on page 401 of the Hebrew edition.

34. Kutscher, *Isaiah*, 57. The confusion between *aleph* and *ʿayin* on the one hand

Kutscher backs his statement up with numerous examples of slips that the scribes of 1QIsa^a made in representing the etymological gutturals, as well as cases where gutturals were introduced where they are not part of a word's etymology. He specifies that this phenomenon (that "laryngeals and pharyngeals were indistinguishable") was not pervasive in all dialects of Hebrew and Aramaic in Palestine.[35]

Qimron emphasizes that although there are eighty cases (among the corpus he studied) of words containing gutturals that are misspelled, misspellings are "chiefly with *alef*, less often with *he*, *ayin*, and *ḥet*."[36] Despite the lopsided data, Qimron comes to a conclusion similar to that of Kutscher: "gutturals in the Qumran pronunciation were weakened."[37] He clarifies what he means by "weakened," at least in relation to the dialect of 4QMMT, when he notes in his summary of the language of the text that "gutturals were 'weakened,' i.e., often so little pronounced as to be imperceptible."[38] Notice, however, that Qimron is less specific than Kutscher and does not indicate explicitly, for example, that *ʿayin* had disappeared to the degree that *aleph* had. In fact, Qimron is quite explicit that he views *aleph* as totally quiesced in intervocalic position.[39] He does not say this about the other gutturals.

Things become more muddled when comparing these evaluations with those of other scholars. Goshen-Gottstein, for example, does not describe the falling together of *aleph* and *ʿayin*, but, instead, implies the falling together of *aleph* and *heh*.[40] Murtonen seems to agree with Goshen-Gottstein's view, asserting that the *ḥeth* and *ʿayin* were preserved longer than *aleph* and *heh*, and suggests that since confusion between words containing *ḥeth* and *ʿayin* occurs primarily in the first half of 1QIsa^a, the scribe

---

and *heh* and *ḥeth* on the other is the same confusion recounted in the Jerusalem Talmud for people in the towns of Haifa, Beth-Shean, and Tibeon (see ibid., 58).

35. Ibid., 59.

36. Qimron, *HDSS*, 25.

37. Ibid.

38. Qimron, "The Language," in DJD 10:69. Does he mean that there was not a distinction between laryngeals and not a distinction between pharyngeals? Or, does he mean that the gutturals had all collapsed to a single phoneme?

39. Qimron, *HDSS*, 31.

40. Goshen-Gottstein refers to the "collapse of the laryngal-pharyngal system, especially of the weakening of the laryngals [i.e., א and ה]" ("Linguistic Structure," 108–9).

of this portion of the scroll did not pronounce them, while "the writers of the model exemplars probably still did."[41]

Although statements asserting the weakening of gutturals in the Hebrew of the DSS are frequent, most words in the DSS are spelled correctly with *heh*, *ḥeth*, and *ʿayin*, as Qimron and others specify.[42] The simplest explanation for this is that the writers of the DSS, with some possible exceptions (like the scribes who copied 1QIsa^a^), still knew the standard or "correct" pronunciation of the respective letters. They perhaps did not recognize the twofold pronunciation of *ḥeth* (as /ḥ/ and /ḫ/) and of *ʿayin* (as /ʿ/ and /ġ/), but they would have recognized /h/, /ḥ/ and /ʿ/ as distinct, at least when writing and reading texts carefully.

Although a consistency in spelling certain words with particular letters might be the result of a conservative spelling tradition (that is, "light" was always spelled with an *aleph*, אור, and "skin" always with an *ʿayin*, עור), there are several factors that suggest consistency is not only attributable to a spelling tradition. First, it should be recognized that although Hebrew had a spelling tradition involving the writing of etymological *aleph*s (even when these were no longer pronounced, as in ראש "head"), the scribes often did not follow it (and wrote רוש instead). They did this even though this created graphic ambiguity (compounding the already existing phonetic ambiguity) with the word "poor" רוש.[43] Thus, one would assume that if the other gutturals were as weak as *aleph*, then the scribes would also not follow the spelling conventions of preceding generations and would have regularly spelled words like מעשה "deed" as *משה. However, words that have an etymological *heh*, *ḥeth*, and/or *ʿayin* root consonant are not routinely misspelled.[44] Second, while (mis)spellings with *aleph* occur in a number of different permutations these do not occur with *heh*, *ḥeth*, and *ʿayin*. For example, though ראשית "beginning" may be spelled רשית and

41. A. Murtonen, "A Historico-Philological Survey of the Main Dead Sea Scrolls and Related Documents," *Abr-Nahrain* 4 (1963–1964): 72.

42. Qimron, *HDSS*, 25, and Abegg, "Hebrew of the Dead Sea Scrolls," 327.

43. In at least one instance this lead to a scribe writing the word for "poor" like the word for "head" ראש (4Q416 2 iii, 2). The word ראש "head" is spelled without *aleph* around thirty-four times in the biblical and nonbiblical scrolls and שארית is spelled without *aleph* around ten times.

44. For example, for *ʿayin*, the closest one comes to a repeated mistake is the form "he did" ויעש and "may he do" יעשה both misspelled in 1QIsa^a^ as וישה and the forms "he/it/they (will) pass" (עבר) spelled יבר in 1QIsa^a^, יאבורו in 1QS, and אברו in 4Q55 (4Isa^a^) (for details, see the subsection on *ʿayin*). Compare the frequency of רוש.

רישית, it is never spelled with *heh*, *ḥeth*, or *ʿayin* (as *רהשית, *רחשית, *רעשית, respectively). Similarly, although גוים "peoples" might be written גואים, it is never written *גוהים, *גוחים, or *גועים.

The situation in DSS Hebrew might be compared to that in DSS Aramaic, as described by Muraoka:

> Though the weakening of gutturals in Q[umran] A[ramaic] appears to be an indisputable fact, it does not necessarily follow that all the three letters, <ח, ה, א>, carried the same phonetic value everywhere nor that they carried no phonetic value at all. Though the four possible spellings—ברה טבה, ברא טבא, ברה טבא, ברא טבה—may have all sounded in QA exactly the same and meant exactly the same thing, 'the good son,' it does not necessarily follow that Afel אקים and Hafel הקים were every bit phonetically identical.[45]

I wonder whether for DSS Hebrew the *ʿayin* was also distinguished, especially in certain texts. In short, my view is that for the writing/reading register of the DSS scribes, *aleph* and *heh* are usually preserved at the beginning of a word and when directly preceded by a full vowel; *ʿayin* is usually preserved, but occasionally is lost at syllable end and where it is directly preceded within a word by a consonant or muttered vowel; *ḥeth* is only rarely lost at syllable end, suggesting in most cases it had not weakened (the dialect of the scribes of 1QIsa[a] being a possible exception in this regard).

So, what evidence has been assembled to convince "all Hebraists" that the gutturals had undergone weakening? In what follows, I lay out the evidence presented by Qimron and Kutscher, as well as additional examples I have found. In general, the evidence is based on spelling mistakes. Although an imprecise articulation of the gutturals may have been a contributing factor in some instances, often other circumstances can explain the misspellings. The end result is that the case for the weakening of the gutturals is not so wide-ranging as most assume. It is likely that in the spoken idiom of some of the writers and scribes the gutturals were not clearly distinguished. But, that no distinction was ever made seems highly unlikely. This means that one should not take at face value the kind of summary statements that one often finds in sketches of DSS Hebrew. The situation was more complex than is often presented.

---

45. Muraoka, *GQA*, 14.

As a preface to the following analysis, two brief remarks should be made about morphophonemic and lexicophonemic conditioning and about the use of 1QIsa[a] in determining guttural weakening. First, although the elision of a guttural will sometimes be cited as evidence of its disappearance from the language, not all examples are equal. For instance, in some cases the loss of *heh* is conditioned by the particular verbal forms from which it disappears (e.g., the infinitives of the *niphal* and *hiphil* when preceded by the *lamedh* preposition).[46] In other cases, the exchange of gutturals *aleph* and *ʿayin* is due to confusions between similar words, like the prepositions אל and על, which can be used in the same context with little distinction in meaning.[47] Even in cases where two words are semantically different (as with אתה "you" and עתה "now"), the similar syntactic slots in which they are used mean that one appears in the MT version of Isaiah and the other appears in 1QIsa[a], though this does not necessarily imply anything about a confusion of gutturals.[48] Second, 1QIsa[a] seems often to replace a word of the MT tradition with another (often commoner, simpler) word. Kutscher

46. Goshen-Gottstein, "Linguistic Structure," 109.

47. Ibid., 108. See also BDB, sub אל, note 2 and Bruce K. Waltke and M. O'Connor, who write in relation to על: "This sense [i.e., 'on, to, onto'] is shared by *ʿl* and *ʾl*; from it other senses of the two prepositions come to overlap by analogy. Futile is the tendency to emend the MT in order to eliminate some or all of these senses, although there may be cases in which the prepositions have been confused in the development of the text" (*Introduction to Biblical Hebrew Syntax* [Winona Lake, Ind.: Eisenbrauns, 1990], 216). Note the preposition אל in 1 Sam 31:3 and 2 Sam 6:3 and על in the corresponding verses from 1 Chr 10:3 and 13:7, as well as in 4Q51 (4QSam[a]) (see Ulrich et al., *Biblical Qumran Scrolls*, 289, 297). An analogous confusion is found between על in 4Q51 (4QSam[a]) at 2 Sam 2:6 and in the MT and ל in the MT at 1 Chr 17:24 (ibid., 299).

48. Consider, e.g., that וְעַתָּה appears at 1 Kgs 1:18 in the MT (Leningrad Codex), though other medieval manuscripts, the LXX, Targum, and Syriac attest or presume וְאַתָּה (this confusion in the MT is perhaps due to dittography); note, too, 1Q8 (1QIsa[b]) at Isa 41:8 has ועתה, while the MT and 1QIsa[a] have ואתה. One also finds in the MT at Gen 26:29 אַתָּה עַתָּה while LXX has νῦν σὺ (in contrast to 1 Kgs 12:4 and 21:7 [= LXX 20:7], where MT and LXX have the same word order); the MT at Isa 37:20 has וְעַתָּה though the LXX has σὺ δέ. The reverse relationship also exists, as in the MT at Dan 8:26 וְאַתָּה vs. LXX καὶ νῦν; in the MT at 1 Chr 28:9 וְאַתָּה vs. LXX καὶ νῦν. Similarly, note the confusion between the MT and LXX at Isa 28:22, where the MT has וְעַתָּה and the LXX καὶ ὑμεῖς; this suggests that the confusion was not exclusively phonetic, since the Hebrew presumed by the LXX is וְאַתֶּם (in 1QIsa[a], however, the reading ואתה in this verse may, in fact, reflect phonetic confusion, though a similar contextual confusion is possible). For other examples, see Delitzsch, *Lese- und Schreibfehler*, 123–24.

frequently suggests that this substitution is due, in part, to the weakening of the gutturals.[49] This may be the case, but other reasons may be more important and the correspondence in sound between the words may only be partial. As Kutscher himself says, the scribe's replacement of one word for another does not presume identical sense: "if the scribe did not understand a word or form he did not hesitate to substitute a more common one which he knew, regardless of whether or not its meaning was appropriate."[50] Given this fact, it is not surprising that the words (that is, the one introduced by the 1QIsa^a scribes and the one found in the MT), although often exhibiting similar sounds, are hardly ever exact homonyms of each other. Sometimes the words are not even phonetically similar. Consider some of the examples that Kutscher cites: יודיע "he will make known" (1QIsa^a at Isa 42:13) for MT יָרִיעַ "he will shout"; פתחו "they are open" (at Isa 42:20) for MT פָּקוֹחַ "open"; טוב "good" (at Isa 45:7) for MT שָׁלוֹם "well being"; מטלים "those hammering" (at Isa 50:6) for MT מֹרְטִים "those polishing"; וינקו ידים "they clean hands" (at Isa 65:3) for MT וּמְקַטְּרִים "they make sacrifices." And, it should be noted, Kutscher himself often remarks on the many possible reasons that a scribe might substitute one word for another, only one of which is the weakening of the gutturals. Given the many reasons one word might be substituted for the other, and given the merely approximate correspondence in sound between the 1QIsa^a word and the MT word, such substitutions provide limited evidence for the weakening of gutturals. In what follows, I first address the phonemes /ʾ/ and /ʿ/, then /h/ and /ḥ/.

Quiescence of *Aleph*

The quiescence of the glottal stop (which is distinct from the elision of the graphic symbol *aleph* in the spelling of a word) is a phenomenon that took place repeatedly (or continuously) over the course of centuries. For example, the word ראש, based on comparative evidence (Phoenician *rʾš*, Arabic *raʾs*), is commonly assumed to have begun as **raʾš* then through the quiescence of the glottal stop and compensatory lengthening to have

49. See, e.g., Kutscher, *Isaiah*, 259–60, 273, 289.

50. Kutscher, *Isaiah*, 34. On page 30, he writes: "He [i.e., the scribe] was likely—both consciously and subconsciously—to substitute one common word for another, and an unusual one by a word known to him either from current use or because of its frequency in scripture."

become **rāš* before then undergoing the Canaanite Shift and becoming *rōš*. (A similar development might be postulated for some I-*aleph* verbal forms like יֹאמַר *yōmar* < **yāmar* < **ya'mar*.)[51] That the word for "head" is found in the Amarna texts (ca. 1350 BCE) with a spelling that presumes the pronunciation *rōš*, implies the antiquity of the quiescing of the glottal stop in a syllable closed by two consonants (as well as the antiquity of the spelling tradition that preserved the *aleph* for centuries).[52]

After the quiescence of the glottal stop in environments like that found in **ra'š*, there appears to have been a second, later phase when the glottal stop elided at the end of words and resulted in compensatory lengthening, resulting in developments like **maθa'a* > **maṣa'a* > **maṣa'* > **maṣā* > *māṣā* or מָצָא "he found." At this point the Canaanite Shift no longer affected the /ā/ vowel and, thus, it did not shift to /ō/. Similarly, note the loss of the glottal stop within words at the end of syllables, as in מָצָאתָ "you found." The loss of the glottal stop after a shewa, as in שְׁאֵרִית/שֵׁרִית "remainder," is perhaps part of this second phase of quiescing or perhaps a third phase.[53] That the glottal stop continued in this trajectory during the late Second Temple era and that the *aleph* was frequently not written within words and at the end of words does not seem surprising. Qimron goes so far as to write that "it is doubtful whether intervocalic *alef* was pronounced at all in DSS Hebrew."[54] The *aleph*, when it appears intervocalically, he believes is rather "an orthographic device to designate two consecutive vowels," that is, *aleph* is only a graphic means of indicating

---

51. See Blau, *Phonology and Morphology*, 87, 240.

52. By the time of the DSS, the writing tradition had begun to change such that the word for "head" was sometimes spelled with a *waw mater* before the *aleph*, sometimes with a *mater* after the *aleph*, and sometimes with only a *waw mater* (the *aleph* dropping out). For a slightly different explanation for the elision of the glottal stop, see Blau, *Phonology and Morphology*, 87–88. For a different explanation of the development of the word "head," see Elisha Qimron, "ראשׁ and Similar Words" (Hebrew), *Leshonenu* 65 (2003): 243–47.

53. The time when these shifts take place is hard to know. Many other examples can be cited, e.g., תוֹמִם (Gen 25:24, for expected תְּאוֹמִים, as in Gen 38:27), חֹטְאִים (1 Sam 14:33), לַהְשׁוֹת (2 Kgs 19:25, for expected *לְהַשְׁאוֹת), כַּאבִּיר (Isa 10:13) (see Andersen and Forbes, *Spelling*, 85–91).

54. Qimron, *HDSS*, 31. He does suggest, however, that the word שאול "Sheol" retained the glottal stop (ibid., 39 and Qimron, *Grammar*, 89, 118). Kutscher suggests a similar loss even for the liturgical register (*Isaiah*, 499). For the spelling of גוים with an *aleph* as גואים, see §4.4, "*Aleph* < *Yodh* and *Yodh* < *Aleph*."

hiatus.[55] Although other scholars seem to assume the preservation of an intervocalic glottal stop (even if just a glide), the precise reasons why they believe this are typically not spelled out.[56] The following will specify where the glottal stop typically is lost and what evidence exists to suggest that the glottal stop was still articulated in some environments.

Among the DSS, *aleph* as a graphic component of a word is not always dropped from words, only sometimes. If the letter is dropped from the spelling of a word, it is typically in the same environments as those described immediately above, in words like ראש (רוש *rōš* 4Q403 1 i, 1 versus ראש *rōš* 4Q216 I, 4), in words where the glottal stop would have occurred at the end of a syllable (within words ברתנו *bərātānū* "you created us" 4Q495 2, 1 versus בראתנו *bərātānū* 1Q34bis 3 i, 7; and at the end of words הנבי *hannābī* "the prophet" 4Q175 7 versus הנביא *hannābī* 4Q174 1–2 i, 15 and יבו *yābō* "he will come" 4Q266 8 i, 7 versus יבוא *yābō* 4Q268 1, 3),[57] as well as in places where the glottal stop would have been immediately preceded by a consonant (שו *šāw* "nothingness" 1QH^a XV, 37 versus שוא *šāw* 1QH^a X,30) or a vocal shewa (שרית *šērīt* "a remainder" 1QH^a XXVI, 27 versus ושארית *ūšəʾērīt* 1QH^a XIV, 11; ונצה *wənāṣā* "and contempt" 4Q175 28 for *ונאצה *ūnəʾāṣā*; רויה "what was seen" *rūyā* 11Q19 LXVI, 9 for *ראויה *rəʾūyā*).[58] In all these environments except the first (רוש), *aleph* is some-

55. Qimron, *HDSS*, 32.

56. Commenting on a form of the word גוי from HazGab 13, Gary A. Rendsburg ("*Hazon Gabriel*: A Grammatical Sketch," in *Hazon Gabriel: New Readings of the Gabriel Inscription* [ed. Matthias Henze; SBLEJL 29; Atlanta: SBL, 2011], 66) and Bar-Asher ("*Vision of Gabriel*," 500 n. 54) presume the existence of a pronounced glottal stop. Muraoka also confirms the possible existence of a consonantal glottal stop in the Aramaic of the DSS, though he admits the *aleph* might instead function as a vowel carrier or indicate a glide (*GQA*, 29).

57. Note some other cases where the *aleph* drops from the end of a word, as in נשי in 1QM III, 15 and IV, 1 for *נשיא; הנבי in 1Q4 (1QDeut^a) at Deut 13:4 for MT הַנָּבִיא; להבי in 4Q394 [4QMMT] 8 iv, 8 for *להביא; contrast the other occurrences of this loss of *aleph* which seem occasioned, in part, by a following *aleph* in 1QS I, 7 and 4Q331 1 i, 7. For similar cases in the MT, also involving a following *aleph*, see R. Gordis, *The Biblical Text in the Making: A Study of the Kethib-Qere* (New York: Ktav, 1937), 95.

58. Some of the examples come from Qimron, *HDSS*, 25. Other examples include ובירות (11Q20 XII, 25) for what would be in the MT וּבְאֵרוֹת; משרו (4Q386 1 ii, 4) for what would be מִשְׁאֵרוֹ; שיר (4Q477 2 ii, 8) for שְׁאֵר; בית שן (4Q522 8, 3) for בֵּית שְׁאָן. Some cases are ambiguous; נושיאי[ם] "those bearing" (4Q364 11, 3 at Gen 45:23 for MT נֹשְׂאִים) might imply an initial pronunciation *nōsīm* corrected to reflect *nōsəʾīm* (with the first spelling uncorrected), or, alternatively, the spelling with two

times dropped from the orthography of certain words in the MT too (e.g., מָצָתִי "I found" Num 11:11; הֶחֱטִי "he sinned" 2 Kgs 13:6; בַּשָּׁו "in nothingness" Job 15:31; שֵׁרִית "remainder" 1 Chr 12:39; הַנָּוָה "the lovely" Jer 6:2), though the elision is certainly more common and widespread among the scrolls (found in DSS-SP9, DSS-SP1c, and DSS-NSP texts). Note also that some words that routinely lose the glottal stop in the MT routinely lose *aleph* in the DSS: חטותיהא *ḥaṭṭōtehā* "her sins" (4Q176 1–2 i, 6) and חטתיכמ *ḥaṭṭōtēkem* "your sins" (11Q1 [11QpaleoLev[a]] at Lev 26:18) for MT חַטֹּאתֵיכֶם; in the MT such loss is restricted to certain common words (other major examples being רָאשִׁים < **rəʾāšīm* "heads" and בּוֹר < **buʾr* "cistern").[59] In addition, in the majority of I-*aleph* and II-*aleph* verbs, the *aleph* is preserved, except where the MT shows the loss of the glottal stop and/or the elision of the *aleph* (e.g., ויומר "and he said" 4Q200 4, 6 and passim versus MT תֹּמְרוּ 2 Sam 19:14; ותוסף "it is gathered" 1QH[a] XIII, 16 versus MT תֹּסֵף Ps 104:29).[60] Due to the parallels with MT orthography it is my assumption that the orthography of the DSS reflects a phonetic realization of the *aleph* similar to that found in the MT. In other words, the letter represents a historical writing (and not a glottal stop) where it occurs at the end of a syllable (מצאת) or within a word when directly preceded by a consonant (as in שוא); but the *aleph* does represent a glottal stop when it occurs at the beginning of a syllable. In some words where the glottal stop would have come after a muttered vowel, it sometimes quiesces and the

---

*yodh*s might be interpreted as a scribal error of metathesis. The case of זכרתה (4Q24 [4QLev[b]] at Lev 2:16) for MT אַזְכָּרָתָהּ is another example; this could reflect the loss of the initial glottal stop or, conceivably, be attributable to sandhi with the preceding definite direct object marker את.

59. The plural forms of חַטָּאת with suffix and the construct plural forms of the same word do not reflect the glottal stop in the MT: חַטֹּאתֶיהָ (Isa 40:2), and חַטֹּאתֵיכֶם (Lev 26:18 and passim), for what should be **ḥaṭṭəʾōtehā* and **ḥaṭṭəʾōtēkem*, respectively. In the DSS, the plural of "head" occurs rarely without the *aleph*, according to Accordance: in 4Q171 1 + 3–4 iii, 5 and 4Q328 1, 1; the *aleph* is inserted interlinearly in 11Q5 (11QPs[a]) at Ps 139:17. Other words that have lost the glottal stop in the MT include מָאתַיִם, מְלָאכָה, and a variety of other words, including some where the loss of the glottal stop occurs with the prefixing of a particle as in לֵאמֹר and לֵאלֹהִים, but also וַאעַנֶּה (1 Kgs 11:39). See Joüon-Muraoka §24e–f, and Andersen and Forbes, *Spelling*, 85–91. *Aleph* is sometimes lost in such words in the DSS: מלאכי (4Q216 V, 5–8 [three times]); לאמר (4Q49 [4QJudg[a]] at Judg 6:13); ואענה (11Q5 [11QPs[a]] at Ps 119:42).

60. See Stegemann, Schuller, Newsom, DJD 40:171 on יורבו (similar to וַיָּרֶב [from ארב] in 1 Sam 15:5).

aleph is subsequently not written (e.g., שרית *šērīt*), but it can also be preserved in this same environment, in which case *aleph* is preserved in the orthography (שארית *šəʾērīt*). The reason that the *aleph* likely represents a glottal stop in this and other environments is outlined below.

First, the place of the *mater* in words like מאור "light," שאול "Sheol," נפלאות "wonders," הביאותה "you brought" does not vary as it does in environments where the etymological /o/ or /u/ vowel is directly preceded by a consonant and followed by an etymological *aleph* (רוש/ראוש/רואש "head" and יבו/יבאו/יבוא "he came").[61] This suggests that *aleph* had not quiesced in words like מאור. If it had quiesced, one would expect to encounter frequent examples of misspellings like *מואר and *מוור. When letters are used solely as a graphic means of indicating etymology (as historical spellings, like the *aleph* in ראש) or as indicating number (as in the *yodh* of the 3ms suffix on plural nouns, יו-), they frequently are either elided (רוש, ו-) or misplaced (ראוש) in the orthography of DSS-SP9 texts.[62] Elision of *aleph* happens only extremely rarely with words similar to מאור (e.g., רובן *rəʾūbēn* > *rūbēn*), and the misplacement of the *mater* almost never happens. Rare cases like צבואת (*ṣəbāwōt* "hosts" 11Q19 LXII, 5 corrected to צבאות) and הטמואת (*haṭṭōmāwōt* "the impurities" 11Q19 LI, 6 corrected to הטמאית) can be explained either as examples of metathesis or as examples of the occasional assimilation of the glottal stop to a neighboring vowel. These do not necessarily imply that the glottal stop always quiesced in this environment since similar assimilation takes place with other consonants (like *heh* and *yodh*) and these consonants usually are preserved in this environment and others (to judge from the orthography).[63] The more

61. See §3.5, "Digraphs." The spellings of the *qal* 3ms imperfect of בוא are found in different texts: יבוא (1QS V, 13 and passim), יבאו (1Q8 [1QIsa^b] at Isa 26:2; 4Q73 [4QEzek^a] at Ezek 23:44; 4Q76 [4QXII^a] at Mal 3:1), יבו (4Q266 8 i, 7). In the text 4Q266 (a copy of the Damascus Document), the verb is consistently spelled without the final *aleph*: *qal* infinitive בו (4Q266 6 ii, 4 and 9 ii, 14); *hiphil* infinitive הבי (4Q266 1a–b, 3 and 1c–f, 4).

62. This is so, even though such spellings produce ambiguity, like in יבאו "he came."

63. Note, תהוו (*tōhū* >) *tōwū* "emptiness" (4Q504 1–2 iii R, 3 and 1QIsa^a at Isa 40:17) for MT תֹּהוּ; דניל (*dānīʾēl* >) *dānīyēl* "Daniel" (6Q7 [6QpapDan] at Dan 10:12) for MT דָּנִיֵּאל. See the subsection "Quiescence of *Heh*" in this section as well as "*Aleph* < *Yodh* and *Yodh* < *Aleph*" (§4.4). Assimilation of *aleph* to *waw* and vice versa is explained in §4.5, "*Aleph* < *Waw* and *Waw* < *Aleph*." The shifts between these consonants happen in fairly predictable environments and do not imply a free interchange among glides and approximants.

common shift of etymological *yodh* to *aleph* can, by contrast, be explained through dissimilation. Although Qimron asserts that the *aleph* in words like כתיאים "Kittim" marks hiatus or a "glide of unclear character," the tendency for such *aleph*s to appear between /ī/ vowels (*-īyī-* > *-īʾī-*) and where a diphthong might have formed between the preceding vowel and the *yodh* consonant (*-āyī-* > *-āʾī-*, as in פתאים; *-ōyī-* > *-ōʾī-*, as in גואים) suggests that the *aleph* is used to preserve the syllable structure of words and, thus, that it was pronounced in these intervocalic positions.[64]

Second, Qimron notes that elision of *aleph* is especially found in "non-formal manuscripts." The absence of such spellings from formal texts is due to the "effort made to preserve the historical spelling."[65] This suggests to me that some scribes also took care to preserve the historical pronunciation in some contexts; this point is even relevant if the copying of texts was not accompanied by an actual pronunciation of the words since in writing and reading silently we often experience an *innere Aufführung*.[66]

Third, one must note that although the glottal stop was liable to quiesce in certain words and in certain environments in the MT, it was also preserved in the same words/environments according to the Tiberian tradition: שֵׁרִית (1 Chr 12:39) for שְׁאֵרִית (1 Chr 4:43); וַתַּזְרֵנִי "you girded me" (2 Sam 22:40) for וַתְּאַזְּרֵנִי (Ps 18:40).[67] The preservation and loss of

---

64. Qimron, *HDSS*, 32. See "*Aleph* < *Yodh* and *Yodh* < *Aleph*" (§4.4).

65. Ibid, 25.

66. The phrase is Goethe's, as cited by A. K. Gavrilov, "Techniques of Reading in Classical Antiquity," *Classical Quarterly* 47 (1997): 69. In this article, Gavrilov demonstrates silent reading was not as uncommon in the ancient world as is often thought. Although Tov suggests that the copying out of scrolls through dictation was rare at the time of the DSS, he does allow for this possibility (*Scribal Practices*, 11). Furthermore, other scholars, like Jonathan Norton, do not agree with Tov's assessmnet ("The Question of Scribal Exegesis at Qumran," in *Northern Lights on the Dead Sea Scrolls: Proceedings of the Nordic Qumran Network 2003–2006* [ed. Anders K. Petersen et al.; STDJ 80; Leiden: Brill, 2009], 151 n. 31).

67. See GKC §23c and f for more examples. Qimron also recognizes this similarity between the DSS and MT (*HDSS*, 25). Bergsträsser's comment that such misspellings in the MT suggested the disappearance of this phoneme from the "living language" might be taken to imply that the phoneme was preserved in the writing/reading register of the language (*Hebräische Grammatik*, 1:92). I assume that the pronunciation of a glottal stop by the MT vocalizers was not an archaizing tendency by the scribes; Blau remarks that had the Masoretes "restored the laryngeals and pharyngeals, they would have done so in a more uniform and comprehensible way" (*Phonology and Morphology*, 86).

the glottal stop in the MT tradition suggests something similar could have taken place among the DSS.

Fourth, modern Semitic languages provide further examples of how it is possible for the glottal stop to be preserved in some environments within words, even if it is lost in others. For example, although in most modern dialects of Arabic, the glottal stop is generally lost (with the exception of those times when a word with an etymological glottal stop begins an utterance), it is preserved in word-medial position when it occurs between two identical vowels.[68] In contemporary Israeli Hebrew, similarly, the glottal stop is lost in most environments, but it is optionally preserved "as onglide to a heavily stressed syllable," as in *ša(ʾ)ul* ("borrowed"), and even where another guttural was etymologically present, as in *giv(ʾ)a*, *gva(ʾ)ot* ("hill") and *dim(ʾ)a*, *dma(ʾ)ot* ("tear").[69] Even in the tradition of Samaritan Hebrew, which is often cited as a Hebrew dialect in which gutturals weakened, the glottal stop is still present at the beginning of syllables, though this is not always from an etymological *aleph*.[70] This suggests, therefore, that although *aleph* as a glottal stop might have been lost in certain environments in DSS Hebrew, this does not imply its loss in all environments. Similarly, the absence of a glottal stop in the spoken vernacular of some (most?) writers and scribes of the DSS, does not imply that they did not articulate this phoneme when reading texts, especially scriptural texts. The observation of Blau on the pronunciation of II-*aleph* nouns is relevant here: "[I]n vernacular speech the *aleph* of such nouns was elided, so that original **biʾr* became **bēr*, yet in the higher language the ʾ was preserved. On the analogy of biblical forms … a more elegant pseudo-form was coined for **bēr*, viz., בְּאֵר."[71]

---

68. Janet C. E. Watson, *The Phonology and Morphology of Arabic* (Oxford: Oxford University Press, 2002), 18.

69. Shmuel Bolozky, "Israeli Hebrew Phonology," in *Phonologies of Asia and Africa* (ed. Alan S. Kaye; 2 vols.; Winona Lake, Ind.: Eisenbrauns, 1997), 288; examples drawn from 297 and 309. See also Christopher Farrar and Yehiel Hayon, "The Perception of the Phoneme *Aleph* (/ʾ/) in Modern Hebrew," *HAR* 4 (1980): 53–78.

70. Ben-Ḥayyim writes: "אל"ף (< אהח"ע) … appears at the beginning of a syllable: *ʾilla* אלה, *ʾinna* הנה, *ʾikma* חָכמה, *ʾirbəm* ערבים, *ʾå:rəṣ* ארץ, *ʾå:šən* חשן, *ʾam* עם, *ʾoṣ* עוץ, *ʾor* אור, *ʾūr* אוּר, … *yišrå:ʾəl* ישראל, *kå:ʾən* כהן, *yišmå:ʾu* ישמעו, *yērēʾi* יראה" (*A Grammar of Samaritan Hebrew: Based on the Recitation of the Law in Comparison with the Tiberian and Other Jewish Traditions* [Jerusalem: Magnes, 2000], 38–39).

71. Blau, *Phonology and Morphology*, 55. See also Blau, *On Pseudo-Corrections*, 28–29.

Finally, that the gutturals in general and the glottal stop in particular are evidenced in traditions later than the DSS (not only the MT, but also Origen's Secunda) suggests that the *aleph* was recognized by some Judeans as a glottal stop.[72]

The parallels between the DSS and the MT suggest that such loss of the glottal stop is a regular tendency in the language, especially the later stages of the classical language. The more frequent elision of *aleph* in the DSS presumably reflects a slow movement toward the total loss of the phoneme in the spoken dialect. This tendency is exemplified in some texts like 1QIsa[a] where one sees numerous mistakes relating to *aleph*, as well as in even shorter texts like 4Q175, in whose thirty lines there are at least six mistakes relating to the quiescence of *aleph* (not to mention another three related to the use of the *aleph* as a *mater*).[73] Nevertheless, I assume in the DSS that in the reading of texts by most individuals the glottal stop was still pronounced at the beginning of words and within words at the beginning of syllables, often even where a muttered vowel directly precedes the *aleph*. The following paragraphs explain some apparent exceptions to this conclusion.

The absence of *aleph* in מוד/מודה "much" (= MT מְאֹד) and תר/תור "form" (= MT תֹּאַר) is perhaps due to analogy with רוש/ראש, if not also with other words (see §5.5, "**quṭl* Nouns"). As with ראש, the spellings without *aleph* are concentrated in nonbiblical manuscripts of the DSS-SP9 and DSS-SP1c text groups.

The absence of *aleph* in the word מוזנים "scales" (4Q415 9, 11; 4Q418 127, 6; 4Q418 167a + b, 2; 4Q511 30, 5; 1QIsa[a] at Isa 40:12, 15 = MT מאֹזְנַיִם) is not entirely clear.[74] It might reflect the fact that *aleph* was perceived as quiescent (as in ויומר "he said"), might reflect Aramaic influence (where

---

72. That *aleph* is realized as a glottal stop is the consensus opinion, and is confirmed in the study by Khan ("Tiberian Pronunciation," 3). That the Secunda gives evidence for the preservation of gutturals is underlined by Janssens, *Studies in Hebrew*, 41–43 and Yuditsky, "Weak Consonants," 239.

73. The mistakes relating to quiescence include: נבי (for נביא twice); וישה corrected to וישא; היש (for *האיש); ואנה (for *והנה); נצה (for *נאצה). Abegg also notes the frequent elision of *aleph* in the phylactery texts ("Linguistic Profile," 27).

74. The word appears with the *aleph* once (4Q418 207, 4), but six times without it. In all but one instance where it is spelled without an *aleph*, it has a *waw mater*. Note also the spelling without *aleph* or *waw mater* in 1Mas h IV, 9 (= Sir 42:4).

the word does not bear an *aleph* typically), and/or reflect an etymologically more reliable form.[75]

In some rare cases, the *aleph* is lost at the beginning of a syllable, when it would have been preceded by and followed by a full vowel: הרץ "the land" (1QpHab XIII, 1 and 4Q79 [4QXII^{d}] at Hos 2:2) for MT הָאָרֶץ; והספם "and their assembling" (*niphal* infinitive construct; 1QSa I, 1) for *והאספם; היש "the person" (4Q175 22 and perhaps 4Q186 1 i, 6) for what would be in the MT הָאִישׁ.[76] This is relatively rare in the DSS and occurs at least once in the MT: הָשֲׁפּוֹת "the refuse" (Neh 3:13) for *הָאַשְׁפּוֹת (which is attested in Neh 3:14).[77] Again, the parallel in the MT suggests the loss of *aleph* in this environment is associated with the natural weakness of the phoneme.

In other cases, the *aleph* elides after a full vowel when it would have been followed by a *hatef*-vowel in the MT (that is, by a reduced historical short vowel): הרצות "the lands" (4Q374 2 i, 4) for *הארצות; הנשים "the men" (1QSa I, 27) for *האנשים; הבנים "the stones" (1QH^{a} XXIII, 28) for *האבנים; הזין "he did (not) listen" (4Q364 22, 2 at Deut 1:45) for MT הֶאֱזִין.[78] The phenomenon is slightly more common in the DSS than in the MT: הָסּוּרִים "those bound" (Qoh 4:14) for *הָאֲסוּרִים and הָרַמִּים "the Arameans" (2 Chr 22:5) for *הָאֲרַמִּים.[79] The parallels with the MT suggest again the loss of *aleph* in these environments is a common phenom-

75. The root of the word is apparently יזן, though it was reanalyzed as from אזן (see *HALOT*). Kutscher (*Isaiah*, 187–88) comments on the forms in 1QIsa^{a} and suggests they are due to Aramaic influence, though it seems just as likely that they are due to the perception that the nonetymological *aleph* had quiesced.

76. Some of the examples derive from Qimron, *Grammar*, 83. The example of היש in 4Q175 may also be attributable to the shift of *aleph* > *yodh*, discussed in §4.4, "*Aleph* < *Yodh* and *Yodh* < *Aleph*." The possible example from 4Q186 may be attributable to the reverse-writing in this text. The spelling תוצוו (1QIsa^{a} at Isa 22:4) for MT תָּאִיצוּ "do (not) rush" likely has another explanation; see §4.4.

77. Andersen and Forbes, *Spelling*, 86. This is not including cases like תְּלוֹם (2 Sam 21:12) where the disparity between *qere* and *kethib* presumes confusion between III-*yodh* and III-*aleph* by-forms.

78. Qimron also lists ופריי (1QM VII, 11) for *ופאריי (*Grammar*, 83). Note also נוה for MT נָאוָה in 4Q84 (4QPs^{b}) at Ps 93:5, which might be construed as the absolute or construct form for "abode" (= MT נָוֶה).

79. See Andersen and Forbes, *Spelling*, 86. As an example of where the *aleph* is lost when it is followed by a *hatef* vowel in the MT, though it is not a historical vowel, see מַכֹּלֶת (1 Kgs 5:25) for *מַאֲכֹלֶת.

enon among different dialects and is attributable to the natural weakness of the phoneme.

Sometimes the loss of *aleph* is due to confusion over marking the preceding vowel. Thus, a III-*aleph* verb is rarely found marked with final *heh*, as in וירה "he feared" (4Q381 50, 4) for *ויראה; similarly III-*aleph* words in construct sometimes take a *yodh* in place of an *aleph* (וחוטי נפשכה "incurring the penalty of your life" 1QpHab X, 2, quoting Hab 2:10: וְחוֹטֵא נַפְשֶׁךָ), something seen more commonly in III-*waw*/*yodh* words (see §3.2, "*Plene* Orthography"). Although a similar tendency is quite common in DSS Aramaic where the root types have truly become confused, this phenomenon in Hebrew is relatively rare. The variations in spelling in the words above are reflective of the loss of the glottal stop at the end of syllables, but also probably of the confusion over how best to represent the final vowel.[80]

Also rare are those cases where *aleph* is introduced erroneously into the text, as in ונאלכה "that we may go" (1QIsa[a] at Isa 2:3) for MT וְנֵלְכָה and נאכר "foreign" (4Q372 1, 11 and 15 and 4Q387 3,6) for what is usually נכר (= MT נֵכָר).[81] As mentioned above in §3.2, "*Aleph* as Internal *Mater*," the *aleph* may function as a *mater* in these cases. In some cases the introduction of an *aleph* may be based on parallel by-forms in the MT: ימאס "it will melt" (4Q56 [4QIsa[b]] at Isa 13:7) for MT יִמָּס, perhaps influenced by וַיִּמָּאֵס "it ran (lit., melted)" and יִמָּאֲסוּ "let them run (lit., melt)" in Job 7:5 and Ps 58:8, respectively.[82] In rare cases, the introduction of a nonetymological *aleph* may suggest another version of a text, as in ולוא יכנפו עוד מוראיך (1QIsa[a] at Isa 30:20) for MT וְלֹא יִכָּנֵף עוֹד מוֹרֶיךָ "your teacher will never again hide himself."[83] The text in 1QIsa[a] presumes "and your fears will never again gather (or, be gathered)," the meaning of כנף in the *qal* or *niphal* being borrowed from Aramaic where the verb in the G-stem and tD-stem means "assemble" and "be assembled." Sometimes a word which contains an etymological *aleph* will attest this letter in the wrong place,

80. For Aramaic, see Muraoka, *GQA*, 123: "This tendency of verbs with /ʾ/ as their R3 to merge with those with /y/ in the same slot that had started earlier in the history of Aramaic appears to be a *fait accompli* in our idiom."

81. See Morgenstern, "Notes on the Language of the Qumran Scrolls," 161–62.

82. These last two biblical verbs are usually parsed as from מאס II "to flow" or "err," i.e., as by-forms of מסס. Note the similar addition of *aleph* in the MT יָנֵאץ (Qoh 12:5), though the root is נצץ.

83. See Kutscher, *Isaiah*, 253–54.

suggesting the quiescence of the letter as well as the scribes' inattention to etymological spelling; for example, תפראת (1QIsa[a] at Isa 13:19) for MT תִּפְאֶרֶת.[84]

To reiterate, the above rare cases where *aleph* is elided do not demonstrate that etymological glottal stops had entirely vanished from the phonemic inventory of most writers and readers of the DSS. It was still usually pronounced at the beginning of words and within words at the beginning of syllables. Only in some environments (e.g., at the end of syllables) had the glottal stop vanished, or could vanish (when preceded by a consonant or muttered vowel).

By way of conclusion, it should be noted that the many parallels between the MT orthography and that of the DSS suggest that the writing of the word ראש without *aleph* in the DSS is something unexpected, even innovative, in the orthography of Hebrew. This innovation is, in part, reflected in the distribution of the spelling רוש.[85] The spelling without *aleph* appears relatively rarely (at least six times) in the biblical scrolls, in 1QIsa[a] at Isa 40:21, 41:26, 48:16; 4Q80 (4QXII[e]) at Zech 4:2 (twice); 4Q88 (4QPs[f]) at Ps 109:25 (both DSS-SP9 and DSS-NSP [4Q88] texts). But, it is spelled without *aleph* over twenty times in the nonbiblical scrolls (always in the DSS-SP9 and DSS-SP1c texts).[86]

Quiescence of *ʿAyin*

The loss of the voiced pharyngeal fricative from the spoken and written language of certain scribes and writers is implied where *ʿayin* is dropped entirely from a word or where the letter is initially not written but then added interlinearly as a correction. Cases where *aleph* is written for etymological *ʿayin* suggest this same loss, though perhaps also a memory of some guttural consonant. On the other hand, the fact that words with *ʿayin* are not routinely misspelled and that there are only a few cases where *ʿayin* is

---

84. See Kutscher, *Isaiah*, 57.

85. The spelling without *aleph* is, however, apparently attested in Moabite (see *HALOT*, s.v., and references there); furthermore, note that the *aleph* is lost in similar environments in other words from the MT, like מוֹסֵרוֹת from אסר and בּוֹר from באר (see Bergsträsser, *Hebräische Grammatik*, 1:90). For more on the texts that contain the different spellings of ראש, see footnote 125 in the section "Digraphs" (§3.5).

86. By contrast, the word occurs with *aleph* around fifty times among the nonbiblical texts.

written for etymological *aleph* suggest that this phoneme (or some distinct sound associated with the letter) was not universally lost. If *aleph* and *ʿayin* represent indistinguishable sounds, one would expect an equal number of examples where one letter replaces the other. In anticipation of the conclusions, it can be said that *ʿayin* is weakest in the dialect of those writing DSS-SP9 texts, where it tends to elide occasionally at the ends of syllables and when preceded by a consonant or a muttered vowel—the same positions in which *aleph* elides. But, the elision of *ʿayin* is never so common as the elision of *aleph*. And, even in the dialect (or set of dialects) represented by DSS-SP9 texts, the *ʿayin* is still a clear phoneme at the beginning of syllables. In DSS-NSP texts, the *ʿayin* and its associated phoneme are preserved; the handful of spelling errors associated with the *ʿayin* in these texts can be attributed, in part, to the natural weakness of the voiced pharyngeal fricative.

First, it should be admitted that some scholars have identified examples in the biblical Hebrew lexicon that suggest a correspondence between the phonemes represented by *aleph* and *ʿayin*.[87] The best evidence for this is the roots גאל II (*niphal*: "to be defiled") and געל (*niphal*: "to be defiled"). Another example is פִּתְאֹם ("suddenly") as possibly derived from פֶּתַע ("moment").[88] Although such alterations of original *ʿayins* to *alephs* may exist, their very rarity in the MT suggests that the tradition that eventually developed into the Tiberian MT preserved very well a distinction between the glottal stop and the voiced pharyngeal fricative.

The total loss of *ʿayin* in the DSS is found clearly in the following cases:

נשנתי — (1QH[a] XIX, 35) for *נשענתי "I leaned"[89]
שבעשרה — (3Q15 [Copper Scroll] I, 4) for *שבע עשרה "seventeen"[90]

87. See *HALOT*, *sub* א.

88. See Joüon-Muraoka, §102b. Another example, cited by *HALOT*, is תאב II (only once, in the *piel* "to desecrate") and תעב (*piel*: "to abhor"), though, as they note (*sub* תאב II), this single example of a root may be due to scribal interference.

89. This is cited by Qimron, *Grammar*, 83. Another example is also cited by him: תשת שע (1QH[a] XII, 8) for *תשתעשע. In this example, there is a space where the *ʿayin* should go; there is a dot above the space, which may be a scribal mark or defect in the leather (Stegemann, Schuller, Newsom, DJD 40:229). As Stegemann and Schuller note, "[i]t is unclear whether he [the scribe] 'forgot' to write the letter … or left the space uninscribed due to a defect in the leather" (ibid.).

90. For this and the following example, see Puech, "Le Rouleau de Cuivre de la Grotte de Qumran (3Q15)" in *Le Rouleau de cuivre de la grotte 3 de Qumran (3Q15):*

שלושרא — (3Q15 [Copper Scroll] IX, 2) for *שלוש עשרא "thirteen"
המרב — (3Q15 [Copper Scroll] XII, 1) for *המערב "the west"[91]
שבו — (4Q216 II, 3) for *שבעו "they were satisfied"[92]
ממוד — (4Q266 10 i, 12) for *מעמוד "post, standing"[93]
וישה — (1QIsa[a] at Isa 5:4) for MT וַיַּעַשׂ "it made"[94]
יבור — (1QIsa[a] at Isa 28:15) for MT *qere* יַעֲבֹר "it will cross"
וישה — (1QIsa[a] at Isa 48:14) for MT יַעֲשֶׂה "he will do"

Expertise—Restauration—Epigraphie, by Daniel Brizemeure, Noël Lacoudre, Emile Puech (2 vols.; STDJ 55; Leiden: Brill, 2006), 1:179, 195. The first is likely due to sandhi and the second to haplography.

91. See Puech, "Rouleau de Cuivre," 1:204–5. Note that the mistake of דמ for *דמע in IX, 6, read by Milik ("Rouleau de Cuivre," 293), is no longer read by Puech in this way, but rather as ר(ו)מחצא (Puech, "Rouleau de Cuivre," 1:194–96). Also, Accordance's reading ארבב (3Q15 XI, 10) for *ארבע is read by Puech ("Rouleau de Cuivre," 1:200, 203) as "(?) א[[ר]]ז/אר."

92. VanderKam and Milik, "216. 4QJubilees[a]," in DJD 13:10. Although this seems to be a likely example of elision, the immediately following words [ופנו] אחר אלהים [אחר]ים suggest perhaps that confusion was not due solely to an aural lapse but rather also to the sense that שבו gives to the passage: "they turn (back) [reading שָׁבוּ] [and turn away] after other god[s]."

93. Presumably this is a **maqṭul* variant of the word מעמד "standing," similar to how it is used in 1QH[a] XII, 37 (see §5.4, "*Waw* Marking /u/ Class Vowel in Nouns Where MT Has No /u/ Class Vowel").

94. Unless this is a mistake for וישא "it yielded," as in the initial mistake of וישה in 4Q175 9 (see Ezek 36:8 for נשא plus פרי). For this and the other examples from 1QIsa[a], see Kutscher, *Isaiah*, 507. Kutscher only lists the passage from 48:14 on page 507, but lists the passage from 5:4 on page 328 as an example of where 1QIsa[a] contains a long form where the MT has a short form. Another example he might have cited on page 507 is יודינו (at Isa 40:14) for MT יוֹדִיעֶנּוּ, which he cites on page 516; however, his reading is incorrect and Accordance and Ulrich et al. (*Biblical Qumran Scrolls*, 408) read יודיענו with the last three letters slightly damaged. Kutscher also cites (*Isaiah*, 507) משתריים (at Isa 28:20) for MT מֵהִשְׂתָּרֵעַ, which can also be explained as due to the replacement of one word with another by the scribe, perhaps due to a different tradition, perhaps also due to confusion with the preceding word מַצָּע "couch" (the latter perhaps calling to the mind of the scribe the more common מַצָּה "strife"). The word in 1QIsa[a] is presumably the *hithpael* participle from שׂרה "those persevering" or "those fighting," a similar tradition being reflected in the LXX's *μάχεσθαι* "to quarrel" (see Kutscher, *Isaiah*, 289 and, below, in the discussion concerning the quiescence of *heh* and *ḥeth*).

Such elision also happens in documentary texts: לול[ם] (KhQ1 5) for *לעולם "forever." Another example of *ʿayin* disappearing in pronunciation may be represented in נעוו לשכר (1QIsa[a] at Isa 29:9) for MT נָעוּ וְלֹא שֵׁכָר "they staggered, but not from strong drink," in which case the double *waw* at the end of the first word would indicate the assimilation of *ʿayin* to /ū/, similar to the assimilation of *aleph* in באוו *bāwū* "they came" and ראוו *rāwū* "they saw."[95] Such seems to be the interpretation presumed in the edition of 1QIsa[a] in Accordance and in *Biblical Qumran Scrolls*.[96] Nevertheless, Kutscher suggested reading נעוו as the *niphal* of עוה (*naʿăwū*) "they were perverted" and conjectured that the scribe perhaps understood the text to mean something like חטאו לשכר "they sinned in becoming drunk."[97] Alternatively, it seems possible to understand this verb as an imperative in line with the more explicitly marked שועו "be blind" that precedes it; in this case, the spelling might be a scribal mistake of metathesis for נועו "be tottering."[98]

Related to the above examples are the spellings from 1QIsa[a] in which the *waw mater* seems to indicate that the *ʿayin* was no longer pronounced: פועלתי "my work" (1QIsa[a] at Isa 49:4, MT פְּעֻלָּתִי), פועלתמה "their work" (1QIsa[a] at Isa 65:7, MT פְּעֻלָּתָם).[99] These, however, are better explained as words where one /u/ vowel has engendered another, preceding /u/ vowel.[100] Although the example of צעור "Zoar" in 1QIsa[a] at Isa 15:5 for MT צֹעַר might at first seem to suggest that the displacement of the /o/ or /u/ vowel

95. See the discussion in §4.5, "*Aleph* < *Waw* and *Waw* < *Aleph*." Alternatively, the double *waw* in נעוו could be an example of a *mater* written twice (see §3.1).

96. Ulrich et al, *Biblical Qumran Scrolls*, 384. This is the explicit explanation offered by Qimron ("*Waw* as Marker for a Glide" [Hebrew], in *Homage to Shmuel: Studies in the World of the Bible* [ed. Zipora Talshir et al.; Jerusalem: Bialik Institute, 2001], 368).

97. Kutscher, *Isaiah*, 271.

98. Note the similar instances where a *mater* is misplaced in the examples cited in "Scribal Mistakes" (§3.1). If one supposes that the spelling reflects the quiescence of *ʿayin*, then interpreting it as an imperative is still possible: the spelling נעוו should perhaps be changed to נעיו since we would expect a dissimilation such that *nūwū* would become *nūyū*. All of these suggestions, of course, explain only the possible understanding of one (later) scribe, which depends, presumably, on another (earlier) scribal mistake where ולא was broken apart, the *waw* attached to the preceding verb, the *aleph* dropped, and the *lamedh* attached to the following noun.

99. Kutscher, *Isaiah*, 498; Abegg, "Linguistic Profile," 30.

100. See "*Waw* Marking /u/ Class Vowel in Nouns Where MT Has No /u/ Class Vowel" (§5.4) and "Digraphs" (§3.5).

was, in fact, caused by the near quiescence of *ʿayin*, this place name seems to have known several forms from relatively early times.[101] The case of ואתועדדה "I will stand up" (4Q382 23, 1) for *ואתעודדה may reflect the weakness of *ʿayin*, if not also a graphic mistake of metathesis.[102]

In the following words, *ʿayin* was initially forgotten, then added later.

מערכת — "battle line" (1QM V, 3 and VI, 5)
בעדת — "in the congregation of" (1QHª XV, 37)[103]
[מ]ע[נה] — "response" (1QHª XIX, 31)
אלמעונתו — "to his dwelling" (1QHª XX, 10)
תגער — "you will rebuke" (1QHª XXII, 25)[104]
דמע — "tithe" (3Q15 [Copper Scroll] XI, 4 [once, perhaps twice])[105]
בעץ — "in a tree" (4Q163 23 i, 17)
לידעתיכהו — "I did not know you (?)" (4Q175 16)[106]
בעצה — "with (no) counsel" (4Q261 5a–c, 3 [though the *ʿayin* is very damaged])[107]
דעה — "knowledge" (4Q426 1 i, 4)
הרישנה עם — "the first with" (4Q514 1 i, 8 [though the text is very damaged])[108]
העלות — "to lift" (11Q19 XLII, 16) [109]

101. See Kutscher, *Isaiah*, 69–71.

102. See "Scribal Mistakes" (§3.1).

103. See Malachi Martin, *Scribal Character of the Dead Sea Scrolls* (Louvain: Publications universitaires, 1958), 481.

104. Qimron, *HDSS*, 25. Stegemann, Schuller, Newsom (DJD 40:273) refer to this *ʿayin* as "quiescent" as does Martin, *Scribal Character*, 486.

105. For the tabulations below, only one instance of this spelling is considered.

106. The reading of the form in 4Q175 is debated. Allegro transliterates לידעתיכהו and comments: "The first *yōdh* was written over a previous *ʾāleph*, and the *ʿayin* inserted above the line by the same hand. MT has [at Deut 33:9] לא ראיתיו" (DJD 5:59). By contrast, *DSSSE* transliterates לא דעתיכהי and translates "I have not known you." Presumably, this reading implies an elided initial *yodh* followed by the 2fs suffix. Accordance follows the understanding of Allegro.

107. Alexander and Vermes, DJD 26:181.

108. See Baillet, DJD 7:296.

109. There is an erased letter preceding the *heh*, either an *ʿayin* (so, Yadin, *Temple Scroll*, 2:180) or another *heh* (so, Lawrence H. Schiffman "Temple Scroll" in *The Dead Sea Scrolls, Hebrew, Aramaic, and Greek Texts with English Translations, Volume 7: Temple Scroll and Related Documents* [ed. James H. Charlesworth; Princeton Theological Seminary Dead Sea Scrolls Project 7; Tübingen: Mohr Siebeck, 2011], 104).

ישעיהו — "Isaiah" (1QIsa[a] at Isa 1:1)
בעיניהם — "in their eyes" (1QIsa[a] at Isa 5:21)[110]
יעקוב — "Jacob" (1QIsa[a] at Isa 9:7 and 17:4)
לעשק — "to oppress" (4Q82 [4QXII[g]] at Hos 12:8)[111]

Another example is less likely attributable to aural confusion: מעם "from with" in 11Q5 (11QPs[a]) at Ps 121:2. Rather, this mistake is likely due to the similarity in shape between the top parts of the *mem* and *ʿayin.*

In these following words, *aleph* is written for an etymological *ʿayin* and left uncorrected.

אם — (1QS VIII, 2) for *עם "with"[112]
מושיא — (4Q365 6a ii + 6c, 3) for *מושיע "one delivering"[113]
שש אסר — (4Q394 [4QMMT] 1–2 iv, 3) for *ששה עסר "sixteen"[114]
וכאפר — "and like ashes" (4Q434 7b, 3) for *וכעפר "and like dust"[115]
ואתה — (1QIsa[a] at Isa 5:5) for MT וְעַתָּה "and now"
אצית — (1QIsa[a] at Isa 25:1) for MT עֵצוֹת "counsels of"[116]
ואתה — (1QIsa[a] at Isa 28:22) for MT וְעַתָּה "and now"
ואשא — (11Q5 [11QPs[a]] at Ps 119:117) for MT וְאֶשְׁעָה[117]

Yadin (*Temple Scroll*, 2:180) explains: "Seemingly the scribe first wrote עד ע, then erased *ʿayin* and wrote הלות, and finally suspended *ʿayin* above the line in correction."

110. The scribe's missing of the *ʿayin* in בעיניהם is perhaps due to the similarity with the expression "between them"; understanding the letters as "between them" would make sense with the prepositional phrase of the second colon: נגד פניהם, found in both the MT and 1QIsa[a].

111. See Russel E. Fuller, "82. 4QXII[g]," in DJD 15:286–87.

112. Note the similar mistake of אם for *עם in 1Mas h VII, 11 (= Sir 44:11).

113. See Tov and White, DJD 13:269. They note (ibid., 271) that Puech has suggested an alternative reading of תושיא, also from ישע.

114. Qimron, *HDSS*, 25. See also Qimron and Strugnell, DJD 10:7. Note, however, that the *aleph* is slightly damaged. The editors note that the marks read as *aleph* do not resemble those of other *ʿayins* in the calendar; nevertheless, they admit that they do resemble "a type of *ʿayin* found in the other columns of the manuscript" (ibid.). The loss of *ʿayin* in שש אשר may have been encouraged by sandhi, the multiple syllables presumably being pronounced with a single stress.

115. We would expect the word with *ʿayin* since the following verb is שחק and this verb occurs with כעפר in two passages from the MT (2 Sam 22:43, Ps 18:43). Quite possibly, the two words אפר and עפר had become semantically confused.

116. The meaning of אצית is not clear (Kutscher, *Isaiah*, 221).

117. The spelling ואשא may be attributable to a conscious alteration of the bibli-

Excluded from this list are וכארום "they will disgust them" (4Q169 3–4 iii, 4) for *וכערום.[118] The word וכארום is paralleled by the passive participle two lines preceding in 4Q169 3–4 iii, 2 כאורה "a disgusting thing." In Rabbinic Hebrew, the *qal* passive participle of this verb is sometimes found spelled with *aleph*, while the finite forms of the verb are spelled with *ʿayin*. That this is the case suggests that there are perhaps two complementary roots, one with *aleph* and one with *ʿayin*. Confusion between the two, if this is what is happening in 4Q169 3–4 iii, 4, may not be related directly to the phonetic identity of *aleph* and *ʿayin*, but rather a reflection of confusion between the two roots.

In addition, not considered are the examples Kutscher gives of the confusion between the prepositions אל and על, which do not relate (at least solely) to phonetic confusion.[119] Similarly, another example of ואתה for MT ועתה (at Isa 64:7) is not listed since this mistake seems likely triggered by the following occurrence (three words later) of the second-person masculine singular pronoun. It might be mentioned also that the two examples of ואתה for MT ועתה listed above might, in part, be due to dittography, the following words in each verse beginning with *aleph*.[120]

Although Accordance and the *Dead Sea Scrolls Concordance* suggest that the Copper Scroll contains another example of the numeral "ten" written אסר (in 3Q15 VIII, 3), the marks are not read in this way by Puech or in *DSSSE*.[121] Additional examples of *aleph* written for *ʿayin* include עתה

cal text (so that it implies "I will lift your statutes [חוקיכה]" instead of MT "that I may gaze on your statutes [בְחֻקֶּיךָ]); note that this scroll exhibits other differences from the MT text: חונני "show me favor" for MT חַיֵּנִי "make me live," as in 11Q5 (11QPs[a]) at Ps 119:37 and passim. Note also the apparent spelling נאנש for *נענש in 1QS VI, 27, though the *aleph* is attested only by a slight vertical mark. The word גדאו is read for *גדעו in 4Q159 2–4, 1 by Accordance and the *Dead Sea Scrolls Concordance*; it is read, instead, as גר או "foreigner or" in *DSSSE*. The reading צבאי in 1QH[a] XV, 32 is disputed and unclear (see Stegemann, Schuller, Newsom, DJD 40:209–10).

118. Qimron, *Grammar*, 84. Note the discussion on this word in Menahem Kister, "Some Observations on Vocabulary and Style in the Dead Sea Scrolls," in *Diggers at the Well*, 140–41. Another example may be זאף for *זעף "grew angry" in 4Q184 2, 6, though it is read as ואף אף by Allegro (DJD 5:84).

119. Kutscher, *Isaiah*, 507.

120. Kutscher, *Isaiah*, 507. Confusingly, Kutscher lists one of these passages, Isa 64:7, under the paragraph in which he lists cases where the MT has *aleph* and 1QIsa[a] has *ʿayin*, as though the scroll contained עתה for MT אתה (*Isaiah*, 506). It does not.

121. Puech, "Rouleau de Cuivre," 1:192–93.

for *אתה in 4Q223–224 2 v, 3, though the text is very fragmentary and, thus, the word's identification less certain.[122]

Examples of words where what should have been an *ʿayin* was written initially as *aleph* or some other letter, but then corrected to *ʿayin* include the following:

יאבורו — (1QS I, 16) corrected to יעבורו "they will pass"[123]
שר[ו]א — (4Q24 [4QLev^b] at Lev 22:23) corrected to [ש]רוע "extended"[124]
ואואר — (1QIsa^a at Isa 42:19) for MT עִוֵּר; corrected to ועואר "blind"
אברו — (4Q55 [4QIsa^a] at Isa 23:2) for MT עֹבֵר; corrected to עברו "they crossed"[125]

Not considered are the spellings of the preposition אל (1QS V, 2; VI, 20; VII, 3) corrected to על; ל (1QH^a XI, 29) corrected to על; °רות (1QH^a XX, 28) corrected to ערות "nakedness of."[126]

Examples of *ʿayin* written for an etymological *aleph* are much rarer, but include the following, two of which were corrected by ancient scribes.

נרעתה — (1QS VII, 14) corrected to נראתה "it appears"[127]
ועל — (1QIsa^a at Isa 6:9) for MT וְאַל "and not"; twice in the same verse

---

122. VanderKam and Milik, "223–224. 4QJubilees^h," in DJD 13:126.

123. Qimron, *Grammar*, 85 and Elisha Qimron and James H. Charlesworth, "Rule of the Community," in *Dead Sea Scrolls … Rule of the Community and Related Documents*, 8.

124. Eugene Ulrich, "24. 4QLev^b," in *Qumran Cave 4.VII: Genesis to Numbers* (ed. Eugene Ulrich et al.; DJD 12; Oxford: Clarendon, 1994), 182–83.

125. See Skehan and Ulrich, DJD 15:9.

126. Qimron, *Grammar*, 85. Another example he cites seem less certain to me, וענם (1QS VII, 11) corrected to וחנם. In this case, the correction and reshaping of another earlier mark leaves the earlier mark obscure. As observed above, confusion between אל and על is, in large part, due to confusion in the usage of the two prepositions; a similar situation pertains to ל. In relation to the correction in 1QH^a XI, 29 (ל corrected to על), Stegemann and Schuller note that the original marks might also have been read as ולכ, suggesting that the mistake was perhaps visual and not aural (Stegemann, Schuller, Newsom, DJD 40:151).

127. Qimron and Charlesworth, "Rule of the Community," 32.

מנעציך — (1QIsaᵃ at Isa 60:14a) as a mistake for MT מְנַאֲצָיִךְ "those despising you" (at Isa 60:14b)[128]

על — (4Q99 [4QJobᵃ] at Job 37:5) for MT אֵל "God"[129]

Other examples, cited by Kutscher, relate mostly to the confusion of the prepositions אל and על.[130] In addition, there is the ambiguous case of עמ (1QIsaᵃ at Isa 53:9) corrected to עת, for MT אֶת־ (prep.); the *mem* in the scroll is corrected to *taw*, though the ʿ*ayin* is not corrected. Qimron lists a passage (4Q491 8–10 i, 8) where the 2ms independent pronoun, ואתה, is spelled ועתה; however, Maurice Baillet translates this as "Et maintenant," which seems to fit the context well.[131] The word צוּאָר in the MT at Isa 8:8 is rendered צער (presumably "Zoar") in 4Q59 (4QIsaᵉ); here one cannot discount the possibility of phonetic confusion, but the place name also makes sense in the text, which mentions Zoar next in 15:5. Note also ויעוה "it will distort" (4Q109 [4QQohᵃ] at Qoh 7:7) for MT וְיְאַבֵּד "it will destroy," which seems only partially attributable to an aural confusion.[132]

Other confusions are less common. The significant examples are the following.

על יפות — (1QS VI, 7) for חליפות "substitutes of"[133]

---

128. Kutscher, *Isaiah*, 506. The word מנעציך is crossed out in the scroll and appears in the first colon just before מעניך (= MT מְעַנַּיִךְ "those oppressing you"). Thus, מנעציך would seem to be a mistaken conflation of the two words מעניך and מנאציך, a mistake perhaps occasioned by the similarity in the sounds represented by *aleph* and ʿ*ayin*, but not necessarily their identical articulation. Kutscher's listing of עתה from Isa 64:7 on page 506 is a mistake, as noted earlier.

129. Note that the spelling עאל (4Q222 1, 4) (with two correction dots over the ʿ*ayin* indicating it should be ignored) for intended *אל "God" is perhaps not due primarily to the confusion of sounds, but due to the following word עליון (see VanderKam and Milik, DJD 13:91). Note also הע for *הא in 1Mas h III, 2 (= Sir 41:2).

130. Kutscher, *Isaiah*, 506. He also suggests more tentatively the possible correction of עלמנה to אלמנה and of צואה to צועה in 1QIsaᵃ at Isa 47:8 and 63:1, respectively (*Isaiah*, 508, 536).

131. Qimron, *Grammar*, 83 and Maurice Baillet, DJD 7:23. Other translations, like that of *DSSSE*, follow Baillet.

132. Note the similar confusion in the same scroll of תעזר (4Q109 [4QQohᵃ] at Qoh 7:19) for MT תָּעֹז, which is supported by the LXX and seems not related to a weakening of ʿ*ayin*'s pronunciation.

133. See Qimron, *Grammar*, 84–85. Compare תתחנג in Sir 37:29, MS Bm, for perhaps *תתענג (Miguel Pérez Fernández, *An Introductory Grammar of Rabbinic*

ההולה — (4Q365 12a–b ii, 2 at Exod 38:1) for הָעֹלָה "the burnt offering"[134]
[ר]שהה — (4Q379 22 ii, 13) corrected to [ר]שעה "evil"[135]
מסלה — (1QIsa^a at Isa 16:1) for MT מִסֶּלַע "from Sela"[136]
שעיס — (1QIsa^a at Isa 37:30) for MT שָׁחִיס "grain"[137]

Another "doubtful" example where *ḥeth* is written for etymological *ʿayin* is יכחס (1QS VII, 3) for what should be *יכעס "he will be angry."[138] Kutscher lists an additional example: סחורה "one traded" at Isa 54:11 for MT סֹעֲרָה "one stormed upon," though here the word in the scroll makes perfect sense and seems to be a case of the scribe choosing a word more common than the one in the MT tradition, one that is phonetically similar to the MT word, but not identical in sound.[139] Kutscher lists one example where *ʿayin* is written for an etymological *heh*, עמוסים "loads" for MT הֲמָסִים "brushwood" at Isa 64:1, though this seems again to be a case of the scribe writing a more common word ("loads") for an obscure word in the MT; note that the LXX, Targums, and Peshitta do not translate הֲמָסִים.[140] The example of מעשבת (1QS IV, 4) corrected to מחשבת "thought of" is likely due to a visual slip; the first word of the line is מעשי "deeds of" and the word immediately following מעשבת is מעשה.[141]

Kutscher also cites examples of the scribes introducing *ʿayin*s into words that do not contain an etymological guttural. His presentation seems

Hebrew [Leiden: Brill, 1999], 11–12), though the same misspelling appears to be found in MS D (with, however, the crucial letter heavily damaged), and despite the correct spelling in the same verse of תענוג.

134. Tov and White note: "Above the unusual second letter of this word the scribe wrote a sign or letter, the nature of which is unclear" (DJD 13:279).

135. One wonders if the mistake was partially visual, the result of the following *heh*.

136. Kutscher, *Isaiah*, 112, 507. Kutscher also lists ההם at Isa 9:12 for MT העם, though the word is read as העם in the scroll by Accordance and Ulrich et al., *Qumran Biblical Scrolls*, 349.

137. Kutscher, *Isaiah*, 507.

138. Qimron, *Grammar*, 84. He notes that this is more likely a mistake for יכחש "he will deceive."

139. Kutscher, *Isaiah*, 507. Kutscher does not discuss the possibilities relating to why the scribe wrote סחורה, other than a scribal slip for סערה.

140. Kutscher, *Isaiah*, 506. Notice that the passive participle of עָמַס "to burden" appears in Isa 46:1; there it is used in reference to false gods, while in Isa 64:1 it would presumably have a generic meaning "loads."

141. See Qimron, *Grammar*, 84–85.

somewhat misleading. He writes: "As a result of the weakening of the laryngeal-pharyngeals the scribe … might even add them [that is, laryngeal or pharyngeal consonants] to words which did not have these as consonants at all."[142] In relation to *ʿayin*, he cites as examples of this נעשף (at Isa 40:24 for MT נָשַׁף "he blows"), which seems to have begun as עשו "they made" and then was partially corrected with initial *nun* and final *peh*, but leaving the *ʿayin*;[143] ממעיכה "from your womb" (at Isa 39:7) for MT מִמְּךָ "from you"; ותעלוז "you exulted" (at Isa 30:12) for MT וְנָלוֹז "what is crooked."[144] Nevertheless, in his explanation of these specific substitutions, he notes many possible reasons for the chosen word of the scribe, the weakening of the gutturals sometimes being only tangential to the scribe's choice. In relation to עשו (> נעשף) and תעלוז, Kutscher references the scribe's tendency to replace an obscure word with a more common one, even if the common one does not fit the context.[145] In relation to תעלוז he notes as an aside "By the way, this change was rendered easier because of nonpronunciation of the pharyngeals."[146] With regard to ממעיכה for MT מִמְּךָ, he notes that "the lack of differentiation in the pronunciation of the pharyngeals" made the two different phrases sound "identical."[147] Although this might be the case, notice that Kutscher has also provided the grounds for a second (and better) reason ממעיכה might replace ממך, namely the fact that in Isa 39:7 the phrase in question is preceded by יצא "to go forth" and that the expression יצא + מן + מעים is found in three other passages (Gen 15:4, 2 Sam 7:12, 16:11), while יצא + מן is found in only two other passages (Gen 17:6, 2 Kgs 20:18).[148] As Kutscher himself writes, the scribes' practice was sometimes to replace one word with another equally common word. And, even if phonetic similarity played a role in the substitution of one word for another, this does not imply identical pronunciation, just as the substitution of פתחו "they opened" at Isa 42:20 for MT פָּקוֹחַ "open" does not presuppose that *taw* was articulated like *qoph*.

142. Kutscher, *Isaiah*, 509.

143. See Ulrich et al., *Biblical Qumran Scrolls*, 408.

144. Kutscher, *Isaiah*, 507.

145. Ibid., 274, referring back to page 34.

146. Ibid., 273. He also notes the possibility that the word the scribe had intended was לעז, the weakening of the pharyngeals causing the misplacement of the *ʿayin*.

147. Ibid., 259–60.

148. Ibid., 259.

As a point of comparison, one can refer to the situation in the Aramaic of the DSS as well as the interlinear *ʿayin*s in the MT. There are only a few examples of a possible elision of *ʿayin* in the Aramaic of the scrolls: שתא (4Q550 1, 3 and 4Q552 1 i + 2, 7) for *שעתא "the hour"; and שמון (Jer 3ver,1) for *שמעון "Shimeon," though there are other possible explanations for the form of the name that do not depend on elision of *ʿayin*, namely that it could be an alternative spelling of סמון "Simon."[149] Muraoka also cites examples where etymological *ʿayin* is represented by *aleph*, as in מארבא (4Q209 23, 4) corrected to מערבא "west" and אסר (4Q201 3, 10) corrected to עסר "ten."[150] In the MT, one finds three cases of an *ʿayin* suspended above the line perhaps reflecting their omission and subsequent addition in an earlier manuscript (מִיָּעַר Ps 80:14; רְשָׁעִים Job 38:13 and 15).[151] Such possible omissions reflect either the influence of subdialects of Hebrew that did not preserve the *ʿayin* and/or the inherent weakness of the consonant.

Of those Hebrew examples listed in the columns above, there are nine cases where the *ʿayin* is totally lost and an additional seventeen instances where it is initially not written and then added later. Of these twenty-six cases, fifteen derive from 1QIsa[a], 1QH[a], and the Copper Scroll; ten derive from other DSS-SP9 and DSS-SP1c texts. Only one comes from a DSS-NSP text (4Q514). There are twelve cases where *aleph* is written for etymological *ʿayin*, four of which have been corrected to *ʿayin*. Four of these eleven words appear in 1QIsa[a]; the remaining eight appear in other DSS-SP9 and DSS-SP1c texts, with only two in a DSS-NSP text (4Q24 [4QLev[b]]; 4Q55 [4QIsa[a]]). The remaining ten passages listed attest to an apparent confusion between *ʿayin* and *aleph*, *heh*, and *ḥeth* in two passages from 1QS and four from 1QIsa[a]. Again, only one passage is from a DSS-NSP text (4Q379). Considering all these misspellings, most derive from DSS-SP9

149. On שתא, see Émile Puech, *Qumran Grotte 4.XXVII: Textes araméens, deuxième partie: 4Q550–575a, 580–587 et appendices* (DJD 37; Oxford: Clarendon, 2009), 13 and 63. On שמון, see E. Eshel and H. Eshel, "Jericho papDeed of Sale ar," in *Miscellaneous Texts from the Judaean Desert* (ed. James Charlesworth et al; DJD 38; Oxford: Clarendon, 2000), 41.

150. Muraoka, *GQA*, 14. The weakening of *ʿayin* in numerals twelve through nineteen is also found in Judean Aramaic, e.g., תליסר and תלתיסר, as cited by Milik, "Rouleau de Cuivre," in DJD 3:229. The case of יחאכון for יחעכון in 11Q10 VII, 5 is more complicated than simply the quiescence of *ʿayin* and may reflect a complicated development, for which see Muraoka, *GQA*, 6 and the literature cited in 6 n. 34.

151. See Tov, *Scribal Practices*, 217. Cf. נִשְׁקְָה for *נִשְׁקְעָה in Amos 8:8.

texts.[152] Cumulatively, twenty-four of the forty-eight instances of misspellings derive from 1QIsa^a, 1QS, and 1QH^a which suggests that the weakening of *ʿayin* was especially prevalent among sectarian scribes, though it should be emphasized that this weakening is by no means as frequent or as pervasive as the quiescence of *aleph* (see below). The weakening of *ʿayin* in a documentary text suggests it was perhaps part of the spoken dialect, certainly part of a less literary register. The numerous cases of confusion in 1QIsa^a, together with the more circumstantial evidence cited by Kutscher, suggests that the *ʿayin* was weakest in the idiolects of this scroll's scribes.

Several more details should be noticed in relation to the weakening of *ʿayin*. First, in twenty-two out of the twenty-six cases where *ʿayin* is entirely lost, or lost initially and then inserted as a correction, it is in the environment where *aleph* quiesces, that is, where it would close a historically closed syllable (יעקוב, ישעיהו, [מ]ע[נה], מערכת, ממוד, יבור, ישה, העלות, לידעתיכהו) or where it is preceded by a consonant or a vocal shewa (according to the MT vocalization) (אלמעונתו, מרב, שבעשרה, שבו, נשנתי, בעצה, בעץ, לעשק, בעיניהם, תגער). Furthermore, in seven cases where *aleph* replaces an etymological *ʿayin*, *ʿayin* would close a syllable (יאבורו, מושיא, שר[ו]א) or precede a shewa (ואתה, ואואר, וכאפר) and in three cases where *ʿayin* replaces etymological *aleph*, *aleph* would be preceded by a shewa (ועל, נרעתה).

The similarity in phonetic environments where *aleph* and *ʿayin* are lost or confused reflects a common weakness in pronunciation, though one should note the limited number of cases where *ʿayin* is lost and the comparative frequency of *aleph*'s loss. With the exception of a few misspellings like יעשה as ישה in 1QIsa^a, words with *ʿayin* are not repeatedly misspelled.[153] In fact, no single word is misspelled more than three times among the DSS. Second, one should notice that with the exception of על יפות, עם, אצית, and על (in 4Q99), *ʿayin* is only lost or confused when it occurs in the middle or at the end of words (including when it is preceded by a morphological affix or enclitic particle). This distribution suggests that the *ʿayin* at the beginning of a word or when it occurs within a word preceded by a full vowel was likely pronounced relatively clearly and distinctly. Third, that the *ʿayin* had not totally quiesced is also suggested by

152. Only three texts (not including the Copper Scroll) do not come from DSS-SP9 or DSS-SP1c texts (4Q24, 4Q99, 4Q379).

153. Particles like עתה and על should not be considered as misspellings on par with others.

the few examples where one finds *ʿayin* and *ḥeth* confused (e.g., על יפות and שעיס). Note too the apparent phonetic spelling למעאן in 4Q175 4 (for what would be in the MT לְמַעַן), in which *aleph* presumably marks a preceding /a/ vowel; if this is so, then this presumes the presence of an epenthetic vowel (as in the MT form of the word), one purpose of which might have been to preserve the pronunciation of *ʿayin*. Finally, the confusion and interchange of the two consonants *aleph* and *ʿayin* is not equal. *Aleph* could be written for *ʿayin*, especially in the specific environments where *ʿayin* would likely be weakest in pronunciation or even elided. But, *ʿayin* is less often written for *aleph*; there are just four examples of this (על, ועל [twice], מנעציך, נרעתה), two of which probably were influenced by the frequent interchange of the graphically similar prepositions אל and על and/or the confusion of the words "God" אל and "Most High" עליון. Thus, one should not characterize the two consonants or phonemes as interchangeable.

Quiescence of *Heh*

The glottal fricative phoneme (*heh*) is dropped in essentially the same environments that the glottal stop (*aleph*) is dropped, though less frequently. It is best to conclude that this is partially attributable to the inherent weakness of this phoneme, reflected in numerous ways in the Tiberian tradition, and partially attributable to the quiescence of this phoneme in certain other environments in the dialect(s) of the scribes and writers. We should also note in passing the various I-*aleph* and I-*heh* words that share similar meanings: אדר *niphal*: "be glorious" versus הדר *niphal*: "be honored"; אַוָּה versus הַוָּה "desire"; אוֹן "power, wealth" versus הוֹן "wealth." These pairs perhaps reflect a natural correspondence between the sounds of the respective phonemes in the minds of early Hebrew speakers; they do not suggest the absence of a distinction between the phonemes.

The following words clearly attest the elision of *heh* where the letter's loss is most likely reflective of the quiescence of the glottal fricative. The list shows representative examples.

ולהתלך — "and to walk about" (1QS V, 10 = MT *וּלְהִתְהַלֵּךְ)[154]

154. Qimron, *Grammar*, 83 and idem, *HDSS*, 25. Many of the other examples are derived from these pages of Qimron's *Grammar* and *HDSS*. Another case listed by Qimron is הטל הראישון (1QM VIII, 15) as a mistake for *הַהֶטֵּל הראישון; however,

משא עדה — “a burden of the congregation” (1QSa I, 20)
לוגיע — “to make weary” (1QpHab X, 11) for *להוגיע
על אות הראישונה — “upon the first banner” (1QM IV, 9)[155]
על אות השנית — “upon the second banner” (1QM IV, 9)
שלבתה — “its flame” (1QH^a XVI, 31 = MT *שַׁלְהַבְתָּהּ)[156]
ואזינו — “and give ear” (1QIsa^a at Isa 1:10) for MT הַאֲזִינוּ[157]
מתלות — “mockeries” (1QIsa^a at Isa 30:10) for MT מַהֲתַלּוֹת
לנפה — “to shake” (1QIsa^a at Isa 30:28) for MT לַהֲנָפָה
ונע — “and Hena” (1QIsa^a at Isa 37:13) for MT הֵנַע
לשאוות — “to destroy” (1QIsa^a at Isa 37:26) for MT לְהַשְׁאוֹת
ולחיות — “to revive” (1QIsa^a at Isa 57:15 [twice]) for MT וּלְהַחֲיוֹת
לשמיע — “to make heard” (1QIsa^a at Isa 58:4) for MT לְהַשְׁמִיעַ
תומות — “depths” (1QIsa^a at Isa 63:13) for MT תְּהֹמוֹת

With one exception where the *heh* as a root consonant would have come at the end of an etymologically closed syllable (מתלות), all these words exhibit the dropping of the *heh* where it would have occurred after a syllable that ends in a consonant or a syllable that ends in a vocal shewa, the latter environment being the same in which the *heh* of the definite article frequently elides in the MT. In three cases, the definite article elides before another guttural (משא עדה, על אות הראישונה, על אות השנית); in the rest of the examples, the *heh* is a root consonant or verbal prefix. The *heh* is initially lost and then added as a correction in identical phonetic environments.[158] Note that all the texts are DSS-SP9, though this same phenomenon appears in DSS-NSP texts too (e.g., לשמיע “to declare” 4Q381 76–77, 10; לשכיל “to teach” 4Q381 80, 1; ולבדל “and to be separated” 4Q258 I, 2).

It should be observed, that in some cases what appears to be the elision of the *heh* really occurs for reasons other than the weakness of the conso-

---

this phrase can be read not as Qimron does, but rather as a defective *hiphil* infinitive construct (or infinitive absolute used as a construct) from טול “to throw.”

155. Interpreting this and the following example as cases of construct chains (as Accordance does) seems less likely given the consistency with which the ordinal numbers are used in attributive adjectival constructions with preceding nouns in the DSS.

156. See Stegemann, Schuller, Newsom, DJD 40:222, who also note that the word looks like שלכתה.

157. For this and the following examples from 1QIsa^a, see Kutscher, *Isaiah*, 506.

158. Before a shewa (ו˺ה˹אזינו in 1QIsa^a at Isa 8:9), and at the end of a historically closed syllable (ולטו˺ה˹רה in 1QS VI, 22; בא˺ה˹ב[ה] in 462 1, 6).

nant. For example, the spelling יופכו "they overthrew" (4Q501 1, 4) for an assumed root הפך does not necessarily imply the weakness of the glottal fricative, since the DSS seems to have known another synonymous verbal root, אפך, also found in RH and Aramaic, which verb (specifically in the Mishnah) takes an /o/ vowel after the prefix in the *qal* imperfect, similar in this sense to אמר. The spelling יהופכו (4Q432 4, 1) is presumably due to confusion between הפך and אפך.[159]

In other cases, the *heh* seems to assimilate to a preceding or following vowel, as *aleph* does in forms like דניל (*dānīʾēl* >) *dānīyēl* "Daniel" and בוו (*bāʾū* >) *bāwū* "they came" (see §§4.4–5, "*Aleph* < *Yodh* and *Yodh* < *Aleph*" and "*Aleph* < *Waw* and *Waw* < *Aleph*"). The following represent the most relevant examples:

לאביו — "to his fathers" (4Q175 15 and passim)
אלויכה — "your God" (4Q219 II, 32 = MT *אֱלֹהֶיךָ)
וירמסוויו — "they will trample him" (4Q368 10 ii, 7)
תהוו — "emptiness" (4Q504 1–2R iii, 3 and 1QIsa[a] at Isa 40:17) for MT תֹּהוּ[160]
אלוים — "God" (8Q4 [8QMez] 35) for MT אֱלוֹהִים[161]

The spelling of the word "his father" (אביו) reflects *ʾābīyū* from an earlier **ʾābīhū*, as explained in §4.10, "Diphthongs and Triphthongs." The two misspellings of the word "God" presumably reflect something like *ĕlōyekā* and *ĕlōyīm* (note too *ĕlōyē* from HazGab). With regard to the spellings תהוו (*tōwū*), the one from 4Q504 might be a case of dittography, since the following word begins with a *waw* (ואסף "and nothing"), though the

159. See Kutscher, Isaiah, 251. For more on this verb in Aramaic, see Matthew Morgenstern, *Studies in Jewish Babylonian Aramaic Based upon Early Eastern Manuscripts* (HSS 62; Winona Lake, Ind.: Eisenbrauns, 2011), 170–71. See also the subsection "Lexicon" in §5.6, "Verbs."

160. Qimron, *HDSS*, 26. The development is *tōhū* > *tōwū*; the *heh* is a historical writing. Note the lack of spacing in the phrase תהווב[הו] in 4Q303 1, 5.

161. Qimron, "Diphthongs and Glides," 273. His other examples are not as convincing. Note also אלי "God of" (HazGab, 68; = MT *אֱלֹהֵי). See Qimron and Yuditsky, "Notes," 36; Bar-Asher, "On the Language" (2008): 499–500; Rendsburg, "Grammatical Sketch," 66; Yardeni and Elizur, "Hebrew Prophetic Text," 68. Bar-Asher and Yardeni and Elitzur also find this same spelling in line 84. Note that אלי "gods of" is restricted mostly to the Songs of the Sabbath Sacrifice and is used in reference to divine beings, not as a reference to God.

example from 1QIsa[a] is not followed by a *waw* and its spelling, therefore, cannot be explained in this way.[162] I assume, furthermore, that this is not a case of a double *mater*, since this phenomenon is rather rare. The strange form וירמסוויו "they will trample him" from 4Q368 presumably began as **wəyirməsūhū* and then developed to **wəyirməsūwū* through assimilation; the suffix was then further altered through dissimilation to *wəyirməsūyū*, the double-*waw* in וירמסוויו being due to a visual mistake of dittography or metathesis (for an intended *וירמוסויו *wəyirmōsūyū*).[163] These examples are attested not only in DSS-SP9 texts, but also in DSS-NSP (4Q368, 8Q3).

Sometimes *aleph* is written for etymological *heh*.[164] The following represents only some of the examples.

באמרות — (1QS VI, 26) for *בהמרות "when he disobeys"
באופיע — (1QS X, 2) for *בהופיע "when [they] shine"
ואנה איש ארור אחד (4Q175 23) for *והנה איש ארור אחד "Now, an accursed person"
אנבא — (4Q385 2, 7) for *הנבא "prophesy" (*niphal* imperative)
יאודה — (4Q504 1–2 iv, 6) for *יהודה "Judah"
אוגו — (4Q523 1–2, 2) for *הוגו "they thrust away"[165]
אודו — (1QIsa[a] at Isa 12:4) for MT הוֹדוּ "give thanks"[166]
אילילו — (1QIsa[a] at Isa 23:1) for MT הֵילִילוּ "wail"
אושיענו — (1QIsa[a] at Isa 37:20) for MT הוֹשִׁיעֵנוּ "deliver us"
אחשיתי — (1QIsa[a] at Isa 42:14) for MT הֶחֱשֵׁיתִי "I was quiet"
אקשיבו — (1QIsa[a] at Isa 51:4) for MT הַקְשִׁיבוּ "pay attention"
ארחיבי — (1QIsa[a] at Isa 54:2) for MT הַרְחִיבִי "broaden"

---

162. The form תוה (1QIsa[a] at Isa 49:4 for MT תֹּהוּ) is vocalized by Qimron (*HDSS*, 17) as *tō* (and thus perhaps provides further evidence for the quiescence of word-internal *heh*); all the same, this spelling is perhaps to be explained, rather, as a case of haplography since the following word begins with *waw*: ולהבל.

163. Or did the object suffix have the form *-ēhū*, as on the singular, thus leading to **yirməsūēhū* > **yirməsūwēhū* > *yirməsūwēyū*. Note the spelling [ויר]מ׳סהו "he trampled him" (4Q113 [4QDan[b]] at Dan 8:7) for MT וַיִּרְמְסֵהוּ; all the letters except *waw* are hard to read in the scroll.

164. Qimron, *Grammar*, 84.

165. The surrounding text around this word is very damaged and Puech notes many alternative understandings (*Qumran Grotte 4.XVIII: Textes hébreux (4Q521–4Q528, 4Q576–4Q579)* [DJD 25; Oxford: Clarendon, 1998], 78).

166. Kutscher, *Isaiah*, 506.

אשקיט — (1QIsa[a] at Isa 57:20) for MT הַשְׁקֵט "to be quiet"
אחזיק — (1QIsa[a] at Isa 64:6) for MT הַחֲזִיק "to grasp"
איות — (4Q85 [4QPs[c]] at Ps 50:21) for MT הֱיוֹת "to be"[167]

These mostly involve possible dittography (אנה) and/or influence from Aramaic's variation between causative *haphel* and *aphel* stems.[168] It should be emphasized that the assumption that the *aleph/heh* exchange in 1QS and 1QIsa[a] listed above is due to analogy with Aramaic *haphel/aphel* is based, in part, on the fact that the use of *aleph* in place of the prefix *heh* for the *hiphil* occurs primarily in 1QS and 1QIsa[a], texts in which one finds other causative stem forms that bear Aramaic traits (see the subsection "Conjugations" in §5.6, "Verbs," for further details). As Muraoka notes for DSS Aramaic, the variation between *haphel* and *aphel* does not necessarily imply an identical pronunciation for the two letters.[169] On the other hand, the case of יאודה for יהודה does seem like evidence for the confusion of the two phonemes, as does איות for MT הֱיוֹת and אנבא for הנבא. In some cases, what appears to be a case of *aleph* for *heh*, may be due to a scribal mistake like metathesis, as in עליאה (4Q369 1 ii, 3) (cf. עליהא in 1QIsa[a] at Isa 34:11, 37:33, 42:5, 45:12, and 66:10). Most of the examples are again DSS-SP9 texts, though some (4Q523, 4Q85) are DSS-NSP.

In rare cases, *heh* is written for etymological *aleph*. The best examples, cited by Qimron, all derive from 1QS.[170]

הנשי — (1QS VIII, 13 for אנשי "men of")[171]

---

167. Note that the *aleph* is very damaged; see Patrick W. Skehan, Eugene Ulrich, Peter Flint, "Psalms," DJD 16:58.

168. The *haphel* and *aphel* are both present in Biblical Aramaic and the Aramaic of the DSS, and conceivably these variant forms suggested to the scribes of 1QS and 1QIsa[a] a similar variation for Hebrew. Note also the possible example of ואסיג (1QIsa[a] at Isa 59:14 for MT וְהֻסַּג "it will be turned back"); the scroll's word could reflect either "he will turn back" or "I will turn back." Influence from other Aramaic words include אנה אנוכי at Isa 8:18 for MT הִנֵּה אָנֹכִי; אדס at Isa 55:13 for MT הֲדַס. Other reasons for the confusion include a different understanding of the passage (e.g., אסיר "I will turn aside" at Isa 5:5 for MT הָסֵר "turning aside").

169. Muraoka, *GQA*, 14.

170. Qimron, *Grammar*, 83–85.

171. Confusion of the two consonants, *aleph* and *heh*, is also found in the MT, especially in names: אֲדֹרָם in 1 Chr 10:18 for הֲדֹרָם in 1 Kgs 12:18; הַהֲרָרִי in 1 Chr 11:35 for הָאֲרָרִי in 2 Sam 23:33; and הֵיךְ in 1 Chr 13:12 for אֵיךְ in 2 Sam 6:9. For these,

הברכנו — (1QS X, 6 for אברכנו "I will bless him")
הבחרה — (1QS X, 12 for אבחרה "I will choose")[172]

Although Kutscher lists other instances of this phenomenon in 1QIsa[a], all can be attributed to other factors, or, at the least, to circumstances that might have significantly contributed to the confusion between laryngeals. The factors are: the difficulty of the original words (e.g., הדש "thoroughly [trampling]" the *hiphil* infinitive absolute of דוש followed by *qal* imperfect of דוש, at Isa 28:28 for MT אָדוֹשׁ "trample," which is an unprecedented *qal* infinitive absolute of דוש; הכ׳נכה "he established you [with a name]," *hiphil* of כון, at Isa 45:4 for MT אֲכַנְּךָ "I named you [your name]"; הוררט "Horarat (?)" at Isa 37:38 for MT אֲרָרָט "Ararat"); a separate understanding of the word or passage, twice where 1QIsa[a] introduces a syntax with infinitives more common to DSS Hebrew (e.g., השיב "[my hand] turned," *hiphil* infinitive, at Isa 1:25 for MT אָשִׁיבָה; העד "make testify," *hiphil* imperative, at Isa 8:2 for MT אָעִידָה; הנשא "to be lifted," *niphal* infinitive, perhaps due to dittography, at Isa 33:10 for MT אֶנָּשֵׂא), or the influence of Aramaic words (e.g., היכה "alas" at Isa 1:21, 14:12 for MT אֵיכָה; הכן "indeed" at Isa 40:7 for MT אָכֵן).[173] Another possible example from another scroll is ויהיר in 4Q381 1, 5 for what should be ויאיר "he will light up," though ויהיר may also be the *hiphil* of נהר "he will make shine."[174] In the end, since other factors might have contributed significantly to the confusion, one should

see Alexander Sperber, "Hebrew Based Upon Biblical Passages in Parallel Transmission," *HUCA* 14 (1939): 161. As for the second example, note that confusion on the part of the Chronicler might have been occasioned by the occurrence of ההררי earlier in 1 Sam 23:33.

172. Note that הבחרה can be explained as a *niphal* infinitive construct used as a finite verb, as Mark S. Smith has tentatively indicated ("The Infinitive Absolute as Predicative Verb in Ben Sira and the Dead Sea Scrolls: A Preliminary Survey," in *Diggers at the Well*, 264).

173. For the list of these interchanges, see Kutscher, *Isaiah*, 505. On הוררט, see ibid., 102. The reading of 1QIsa[a] at 45:4 is supported by numerous versions (for which see ibid., 247); for the passages with infinitives in Isa 1:25 and 33:10, see the comparable uses of the infinitive in Smith's "Infinitive Absolute," 264. The writing of an interlinear *heh* in מה־איבו at Isa 1:24 for MT מֵאוֹיְבָי is, as Kutscher suggests, misplaced from the preceding word ואנקם (= MT וְאִנָּקְמָה) (ibid., 505). The Aramaic influence of היך on איך is seen even in the Bible, where it occurs at Dan 10:17 and 1 Chr 13:12. See also Aramaic-like היככה in 4Q223–224 2 iv, 5 and 4Q385 2,3 in contrast to Hebrew איככה in 4Q200 4, 6; 4Q381 31, 6; 4Q388 7, 5 and 4Q453 1.

174. See Schuller, DJD 11:95.

not draw from these examples the conclusion that the phoneme /h/ had entirely quiesced, disappeared, or merged totally with the glottal stop.

Additionally, Qimron considers the rare instances of לוהב "flame, blade" spelled להוב in the absolute (in 1QHª XI, 31 and 4Q169 3–4 ii, 3) as further evidence of the weakness of *heh*.[175] This seems likely and would imply a variation in II-*heh* **quṭl* nouns similar to that found in II-*aleph* nouns like ראש. Newsom notes a similar possible variation in phrases like טוהר טהורים "purity of purities" (4Q403 1 i, 42), מלך הטהור "the king of purity" (4Q403 1 ii, 26), and ממולח טוהר "one blended purely" (4Q405 19, 4; 20 ii–22, 11; 23 ii, 10; 11Q17 IX, 7, corresponding to מְמֻלָּח טָהוֹר in Exod 30:35), though for these scrolls, one must recall the alternation between genuine **quṭl* and **qaṭul* forms, as in קדושי קודש קודש[ים] "holy ones of the holy of holies" (4Q400 1 ii, 6), which seems, in part, stylistic.[176]

The glottal fricative represented by *heh* clearly quiesced in some instances, especially after a shewa. Although in the MT the phoneme is lost in this same environment, this loss is primarily restricted to certain words and forms (after the prefix prepositions ב, כ, ל; in the prefix of the *hiphil* imperfect, **yəhaqṭīl* > *yaqṭīl*). In the DSS, the loss of *heh* after what would be a shewa seems to be found more frequently (e.g., ו^האזינו, ואזינו; ונע; תומות; יאודה) and is found in both DSS-SP9 and DSS-NSP texts. In addition, the *heh* is lost in other environments as well, like at the end of a syllable within a word (מ^אפכת and מאפכת, מתלות); it even sometimes replaces *aleph* at the beginning of a word (הנשי, הברכנו). Some confusions seem restricted to certain texts; for instance, *heh*'s replacement by *aleph* in the prefix of *hiphil* verbs is almost exclusively in 1QS and 1QIsaª; the spelling of *heh* for *aleph* at the beginning of a word is found primarily in 1QS. Such things do not mean, however, that the glottal fricative disappeared entirely from the language; it was probably preserved in more careful speech, reading, and writing by scribes of most DSS-SP9 texts (not 1QS, 1QIsaª). It bears mentioning, in relation to this, that words that contain an etymological *heh* as a third root consonant consistently attest this consonant, as in the absolute singular form of "God" אלוה (about twenty times); the verb "to be high" גבה (fifteen times), the abstract noun "height" גובה/גבה (about twenty times), and the adjective "high"

175. Qimron, *HDSS*, 37.

176. In 4Q400 1 ii, 6, the initial word is **qaṭul* and the following words are **quṭl*. See Newsom, DJD 11:254, 342. For the phrase of 4Q405 20 ii–22, 11, note the haplography, described above in "Scribal Mistakes" (§3.1).

גבוה/גבה (eighteen times); the verb "to shine" נגה (eight times) and the abstract noun "brightness" נוגה/נגה (eighteen times). Also note that the words (excluding the plural of אלוה) are spelled with *heh* not only when *heh* would be the last consonant of a word, but also when *heh* is followed by suffixed pronouns and morphemes attached to them. The consistency in spelling perhaps provides some small evidence that the scribes pronounced the *heh* as distinct from *aleph*.

Quiescence of *Ḥeth*

Of the four guttural consonants, there is the least evidence for *ḥeth*'s weakening. Although it is certain that the unvoiced pharyngeal fricative did weaken in certain environments and in certain texts, it seems equally certain that it was usually preserved, even, we may assume, in speech.

The examples from the MT lexicon of a supposed alternation between *ḥeth* and *heh* are dubious.[177] The correspondences asserted for *ḥeth* and *ʿayin* in the Hebrew lexicon are mostly late and probably influenced from Aramaic.[178]

The number of examples where *ḥeth* is elided is rather small: צצחות (1QIsa^{a} at Isa 58:11 for MT צַחְצָחוֹת "parched land")[179] and אזתמ (11Q1 [11QpaleoLev^{a}] at Lev 25:32 for MT אֲחֻזָּתָם "their possession").[180] Other examples are debateable, like that proposed by Wernberg-Møller: י(ח)שב "he will be thought" (1QS XI, 21) instead of ישב.[181]

---

177. See *HALOT*, *sub* ח, which suggests an alternation with *heh* in the roots גבה/גבח. The apparent correspondence between the Hebrew גִּבֵּחַ "bald" and Arabic *ʾajbah* "with a high forehead" (see *HALOT*, *sub* גִּבֵּחַ) I assume is coincidental.

178. See *HALOT*, *sub* ח, which lists alternations between לְחִי "jaw" and לוֹעַ "jaw," the latter occurring at the earliest only in Amoraic texts. Note לוחיי in 1QIsa^{a} at Isa 30:28 for MT לְחָיֵי "jaws" as a possible mistaken conflation of the Aramaic and Hebrew words (see Kutscher, *Isaiah*, 250), though it seems easier to assume that the form in 1QIsa^{a} is another example of a DSS word with a **quṭl* base where the MT reflects a **qaṭl* base. A possible case of this confusion in the MT lexicon is the writing חֵץ in 1 Sam 17:7 for *עֵץ.

179. Kutscher, *Isaiah*, 221–22, 506. Kutscher actually cites a third example: מת at Isa 10:9 for MT חֲמָת, but this is now read as חמת with a heavily damaged *ḥeth* (see Accordance and Ulrich et al., *Biblical Qumran Scrolls*, 350).

180. Could this perhaps be caused by visual confusion between the paleo forms of *aleph*, *ḥeth*, and *zayin*?

181. P. Wernberg-Møller, *Manual of Discipline: Translated and Annotated with*

An initial loss of *ḥeth* and subsequent correction is found more frequently.

להוכי[ח] — "to reprove" (1QS V, 24)
ה[ח]נינה — "the favor" (1QH[a] XIX, 32)[182]
ה[ח]דר — "the chamber" (4Q365a 2 ii, 8)
תשמ[ח] — "do (not) rejoice" (4Q417 2 i, 10)[183]
נ[ח]שת — "copper" (4Q33 [4QDeut[f]] at Deut 8:9)
וה[ח]זיקה — "they will seize" (1QIsa[a] at Isa 4:1 for MT וְהֶחֱזִיקוּ)[184]
למ[ח][תה] — "for a ruin" (4Q70 [4QJer[a]] at Jer 17:17).[185]

These examples do suggest the weakness of *ḥeth*, though sometimes other reasonable explanations present themselves, like a confusion over what the text should say (תשמ[ח] "do [not] be forlorn" versus "do [not] rejoice") and haplography due to the similarity in shape between *heh* and *ḥeth* (ה[ח]נינה, ה[ח]דר, וה[ח]זיקה).

I could find only one clear example, in a fragmentary context, where *aleph* is written for etymological *ḥeth*, א[י]ת (4Q82 [4QXII[g]] at Hos 2:14 for MT חַיַּת "animals of").[186] However, examples of *heh* written for etymological *ḥeth* and vice versa are slightly more plentiful. Although these

---

an Introduction (STDJ 1; Leiden: Brill, 1957), 154. He is followed more recently by *DSSSE*. Qimron and Charlesworth, on the other hand, read as the verb ישב ("Rule of the Community," 50–51).

182. Stegemann and Schuller note that Scribe C seems to have started an *aleph*, then changed it to a *ḥeth* (Stegemann, Schuller, Newsom, DJD 40:241).

183. The final *mem* suggests that the scribe thought initially that the word ended with this letter. Strugnell and Harrington write, "to determine what the scribe initially intended with his תשם is difficult—it may well have simply been a mistake" (DJD 34:181). Despite this, it seems likely to me, based on the context, that the scribe thought the text should read "do not be forlorn (= MT *תֵּשֹׁם or *תֵּשָׁם, from שמם) in your mourning (באבלכה)." The two words (i.e., the verb שמם and the noun אבל) occur together in, e.g., Jer 12:11 and Lam 1:4.

184. See Kutscher, *Isaiah*, 506. This mistake may be due to haplography.

185. The reading סלה לה (4Q416 2 iv, 10) is ambiguous. It may be a case where *ḥeth* is written like a *heh* and thus we should read סלח לה. See Strugnell and Harrington, DJD 34:124–25.

186. Kutscher also lists an example where *aleph* is written for *ḥeth*, in the phrase לשון אש ואש לוהבת in 1QIsa[a] at Isa 5:24 for MT לְשׁוֹן אֵשׁ וַחֲשַׁשׁ לֶהָבָה (*Isaiah*, 506). For this mistake, Kutscher cites "the weakness of the pharyngeal" and the precedent of the phrase אש להבה "flame of fire" in Isa 4:5 (as well as elsewhere) and other similar

may reflect *ḥeth*'s weakening, one must recognize that all such mistakes may not reflect aural mistakes, but rather visual gaffs, the two letters being so similar in shape.[187] Examples of *heh* written for etymological *ḥeth* are listed here. Notice that almost all of the examples are from 1QS and 1QIsa^a.

מהשבתם — (1QS III, 15) corrected to מחשבתם "their thoughts"[188]
ישהק — (1QS VII, 14) corrected to ישחק "he will laugh"
להפצ — (1QS VI, 11) for *לחפץ "to the desire of"[189]
הגורה — (1QIsa^a at Isa 3:24) for MT חֲגוֹרָה "girdle")
השקי — (1QIsa^a at Isa 21:4) for MT חִשְׁקִי "my desire"
ה̇רבות — (1QIsa^a at Isa 21:15) for MT חֲרָבוֹת "swords"[190]
נרהב — (1QIsa^a at Isa 30:23) for MT נִרְחָב "broad"
מהשוכים — (1QIsa^a at Isa 42:16) for MT מַחְשָׁךְ "darkness"
השילה — (4Q59 [4QIsa^e] at Isa 8:6) for MT הַשִּׁלֹחַ "the Shiloah"

One example proposed from the Vision of Gabriel text is uncertain; Bar-Asher argues that הביב is written for חביב "loved one" in line 64 of the text, though the editors and Yardeni in particular seem to favor the reading חביב.[191]

---

expressions (ibid., 221). However, the change in 5:24 seems more likely due to dittography and/or the substitution of a simpler word for an obscure MT word.

187. See Tov, *Textual Criticism*, 231; he notes that such mistakes may also have a phonological component. Cross and Eshel note the graphic confusion of the two letters in many inscriptions from the first century C.E. (Frank Moore Cross and E. Eshel, "1. KhQOstracon," in *Qumran Cave 4.XXVI: Cryptic Texts and Miscellanea, Part 1* [ed. S. J. Pfann et al.; DJD 36; Oxford: Clarendon, 2000], 497). Similar confusions occur in the MT: יִפְרֶה (Isa 11:1) for *יפרח; מְבֹחֶלֶת (Prov 20:21) for *מבהלת; ולחתם *kethib* (Dan 9:24) for וּלְהָתֵם *qere* (Delitzsch, *Lese- und Schreibfehler*, 109); perhaps also וְרָהְבָּם (Ps 90:10) for *רחבם (cf. רחוב 1QIsa^a at Isa 51:9 for MT רַהַב).

188. Qimron, *Grammar*, 85. Note that Qimron and Charlesworth seem more hesitant about this correction and write "original ה perhaps corrected to ח" ("Rule of the Community," 14).

189. Qimron, *Grammar*, 84.

190. For this and the other examples, see Kutscher, *Isaiah*, 506. This mistake may be due to confusion with הָרְבּוֹת or הָרַבּוֹת. What Kutscher lists as יהיה is to be read (like the MT) as יחיה (see Accordance and Ulrich et al., *Biblical Qumran Scrolls*, 344).

191. Bar-Asher, "*Vision of Gabriel*," 500. Apparently, Yardeni and Elitzur first were unsure which letter should be read, then Yardeni (in a personal conversation) said she thought it was a *heh*, and then later said that she prefers the reading with a *ḥeth* (ibid., 500 n. 55).

There are fewer convincing examples of *ḥeth* written for an etymological *heh*.

וחלחם — (4Q369 2, 2) for *והלחם "to fight"
מנחל — (1QIsa[a] at Isa 51:18) for MT מְנַהֵל "one to guide"
לנדוח — "for banishing (their children)" (4Q111 [4QLam] at Lam 1:17) for MT לנדה "impure thing"

Other examples are less certain: חפר "be ashamed" (4Q416 2 iv, 9) corrected to הפר *hāfēr* "annul" (*hiphil* imperative of פרר) may, as Strugnell and Harrington note, reflect no correction, but simply an unusually formed *heh*.[192] The example of עיר החרס "the city of the sun" (presumably, Heliopolis) in 1QIsa[a] and 4Q56 (4QIsa[b]) at Isa 19:18 for MT עִיר הַהֶרֶס "the city of destruction" either reflects the earlier text from which the MT derives through wordplay (between הֶרֶס and חֶרֶס) or the fact that the scribes of 1QIsa[a] and 4Q56 failed to recognize the pun and replaced the less common הרס "destruction" with the more common חרס "sun."[193] Kutscher cites other examples where *ḥeth* is written for etymological *heh*, but these are either no longer read as *ḥeth* (e.g., אשיתחו at Isa 5:6 is now read as אשיתהו "I will render it");[194] are due to an obscure word in the MT (כחדוש "like the month of" at Isa 25:10 for MT כְּהִדּוֹשׁ "as the threshing of"; תפתח "opening" or "you will open" at Isa 30:33 for MT תָּפְתֶּה "Topheth"; חוברי "conjurers of" at Isa 47:13 for MT *kethib* הברו "they astrologize" [*qere* implies הֹבְרֵי "those astrologers"];חוזים "they who see" at Isa 56:10 for MT הֹזִים "those who talk incomprehensibly"); or are the result of confusion between common words (רחוב "Rehob" or "plaza" at Isa 51:9 for MT רַהַב "Rahab").[195]

A weakening of *ḥeth* is implied, according to Qimron, in the single form רחובו "its width" (4Q365 12b iii, 9) for what would otherwise be רוחבו, as in 4Q365a 2 ii, 10.[196] This might be the case, but I think the evidence for the quiescing of *ḥeth* in this kind of environment is weak and the example of רחובו may simply be a visual error, similar to other cases where

192. See Strugnell and Harrington, DJD 34:124–25. Accordance reads the form as the *hiphil* 3ms perfect of פרר "he annulled."

193. Kutscher, *Isaiah*, 507.

194. Accordance and Ulrich et al. in *Qumran Biblical Scrolls*, 338.

195. Kutscher, *Isaiah*, 506. On חרס, see ibid., 116; on חוזים, see ibid., 235.

196. Qimron, *HDSS*, 37.

a *mater* is put in the wrong place (see the examples listed above in §3.1, "Scribal Mistakes") or due to the scribe initially thinking he was writing the construct form of the word "width" and then, after adding the suffix, not bothering to correct the spelling.[197] The example of שחוד "bribe" from 1QIsa[a] at Isa 5:23 and 33:15 (as an absolute noun) is also exceptional and might be evidence for the weakened *ḥeth* in the dialect of the scribes of 1QIsa[a], though it could also be a mistake perhaps due to influence from Aramaic orthography.

The likelihood that *ḥeth* was not quiescent is perhaps also suggested by the misspelling, erasure, and correction in three texts (if these are not due to visual slips). The word יאכלו "they will eat" (4Q514 1 i, 6) was first spelled with a *ḥeth*, as יאחלו. The word החול "the sand" (4Q225 2 i, 6) was first written הכול. The word + suffix ניחוחיכם "your pleasing sacrifice-odor" (4Q270 7 i, 18) was first written without the *kaph*. Although *ḥeth* represented a sound distinct from *kaph* at the turn of the era (even spirantized *kaph*), such mistakes suggest that the *ḥeth* was not quiescent. It bears mentioning that the three scrolls represent the three categories of texts, DSS-SP9 (4Q225), DSS-SP1c (4Q270), and DSS-NSP (4Q514).

Like the other gutturals, *ḥeth* could drop at the end of a word or syllable. Likewise, its confusion with *heh* is sometimes at the end of a syllable, though there are also cases where the two letters are confused at the beginning of a syllable too. The inherent weakness of the phoneme, the phonetic similarity with /h/, and *ḥeth*'s graphic similarity to *heh*, all help to explain many of the examples cited above. And, much evidence cited for this variation derives from 1QIsa[a], which implies the peculiarity of this phenomenon to this text and its scribes. That the unvoiced pharyngeal fricative weakened in the dialects (and idiolects) of all or even most scribes seems unlikely. The rarity of the letter's elision together with the fact that it is sometimes confused with *kaph* suggest that the letter still represented a sound distinct from the glottal stop (*aleph*) or glottal fricative (*heh*).

Summary

If we look at all the evidence for the weakening of gutturals, we come up with the following picture: the gutturals had "weakened," but they had not

197. For a discussion of this and related forms, see also § 5.5, "**quṭl* Nouns."

all become weak to the same degree. The most likely environment for a guttural to be pronounced is at the beginning of a word; its loss or mispronunciation is most common in the middle or at the end of a word, especially where it closes a syllable and where it is immediately preceded by a consonant or vocal shewa.

Nor are the gutturals all interchangeable with each other in every text, register, and idiolect. Over all, gutturals are particularly weak in 1QS, 1QIsa[a], and the Copper Scroll (3Q15). Some texts seem to reflect a particular difficulty with certain sounds and letters. For instance, 1QH[a] attests numerous cases of misspellings involving *ʿayin*, but comparatively few with *heh* or *ḥeth*. Also, note the frequency with which *heh* is written for *ḥeth* in 1QS and 1QIsa[a]. Such distributions may be only coincidental, but perhaps reflect a range of different kinds of guttural weakening in the dialects or idiolects of the scribes and/or in the different registers of the texts.

Aleph was often elided in writing of all kinds, presumably reflecting the loss of the glottal stop in many different environments. This loss was probably frequent in speech as well, though this does not mean that the phoneme was never articulated. When it is missing, it is most often in the middle of a word when it is not preceded by a full vowel (that is, when it is preceded, according to the Tiberian tradition, by a consonant or a vocal shewa) or when it would have come at the end of a syllable. When preceded by a full vowel at the beginning of a syllable, however, the *aleph* is usually retained and presumably represents a glottal stop. When the *aleph* is followed by an /o/ or /u/ vowel it is often retained, even when preceded by a vocal shewa. Occasionally in the writings associated with the sect (especially 1QpHab, 1QSa, 1QH[a]) the *aleph* is dropped before a full vowel.

The *ʿayin* is, compared to *aleph* and *heh*, only rarely elided; when it is dropped, it is often in the same environment where these other gutturals are dropped. In contrast to the situation with *aleph*, there are no cases where an individual word with *ʿayin* is misspelled consistently (in more than three separate passages). Its loss is most frequent in 1QS, 1QH[a], 1QIsa[a], and 3Q15 (the Copper Scroll).

The *heh* was often lost too, frequently in environments where it is also lost in the MT, but to an even greater degree. This suggests the loss of the corresponding phoneme, the glottal fricative, in certain environments. Such loss is partially a consequence of the phoneme's inherent weakness, but also the weakening of its pronunciation especially as reflected in 1QIsa[a] and 1QS. Its loss is also suggested through a variation in spelling, where *aleph* sometimes replaces *heh*. However, in many cases where such variation occurs with the *heh* of the *hiphil* prefix, the reason is not necessarily aural confusion, but may be due to analogy with the alternation in Aramaic between *haphel* and *aphel* causative stems; such variation is most obvious in 1QIsa[a] and 1QS and coincides with other parallels between *hiphil* and *haphel* forms in these texts. The assimilation of *heh* to a neighboring vowel (like the analogous assimilation of *aleph*, *waw*, and *yodh*) is only an occasional reflex of the phoneme's inherent weakness. In the end, I find it unlikely that the *heh* phoneme was entirely lost in word-medial position in the speech or in the writing/reading registers of most scribes and writers of the DSS. As in the MT, the *heh* could elide in certain positions or be retained.

The *ḥeth* phoneme shows some signs of having weakened. The best evidence again comes from 1QS and 1QIsa[a] and reflects the peculiar pronunciation or dialect of its scribes. Confusion with *kaph* in three separate texts suggests that it had not weakened in the dialect(s) of other scribes.

As for Kutscher's characterization of the situation, that the phonemes represented by *aleph* and *ʿayin* had fallen together and those represented by *heh* and *ḥeth* had fallen together, the evidence from the entire corpus of scrolls does not reflect this. Most cases in which these groups of consonants are confused reflect either the common weakness of the grouped consonants, the similarity in their sound, or even (in the case of *heh* and *ḥeth*) the similarity in the graphic shape of the respective letters. Notice, as a comparison, the confusions cited in "Scribal Mistakes" (§3.1) between letters representing velar/uvular consonants (*gimmel*, *kaph*, *qoph*); to my knowledge no one has suggested that the scribes of the DSS had lost the distinction between these consonants. This is not to deny, however, that the situation in 1QS and 1QIsa[a] does seem to reflect a relatively high degree of confusion between all the gutturals.

The characterization of Goshen-Gottstein, among others, that the phonemes associated with *aleph* and *heh* were often confused does seem to be true, but primarily at the end of words and syllables where the articulation of the two phonemes would be more difficult to make and/or hear. The frequent variations of *aleph* and *heh* at the beginning of words do reflect a weakening of /h/, though many of these examples may also be influenced from Aramaic morphology (*aph*el instead of *haphel* causative stem) and Aramaic words (היכה instead of Hebrew איכה). There is no reason to believe that *ḥeth* and *ʿayin* were typically confused. The few instances where one is written for the other suggest the common place of their articulation (the pharynx); that *ḥeth* is confused with *ʿayin* may offer further evidence for the preservation of a sound associated with *ʿayin*, one distinct from that of *aleph* and *heh*.

4.4. *Aleph* < *Yodh* and *Yodh* < *Aleph*

In the Hebrew of the DSS, as in the Hebrew of the MT, an etymological *yodh* can shift to *aleph* or the reverse can happen: an etymological *aleph* can shift to a *yodh* or *aleph* + *yodh*.[198] These shifts are parallel to shifts between *aleph* and *waw* discussed below. Since such variations in spelling occur in the MT, scholars have offered various explanations for them over time.[199] Examples of the shift from etymological *yodh* to *aleph* are found in the MT among the plural forms of gentilics and of words whose final etymological root consonant is *yodh*. To understand these shifts fully, especially in relation to the gentilics, it is useful to understand a bit of the history of Hebrew nouns.

Evidence from the MT of *Aleph* < *Yodh*

Based on comparative evidence, it seems that the gentilic nouns at one time had the ending **-iyyu*.[200] This was then shortened to *-īy*, which would sound almost identical to /ī/.[201] Thus, for the masculine singular absolute in the MT one finds words like עִבְרִי *ʿibrī* "Hebrew." For feminine singular

198. Such shifts are distinct from the shifts suggested through the biblical Hebrew lexicon, as in אֵבָל "canal" (< יבל "to bring"), a by-form of יוּבַל, as well as אִשׁ and יֵשׁ (see *HALOT*, s.v.). In these cases, the evidence for development (from *yodh* to *aleph* or vice versa) is usually encumbered by ambiguities. E.g., for the word "canal," note the verb אבל "to be dry" and for the particle of existence: Ugaritic *ʾit* versus Phoenician *yš*. Conceivably, these pairs of words reflect the inherent similarity of the phonemes.

199. For a lucid and insightful study of analogous exchanges in MH, see Yohanan Breuer, "Intervocalic *Alef/Yodh* Interchanges in Mishnaic Hebrew," *Revue des Études juives* 159 (2000): 63–78.

200. On the Arabic gentilic, for example, see W. Wright, *A Grammar of the Arabic Language* (3rd ed.; 2 vols.; Cambridge: Cambridge University Press, 1896–1898), §249. The class of gentilic nouns is part of a broader group of nouns with the same morphology that are called "relative adjectives" in Arabic grammar and sometimes also in Hebrew grammar (see Blau, *Phonology and Morphology*, 276).

201. Ben-Ḥayyim (*Grammar of Samaritan Hebrew*, 64 n. 89) writes in relation to Tiberian Hebrew: "As is well known, there is no distinction between *-īya* and *-iyya*." Blau notes that Hebrew ִי - can mark either *-iyy* or *-īy* (*Phonology and Morphology*, 276).

and masculine plural nouns the etymological *yodh* consonant of the gentilic ending is only rarely preserved (e.g., הָעִבְרִיָּה *hāʿibrīyā* Deut 15:12, and כִּתִּיִּים *kittīyīm* "Kittim" Jer 2:10).[202] More often, the feminine singular and masculine plural do not show an etymological *yodh* but do exhibit a long /ī/ vowel (e.g., עִבְרִים *ʿibrīm*, כִּתִּים *kittīm*, and עִבְרִית *ʿibrīt*). The feminine plural, on the other hand, regularly has an etymological consonantal *yodh* (e.g., הָעִבְרִיֹּת *hāʿibrīyōt*, Exod 1:15).

The reason for the variations in the feminine singular and masculine plural nouns is unclear. Based on the historical form of the gentilic ending, it seems likeliest that words without the consonantal *yodh* have undergone some truncation (that is, *-īyī-* > *-ī-*), while those with the *yodh* preserve a vestige of the etymological form of the ending.[203] Similar cases of truncation are regularly found for other etymological III-*yodh* words (e.g., with participles, **bāniyīm* > *bōnīm* = בֹּנִים "they who build" and **bāniyāt* > *bōnōt* = בֹּנוֹת).[204] Although not denying the etymological development of the affix, Bergsträsser notes that there might not really be a significant phonetic difference between those forms that end ִיִּים - and those that end

202. Alternatively, they may represent *ʿibriyyā*, *kittiyyīm*. The similar writing of **qaṭīl* base nouns/adjectives like נְקִיִּים must reflect *nəqīyīm* (not **nəqiyyīm*) since there is no reason to believe that such adjectives ended with two consonantal *yodhs*. Similarly, לְוִיִּם should imply *ləwīyīm*. That the MT Hebrew forms like הָעִבְרִיָּה (Deut 15:12) and כִּתִּיִּים do not reflect the etymological form of the gentilics, *-iyy*, is something remarked on by Blau (ibid., 276), who notes that the Aramaic gentilic ending, *-āy*, suggests that Hebrew gentilics are characterized by a long vowel followed by a single *yodh*: *-īy*. One wonders, on the other hand, if both forms of masculine plural nouns (gentilics like כִּתִּיִּים and III-*yodh* **qaṭīl* base nouns/adjectives like נְקִיִּים) could be due to spontaneous gemination, like that found more commonly after /a/ vowels, as in גְּמַלִּים, but also after /i/ vowels as in אִסָּר (see Joüon-Muraoka §18f and §96Bb and Blau, *Phonology and Morphology*, 124, 132), perhaps analogously with *qal* fs participles like הֹמִיָּה (for more examples, see *HGhS*, 590h).

203. Bauer and Leander consider the MT forms with *-īyī-* and *-īyā* as preservations of earlier, etymological forms; they explain the shorter endings, *-īm* and *-īt*, as the result of truncation of the earlier morpheme (what they and Brockelmann call "haplography") (*HGhS*, 217f–g).

204. As Brockelmann illustrates, earlier in the development of the Semitic languages, intervocalic /w/ or /y/ often disappeared; he cites verbal forms like **qawama* becoming *qāma* (in Hebrew, the *qal*, 3ms perfect of קום) and similarly **saluyū* becoming *salū* (C. Brockelmann, *Grundriss der vergleichenden Grammatik der semitischen Sprachen* [2 vols.; Berlin: n.p., 1908–1913; reprinted Hildesheim: Georg Olms, 1961], 1:57 §39w).

with ִים-; in both cases the spelling may simply indicate an ultralong /i/ vowel: *-īm*, and, in any case, he observes, *-īyī-* and *-ī-* are practically identical in their sound.[205] It bears mentioning that those gentilics that exhibit the *-īyī-* etymological ending (like כִּתִּיִּים) are from a diverse range of texts, some early and some late; there is often not consistency within a given text.[206] This implies that for a certain period of time both forms for feminine singular and masculine plural words were optional pronunciations and/or spellings.

In any case, there seems to have been another development that followed the shift from *-īyī-* > *-ī-* (or, alternatively, a simultaneous and parallel development), whereby the *yodh* of *-īyīm* is written as *aleph*, reflecting, presumably, a shift to a glottal stop or glottalized glide, to become *-ī'īm*. There are two gentilics that exhibit this shift in the MT; the first is הַהַגְרִיאִים "the Hagarites" in 1 Chr 5:19, 20 and הַהַגְרִאִים in 1 Chr 5:10, the expected form being הַגְרִים (in Ps 83:7); and the second is הָעַרְבִיאִים "the Arabians" in 2 Chr 17:11, but more commonly עַרְבִים in Neh 4:1, 2 Chr 21:16, 22:1 (note עַרְבִיים in 2 Chr 26:7, *kethib* implying עַרְבִיִּים). These MT forms with *aleph* are usually explained by scholars as reflecting a shift in pronunciation, associated with glide or dissimilation. Bergsträsser, for example, describes the *aleph* in forms like הַגְרִיאִים as representing a "Gleitlaut" that had developed from an earlier *yodh*.[207] Bauer and Leander, on the other hand, characterize the *aleph* as resulting from dissimilation, by which they mean a phonetic transformation brought on by the similarity in sound between the *yodh* and the preceding and/or following /i/ vowels.[208]

205. Bergsträsser, *Hebräische Grammatik*, 1:102.

206. The simpler ending also occurs in later books. For example, the vocalization reflecting *kittīyīm* occurs in Jer 2:10 and Ezek 27:6, while the vocalization reflecting *kittīm* occurs in six passages in Genesis, Numbers, Isaiah, Daniel, and 1 Chronicles (in Isa 23:12 the *kethib* presumes the vocalization with *yodh*, though the *qere* presumes that without). The vocalization *ʿibrīyā* appears twice, in Deut 15:12 and Jer 34:9, the alternative form does not occur; the plural *ʿibrīyīm* occurs only in Exod 3:18, though the shorter form occurs in Exodus and 1 Samuel. The form פלשתיים occurs once in Amos 9:7, but everywhere else פלשתים; ארמיה appears in 1 Chr 7:14, while the short plural form (ארמים) appears in 2 Kgs 8:28, 29, 9:15; כושיים appears in Amos 9:7, but everywhere else כושים; אדומיים appears in 1 Kgs 11:17, while the shorter form appears in 2 Kings and 2 Chronicles.

207. See, Bergsträsser, *Hebräische Grammatik*, 1:93, 1:102–3.

208. Bauer and Leander, *HGhS*, 215g. In this paragraph, Bauer and Leander men-

Presumably, both interpretations could be correct.[209] In either case, the glottal stop between /i/ vowels helps to distinguish the ultimate and penultimate syllables, which might otherwise have contracted to a simple long /i/ vowel. In this case, we might think of the glottal stop that appears here as a kind of epenthetic consonant, separating the surrounding vowels or breaking up the potential hiatus.[210]

Most nouns, adjectives, and participles that are from etymological III-*yodh* roots exhibit a truncation in the plural and feminine forms, as mentioned above (**bāniyīm* > *bōnīm* = בֹּנִים and **bāniyāt* > *bōnōt* = בֹּנוֹת). This is the normal development, according to the basic model for III-*yodh* roots; the sequence Vowel + *y* + Vowel contracts to just Vowel. Words of III-*yodh* roots that exhibit a consonantal *yodh* instead of contraction, as in עֹטְיָה "one who wraps" (Song 1:7), are therefore unexpected.[211] Scholars like Bergsträsser and Bauer and Leander explain such forms as based on analogy to similar words from strong roots.[212] For example, the above feminine singular participle עֹטְיָה is formed on analogy to other *qal* feminine singular participles like אֹכְלָה "one which eats" (Deut 4:24) and שֹׁפְטָה "one who judges" (Judg 4:4). In the same way, masculine plural III-*yodh* nouns/adjectives from a **qaṭl* or **qiṭl* base like צְבִי "gazelle," should have gone from **ṣabayīm* to **ṣābīm* = *צָבִים through contraction, but, instead, they formed plurals like הַצְּבָיִם (2 Sam 2:18) and פְּתָיִם (Prov 1:22, singular פְּתִי "simple"), as well as פְּתָיִים (Ps 119:130), on analogy to **qaṭl* and **qiṭl* plurals like מְלָכִים "kings" and סְפָרִים "books."[213] In contrast to the

tion only nouns like חֲלָאִים discussed below, but on page 564 they list the above gentilic nouns with *aleph* and refer the reader to page 215 §g.

209. See Blau's comments on the similar צבאים (*Phonology and Morphology*, 89).

210. The use of glottal stops for epenthesis is found cross-linguistically. Christian Uffmann writes: "Glottal stops are frequently found in the world's languages.... In addition, they are typically found ... intervocalically, as a hiatus breaker.... Glottal stops are found epenthetically in onsets of initial or stress syllables, that is, in prominent positions" ("Intrusive [r] and Optimal Epenthetic Consonants," *Language Sciences* 29 [2007]: 457). Note also that the glottal stop sometimes appears in Israeli Hebrew in similar contexts, as "onglide to a heavily stressed vowel" (Bolozky, "Israeli Hebrew Phonology," 288).

211. Such forms are also occasionally found in the Hebrew of the DSS, as in כליו (4Q83 [4QPs[a]] at Ps 69:4 for MT כָּלוּ).

212. Bergsträsser, *Hebräische Grammatik*, 1:102 and Bauer and Leander, *HGhS*, 215g.

213. See also Joüon-Muraoka §96Aq. Another example is שְׁפָיִם (Jer 3:2) and

analogically formed III-*yodh* participles which are rare, these analogically formed segholate plurals are common. Similarly, although some III-*yodh* nouns/adjectives of the **qaṭīl* base, like שָׁנִי "scarlet," exhibit contraction in the plural (שָׁנִים Prov 31:21), more often such words in the feminine singular and plurals are formed on analogy to the strong root. Thus, נָקִי "innocent" becomes נְקִיִּם (Josh 2:17) as well as נְקִיִּים (Jer 2:34), both vocalized *nəqīyīm*, on analogy to adjectives like חָסִיד "pious" which is חֲסִידִים in the masculine plural.[214]

Although the participles and **qaṭīl* base nouns/adjectives in the MT do not exhibit a shift from etymological *yodh* to *aleph*, like that found in הָעַרְבִיאִים, III-*yodh* segholate nouns/adjectives do (that is, those from **qaṭl*, **qiṭl*, **quṭl* bases). Usually these are plural forms where the vowel preceding the historical *yodh* is /ā/, such that the shift is usually *-āyīm* > *-āʾīm* or *-āyōt* > *-āʾōt*. In the MT, these include the word צְבָאִים "gazelles" (1 Chr 12:9, *kethib* presuming *ṣəbāʾīm*), and צְבָאוֹת (Song 2:7, 3:5); פְּתָאִים "simple" (Ps 116:6, *kethib*); מְנָאוֹת "shares of" (Neh 12:44, cf. מְנָיוֹת in Neh 12:47, sing. *מְנָת), חֲלָאִים "ornaments" (Song 7:2, sing. חֲלִי; compare the plural forms of חֳלִי "sickness" חֳלָיִם in Deut 28:59 and חֳלָיִים in 2 Chr 21:15); עֳפָאִים "foliage" (Ps 104:12, *kethib*, sing. *עֳפִי); בְּלוֹאֵי "worn out" (Jer 38:12, compare בְּלוֹיֵ in Jer 38:11, sing. *בְּלוֹי).[215] Other examples include words from **qaṭal* bases like טְלָאִים "lambs" (Isa 40:11, sing. טָלֶה); the odd by-form of צֹאן "flock," צֹנַאֲכֶם (Num 32:24, sing. צֹנֶה Ps 8:8); and the **taqṭūl*

שְׁפָיִים (Jer 3:21). Perhaps, the inclusion of the *yodh* as a consonant in these words served the purpose of distinguishing such words from other, similarly shaped words, like masculine plural participles from II-*waw/yodh* roots, e.g., קָמִים. The tendency for III-*yodh* **qaṭīl* base adjectives to also include a consonantal *yodh* in the feminine and plural forms may be for similar reasons.

214. Similarly, עָנִי "afflicted" becomes עֲנִיִּים (Isa 3:15). See Joüon-Muraoka §88Eb and §96Db. Compare the participles בֹּכִיָּה (Lam 1:16) and הֹמִיָּה (Prov 7:11), which seem to follow the forms of III-*yodh* nouns/adjectives (*HGhS*, 590h and GKC §75v).

215. See Bauer and Leander, *HGhS*, 579p'. Forms like צְבָיִם, similar to גּוֹיִם, do not, typically, have a *mater yodh* for the long /ī/ (see GKC §8k). The form צְבָאִים must reflect the interchange under discussion, *ṣəbāyīm* > *ṣəbāʾīm*, which was later "corrected" by the Masoretes to reflect *ṣəbāyīm*, perhaps with the *aleph* construed as a *mater*. Bergsträsser also lists מִי אֲנַחֲמֵךְ (Isa 51:19) for *מִי יְנַחֲמֵךְ, which seems supported by the version in 1QIsa[a]: מי ינחמך (*Hebräische Grammatik*, 1:102). Note too the spelling חֵלְכָּאִים in Ps 10:10, the plural of חֵלְכָה (in Ps 10:8, 14), as well as תַּאֲמִינוּ "you go to the right" in the MT at Isa 30:21, for *תֵּימִינוּ (cf. וְאֵימְנָה Gen 13:9) or *תַּיְמִינוּ (cf. מַיְמִינִים 1 Chr 12:2). Perhaps the last example is due to orthographic confusion with תַּאֲמִינוּ "you will trust."

noun in the plural תַּחֲלֻאִים "sickness" (Jer 16:4 and 2 Chr 21:19), from the root חלה.[216] Bergsträsser, again, describes the *aleph* in צְבָאִים as representing a "Gleitlaut" that developed from an earlier *yodh*, Bauer and Leander characterizing the *aleph* as resulting from dissimilation.[217] Blau suggests that such words may "represent a combination of dissimilation and glide."[218] Notice that in most examples where there is a shift from an etymological *yodh* to *aleph*, the text is exilic or postexilic. This suggests that this shift is one that occurs during the exilic or Second Temple era.

One sees a similar shift also, incidentally, in Aramaic where it happens more regularly. For example, the shift happens in Biblical Aramaic and in DSS Aramaic in the masculine singular participle of II-*waw*/*yodh* roots, which should be realized as **qāyēm*, but are instead קָאֵם. It also occurs in Aramaic gentilics, like כַּשְׂדָּאִין "Chaldeans" (Dan 3:8) and יְהוּדָאִין "Judeans" (Dan 3:12, *kethib*), which should be *kaśdāyīm* and *yəhūdāyīm* (cf.יְהוּדָיֵא "the Judeans" in Dan 3:8). Similarly, in DSS Aramaic, one finds אמוראא "the Amorites" in 1Q20 XXI, 21 for what one would expect as *אמוריא; and with similar nouns נכראין "foreigners" in 4Q542 1 i, 5.[219]

EVIDENCE FROM THE DSS OF *ALEPH* < *YODH*

In the DSS, the tendency for etymological *yodh*s to appear as *aleph*s is more common than it is in the MT. This shift is seen not only with gentilics (כתיאים "Kittim") and III-*yodh* segholate nouns/adjectives (פתאים "simple"), but also with III-*yodh* nouns/adjectives from a **qaṭīl* base like נקי "pure," and still other III-*yodh* nouns like גוי "nation," and even the II-*yodh* noun איב "enemy." It does not appear, however, where no *yodh* appears in the singular form of a noun; for example, forms with *aleph* do not generally occur on masculine plural participles of III-*yodh* verbs (the

216. The *hiphil* participle "those shooting" מוֹרְאִים (2 Sam 11:24) seems like an error due to confusion of III-*aleph* and III-*yodh* roots. Similarly תְּלֻאִים (Deut 28:66) is likely due to a III-*aleph* by-form, implied also in the *qere* of תְּלָוּם (2 Sam 21:12) (see *HALOT*, s.v.).

217. Bergsträsser, *Hebräische Grammatik*, 1:93, 1:102–3; and Bauer and Leander, *HGhS*, 215g–h. In this paragraph, Bauer and Leander mention specifically חֳלָאִים/חֳלִי and עֳפָאִים/עֳפִי.

218. Blau, *Phonology and Morphology*, 89.

219. For these and more examples, see Muraoka, *GQA*, 18.

exception being *qal* passive participles, like [ה]נטוא and שבאים described below).[220]

Masculine plural gentilic nouns in the DSS, as in the MT, reveal three possible orthographic forms: with a single *yodh*, with two *yodhs* (the second functioning as *mater*), and with a *yodh* + *aleph* + *yodh* (*mater*).[221] Several gentilic nouns in the DSS evidence one or more of these forms. For example, MT כִּתִּים "Kittim," and פְּלִשְׁתִּים "Philistines" can be spelled with one *yodh* פלשתים (1QIsa[a] at Isa 2:6); with two *yodhs* כתיים (1QM I, 4, and passim), פלשתיים (1QIsa[a] at Isa 11:14 and 6Q9 32, 1); or with *yodh* + *aleph* + *yodh* (*mater*) כתיאים (1QpHab II, 12 and passim).[222] The same options are found for words that end with an etymological *-īy*, including one example of a noun/adjective of the **qaṭīl* base (נקי "innocent"), though not all options are attested for all types of words. The masculine plural **qaṭīl* base noun/adjective נקי is spelled נקיאים (4Q266 8 i, 3; 4Q284a 2, 6 = MT נְקִיִּם / נְקִיִּים).[223] One finds the MT form לְוִיִּם "Levites" as לוים (1QM XVI, 7 and four other times in nonbiblical texts), לויים (1QM VII, 15 and at least thirty other times in nonbiblical texts), and לויאים (4Q491 13, 6 and partially preserved in 4Q285 3, 2).[224] One finds נכריאים "foreigners" (1QIsa[a] at Isa 2:6) and נוכריאים (5Q6 [5QLam[a]] at Lam 5:2).[225]

220. Accordance counts 144 examples of masculine plural participles from III-*yodh* roots (including construct forms, but not suffixed forms). Only one contains the double *yodh*, נלויים in 1QIsa[a] at Isa 56:6. All the rest have just one *yodh*.

221. A fourth possibility, noted by Qimron ("Diphthongs and Glides," 264 and *HDSS*, 33), is the spelling of gentilics with three *yodhs*; Qimron lists לוייים in 4Q491 1–3, 17. The same form also apparently occurs in 4Q491 1–3, 9, though it is partially reconstructed: לויי[י]ם. These seem like *plene* spellings of לוים and לויים, each of which would have been pronounced the same: *ləwīyīm*. The spelling with three *yodhs* is peculiar to this word and text.

222. Other plural gentilics include כנעניים (PAM 43692 85,1); מ[צ]ריים (4Q22 [4QpaleoExod[m]] at Exod 7:18 and passim).

223. The fact that the masculine singular of נקי appears in the MT twice with a final *aleph*, נָקִיא (Joel 4:19 and Jon 1:14), may imply that there was confusion about the correct etymology of this word. In the DSS, the word is spelled correctly in the singular twice (11Q19 LXIII, 7 and 8) and once with *aleph* (1QIsa[a] at Isa 59:7). If there was confusion over this word's etymology, then the inclusion of an *aleph* in the plural forms is not necessarily due to a phonetic phenomenon. Note that the other nouns/adjectives from this same **qaṭīl* base (e.g., עני) do not attest an *aleph* in the plural in the DSS, as does נקי.

224. Note also לוייים in 4Q491 1–3, 9 and 17, mentioned in a preceding note.

225. Qimron, "Diphthongs and Glides," 262. Qimron cites the second instance as

As in the MT, segholate (**qaṭl/*qiṭl/*quṭl* base) nouns/adjectives, like MT פְּתָיִם can be spelled פתיים (4Q424 1, 13), and פתאים (4Q381 1, 2).[226] Other examples are MT שְׁפָיִם "bare places" and שְׁפָיִים (sing. שְׁפִי) spelled [ש]פיים (1Q8 [1QIsa^{b}] at Isa 41:18), שפאים (1QIsa^{a} at Isa 41:18 and 49:9), and שפאים (4Q70 [4QJer^{a}] at Jer 14:6) corrected to שפים.

In DSS Hebrew, other kinds of words exhibit similar endings, with one *yodh*, two *yodh*s, and *aleph* + *yodh* (*mater*). For example, MT גּוֹיִם "peoples" is written גוים, גויים, and גואים.[227] The feminine adjective "dry" is perhaps another example ציאה (1QIsa^{a} at Isa 41:18, 53:2), **ṣiyyā* > *ṣīyā* (MT) > *ṣīʾā*.[228] A more certain example is אואב for MT אוֹיֵב "enemy" (4Q98g [4QPs^{x}] at Ps 89:23); as well as אואבים (4Q88 [4QPs^{f}] X, 11); and אואביהם (4Q434 7b, 3).[229] Another example is עאף (1QH^{a} XVI, 37) in an allusion to Isa 50:4 where the MT has יָעֵף "weary," though the form in 1QH^{a} seems to assume the synonymous word in the MT, עָיֵף "weary." Note too נטוא[ה] 4Q51 (4QSam^{a}) in an addition to 2 Sam 24:16 for what would be in the MT *נְטוּיָה; שבאים "those captured" (4Q385a 18 ia–b, 3) for what would be *שְׁבוּיִם (as in Isa 61:1);[230] נבאות (1QIsa^{a} at Isa 60:7) for MT

נוכריאים though both Accordance and Ulrich et al. (*Biblical Qumran Scrolls*, 753) read without the second *yodh*. Note also the anomalous תענייות "humiliations" (4Q511 8, 5 and 121, 2 [with interlinear second *yodh*]).

226. Additionally, one finds spellings with a *waw mater*: פ֯ותיים (4Q439 1 i + 2, 7) and פותאים (1QH^{a} V, 13). For the morphology of this word, see "Waw Marking /u/ Class Vowel Where MT Has No /u/ Class Vowel" (§5.4).

227. The spelling גוים predominates in most biblical DSS scrolls, though גויים is found in 4Q51 (4QSam^{a}) at 2 Sam 22:44; 4Q78 (4QXIIc) at Joel 4:9, 12; 4Q96 (4QPs^{o}) at Ps 115:4; 4Q87 (4QPs^{e}) at Ps 126:2; 11Q5 (11QPs^{a}) at Ps 126:2, 149:7; and perhaps at Mur88 at Zeph 3:6, while גואים is found only in 1QIsa^{a}, at Isa 2:2, 4, 5:26, 8:23, 10:7, 11:10, 12, 13:4, 14:6, 9, 18, 26, 23:3, 25:7, 29:7, 8, 30:28, 34:1, 2, 36:18, 37:12, 40:15, 17, 41:2, 42:1, 6, 43:9, 45:1, 20, 49:6, 22, 52:10, 15, 54:3, 60:3, 5, 11, 12, 16, 61:6, 9, 11, 62:2, 64:1, 66:12, 18, 19 (twice), 20. For other words where this phenomenon takes place, see Qimron, "Diphthongs and Glides," 262.

228. Qimron cites this form in "Diphthongs and Glides," 263 along with עליאה (4Q369 1 ii, 3) which might be an example of *-ēhā* becoming *-ēʾā*, but more likely a case of metathesis (see the subsection "Quiescence of *Heh*" in §4.3, "Weakening of Gutturals").

229. Qimron cites these forms in "Diphthongs and Glides," 263. Note ωεβη in the Secunda at Ps 35:19 for MT אֹיְבַי (Yuditsky, "Weak Consonants," 234). The Secunda also preserves the same shift in εγγαων at Ps 9:17 for MT הִגָּיוֹן (ibid.).

230. It seems less likely that שבאים could be interpreted as a plural of שבי "captivity, captive" since this word always is used in the singular as a collective. See Devorah

נְבָיוֹת "Nebaioth"; as well as שפאותיכה "your lips" (1QIsa[a] at Isa 37:29), which reflects *sifʾōtekā*, possibly from an earlier **sifyōtekā*, but probably from an Aramaic-like base **sifwōtekā*.[231]

The suffixed forms and construct plurals to some of these nouns are also attested with similar variations, גוי (1QM XV, 2 [= MT גּוֹיֵ in 2 Chr 32:13, 17]), גויי (1QM XIV, 7), and, perhaps, גואי (4Q491 8–10 i, 5).[232] Sometimes the form with *aleph* is the only one attested, as with פתאי (1QpHab XII, 4; 4Q169 3–4 iii, 5) and פתאיהם (4Q372 6, 4).[233]

For the more commonly occurring words it is worth mentioning that the three possible forms seem to alternate with each other in individual texts: גוים (4 times in 1QM), גויים (3 times in 1QM), and גואים (twice in 1QM). This suggests a free variation between different pronunciations and/or a common pronunciation represented in different spellings.[234] Since, as explained below, I assume a phonetic distinction between forms like מאיות "soldiers" and מאות "hundreds" where the spelling of the first word presumes a pronunciation with *yodh* (*mēyōt*) and the second with *aleph* (*mēʾōt*), I prefer to assume that the different spellings (גוים versus גואים) reflect different pronunciations. Further explanations of the DSS forms are offered below, in a concluding subsection. Note here that the writing of *aleph* for etymological *yodh* is found in texts of all types, that is, from DSS-SP9 (1QM, etc.), DSS-SP1c (4Q270, 4Q434), as well as DSS-NSP (4Q70, 4Q88, 4Q98g, 4Q284a, 4Q372, 4Q381). This suggests the commonness of this phonological development.

Dimant, "An Apocryphon of Jeremiah from Cave 4 (4Q385B = 4Q385 16)," in *New Qumran Texts and Studies: Proceedings of the First Meeting of the International Organization for Qumran Studies, Paris 1992* (ed. George Brooke; STDJ 15; Leiden: Brill, 1994), 18.

231. See the discussion below in §4.5, "*Aleph* < *Waw* and *Waw* < *Aleph*."

232. On this last form, see the discussion below in "Diphthongs and Triphthongs" (§4.10).

233. 4Q418 223, 3 attests]פתאיה with a heavily damaged *aleph*.

234. Qimron characterizes this as the same pronunciation, though his description seems to suggest a slight, insignificant variation in the nature of the glide: "a glide of unclear character may have been produced between the vowels" (*HDSS*, 32). See below for more on this.

Evidence from the MT of *Yodh* < *Aleph*

The reverse phenomenon, of an etymological *aleph* being written as a *yodh*, is also attested in Hebrew and Aramaic and is presumably precipitated by the inherent weakness of the glottal stop as well as its occasional quiescence word-internally. In the MT, one finds this especially in personal names. For example, the etymologically correct spelling of the name Eliathah (meaning "my God came"), with a consonantal *aleph*, is אֱלִיאָתָה (reflecting *ʾĕlīʾātā*) in 1 Chr 25:4 but the same name is spelled with consonantal *yodh*, אֱלִיָּתָה (reflecting *ʾĕlīyātā*) in 1 Chr 25:27; the name "Daniel" (meaning "God is my judge") is spelled with an etymological, consonantal *aleph*, דָּנִאֵל (reflecting *dānīʾēl*), in Ezek 14:14, 20, 28:3, but it is spelled with consonantal *yodh*, דָּנִיֵּאל (reflecting *dānīyēl*, the *aleph* being a historical spelling) in Ezra 8:2, in the eponymous book, and elsewhere; the name "Doeg" (meaning "one who fears [reverently]") is spelled with its etymological *aleph* דֹּאֵג in 1 Sam 21:8, 22:9, as well as *plene* דּוֹאֵג in Ps 52:2, but is spelled with *yodh* in place of *aleph*, דּוֹיֵג, in 1 Sam 22:18 (twice), 22.[235] Other instances may also exist, for example, the word דַּיָּה, a bird of prey, in Deut 14:13 should derive from the root דאה, based on the verb דָּאָה meaning "to glide," and the noun דָּאָה "bird of prey" in Lev 11:14, though the word דַּיָּה may, in fact, reflect Aramaic influence.[236] Another word is also found with a similar variation. The word for "hundreds," מֵאוֹת, when used to refer to soldiers, is found in three instances written with a *yodh* מֵאיוֹת in the MT (2 Kgs 11:4, 9, 10, the *kethib* reflecting *mēyōt*) and once as מֵיאוֹת (2 Kgs 11:15). The spelling מאיות presumably reflects the end result of the following historical development: **miʾōt* > **mēʾōt* > *mēyōt*. Lastly, there is the case of the *hithpael* of אמר (perhaps) attesting a similar shift in Isa 61:6: תִּתְיַמָּרוּ "you will boast" (spelled in 1QIsa[a] תתיאמרו).[237] In the case of names like Eliathah and Daniel, the sound of a preceding /i/ vowel

---

235. For these examples, see Bergsträsser, *Hebräische Grammatik*, 1:93. See also Blau, *Phonology and Morphology*, 89. On the etymological *aleph* of דאג, compare the verb דאג "to be anxious, concerned" and always appearing with *aleph*; the verb occurs seven times in the MT.

236. Bergsträsser also lists *אֲבִיָּסָף, which is vocalized incorrectly (according to him) in the MT as אֶבְיָסָף (1Chr 6:8, 22:9,19) for אֲבִיאָסָף (Exod 6:24) (*Hebräische Grammatik*, 1:93).

237. Scholars have proposed other roots for this form from time to time (see, BDB, *HALOT*, *s.v.*).

attracts the *yodh* sound due to the similar articulation of *yodh* and /i/.[238] Thus, *-īʾ-* became *-īy-*. Similarly /ē/ attracts the *yodh* sound in מֵאיוֹת. On the other hand, for words like דּוֹיֵג, the *yodh* may mark the development of a glide. In cases like תִּתְיַמָּרוּ, the shift from glottal stop to /y/ may help preserve the syllabic structure of the word, since *aleph* preceded by a shewa could have quiesced leading to an unrecognizable form: **titʾammārū* > **tətammārū* (= *תְּתַמָּרוּ).

In Biblical Aramaic one also sees the writing of *yodh* for etymological *aleph*; the word "your sin" is written without its etymological *aleph* חֲטָיָךְ, though this may be due to the general trend of reinterpreting III-*aleph* roots as III-*waw*/*yodh* in Aramaic.[239]

The shift of *aleph* > *yodh* is attested in texts from a diverse chronological distribution, though many of the examples appear in late books. It also bears mentioning that the shift /ʾ/ > /y/ and the reverse /y/ > /ʾ/ are both attested in 1–2 Chronicles.

Evidence from the DSS of *Yodh* < *Aleph*

The phenomenon of *yodh* appearing for etymological *aleph* is slightly more common in the DSS than it is in the MT, but, as in the MT, seems related to the weakness of the *aleph*. The spelling of the infinitive construct of מלא "to fill" in the *piel* suggests this shift: מליאות (4Q284 2 i, 3) for what would be in the MT מַלְאוֹת.[240] Note also תתיאמרו in 1QIsa^a at Isa 61:6 for MT תִּתְיַמָּרוּ, mentioned just above. This development also seems to be reflected in לביותיו in 4Q169 3–4 i, 4 in a quotation of Nah 2:13 for MT לְבִאֹתָיו "its lionesses" (sing. *לְבִאָה), as well as ימחיו "they will clap" in 1Q8 (1QIsa^b) at Isa 55:12 for MT יִמְחֲאוּ.[241] The spelling of "hundreds" as מאיות (once מיאות) is also found among the DSS in at least nine instances, where the word connotes a group of soldiers or their leaders; the more

238. Blau, *Phonology and Morphology*, 89.

239. Muraoka, *GQA*, 17–18.

240. On this and related forms, see the discussion in the subsection "Infinitives" in §5.6, "Verbs."

241. The first example from 4Q169 is from Qimron, *HDSS*, 26. Alternatively, לביותיו might be construed as the feminine plural of the MT לְבִיָּא (Ezek 19:2), where the shift from *aleph* to *yodh* has already taken place (i.e., **ləbīʾā* > *ləbīyā*, with *aleph* as final *mater*). Qimron (*HDSS*, 26 n. 6 and "*Waw* as Marker for a Glide," 366) suggests reading ימחוו instead of what Accordance and Ulrich et al. (*Biblical Qumran Scrolls*, 538) read as ימחיו.

conventional form, מאות, occurs commonly to indicate the number.[242] That the form with *yodh* consistently denotes groups of soldiers (or their leaders) suggests that we perhaps should distinguish two separate words with distinct pronunciations, one *mēʾōt* "hundreds" and the other *mēyōt* "soldiers."[243] This, in turn, would imply that the *aleph* and *yodh* represent distinct sounds in these environments. Notice that with all but one of the examples above, the *yodh* is followed by a /u/ class vowel.

In the case of the spelling of the name Daniel without the *aleph*, דניל, in 6Q7 (6QpapDan) at Dan 10:12 and the spelling of Eliab (אֱלִיאָב), noted by Qimron, as אליב in 4Q138 (4QPhyl K) at Deut 11:6 (as well as in 8Q3 [8QPhyl] at Deut 11:6), the *aleph* has assimilated to the preceding /i/ vowel and become a consonant (*dānīʾēl* > *dānīyēl*; *ʾĕlīʾāb* > *ʾĕlīyāb*).[244] The shift might seem less obvious in the latter name since in the MT the name is written with a *yodh*, however, the *yodh* is a simple *mater* in the MT form. In the form from the DSS the *yodh* is a consonant, in the same way that the *yodh* is a consonant in דָּנִיֵּאל. More dramatic is the elision of *aleph* and its apparent assimilation to *yodh* in הביו "bring" (1QIsa[a] at Isa 16:3 for MT הָבִיאוּ, *kethib* reflecting mp and *qere* fs) and החטיום "they made them sin" (4Q522 9 ii, 10 for what would be in the MT without assimilation *הֶחֱטִיאוּם).[245] Here too the forms from the Bible (or the corresponding forms) contain a *mater yodh* whereas the DSS forms contain a consonantal *yodh*. Presumably, the respective DSS verbs would be vocalized as *hābīyū* and *heḥĕbīyūm* (written in the Tiberian tradition as *הָבִיּוּ and *הֶחֱטִיּוּם).[246]

---

242. The nine instances of מאיות and מיאות ("soldiers") in the scrolls include the five mentioned by Qimron, 1QM III, 17; IV, 2; 11Q19 XLII, 15; LVII, 4; LVIII, 4 (*HDSS*, 26), as well as 4Q378 3 ii + 4, 7; 4Q491 1–3, 10; 2Q3 (2QExod[b]) at Exod 18:21 for MT מֵאוֹת; and 4Q27 (4QNum[b]) at Num 31:54 for MT מֵאוֹת. See Dimant, "Two Discourses," 56.

243. This assumes, of course, that the *yodh* is not simply a graphic way of indicating the distinction in meaning, which is also conceivable (though less likely). Cf. the use of *yodh* in the 3ms pronominal suffix on plural nouns יו- to graphically mark the distinction from the same suffix on singular nouns; see "Pronouns and Particles" (§5.2).

244. Qimron, *HDSS*, 26.

245. On the first form, see Kutscher, *Isaiah*, 515–16.

246. The similarity to the other forms where *aleph* assimilates into a preceding *yodh* suggests that הביו would not follow precisely the example of Biblical Aramaic הֶעְדִּיו where the /i/ vowel and *waw* form a diphthong /īw/. However, הביו would be close to the pattern assumed for the 3mp perfect of III-*yodh* verbs in Qumran Aramaic

Qimron also suggests the writing היה *hīyā* "she" for *היאה in 1QIsa^a at Isa 30:33, 36:21, where the MT has היא.[247]

Other examples include ישייכה *yaššīyəkā* or *yaššīyekā* "he will deceive you" (1QIsa^a at Isa 37:10) for MT יַשִּׁאֲךָ; נשיי *nəsīyē* "leaders of" (11Q19 LVII, 12) for what would be in the MT נְשִׂיאֵי; and הבריה *habbərīyā* "the creation" (11Q19 XXIX, 9) for what would be in the MT *הַבְּרִיאָה; as well as בריותו *bərīyōtō* "his creations" (4Q216 V, 9) for what would be in the MT *בְּרִיאֹתָיו.[248]

The same phenomenon is also perhaps found in תוצוו (1QIsa^a at Isa 22:4), in which case one should read תוציו.[249] Although the MT has תָּאִיצוּ "do (not) rush" here and although Accordance and the *Dead Sea Scrolls Concordance* parse תוצוו as from the root אוץ "to rush, hasten," the reading תוציו allows for understanding this as from יצא "to go forth." This would provide the following translation for Isa 22:4: "Therefore, I say, 'Turn away from me; let me be embittered through weeping, do not speak (lit., bring forth) to comfort me.…" The figurative use of the *hiphil* of יצא to mean "speak" is found, for example, in Isa 48:20 (not in 1QIsa^a, but in 1Q8 [1QIsa^b] and 4Q58 [4QIsa^d]), as well as elsewhere (e.g., Jer 15:19). The corresponding form of the verb in the MT would be *תּוֹצִיאוּ; if I am correct in this interpretation, it seems to have become *tōṣīyū* here, similar to the development of הביו and החטיום described above. Reading תוצוו as from אוץ presupposes two rather uncommon orthographic phenomena, the loss of *aleph* between two full vowels and a double *mater* for the final /ū/ vowel; for this reason, the proposed solution of reading תוציו seems more likely.[250]

(and other dialects of Aramaic), which attests שריוא *šarrīyū* "they began" (4Q204 4, 3); in this word, it seems more likely that the *aleph* helps to mark a final /ū/ (see Muraoka, *GQA*, 138). On *heḥĕbīyūm*, compare Syriac where a similar phonetic pattern is regularly attested with III-*yodh* verbs in the derived conjugations: *galyūn* "they exiled us" (see Theodor Nöldeke, *Compendious Syriac Grammar* [trans. James A. Crichton; Winona Lake, Ind.: Eisenbrauns, 2001; repr. London: Williams & Norgate, 1904], 145).

247. Qimron, *HDSS*, 26.

248. For the example of נשיי, see the discussion in the subsection below "Explanation of DSS Forms." Note also the very damaged נביים "prophets" in 4Q88 VIII, 14. The pronunciation of the 3ms suffix on plural nouns as /ō/ is discussed in "Diphthongs and Triphthongs" (§4.10).

249. Note that *waw* and *yodh* are, in general, similar in appearance in 1QIsa^a (see Eugene Ulrich and Peter W. Flint, "Introduction to 1QIsa^a," in DJD 32:61).

250. For a discussion of the loss of *aleph*, see the subsection "Quiescence of *Aleph*"

Another possible example of this *yodh* < *aleph* shift relates to להבריך (4Q51 [4QSam[a]] at 1 Sam 2:29) for MT לְהַבְרִיאֲכֶם "for your fattening." In this scroll, the consonants differ from those of the MT not only in the loss of the *aleph*, but also in the loss of the final *mem*. The scroll's version of this verse (and others) parallels that of the LXX in several respects and since the LXX has ἐνευλογεῖσθαι it is likely that the Hebrew represents the *hiphil* of ברך (= *ləhabrīk*) "to bless." However, it is perhaps the case that the MT form was the original or earlier reading and the shift of /ʾ/ > /y/, which would have produced the form *ləhabrīyəkem* (= *להבריכם), led to a scribe misunderstanding the verb as the *hiphil* infinitive of ברך.[251]

Notice, finally, that this shift from *aleph* to *yodh* is found in words in DSS-SP9 and DSS-SP1c (4Q169) texts, as well as DSS-NSP texts (4Q284, 6Q7, 8Q3), again reflecting the widespread nature of this phenomenon.

Explanation of the DSS Forms

Since many of the same words, exhibiting (presumably) the same phenomena (/ʾ/ < /y/ and /y/ < /ʾ/), are observed in the MT, it seems obvious that the same explanations may apply to the forms in the DSS (that is, the development of a glide sound represented by the *aleph*, assimilation, dissimilation). Qimron, however, has offered a slightly different explanation. He suggests, first, that the spelling of the words with and without *aleph*, like כתיים and כתיאים, reflects a common pronunciation *kittiīm*, where the "two identical vowels apparently coalesce into one long vowel," that is, /ī/.[252] Qimron makes the further assertion that wherever this *aleph* appears in other nominal or adjectival forms, it is not representing a glottal stop,

in §4.3, "Weakening of Gutturals"; also, for a list of possible double *maters*, see the section "Scribal Mistakes" (§3.1).

251. Cases like היש (*hāyīš* [?]) (4Q175 22 and perhaps 4Q186 1 i, 6) for what would be in the MT הָאִישׁ may be additional examples (Qimron, "Diphthongs and Glides," 270). However, these seem to me to be further examples of the elision of *aleph* before a full vowel (see "Weakening of Gutturals" [§4.3]) since *aleph* shifts to *yodh* most often when an /i/ vowel or a consonant immediately precedes the *aleph*.

252. Qimron, "Diphthongs and Glides," 264. The translation of the Hebrew is mine. He writes on page 260 of his intention to show "that all the examples of the exchange or addition of *aleph*, *waw*, and *yodh* … are to be interpreted as different writings of a single pronunciation" (my translation). On this idea, see also Y. F. Gumpertz, *Mivṭaʾe Śefatenu: Studies in Historical Phonetics of the Hebrew Language* (Jerusalem: Haraav Kook, 1953), 68.

but either hiatus and/or a glide "of unclear character."[253] Thus, he seems to say that the spelling גואים reflects the pronunciation: *gōim* or the allophonic alternatives *gōʸim*, *gōʷim*, *gōʾim*. The same is true for גוים and גויים. In his article on this subject, Qimron cites a tremendous amount of data and examples not only from the scrolls, but also from different traditions of Hebrew.[254] His general thesis seems possible, though I am skeptical of the existence of hiatus in DSS Hebrew, and believe a simpler way of understanding these different spellings is to consider them different phonetic realizations for the same ending.[255] I prefer to follow the model of Rendsburg who implies that the spelling with *aleph* presupposes a pronunciation with a glottal stop.[256] By contrast, the spelling with *yodh* presumes a /y/ sound. A distinction between the two sounds is implied, as noted above, in the distinction in spelling between מאות *mēʾōt* "hundreds" and מאיות *mēyōt* "soldiers." This does not mean that Qimron is necessarily wrong; כתיים may, in fact, have been sometimes pronounced *kittīm* in the vernacular. Nevertheless, it seems likely to me that the similarity in sound between *-īyī-* and *-ī-* led to some speakers emphasizing the distinct syllables through an intervocalic glottal stop (*-īʾī-*); similarly, a difficulty perceiving /y/ in the sequences *-āyī-* and *-ōyī-* may have encouraged speakers to distinguish the syllables through a glottal stop (*-āʾī-*, *-ōʾī-*).

In relation to the writing of *yodh* for etymological *aleph*, Qimron takes issue with the idea that assimilation and dissimilation involving *aleph* and *yodh* could take place simultaneously. Qimron writes in relation to נשיי

253. Qimron, *HDSS*, 32.

254. Qimron, "Diphthongs and Glides." One point of confusion, however, is his insistence that the *yodh* was not pronounced as a consonant, but only possibly as a glide. As Bergsträsser himself says, the ultralong /i/ vowel, *-ī-*, and *-īyī-* "phonetisch fast identisch sind" (*Hebräische Grammatik*, 1:102).

255. Such difference might be explained by the preference of different subdialects of Hebrew for one pronunciation over another, or to a variation in the language of the writers. Recall that the existence of an intervocalic glottal stop is suggested by the consistent spelling of *aleph* + *waw mater* where the *aleph* is preceded by a full vowel (e.g., in words like מאור "light"); there is no hiatus in these kinds of words (see §3.5, "Digraphs").

256. Rendsburg, commenting on the form גאים from HazGab 13, writes: "One assumes a pronunciation *gōʾīm*" ("Grammatical Sketch," 66). See also Bar-Asher, "*Vision of Gabriel*," 500 n. 54. Muraoka writes in relation to a similar nonetymological *aleph* in DSS Aramaic that it is "consonantal"—though he also refers to it as acting either as a vowel carrier or glide (*GQA*, 29).

"leaders of" (11Q19 LVII, 12) that "it is unlikely that simultaneously *ī'ē* → *īyē* (in נשיאי) while (according to Kutscher) *īyē* → *ī'ē*."[257] This statement ignores the distinctive distribution of these shifts. Although, it is true that the same text may exhibit some cases where *aleph* assimilates to the preceding /i/ vowel to become *yodh* (e.g., דָּנִיֵּאל in 1 Chr 3:1; הביו in 1QIsa[a] at Isa 16:3) and other cases where *yodh* becomes *aleph* through dissimilation or glide (e.g., הָעַרְבִיאִים in 2 Chr 17:11; שפאים in 1QIsa[a] at Isa 41:18 and 49:9), the two phenomena do not occur in every possible environment. Rather, the shift of *yodh* > *aleph* occurs especially between /ī/ vowels (*-īyī-* > *-ī'ī-*, as in כתיאים) and where a diphthong (especially *āy* or *ōy*) might have formed between the preceding vowel and the *yodh* consonant (*-āyī-* > *-ā'ī-*, as in פתאים; *-ōyī-* > *-ō'ī-*, as in גואים).[258] The production of such a diphthong would have made the division of syllables and, also, the spelling of the words less clear. All this suggests that the *aleph*, as a glottal stop, functions to separate vowels or vowel-consonant combinations and that it works as an epenthetic consonant in these environments.[259] The shift *aleph* > *yodh*, on the other hand, is attested primarily where an /ī/ vowel directly precedes the *aleph* and another (non-/i/) vowel follows (*-ī'ă-* > *-īyə-* or *-īye-*, as in ישייכה; *-ī'ā-* > *-īyā-*, as in אליב; *-ī'ē-* > *-īyē-*, as in דניל; *-ī'ū-* > *-īyū-*, as in החטיום). The shift *aleph* > *yodh* is not seen as regularly as *yodh* > *aleph* and is perhaps an occasional reflex of the pronunciation of the /i/ vowel together with the weakness of *aleph* and its capacity to quiesce.

Qimron's thesis regarding these endings is tied in with his belief that the *aleph* was never pronounced intervocalically. If this is the case, then forms like אואבים "enemies" (4Q88 [4QPs[f]] X, 11) and אואביהם "their enemies" (4Q434 7b, 3) perhaps reflect a vocalization where the muttered vowel under the original *yodh* has disappeared and the resulting diphthong /ōy/ was simplified to /ō/, as /ūy/ apparently becomes /ū/ in the *qal* passive participle גלו "what was revealed" (4Q175 11). In that case, the second *aleph* is part of a digraph marking /ō/: *'ōbīm* and *'ōbēhem*. Nevertheless,

257. Qimron, *HDSS*, 32. He also writes that the assimilation of /'/ to a following /i/ or /e/ vowel occurs "regardless of the preceding vowel" (ibid.).

258. The spelling with *aleph* in construct plural forms of these words is probably simply related to the absolute plural spelling.

259. Notice that in the majority of examples *aleph* stands at the beginning of what would be in the MT the accented syllable, the typical phonetic environment for a word-internal glottal stop that functions epenthetically (see Uffmann, "Intrusive [r]," 457).

if the *aleph* in these words was actually pronounced, its use would follow the pattern, described immediately above, wherein an *aleph* helps to break up what might otherwise become a diphthong (**ʾōyēb* > *ʾōʾēb*; **ʾōyəbīm* > *ʾōʾăbīm*). The related form אוביך "your enemies" from 1QIsa[a] (at Isa 62:8) offers the best evidence for the pronunciation with a reduced diphthong, **ʾōyəbekā* > **ʾōybekā* > *ʾōbekā*, though this perhaps just proves the usefulness of *aleph* as an epenthetic glottal stop in the previous forms.[260] The usefulness of the *aleph* in this function is especially relevant to the word איב; if the word "enemy" in the singular had experienced a reduction of the diphthong *ōy* to *ō*, it would be identical in pronunciation to the word "necromancer" or "ghost," אוב (= MT אוֹב).

Qimron also argues, in connection with נשיי, that two *yodh*s written together indicate an /i/ or /e/ vowel; that is, -יי- does not indicate a consonant /y/ followed by a vowel (*-yī-*, *-yē-*), but just the vowel (*-ī-*, *-ē-*).[261] He cites many examples, but these have better explanations than the loss of intervocalic *yodh*. For example, he cites the fact that *qal* 3ms imperfect forms of I-*yodh* verbs are spelled with a single *yodh*, as in ויראו "and they will fear" (11Q19 LVI, 11), instead of with two *yodh*s as is common in the MT. But this defective spelling among the nonbiblical DSS is especially prevalent in just one text, 11Q19, where the spelling ויראו parallels exactly the orthography of the corresponding MT text being quoted or alluded to: 11Q19 LVI, 11 corresponding to Deut 17:13; LXI, 11 to Deut 19:20; LXIV, 6 to Deut 13:12. Furthermore, this same verb does occur with two *yodh*s occasionally (both in DSS-SP9 and DSS-NSP texts): יירא] (4Q487 5, 5, heavily damaged second *yodh*); יירא]ו (11Q11 III, 10); ייראוך (1QIsa[a] at Isa 25:3); ייראו (1QIsa[a] at Isa 59:19); ייראו (4Q84 [4QPs[b]] at Psa 102:16); ייראו (4Q85 [4QPs[c]] at Psa 52:8).[262]

---

260. Alternatively, the form is the result of the scribe writing *waw* when he intended *yodh*; the word occurs rather commonly without a *waw mater*.

261. Qimron, *HDSS*, 32.

262. Ibid. He also cites spellings like כתיים "Kittim," גויים "peoples," גוי "peoples of," לויים "Levites," עשויים "those things done" (*qal* pass. ptc.), עדיים "ornaments" (MT: עֲדָיִים), הויי (Mas 1k i, 2; mp ptc. in construct = *הוֹיֵי), all of which are explainable as the standard (in both the MT and DSS) way of writing this type of word (see "*Plene* Orthography" [§3.2]). Two *yodh*s as a *mater* for a single vowel, by contrast, are explainable as dittographic errors (e.g., ובמעשייכה "in your works" 1QSb III, 27; בפליליים "with judges" 4Q158 9, 5). The correction of the plural of "island" from אם in 1QIsa[a] (at Isa 13:22) to א'ם (for MT אִיִּים), Qimron notes, "makes sense only if this word was not pronounced with consonantal *yod*" (*HDSS*, 33). In other words, the scribe heard

Although Biblical Hebrew does not represent a single dialect and it might be argued that the alternations of *yodh* and *aleph* in the MT are reflective of different dialects or subdialects, this characterization ignores the concentration of forms exhibiting the shift /y/ > /ʾ/ that occur in late texts (many of them in Nehemiah and/or 1–2 Chronicles). It seems that this variation in particular was widespread, the variation continuing and spreading into late Second Temple times and reflected in many of the DSS from all text groups. By contrast, since the shift /ʾ/ > /y/ is one that seems to be attested in texts from the MT that date to different time periods, it seems reasonable to suppose that this shift was one that was a natural reaction to the inherent weakness of the glottal stop, especially when preceded by an /i/ vowel and followed by a vowel of another quality.

4.5. *Aleph* < *Waw* and *Waw* < *Aleph*

As is the case with *yodh*, so *waw* can interchange with *aleph*. The fundamental linguistic reasons are similar. Such variation is also found in the MT. For example, the feminine plural of *נָוֶה "pasture" should be *נָוֹת in the absolute and נְוֹת in the construct due to the same kind of contraction as described above: **nawayāt* > **nawayōt* > **nawōt* > *nəwōt* (plural construct). And, in fact the plural construct is spelled נְוֹת in Zeph 2:6. Nevertheless, it appears as נְאוֹת in eleven other passages of the MT. The common explanation is that it is the result of dissimilation or glide, that is *nəwōt* > *nəʾōt*, in the same way that עַרְבִיים "Arabians" (2 Chr 26:7, *kethib*) could also be realized as עַרְבִיאִים.[263] Another example is רִבֹּאוֹת "ten thousands" (in Dan 11:12 and Ezra 2:69) for what was earlier perhaps *ribbōwōt*.[264]

The DSS attest more examples of this kind of variation, as well as the reverse variation where *aleph* shifts to *waw* due to assimilation to a neighboring /o/ or /u/ vowel. This again suggests that these phonetic

---

ʾīm, not *ʾīyīm*. This is not necessarily true. Perhaps an earlier *-īyī-* had become *-ī-* (as in עִבְרִים), but then again an initial spelling without a consonantal *yodh* does not prove the loss of intervocalic *yodh*, just as the spellings ה׳מים *hayyāmīm* "the days" (4Q252 IV, 2) and וצ׳ה *wəṣiwwā* "and he commanded" (4Q266 6 i, 9) do not presume that the respective words were initially pronounced without a *yodh* or *waw*.

263. See Blau, *Phonology and Morphology*, 89.

264. Ibid. This is often explained as a case of dissimilation and/or glide: **ribbōwōt* > *ribbōʾōt*. Nevertheless, this example is perhaps not the best since the singular of the word sometimes also is accompanied by a final *aleph*, and this might have led to confusion as to the basic form of the word.

shifts represent a trend in Second Temple times. Among those cases of *waw* written for etymological *aleph*, we find באוו *bāwū* "they came" (4Q398 [4QMMT] 11–13, 2 and 3) for what would be in the MT בָּאוּ; בוו *bāwū* "they came" (4Q141 [4QPhyl N] at Deut 32:17) for MT בָּאוּ; ראוו *rāwū* "they saw" (1QIsa[a] at Isa 66:19) for MT רָאוּ; יבאוו *yābōwū* "they will come" in 4Q266 10 i, 3 for what would be in the MT יָבוֹאוּ.[265] Another example may be חטאוו (1QIsa[a] at Isa 27:9), reflecting *ḥeṭwō* "his sin," for what would be in the MT חֶטְאוֹ, though the MT has חַטָּאתוֹ here.[266] In these cases, the *aleph* is often retained as part of a historical spelling, but it was not pronounced. The spelling לשאוות "to destroy" (1QIsa[a] at Isa 37:26) for MT לְהַשְׁאוֹת (from שאה) reflects, perhaps, a similar phonetic development to *lašwōt*.[267] Qimron also suggests the writing הוה *hūwā* "he" in 1QIsa[a] at Isa 7:14 for MT הוא.[268] Although Kutscher suggests that this is a scribal error due to the preceding Tetragrammaton, the example of היה *hīyā* "she" in 1QIsa[a] at Isa 30:33, 36:21 for MT היא suggest that Qimron is right.[269] Qimron also suggests that the emergence of a *waw* for etymological *aleph* might help explain certain misspellings that are subsequently corrected according to the historical form of the words: הטמואת *haṭṭŏmāwōt* (11Q19 LI, 6) corrected to הטמאות *haṭṭŏmāʾōt* "the uncleanness"; צבואת *ṣəbāwōt* (11Q19 LXII, 5) corrected to צבאות *ṣəbāʾōt* "hosts."[270] The above examples derive mostly from DSS-SP9 texts.

Examples of *aleph* written for etymological *waw* include קואי *qōʾē* "those waiting for" (4Q171 1–2 ii 4) in a quotation of Ps 37:9 for MT קֹוֵי, the verb from the same or homonymous root (קוה II in BDB) יקאו *yiqqāʾū* "let them be gathered" (4Q7 [4QGen[g]] at Gen 1:9) for MT יִקָּווּ; and at least six instances of "commandments" spelled with *aleph*, always with a suffix,

265. See Qimron, "Diphthongs and Glides," 270 and idem, "*Waw* as Marker for a Glide," 365–66. The pronunciation of ראוו would presumably make it homophonous with the 3cp perfect of רוה "to be refreshed," which appears as רוו in 3Q15 (Copper Scroll) X, 3 (unless רוי is to be read, see Puech, "Rouleau de Cuivre," 1:197–98).

266. The reading חטאוו is found in Accordance and in the *Dead Sea Scrolls Concordance*, though Ulrich et al. read חטאה (*Biblical Qumran Scrolls*, 380).

267. It seems less likely that the spelling represents the reemergence of the last root consonant (*lašʾăwōt*).

268. Qimron, *HDSS*, 26.

269. Kutscher, *Isaiah*, 184.

270. Qimron, "Diphthongs and Glides," 271. These words are also mentioned in "Digraphs" (§3.5). Although the explanation of assimilation is likely, alternatively, they could be explained through metathesis (see §3.1, "Scribal Mistakes").

always among the Phylactery texts: מצאותי *miṣʾōtay* (4Q129 [4QPhyl B] at Deut 5:10, 29; 4Q137 [4QPhyl J] at Deut 5:29; 4Q130 [4QPhyl C] at Deut 11:13), מצאותו (4Q140 [4QPhyl M] at Deut 6:2; 4Q128 [4QPhyl A] at Deut 10:13).[271] We also find עאון *ʿāʾōn* "iniquity" (1QIsa^a^ part of additional text to Isa 1:15) for what would be in the MT עָוֹן; probably שפאותיכה *sifʾōtekā* "your lips" (1QIsa^a^ at Isa 37:29);[272] רבואותם *ribbōʾōtām* "their ten thousands" (1QM XII, 4); קסאות *qəsāʾōt* "jars" (3Q15 [Copper Scroll] III, 4) for what would be in the MT קְשָׂוֹת.[273] For the last word, one wonders if in the mind of the scribes, the *aleph* was viewed as a *mater* for /ā/.[274] One wonders if עדואתיך in 4Q90 (4QPs^h^) at Ps 119:14 for MT עֵדְוֹתֶיךָ "your decrees," was supposed to be *עדאותיך (*ʿēdʾōtekā).[275] The examples again primarily derive from DSS-SP9 texts, with one exception, 4Q7 (4QGen^g^), from the DSS-NSP texts; one example is from 3Q15, the Copper Scroll. These shifts seem, all things considered, much less common than the similar shifts involving *yodh* and *aleph*. The shift /ʾ/ > /w/ suggests an occasional reflex of assimilation due to the inherent weakness of *aleph* (similar

271. Qimron, "Diphthongs and Glides," 268, 270. Cf. MT מִצְוֹתַי and מִצְוֹתָיו. The spelling is so frequent one wonders of some confusion with the word מוצא "going forth, utterance."

272. The word appears for MT שְׂפָתֶיךָ (dual); the plural + suffix would be in the MT שִׂפְתוֹתֶיךָ. Either שפאותיכה corresponds to the word in Rabbinic Hebrew where etymological *yodh* appears in the plural, שפיות (Kutscher, *Isaiah*, 369), or to the cognate in Jewish Palestinian Aramaic where etymological *waw* appears in all forms, סיפווא (which seems to be Qimron's interpretation, "Diphthongs and Glides," 269). In either case, the earlier *yodh* or *waw* has shifted to *aleph* in שפאותיכה. Kutscher's initial explanation (*Isaiah*, 168) that the *aleph-waw* reflects a digraph is unlikely since this so-called digraph occurs primarily within words that have an etymological *aleph*. Kutscher's second explanation (that it is derived from a form like in Rabbinic Hebrew, שפיות) is unlikely given the plural form in 1QM V, 12 ספות and in 11Q8 (11QPs^d^) at Ps 81:6 שפות, reflecting respectively *səfāwōt* and *sifwōt* (see Qimron, "Diphthongs and Glides," 270). Alternatively, שפות/ספות might represent a new plural form for the word (*sāfōt*), one based on the form of other III-*waw*/*yodh* nouns, in which case the etymological development of שפאותיכה remains unclear.

273. These examples are drawn from Qimron, "Diphthongs and Glides," 269.

274. See §3.3 above, "*Aleph* as Internal *Mater*."

275. See the discussion on this word in "Digraphs" (§3.5). See also קשוא^ות^ in 11Q19 XXXIII, 13 for what would be in the MT קְשָׂוֹת. Qimron reads the latter word as קשוא^ת^ ("Diphthongs and Glides," 268). Presumably the spelling קשוא^ות^ reflects an anomalous use of *waw-aleph-waw* to represent /ō/, or a (partially corrected) mistake for *קשאות.

to the shift /ʾ/ > /y/). The shift /w/ > /ʾ/ appears in places analogous to where *yodh* shifts to *aleph*, that is, between two /ō/ vowels and where the diphthong /āw/ or /ōw/ might otherwise occur; this shift may also reflect assimilation where *waw* initiates a syllable and is followed by an /o/ or /u/ vowel (that is, מצאותי, שפאותיכה).

4.6. *Waw* < *Yodh*

Etymological *yodh* is perhaps written as *waw*, especially where the following vowel is an /o/ or /u/ vowel, as in the MT: נְטוּוֹת "stretched out" (Isa 3:16) where the *qere* presumes נְטוּיוֹת.[276] Among the DSS, Qimron and Yuditsky see this in נטוה, the *qal* fem. sing. ptc. of נטה (4Q137 [4QPhyl J] and 4Q139 [4QPhyl L] at Deut 5:15 for MT נְטוּיָה as well as in HazGab 74).[277] Others read נטיה in the phylactery texts and Yardeni and Elizur tentatively read an entirely different word in the HazGab text: אנשים "men."[278] Presumably, the forms proposed by Qimron and Yuditsky would reflect the pronunciation *nəṭūwā*.[279] This shift is perhaps also found in הרווה "the saturated" (1QS II, 14) for what would be in the MT הָרְוָיָה, as well as בנוות "built" (11Q19 XLII, 9); גדוותיו "its banks" (1QIsa^a at Isa 8:7) for MT גְּדוֹתָיו, but the scroll's form reflecting what should be *גדיותיו (as in 4Q59 [4QIsa^e], [ג]דיות[יו] and like the *kethib* of 1 Chr 12:16, גְּדִיתָיו); חזוון "vision" (1QIsa^a at Isa 22:1) for MT חִזָּיוֹן; יכלוון "they will perish" (1QIsa^a at Isa 31:3) for MT יִכְלָיוּן; יבכוון "they will weep" (1QIsa^a at Isa 33:7) for MT יִבְכָּיוּן; דוות "vultures" (1QIsa^a at Isa 34:15) for MT דַּיּוֹת; ואתוון "come (?)" (1QIsa^a at Isa 41:5) for MT וַיֶּאֱתָיוּן "they came."[280] Given the similarity between *waw* and *yodh*, however, it seems simpler to interpret these as the respective words found in the MT, such that, for example, הרווה be read in 1QS as הרויה *hārəwāyā*.[281]

276. Rendsburg cites this form ("Grammatical Sketch," 66 n. 24). See also עֲשׂוּוֹת (1 Sam 25:18), cited in Qimron, "*Waw* as Marker for a Glide," 363.

277. Qimron, "*Waw* as Marker for a Glide," 363 and Qimron and Yuditsky, "Notes," 36.

278. Yardeni and Elizur, "Hebrew Prophetic Text," 15.

279. See Qimron and Yuditsky, "Notes," 36; and Rendsburg, "Grammatical Sketch," 66.

280. Qimron, "*Waw* as Marker for a Glide," 364.

281. See Qimron, "Waw and Yod," 108.

4.7. Accent or Stress

Although scholars have addressed the possible place of the stress in words in the DSS, suggesting that it was on the ultimate syllable or that it was on the penultimate, the decisive evidence is elusive.[282] To take one example, Ben-Ḥayyim suspects penultimate accentuation due to the frequency of *qal* plural imperfect verb forms with a *waw* between the second and third root consonants (the "so-called pausal forms" like יקטולו).[283] Qimron points out that the Tiberian tradition also has verbal forms with a vowel that would be represented by a *waw* in the DSS, though these same forms are ultimately stressed: וָאֶשְׁקֳולָה "I weighed" (Ezra 8:25), יֶהְדָּפֶנּוּ "he will push him" (Num 35:20), יִשְׁפּוּטוּ "they would judge" (Exod 18:26); תַּעֲבוּרִי (Ruth 2:8).[284] In other words, the *mater* is not assurance of where the accent fell, especially not among the DSS where the *waw* is used to mark any type of /o/ or /u/ vowel. While this is the case, it should also be recognized that the DSS, especially the DSS-SP9 and DSS-SP1c texts, show a preference for forms that correspond to pausal forms in the MT, where the accent or stress usually falls on the penultimate syllable.

In addition to forms like יקטולו, the place of the /o/ or /u/ vowel in geminate imperfects correspond to MT pausal forms: יחונכה "he will favor you" (1QS II, 3 and passim) corresponds to pausal וִיחֻנֶּךָּ (Num 6:25) and וִיחָנֵנוּ (Mal 1:9), and is in contrast to contextual יָחְנְךָ (Gen 43:29, Isa 30:19); also יזומו "they will plot" (4Q171 1–2 ii, 14) stands in contrast to contextual יָזְמוּ (Gen 11:6).[285]

Note too that where a verb in the MT attests an alternation in the imperfect between /a/ and /o/ theme vowels, the orthography of the scrolls (specifically in the DSS–SP9 and DSS-SP1c texts) usually conforms to the theme vowel one sees in pausal forms. Thus, although חפץ "to delight in" takes an /o/ theme vowel in the MT in contextual forms (e.g., אֶחְפֹּץ in Ezek 33:11 and passim) and an /a/ vowel in pausal forms (e.g., אֶחְפָּץ in Job 13:3 and passim), the same verb is always without a *waw mater* in the DSS, both in the biblical (five times [where the MT form has shewa or an /a/

---

282. See Qimron, *HDSS*, 40–42.

283. Ben-Ḥayyim, "Traditions in the Hebrew Language," 202–3. For more on these forms and their explanation, see §5.7, "*Qal* Imperfect + Suffix."

284. Qimron, *HDSS*, 41. See also Kutscher, *Isaiah*, 339–40.

285. The form יזמו (4Q381 45a + b, 2) is ambiguous since in this manuscript we would not expect a short /o/ to be indicated with a *waw mater*.

vowel]) and nonbiblical scrolls (six times), suggesting that the verb always took an /a/ theme vowel in the DSS.[286] Since the verb is often in the singular and attested in DSS-SP9 texts, we would have expected to see a *waw mater* if the theme vowel was an /o/ or /u/ vowel. Although there is some variation in the orthography of imperfect verbs, the number of examples for this verb suggests the spelling without *waw* is not incidental. Note also the reverse pattern: בגד is attested in context with an /a/ vowel (only נִבְגַּד Mal 2:10), but in pause with an /o/ vowel (e.g., תִּבְגּוֹד Isa 48:8 and passim); in the DSS the verb is only attested with a *waw mater* where it occurs without affix (in other words, it presumes an /o/ or /u/ vowel): יבגוד (1QpHab VIII, 3 and 10); ותבגוד (4Q221 16, 5); נבגוד (4Q265 3, 2).

Note a similar preference in the imperative forms of the verb ירש: ראש "possess" (4Q364 24a–c, 4 at Deut 2:31 for MT רָשׁ); ראשו "possess" (4Q364 26a ii, 3 at Deut 9:23 for MT רְשׁוּ), in both cases where the *aleph* is indicating the /ā/ vowel found in the pausal form of the imperative (רָשׁ), in contrast to the contextual רֵשׁ (Deut 1:21).

In nouns with suffixed pronouns too, one sometimes sees a clear preference for what correspond to MT pausal forms, as with רעיכה "your friend" (4Q417 2 ii + 23, 7 and passim), which corresponds to pausal רֵעֶךָ (Deut 5:21) and not contextual רֵעֲךָ (Deut 5:20) (see §5.2, "Pronouns and Particles").[287] While Qimron stresses that one suspects penultimate accent on verbal forms, he cautions that the orthography seems to presuppose ultimate accent on some words, like the *quṭl nouns in construct, just like in Aramaic and in contrast to the accentuation for these words in the MT.[288]

Qimron suggests that the patterns often align with what we would expect from Aramaic (and to a certain extent Mishnaic Hebrew) and seem

286. The nonbiblical scrolls that contain this verb are primarily DSS-SP9 texts (five out of six); the biblical scrolls are from DSS-SP9 (IQIsa[a]) and DSS-NSP texts (1Q8 [1QIsa[b]] and 4Q33 [4QDeut[f]]). The only other verb that falls into this category and is attested in the DSS that I could find is טרף "to tear." In the MT, it is attested mostly in context as יִטְרֹף (Ps 7:3) or something similar and once in pause as יִטְרָף (Gen 49:27); in the DSS it occurs once as יטרפו (1QH[a] XIII, 16). Since the other *qal* 3mp imperfect verbs with /o/ or /u/ theme vowel (and no suffix) in 1QH[a] commonly attest a *waw mater* to mark the theme vowel, it is assumed that the theme vowel of יטרפו is /a/. For a more complete list of these types of verbs, see Jan Joosten, "The Function of the Semitic D stem: Biblical Hebrew Materials for a Comparative-Historical Approach," *Orientalia* 67 (1998): 210–12.

287. Qimron, "Studies in the Hebrew of the Dead Sea Scrolls," 83.

288. Qimron, *HDSS*, 42.

to imply a form of Hebrew that is earlier than that reflected in contextual forms in the MT.[289] While it is also conceivable that the preference among the writers and scribes of the DSS for what are pausal forms in the MT is an artificial and secondary process engendered by mimicking what were perceived to be older, more archaic forms, this makes less sense given the form of **quṭl* nouns in construct. That is, why would scribes and writers choose to mimic archaic-looking verbal forms and nouns + suffixes but not other nominal forms? It seems simpler to suggest that at least for the scribes and writers of the DSS-SP9 texts the accent was similar to the accentuation in Aramaic.[290] All the same, one is left to wonder about the preference for verb forms that parallel pausal forms in the MT, but which do not seem to appear there for reasons of accent or stress (e.g., יחפץ, יבגוד, ראש).

4.8. Vowel Reduction

It is often assumed that propretonic short vowels in open syllables reduced to a muttered vowel in Hebrew sometime in the last half of the first millennium B.C.E.[291] Although it is not obviously evidenced in the DSS, it seems that there is some slight evidence for the reduction of (at least some of) these vowels. The evidence involves the forms described in "Digraphs" (§3.5), specifically the fact that where a word has a full vowel followed by an *aleph* and then an /o/ or /u/ class vowel (e.g., *-āʾō-* or *-āʾū-*), the *aleph* is usually preserved along with a *waw mater* following it (e.g., מאור "light"), whereas when the *aleph* + /o/ or /u/ vowel is preceded by a shewa, then the *aleph* rarely elides, as in רובן for ראובן "Reuben." Furthermore, it seems that the loss of *aleph* occasionally happens in places where it is preceded by a shewa that developed from an earlier short vowel in an open syllable (e.g., שרית for שארית "remainder").

The so-called "Rule of the Shewa," by which is meant the shift from **qəṭə-* to **qiṭ-*, is difficult to perceive through the DSS orthography, though the spelling of לעפים "to weary ones" in 1QH[a] XV, 13 may be evidence of

289. Qimron, "Studies in the Hebrew of the Dead Sea Scrolls," 88–89.

290. See ibid.

291. See Gogel, *Grammar of Epigraphic Hebrew*, 33. On the evidence for a similar reduction in DSS Aramaic, see Muraoka, *GQA*, 31–33. Muraoka notes that most evidence points to the reduction of pretonic short vowels, though perhaps the process was not yet complete.

it. This spelling can be understood as the *lamedh* preposition followed by a defective writing for עיפים *yəʿēfîm* where the *yə-* syllable has coalesced with the preceding shewa of the *lamedh* preposition to form *lî-*. Thus **ləyəʿēfîm* has become *lîʿēfîm* and the etymological *yodh* consonant has been elided. Complicating this assumption, of course, is that the word could also be derived from the synonymous עִיף, in which case one must suppose that the medial *yodh* has dropped out.[292] All things being equal, this seems less likely.

4.9. /å/ < /ā/ < Proto-Semitic /a/

The phonetic shift of Proto-Semitic /a/ to /å/ (= IPA [ɔ]) (the sound in American English "all") is one that is well documented in the history of the Hebrew language. By the time the Masoretes invented their system of vowel notation, short /a/ vowels in etymologically open (tonic and pretonic) syllables had shifted to /å/. Thus, when they pronounced words like דָּבָר "word," what they heard and spoke was *dåbår*. Because this /å/ sound had merged (or become phonemically indistinct) with the sound of the etymological short /o/ (found, for example, in *ḥokmā* "wisdom"), when the Masoretes pointed words like "wisdom," they used the same symbol (*qamets*) to indicate the etymological short /o/ sound in the first syllable and the etymological /ā/ (< /a/) sound in the second: חָכְמָה "wisdom," reflecting the pronunciation *ḥåkmå* (or the allophonic *ḥokmå*). Furthermore, this shift (or a similar one) is known from other languages, such as Phoenician and Aramaic.

That the shift of all etymological short /a/ vowels in open syllables had taken place in Hebrew by the time of the DSS is less clear. Harviainen, in his review of the topic, suggests that the Proto-Semitic /a/ (which had become /ā/ in the early/mid-first millennium B.C.E.) became /å/ only in the 700s C.E., as revealed in Palestinian vocalized texts and in the Tiberian punctuation which dates in its earliest manuscripts to the mid 800s.[293] Additional evidence is derived from Syriac where the *utsatsa* sign ("probably derived from the Greek" *omicron*) indicated etymological /ā/ (< /a/) by

---

292. On the possible explanations of the word and relevant literature, see Stegemann, Schuller, Newsom, DJD 40:202.

293. Tapani Harviainen, *On the Vocalism of the Closed Unstressed Syllables in Hebrew: A Study Based on Evidence Provided by the Transcriptions of St. Jerome and Palestinian Punctuations* (SO 48; Helsinki: Finish Oriental Society, 1977), 108.

"probably" the 700s, if not in the mid-600s when Jacob of Edessa invented the symbol.[294] Other evidence includes the relative absence of the back-pronunciation of historical /a/ (that is, as an /å/, /o/, or /u/ vowel) in the LXX, in Origen's Secunda (where *omicron/omega* appear where MT has *qamets gadol* in only 0.86 percent of occurrences), and the fact that those instances where MT *qamets gadol* is transcribed with an "o" in Jerome are not reliable (that is, are mistakes or quotations from another source) or occur due to the vowel's preceding a *resh*, which results, Harviainen says, in "o" due to a "tendency to provide vowels with labial timbres."[295]

Morag and Meyer, on the other hand, suppose that the shift from /ā/ to /å/ had already taken place in late Second Temple times and is reflected in the DSS.[296] Meyer's examples are, at the least, ambiguous, as Kutscher demonstrates.[297] To give just one instance that is also cited by Harviainen and Morag, כבושים appears in 1QIsa[a] at Isa 5:17 for MT כְּבָשִׂים "lambs."[298] Kutscher believes that the form in 1QIsa[a] reflects a variant tradition which reads not "lambs," but "those subdued" (that is, the *qal* passive participle of כבשׁ, *kəbūšīm*, akin in sense to the LXX translation of this word διηρπασμένοι "those seized").[299] Morag argues, to the contrary, that the context is pastoral and that the LXX word is more likely based on a misunderstanding of a manuscript where the Proto-Semitic /a/ vowel had become /o/ and indicated with a *waw mater*. The words of Isa 5:17a, however, do not necessarily have to be construed as references

294. Ibid.

295. Ibid., 105–6.

296. Rudolf Meyer, "Bemerkungen zu der hebräischen Aussprachetradition von Chirbet Qumrān," *ZAW* 70 (1958): 39–48; Harviainen, *On the Vocalism of the Closed Unstressed Syllables in Hebrew*, 105; Shelomo Morag, "Review of E. Y. Kutscher, *The Language and Linguistic Background of the Isaiah Scroll*" (Hebrew), *Kirjath Sepher* 36 (1960): 29–31; and idem, *The Hebrew Language Tradition of the Yemenite Jews* (Hebrew; Jerusalem: Academy of the Hebrew Language, 1963), 104.

297. Meyer, "Bemerkungen zu der hebräischen Aussprachetradition," 41 and Kutscher, *Isaiah*, 473–74. Kutscher notes, for example, that all the examples (from 1QIsa[a]) Meyer adduces as proof of this shift are not due to "a phonological development, but, generally … a result of variant exegesis" (ibid., 473).

298. Meyer, "Bemerkungen zu der hebräischen Aussprachetradition," 41; Harviainen, *On the Vocalism of the Closed Unstressed Syllables in Hebrew*, 105; Morag, "Review of … *The Language and Linguistic Background of the Isaiah Scroll*," 29–30; idem, *Hebrew … of the Yemenite Jews*, 104.

299. Kutscher, *Isaiah*, 247.

to pasturage and feeding. Instead of reading "the lambs will feed (ורעו) as (in) their pasture (כדברם)" (following the MT), or "those subdued will feed..." (following the LXX), it is possible to read "those subdued have done wrong (ורעו) as they said (they would do) (כדברם)." The people who are subdued are those addressed in the preceding or following verses who ignore or are indifferent to the threat of exile and divine punishment. Since the preceding lines do not mention any pastoral imagery, it would be natural for a reader to interpret the graphically and even phonetically ambiguous letters ורעו as referring to wrongdoing and not feeding. Thus, it is not necessary to argue that the letters כבושים must be interpreted as "lambs" based on the context.

Qimron, in his *HDSS*, lists forms in which the "*Waw* sometimes appears where the Tiberian tradition has *qamets*, *patach*, or *seghol*."[300] (The examples are cited and critiqued in "*Waw* Marking /u/ Class Vowel in Nouns Where MT Has No /u/ Class Vowel" [§5.4].) Qimron goes on to summarize briefly the views of Meyer and Kutscher outlined above and says that since the *waw* can appear in places where the MT has *patach*, or *seghol*, Kutscher's explanation seems more convincing. In other words, if the phonological shift from /ā/ to /å/ in all environments had taken place, the words that have *qamets* in the MT would be the only ones that attest a *waw*; since *waw* also appears in places where the MT contains *patach*, *seghol*, or shewa, there must be another reason for the presence of *waw*. Since the appearance of a /u/ class vowel can be explained as due to the presence of a following (sometimes preceding) bilabial, *lamedh*, *nun*, or *resh*, or a following /u/ vowel, it makes sense to prefer these explanations rather than a general and universal shift of /ā/ > /å/. In addition, it must be observed that if the proposed shift of /ā/ > /å/ had really taken hold, it is surprising that it is so rarely reflected in the writing of the DSS; one might expect a plethora of words attesting a *waw mater* where the corresponding MT word has a *qamets gadol*.

4.10. Diphthongs and Triphthongs

In the above pages, I have already treated a number of examples of phonetic shifts in DSS Hebrew. The following list summarizes most of the transformations that involve vowels.

300. Qimron, *HDSS*, 39.

-C*ʾō*- > -C*yō*-, as in לביותיו "its lionesses" (4Q169 3–4 i, 4 at Nah 2:13)
-C*wō* > -C*ʾō*, as in מ[צ]אותי "my commandments" (4Q129 [4QPhyl B] at Deut 5:10)

-*əʾō* > -*əyō*, as in מליאות "fulfilling" (4Q284 2 i, 3)
-*əʾū* > -*əyū*, as in ימחיו "they will clap" in 1Q8 (1QIsa[b]) at Isa 55:12

-*āʾū* > -*āwū*, as in באוו "they came" (4Q398 [4QMMT] 11–13, 2 and 3)
-*ēʾō*- > -*ēyō*-, as in מאיות "soldiers" (11Q19 XLII, 15)
-*īʾă*- > -*īyə*- or -*īye*-, as in ישייכה "he will deceive you" (1QIsa[a] at Isa 37:10)
-*īʾā*- > -*īyā*-, as in אליב "Eliab" (4Q138 [4QPhyl K] at Deut 11:6)
-*īʾē*- > -*īyē*-, as in דניל "Daniel" (6Q7 [6QpapDan] at Dan 10:12)
-*īʾū*- > -*īyū*-, as in החטיום "they made them sin" (4Q522 9 ii, 10)
-*ōʾū* > -*ōwū*, as in יבאוו "they will come" (4Q266 10 i, 3)
-*ūʾā* > -*ūwā*, as in הוה "he" (1QIsa[a] at Isa 7:14)

-*ōhū* > -*ōwū*, as in תהוו "emptiness" (4Q504 1–2R iii, 3)
-*ūhū* > -*ūwū* > -*ūyū* as in וירמסוויו "they will trample him" (4Q368 10 ii, 7)

-*āwō*- > -*āʾō*-, as in עאון "iniquity" (1QIsa[a] part of additional text to Isa 1:15)
-*ōwē* > -*ōʾē*, as in קואי "those hoping for" (4Q171 1–2 ii, 4)
-*ōwō*- > -*ōʾō*-, as in רבואותם "their ten thousands" (1QM XII, 4)

-*āyī*- > -*āʾī*-, as inפתאים "simple" (4Q381 1, 2)
-*āyē* > -*āʾē*, as inפתאי "simple of" (1QpHab XII, 4) and עאף "weary" (1QH[a] XVI, 37)
-*āyō*- > -*āʾō*-, as in נבאות "Nebaioth" (1QIsa[a] at Isa 60:7)
-*īyī*- > -*īʾī*-, as in כתיאים "Kittim" (1QpHab II, 12 and passim)
-*īyā* > -*īʾā*, as in ציאה "dry" (1QIsa[a] at Isa 41:18)
-*ōyī*- > -*ōʾī*-, as in גואים "peoples" (1QM XII, 14 and passim)
-*ōyē*- > -*ōʾē*-, as in אואב "enemy" (4Q98g [4QPs[x]] at Ps 89:23)
-*ūyā* > -*ūʾā*, as in נטוא[ה] "stretched" (4Q51 [4QSam[a]] in an addition to 2 Sam 24:16)

In addition to these shifts, note the following shifts:

- -*īhū* > -*īyū*, as in אביו "his father" (4Q225 2 ii, 4)
- -*āw* > -*ō*, as in עלו "over him" (1QpHab VIII, 7)
- -*ūy* > -*ū*, as in ראו "it is right" (4Q394 [4QMMT] 3–7 i, 15)
- -*ūy* > -*ūʾī*, as in ראואי "it is right" (4Q394 [4QMMT] 3–7 ii, 1 and 13)
- -*wū* > -*ū*, as in יהו "may they be" (4Q448 II, 7)

The shift -*īhū* > -*īyū* is associated especially with the 3ms pronominal suffix on short nouns like אב "father," אח "brother," פה "mouth," and 1cs perfect verb forms (e.g., קטלתי), in each case where an /i/ vowel comes immediately before the suffix. In the nonbiblical DSS, one commonly finds the 3ms suffix written הו- on such short nouns, where one typically finds in the MT the simple ו-.[301] Thus, one finds פיהו (4Q159 1 ii, 5) instead of פִּיו, the form that is more common in the MT (e.g., Exod 4:15); similarly אביהו (4Q416 2 iii, 16) instead of אָבִיו (e.g., Gen 9:22). Of course, neither the DSS nor the MT is consistent and one finds פיו in the DSS (4Q381 1, 3) and פִּיהוּ in the MT (Exod 4:15 [the same verse where one finds פִּיו]), similarly אביו in the DSS (4Q416 2 iv, 1) and אָבִיהוּ in the MT (1 Kgs 5:15). In the biblical scrolls (many of which are DSS-NSP texts and reflect the MT orthography) the distribution is not surprisingly reversed, ו- is more common than הו- on nouns.[302]

301. The development of the standard MT form is assumed to be *ʾ*ābīhū* > *ʾ*ābīū* > ʾ*ābīw* = אָבִיו. The form אביו occurs in the MT 220 times and אביהו seven times; אחיו occurs 113 times and אחיהו four times; פיו occurs fifty-five times, while פיהו occurs twenty-two times (concentrated in Job, Proverbs, Qohelet, and Lamentations). Among the nonbiblical scrolls, אביו occurs at least four times and אביהו twenty-six times; אחיו occurs two times and אחיהו thirteen times; פיו occurs once (perhaps twice) and פיהו at least thirty times.

302. I.e., according to my search of Accordance, אביו occurs eleven times and אביהו once; אחיו occurs at least fourteen times and אחיהו three times; פיו occurs ten times and פיהו eight times. Note, however, the frequency of the הו- form of the suffix even in the Genizah manuscripts of Ben Sira. The form פיהו occurs in Ben Sira 9:18 (Ms A); 14:1 (Ms A); 39:31 (Mas); 48:12 (Ms B) vs. פיו in 15:5 (Ms A); 39:17 (Ms B); 39:31 (corrected from פיהו) (Ms B). Similarly, רואיהו in 37:24 (Ms D) vs. ראיו in 37:24 (Ms C). The word for "father," however, always appears in the same way with the suffix: אביו in 3:11 (Ms A), 3:16 [twice] (Ms A); 44:22 (Ms B).

Curiously, the suffixes on 1cs perfect verbs do not follow the distributional pattern of nouns; in the nonbiblical DSS, the suffix ו- seems to be slightly more common on 1cs perfect verbs (4Q364 21a–k, 3; 4Q388a 7 ii, 5 [defectively ו-]; 4Q522 9 ii, 11) than הו- (4Q175 16; 11Q19 LIX, 18). In the biblical scrolls, on the other hand, the suffix הו- is slightly more common than ו-, even where the MT has ו-.[303] The presence of both types of 3ms suffix on short nouns and verbs among the DSS should be kept in mind, since previous scholars have made a point of claiming that they do not exist or are attested only in peripheral texts.[304] Although not all words are found in all text groups, some are. The word פיהו, for example, is found in all text types, including DSS-NSP texts (e.g., 4Q372 1, 20 and 4Q381 69, 9); this suggests the possible widespread nature of this orthographic and/or morphological tendency. Notice, however, that the biblical scrolls, though attesting all forms, slightly prefer nouns with ו-.

In any case, the dominance of forms like אביהו in nonbiblical scrolls suggests that where אביו occurs, it is due to the elision of *heh*.[305] If such is the case, then we might suppose a pronunciation like that for the Tiberian tradition, *ʾābīw* (אָבִיו), where the vowel and final consonant form a diphthong. Nevertheless, it is sometimes asserted that the Hebrew suffix was

303. According to Accordance, the suffix הו- occurs eighteen times in the biblical DSS, in all but three cases (1 Sam 1:22, Isa 45:13, 51:23) where the MT has ו-, and even among these three exceptions, in one case the verb in the scroll has no parallel in the MT (1 Sam 1:22) and in another (Isa 51:23) the MT has a 3fs suffix. The suffix ו- appears fifteen times in the biblical scrolls, all but once (1 Sam 16:7) where the MT has ו-.

304. Qimron states categorically "Contracted forms like אביו are not attested" (*HDSS*, 60) and Morag is more specific and mentions that they do not appear in "GQH [= General Qumran Hebrew]" ("Qumran Hebrew," 157). In truth, אביו is attested at least four times in the nonbiblical scrolls and eleven times in the biblical scrolls. In relation to the nonbiblical scrolls, it bears mentioning that of the four sure instances of this spelling (4Q175 15; 4Q225 2 ii, 4; 4Q416 2 iv, 1; 11Q19 LXIV, 2), two occur in texts that also evidence אביהו (4Q416 2 iii, 16; 11Q19 LXIV, 3 and passim). Furthermore, although the appearance of אביו may be explained as part of a quotation of or allusion to various biblical texts (respectively, Deut 33:9, Deut 21:18, Gen 2:24, and Gen 22:7), 4Q225 and 4Q416 do not follow precisely the biblical text; also note that all these texts bear other traits that link them with "GQH" (e.g., the spelling of the pronoun הואה 4Q225 2 i, 4; 4Q416 1, 16, and the *yqwṭl* + suffix pattern, תשופכנו 11Q19 LII, 12]).

305. Note the similar constraction in Aramaic: אחוי "his brothers" (1Q20 XXI, 34) instead of *אחוהי and עלוי "over him" (11Q18 8, 3; 9, 4) instead of *עלוהי (the *heh* being preserved in all other cases). See Muraoka, *GQA*, 40.

pronounced in the DSS, as in Samaritan Hebrew, *-iyyū* or *-īyū*.[306] Support for this supposition is found partly in similar cases where intervocalic *heh* seems to assimilate to a preceding or following vowel, as in תוהו *tōwū* (< **tōhū*) "emptiness" (4Q504 1–2R iii, 3 and 1QIsa[a] at Isa 40:17), as well as in וירמסוויו *wəyirməsūyū* (< **wəyirməsūwū* < **wəyirməsūhū*) or *wəyirmōsūyū* (< **wəyirmōsūwū* < **wəyirmōsūhū*) "they will trample him" (4Q368 10 ii, 7), in the latter word where *waw* has, in turn, dissimilated to *yodh*.[307] Such a tendency for assimilation also seems to be evidenced in the Babylonian tradition where the corresponding form for "his father" is *ʾābīwū*.[308] In the case of DSS אביו, this would mean that the *heh* would assimilate to the preceding /i/ vowel and become /y/: *ʾābīyū*; this assimilation of *heh* is similar to the assimilation of *aleph* in words like הביו *hābīyū* "bring" (1QIsa[a] at Isa 16:3) and החטיום *heḥēṭīyūm* "they caused them to sin" (4Q522 9 ii, 10).[309] As for the DSS spelling אביהו, while it is entirely possible that the suffix was also pronounced *-īyū*, it seems more likely that the cases where the suffix is spelled with a *heh* reflect a pronunciation *-īhū* in the writing/reading register. At the least, it seems inconsistent to argue for a historical spelling with a vernacular pronunciation for אביהו = *ʾābīyū* in a manuscript like 4Q221 that attests numerous other phonetically-inspired spellings like רובן *rūbēn* "Reuben" (4, 9 = MT רְאוּבֵן), ימו *yāmō* "his days" (3, 5 = MT יָמָיו), בנו *bānō* "his sons" (5, 2 = MT בָּנָיו).

These last examples from 4Q221 evidence the contraction *-āw* > *-ō*; such a contraction is commonly assumed for DSS Hebrew based, in part, on the frequent spelling ו- for the 3ms suffix on prepositions and plural nouns which normally take the suffix ָיו- in the MT.[310] Thus, for example, although the preposition + 3ms suffix עליו appears fairly commonly among all the DSS written in its familiar MT fashion, the spelling עלו (presuming *ʿālō*) appears at least eight times among the nonbiblical scrolls (in

306. See Qimron, *HDSS*, 60; Joosten, "Hebrew, Aramaic, Greek," 356.

307. See the subsection "Quiescence of *Heh*" in §4.3, "Weakening of Gutturals."

308. See Israel Yeivin, *The Hebrew Language Tradition as Reflected in Babylonian Vocalization* (Text and Studies 12; 2 vols.; Jerusalem: Academy of the Hebrew Language, 1985), 775.

309. Cf. also Qumran Aramaic שריוא *šarrīyū* "they began" (4Q204 4, 3) (Muraoka, *GQA*, 138). See the subsection "Quiescence of *Aleph*" in §4.3, "Weakening of Gutturals."

310. Since the *yodh* in the MT form is only a historical spelling or, alternatively, a graphic means for distinguishing the singular from the plural nouns, it is not pronounced (see Andersen and Forbes, *Spelling*, 62).

contrast to just twice in the MT 1 Sam 2:10 and 2 Sam 20:8).[311] Another example is the word "face" plus the 3ms suffix, spelled פנו twice (4Q374 2 ii, 8; 4Q405 15 ii–16, 4) and as part of a prepositional phrase לפנו at least eight times (e.g., 4Q266 2 ii, 2).[312] The 3ms suffix on plural nouns is written ו- most frequently in DSS-SP9 and DSS-SP1c texts.[313] Nevertheless, the same suffix is also attested in numerous DSS-NSP texts.[314] The strongest evidence for the contraction to /ō/ comes from 1QIsa[a] where the

---

311. In 1QpHab VIII, 7; 4Q161 8–10, 11; 4Q221 7, 10; 4Q266 6 ii, 2; 8 i, 3 and 5; 4Q270 6 ii, 7; 6 v, 15. Note also אלו "to him/it" in 1QpHab VIII, 5 (twice) at Hab 2:5 for MT אֵלָיו; 4Q398 (4QMMT) 14–17 i, 7. All of these are DSS-SP9 or DSS-SP1c texts.

312. Also in 4Q266 2 ii, 4; 4Q392 1, 4, 5, and 9; 4Q398 (4QMMT) 14–17 ii, 4 and 7; 4Q405 20 ii–22, 7. All of these are DSS-SP9 or DSS-SP1c texts. The appearance of the 3ms ו- suffix on explicitly singular III-*yodh* nouns is comparatively rare: שדו "his field" in 4Q396 (4QMMT) 1–2, iv, 7 and עושו "his maker" (4Q299 3a ii–b, 7 and 8, cf. הָעֹשׂוֹ Job 40:19).

313. The following are from DSS-SP9 and DSS-SP1c texts: אבותו "his fathers" (4Q365 26a–b, 8); אחו "his brothers" (4Q266 5 ii, 4); אלומותו "its sheaves" (11Q5 [11QPs[a]] at Ps 126:6); אלמנותו "his palaces" (1QIsa[a] at Isa 13:22); אפדותו "his ephods" (4Q365 12b iii, 5); גבולותו "its borders" (1QIsa[a] at Isa 28:25) for MT גְּבֻלָתוֹ; דליותו "its branches" (4Q262 B, 1 and 2); חוקותו "his statutes" (4Q138 [4QPhyl K] at Deut 11:1); ימו "his days" (4Q221 3, 5; 4Q270 6 iv, 14; iv, 19); יתדותו "its pegs" (1QIsa[a] at Isa 33:20); מבינותו "his understandings" (4Q417 29 i, 7); מעשו "his works" (1QS VI, 17; 1QSa I, 18 and 22; 4Q261 1a–b, 3; 4Q299 3c, 6); מצותו, מצאותו, מצוותו "his commandments" (1QpHab V, 5; 4Q266 2 i, 4; 4Q128 [4QPhyl A] at Deut 10:13; 4Q138 [4QPhyl K] at Deut 11:1; 4Q140 [4QPhyl M] at Deut 6:2); משלחותו "his sendings" (4Q405 23 i, 13); משפטו "his judgments" (4Q138 [4QPhyl K] at Deut 11:1); סוסו "his horses" (1QpHab III, 6 in a quotation of Hab 1:8 for MT סוּסָיו); עוונותו "his iniquities" (1QS III, 7 and 8); פרשו "his horses" or "horsemen" (1QpHab III, 7, though note the identical spelling of the preceding verb פרשו "they crossed" or "set out"); צדקותו "his righteous acts" (1QS XI, 3); קירותו "its walls" (4Q403 1 i, 43; 4Q404 5, 6); רחמו "his compassion" (4Q434 1 i, 7); תבואותו "its produce" (4Q266 6 iii, 8); תעדתו "his assemblies" (4Q255 2, 6); תשבוחותו "his praises" (11Q17 X, 5).

314. The following are from DSS-NSP texts: אחו "his brothers" (11Q1 [11QpaleoLev[a]] at Lev 21:10) for MT אֶחָיו; איבו "his enemies" (4Q376 1 iii, 2); בריותו "his creatures" (4Q216 V, 9); מלאכו "his angels" (4Q93 [4QPs[l]] at Ps 104:4) for MT מַלְאָכָיו; מעשו "his works" (4Q216 V, 3); מצותו "his commandments" (4Q32 [4QDeut[e]] at Deut 8:2) for MT מִצְוֹתָו; idem (4Q98 [4QPs[q]] at Ps 112:1) for MT מִצְוֹתָיו; מרגלותו "his legs" (4Q114 [4QDan[c]] at Dan 10:6) for MT מַרְגְּלֹתָיו; משבצתו "its settings" (4Q468b 1, 2); נעלו "his sandals" (4Q56 [4QIsa[b]] at Isa 5:27) for MT נְעָלָיו; נערותו "his young women" (2Q16 [2QRuth[a]] at Ruth 2:22) for MT נַעֲרוֹתָיו; רעו "his friends" (4Q472 1, 4). Note also מעלותו "its upper rooms" (Mur88 at Amos 9:6 for MT מַעֲלוֹתָו). Some examples are, of course, ambiguous, as בימו "in his day(s)" (4Q388a 7 ii, 4).

spelling of the 3ms suffix on singular nouns sometimes occurs spelled יו-, as in ידיו נטויה "his hand stretched out" (1QIsa[a] at Isa 5:25, 9:11, 16, 20, 10:4, 14:27, for MT יָדוֹ נְטוּיָה); ריקה נפשיו "his throat is empty" (at Isa 29:8 for MT רֵיקָה נַפְשׁוֹ); אסרחדן בניו "Esarhaddon, his son" (at Isa 37:38 for MT אֵסַר חַדֹּן בְּנוֹ); בראושיו "on his head" (at Isa 59:17 for MT בְּרֹאשׁוֹ).[315] These examples suggest that when יו- appears on plural nouns it is also representing the /ō/ vowel.

However, complicating the assumption that ו- represents /ō/ in forms like עלו is the fact that the MT occasionally attests the 3ms suffix on prepositions like על and on plural nouns without a *yodh*, as in עָלָו "over it" (2 Sam 20:8) and צְבָאָו "his hosts" (Ps 148:2). Also, in very rare cases, the MT evidences יו- when the context and the vowels reflect ו- (see, for example, עֵינָיו "his eye" Qoh 4:8; שְׂפָתָיו "his lip" Prov 16:27).[316] Furthermore, it seems peculiar that the DSS-SP9 texts and DSS-NSP texts should both attest so many examples of the defective spelling. We might expect a peculiar (phonetically inspired) orthography from the former group of texts, but not so with the latter. Given this distribution, it might seem easiest to understand the writing of ו- for the 3ms on plural nouns and suffixes as a simple graphic alternative to יו-. The writing ו- seems to have been the standard writing in preexilic inscriptions and, presumably, this spelling continued down to the time of the DSS, together with the later innovation of writing יו-.[317] Thus, the defective spelling of ו- is not conclusive. We should, however, remember the concentration of this defective spelling in the DSS-SP9 texts, especially with the prepositions (which never occur in DSS-NSP texts) and the frequency with which the spelling is found in some texts that attest other phonetically-inspired spellings, like 1QpHab, 1QS, 4Q417, 4Q221, the Phylactery texts, 1QIsa[a].

There is another factor too that, initially at least, complicates the theory that the 3ms suffix on plural nouns was *-ō*. Notice that the diphthong /āw/ was preserved in some words in the final syllable, even in texts that seem to attest to the contraction of the diphthong in the suffix; as Ben-Ḥayyim notes, the word "nothingness" (= MT שָׁוְא) is spelled with two *waws* שוו = *šāw* in 1QpHab X, 10 and 11, though the same text seems

315. See Kutscher, *Isaiah*, 447 for these examples. This would make the 3ms suffix on singular and plural nouns identical; the same pronunciation is found in Samaritan Hebrew. See Ben-Ḥayyim, *Studies in the Traditions*, 79–82.

316. See Andersen and Forbes, *Spelling*, 62.

317. See Gogel, *Grammar of Epigraphic Hebrew*, 159–60.

to witness the shift *-āw* > *-ō* in, among other places, the word סוסו "his horses" (1QpHab III, 6).[318] Also, as explained above in "*Aleph* as Internal *Mater*" (§3.3), it seems that the diphthong *-āw* sometimes appears in words like עישאו "Esau" (4Q223–224 2 ii, 4, 12; 2 iii, 12; 2 iv, 18; 4Q364 3 ii, 7 for what would be in the MT עֵשָׂו) where *aleph* is used as a *mater* for /ā/.[319] Although the disparity in the preservation of historical /āw/ in these words versus its contraction in the pronoun is puzzling, the peculiar orthography of the above words (שוו, עישאו) may actually offer support for the contraction to /ō/. The fact that the scribes wrote a double *waw* in שוו and introduced *aleph* in עישאו suggests that the *waw* in each word could have been interpreted in the wrong way (namely as /ō/).

Thus, although some of the same words are spelled in the same way in both DSS-SP9 and DSS-NSP texts (e.g., אחו "his brothers"), it seems possible that in some texts (1QIsa[a], 1QS, 1QpHab, 4Q221, 4Q266, 4Q270) the writing of the suffix without *yodh* reflects the contraction of the diphthong to /ō/ while in other texts (e.g., 4Q32, 4Q56, 4Q114) it reflects an older spelling of the uncontracted diphthong /āw/, as sometimes happens in the MT.

One might still wonder why the writers and copyists of the DSS-NSP were so inconsistent in the writing of the suffix. It bears mentioning, therefore, that the suffix without *yodh* appears most commonly on words with the feminine plural ending *-ōt*.[320] In the lists provided in the footnotes above, there are around twenty examples of words ending in *-ōt* that take the suffix ו-, while just ten examples of nouns that would take the absolute plural ending *-īm* (if they did not have a suffix). Observe that the feminine plural ending is clearly marked for plurality in most instances through a *waw mater* (that is, ות-). There is less reason, therefore, to use the expanded 3ms orthography יו-. Similarly, in nouns that do not end in the feminine plural morpheme *-ōt*, the plurality of the noun is usually apparent from the morphology of the noun (e.g., III-*heh* nouns פנו, מעשו, which in the singular would be *פנהו, מעשהו), or from how the noun is used (e.g., רחמו "his compassion").[321]

---

318. Ben-Ḥayyim, *Studies in the Traditions*, 80–81.

319. Other spellings of the name "Esau" seem more ambiguous: עשיו (4Q252 IV, 1), עישיו (4Q215 1–3, 7), עשו (1Q18 1–2, 2, 3; 4Q222 1, 2).

320. Abegg implies that the forms without *yodh* represent 70 percent of the instances of nouns ending in *-ōt* + 3ms suffix ("Hebrew of the Dead Sea Scrolls," 333).

321. Alternatively, the use of ו- was perhaps on analogy to the 3mp suffix ם- and

The resolution of -ūy > -ū is found in ראו "seen" (4Q394 [4QMMT] 3–7 i, 15) as well as גלו in 4Q175 11.³²² This also appears in the MT in צָפוּ "watched" (Job 15:22) and הֶעָשׂוּ "the one made" (Job 41:25), as well as in the Samaritan tradition where the diphthong sometimes shifts to /o/.³²³ In 4QMMT, the preservation of the *yodh* was effected by the insertion of a glottal stop and the shift of /y/ to /ī/: ראואי "seen" (4Q394 [4QMMT] 3–7 ii, 1 and 13), presumably reflecting *rāʾūʾī*. Qimron views the latter case in light of Samaritan Hebrew, which often transforms the diphthong into two separate syllables with a /w/ glide, as in צפואי as *sabbuwwi*; in light of this, it seems easiest to understand the form in 4QMMT as having an epenthetic glottal stop.³²⁴ Nevertheless, there is no reason to assume that all words ending in a similar way would have resolved this diphthong; recall that 4QMMT exhibits numerous idiosyncracies not shared with other texts.³²⁵

The shift of *ōy* > *ō* asserted by Qimron seems unlikely or, at least, extremely rare.³²⁶ He claims that this shift is evidenced explicitly in one form, הוה in 1QIsaᵃ at Isa 1:24 for MT הוֹי. He suggests that cases like מבואי "entrance" (the singular absolute, = MT מָבוֹא) in 4Q405 23 i, 9 and גואי "peoples of" in 4Q491 8–10 i, 5 may evidence the resolution of this diphthong through a suffixed /i/ vowel, which kind of resolution of diphthongs occurs in RH.³²⁷ It seems possible, however, that הוה is, as Kutscher has suggested, another word like הוּא, הֹוֶה, or an abbreviated version of the interjection in Amos 5:16 הוֹ־הוֹ.³²⁸ The example of מבואי

מה- (instead of יהם- or יהמה-) on nouns with the plural -*ōt* ending; the short forms of the 3mp suffix are much more common on nouns ending in -*ōt* in the DSS than the longer forms, as in the MT.

322. Qimron, *HDSS*, 34.
323. Ben-Ḥayyim, *Grammar of Samaritan Hebrew*, 202.
324. For the Samaritan Hebrew example, see Qimron, *HDSS*, 34.
325. For example, Qimron (*HDSS*, 35) suggests שקוי "strong drink" in 1QHᵃ XIII, 36 and 37 (MT abs. שִׁקּוּי) implies the pronunciation *šiqquwi*. It seems easier to assume a pronunciation akin to that of the MT form: *šiqqūy*. The parallel text in 4Q429 3, 7 and 9 preserves שקוי for the first attestation and שק[וי]י for the second (see Schuller, DJD 29:187–89). The second spelling might represent *šiqqūyī* "my drink."
326. Qimron, *HDSS*, 35.
327. See ibid. and his summary of the issue. Moshe Bar-Asher has a similar understanding of the form מבואי in 4Q405 ("Two Phenomena in Qumran Hebrew: Synchronic and Diachronic Aspects" [Hebrew], *Meghillot* 1 [2003]: 173).
328. Kutscher, *Isaiah*, 229.

is perhaps only a mistake influenced by the preceding use of the plural construct of מבוא (that is, מבואי) in the immediately preceding line, more or less directly above the word in question, as well as by the preceding and following words which are both masculine plural nouns in construct (פתחי ... ושערי), not to mention the occurrence of similar phrases such as לפתחי מבואי ... עם כול מוצאי "for the doors of the entrances of ... with all the exits of..." (11Q17 X, 7–8) in other parts of the same work.[329] As for גואי in 4Q491 8–10 i, 5, Qimron asserts that it should be considered not the plural construct (as evidenced in the parallel construction in 1QM XIV, 7, גויי), but rather the singular construct since the preceding verb is in the singular (where the parallel passages in 1QM has a plural verb). However, the simplest explanation to the disparities between these passages, I believe, is to see the singular verb as a mistake and the word גואי reflecting *gōʾē* "peoples of." On the other hand, if Qimron is right, *aleph* is a glide or epenthetic consonant between two vowels, just as one sees an *aleph*, functioning as a glide or epenthetic consonant, interpose itself after the /u/ vowel and before the *yodh* in the passive participle ראואי in 4Q394 [4QMMT] 3–7 ii, 1 and 13.[330] Another example of this phonetic shift may be אוביך "your enemies" from 1QIsa[a] (at Isa 62:8, =*ʾōbekā* [?]), though the spelling might simply reflect an ancient misreading of *waw* for *yodh* = *איביך.[331]

The shortening of -*wū* to -*ū* is found only in the 3mp imperfect of הוה: יהו "may they be" (4Q448 II, 7). Note the similar form in the Mishnah and other Rabbinic writings for the third plural imperfect (יְהוּא).[332] These forms presumably derive from Aramaic, where the earlier form, *yihwū*, is found in an Egyptian Aramaic text from around the fifth or fourth centuries B.C.E.: יהוו (ATNS 26, 6).[333] Qimron draws attention to

329. Newsom, on the other hand, observes that the word could also be read מבואו and the last *waw* explained as dittography, though she prefers what she calls the "simplest" solution which is to read מבואי and understand the spelling as "a combined historical/phonetic orthography" (DJD 11:359).

330. Qimron cites the parallel with Samaritan Hebrew *guwwi* (*HDSS*, 35).

331. See the discussion of this word and related forms in the subsection "Explanation of the DSS Forms" in §4.4, "*Aleph* < *Yodh* and *Yodh* < *Aleph*."

332. By contrast, sometimes it was written *plene*, as found in a Bar Kokhba-era text (שיהוו 5/6 Ḥev 44 16). Note that the form under discussion is distinct from the 3ms shortened imperfect in Eccl 11:3 יְהוּא.

333. See J. B. Segal, *Aramaic Texts from North Saqqâra with Some Fragments in Phoenician* (Texts from Excavations 6; London: Egypt Exploration Society, 1983), 41, text 26, 6.

the same phenomenon attested in the MT with the root חוה where a 3mp imperfect or *waw*-consecutive imperfect is spelled with a single *waw* in the written tradition יִשְׁתַּחֲוֻ (Gen 27:29), וַיִּשְׁתַּחֲוֻ (Gen 43:28), and וַיִּשְׁתַּחֲוּ (1 Kgs 9:9).[334] In these cases, one wonders if such shortening is not due to a phonetic rule, but rather due to confusion over the root consonants.

334. Qimron, "Diphthongs and Glides," 269.

5
Morphology

5.1. Prothetic *Aleph*

In rare cases, an *aleph* appears prefixed to a noun that often appears without it; the nouns that sometimes attest this *aleph* begin with a consonant + shewa. Presumably, the *aleph* functions to break up a word-initial consonant cluster. In the MT the *aleph* is usually followed by a *seghol* (less often *hiriq*), as in אֶתְמוֹל, אֶתְמוּל, אִתְּמוֹל, "yesterday," which occur eight times, versus תְּמוֹל, which occurs twenty-three times, and אֶזְרוֹעַ "arm," which occurs twice, whereas זְרוֹעַ occurs sixty-eight times.[1] Often, it seems, that the *aleph* appears before nouns that are themselves preceded by a preposition or other particle.[2]

Qimron finds this *aleph* in four words.[3] A fifth example is אתמול "yesterday" (4Q251 8, 4 [versus תמול in 4Q366 1, 2]). In three of the five cases, the *aleph* is followed by what would be a consonant + shewa in the MT (אזרוע "arm" in 11Q19 XX, 16 and passim; אשאול "Sheol" in 11Q5 [11QPs[a]] at Ps 141:7; and אתמול). In one case the prothetic *aleph* appears before the word בית "house," as אבית (1QpHab XI, 6).[4] Although the word

1. See Joüon-Muraoka §17a. They feel that the *aleph* was probably not pronounced, though it is difficult to be certain.

2. This happens for אתמול in six of the eight occurrences (1 Sam 10:11, 14:21, 19:7, 2 Sam 5:2, Isa 30:33, Mic 2:8) and for אזרוע in both its occurrences (Jer 32:31 and Job 31:22). Where אתמול is not preceded directly by a particle, the *aleph* separates two *taws* (אתמול is preceded by זאת in 1 Sam 4:7) or stands after a noun in a formulaic phrase (כיום in Ps 90:4).

3. Qimron, *HDSS*, 39.

4. This is also found in the Aramaic of the DSS, 4Q197 4 i, 16, as well as in a Hebrew letter from the Bar Kochba era (Mur. 42, 4), in addition to throughout the Tosefta (e.g., *t. ʿErub.* 8:13; *t. Soṭah* 2:3) and Babylonian Talmud (*b. B. Qam.* 63a; *b. Bek.* 7b).

"house" does not begin with a consonant + shewa, it is best to understand this construction as deriving from an earlier בבית, to which the *aleph* was prefixed.[5] The vocalization of אבדני "forms of" in 1QM V, 6 is unclear.[6] In addition, as in the MT, the words are often preceded by a particle or a word in construct with it. The word אזרוע is frequently preceded by the definite article (4Q524 6–13, 6; 11Q19 XX, 16; 11Q20 IV, 26; V, 3), or another particle (כיא in 4Q171 1–2 ii, 23 and ב in 11Q15 4, 1 [in a broken context]), while אשאול is preceded by לפי, and אתמול by מן. The word אבדני is not preceded by a particle and may, in fact, be due to dittography from the preceding phrase: אבני חפץ "desirous stones." The word אבית seems to have become its own frozen expression and was used in any position. The words largely derive from DSS-SP9 and DSS-SP1c texts.

Qimron asserts that the word "Sheol" was always pronounced as "*ešʾol*" (even where no prothetic *aleph* is present) based on the fact that we would otherwise expect the spelling of the word (שאול) to have varied, as is the case with ראש "head" (spelled ראש, רואש, ראוש, רוש) or מאד "much" (spelled מאד, מאדה, מאוד, מאודה, מואדה, מוד, מודה).[7] The many words that are consistently spelled with the sequence *aleph* + *waw mater*, where an /o/ or /u/ class vowel follows the *aleph* and the preceding vowel is a full vowel or muttered vowel suggest that this is not the case. The word שאול, "Sheol" in its consistent placement of the *waw mater*, simply follows the spelling convention outlined in "Digraphs" (§3.5). The variation in spelling for words like ראש and מאד is due to the lack of a vowel preceding the /o/ vowel. The parallel that Qimron makes to the Samaritan Hebrew oral tradition where prothetic *aleph* appears, though it is often unmarked in the written tradition, seems unlikely given the few examples we have from the DSS and the parallel alternative forms one finds in the MT that presume truly distinct pronunciations (אֶתְמוֹל versus תְּמוֹל).

5. See Pérez Fernández, *Introductory Grammar*, 160; Muraoka, *GQA*, 21; E. Y. Kutscher, "Canaanite, Hebrew, Phoenician, Aramaic, Mishnaic Hebrew, Punic" (Hebrew), *Leshonenu* 33 (1969): 108; Ben-Ḥayyim, "Traditions in the Hebrew Language," 205.

6. The regular form of the word, which is always plural and either in construct with a following word or followed by a possessive suffix, is without an initial *aleph* בדני (e.g., 1QM V, 9).

7. See Qimron, *HDSS*, 39. The word שאול occurs at least twenty times in the nonbiblical scrolls and over fifty times in the biblical scrolls.

In addition to these DSS words, there are words that habitually attest an initial *aleph*. Whether this is for the same phonetic purpose of breaking up an initial consonant cluster or whether the *aleph* functions as a nominal prefix (like *mem* and *taw*) is hard to determine. In either case, the Hebrew of the DSS attests words with this initial *aleph* among the nonbiblical texts. Most are known from the MT: אגרוף "fist" (4Q230 1, 3 and 4Q271 5 i, 3); אזכרה "memorial" (11Q19 VIII, 10); אזרח "native" (1QSa I, 6 and passim); אכזרי "cruel" (1QS IV, 9 and passim); אפרוח "young one" (4Q392 6–9, 5 and twice in 11Q19 LXV, 3); אצבע "finger" (1QS XI, 2); אשמורה/אשמור "watch" (1QS X, 2; 4Q260 II, 1; 4Q437 2 i, 16); אתנם "wages" (4Q166 II, 18), for what would be אֶתְנַן in the MT (see the discussion in "Phonemic Inventory" [§4.1]); though some are not found in the MT like אמצע "middle" (11Q19 XXX, 9), a word found frequently in RH. The biblical texts evidence other words also found in the MT, like אבנט "girdle" (4Q11 [4QpaleoGen–Exod^{l}] at Exod 28:40).

5.2. Pronouns and Particles

The Hebrew pronouns of the DSS largely overlap with the pronouns found in the MT. The common relative pronouns are identical (אשר, ש, זו), as are the interrogative/indefinite pronouns (אי "where," מי "who," מה "what").[8] Various other related pronouns and particles are also found that have parallels in the MT, like אי־זה "which" in 4Q268 1, 2 (= MT אֵי־זֶה); איה "where" in 4Q364 9a–b, 11 (quoting Gen 38:21, where the MT has אַיֵּה); איך "how" in 1QH^{a} VII, 34 and passim (= MT אֵיךְ); איכה "how" in 1QH^{a} VII, 27 and passim (= MT אֵיכָה); איככה "how" in 4Q453 1 (= MT אֵיכָכָה); אנה "to where" in 4Q177 10–11, 9 (quoting Ps 13:3, where the MT has אָנָה); איפה "where" in 1Q27 1 i, 11 and 4Q467 1 + 2, 3 (= MT אֵיפֹה); מתי "when" in 4Q385 2, 9 and passim (= MT מָתַי). One finds Aramaic forms for some of these particles in 1QIsa^{a} היכה "how?" (e.g., 1QIsa^{a} at Isa 1:21; compare היככה "how?" 4Q223–224 2 iv, 5 and passim) and הכן "indeed" (1QIsa^{a} at Isa 40:7).

Like the above pronouns, the prepositions are almost identical to their analogs in the MT, even where suffixes are added. One exception is המן

8. The relative ש is spelled שא in 4QMMT (4Q394 3–7 i, 5, 29; 3–7 ii, 14; 4Q396 1–2 i, 3).

"from" (4Q386 1 ii, 4); the construction is common with suffixes in RH, but occurs here alone without suffixes.[9]

Demonstrative

The demonstrative pronouns in the Hebrew of the DSS are largely identical to those in the MT. The range of simple (that is, without affix) singular pronouns found in the MT (masc.: זֶה, fem.: זֹה, זֹו, זֹאת; masc./fem.: זוּ)[10] seem mostly to be attested in the DSS. Although the orthography prevents us from being certain whether זֹו or זוּ existed in 4Q381 31, 1 and 44, 2, the quotation or allusion to Ps 9:16 (ברשת זו טמ[נו] = MT בְּרֶשֶׁת זוּ טָמָנוּ) in the former passage suggests that this is the demonstrative זו (corresponding to MT זוּ) used as a relative.[11]

The consonants זה usually reflect what corresponds to MT זֶה, though the feminine זה (= MT זֹה) is attested in 4Q109 (4QQoh[a]) at Qoh 5:15. The feminine זאת is attested in various spellings including זאת (1QH[a] XII, 30); זואת (1QS IX, 20); זאות (11Q19 VIII, 10); זות (1QH[a] XX, 35).[12] In addition, the DSS contain another demonstrative in 4Q371 1a–b, 8, read as זן or זך, corresponding to Aramaic דֵּן or דֵּךְ. The sequence of rare demonstratives in the MT that include a prefixed *heh* and *lamedh*, הַלָּז, הַלָּזֶה, הַלֵּזוּ, are only partially attested in the biblical scrolls: [ה]לז (4Q113 [4QDan[b]] at Dan 8:16); [ה]לזו (Mas 1d at Ezek 36:35). As in the MT, the third-person independent pronouns also function as demonstratives, often with the prefixed definite article: ההוא, ההואה, ההיא, ההיאה, ההמה.

In the MT, there are two plural demonstratives, אֵל and אֵלֶּה, the latter being the more common. In the DSS, there are just two clear attestations of אל, only in biblical scrolls, in each case where the MT has אֵלֶּה (4Q129 [4QPhyl B] at Deut 5:22 and 5Q1 [5QDeut] at Deut 7:17). By contrast, in three places where the MT has אֵל, the DSS text has אלה

9. See Moshe Bar-Asher, "המן (= מן) in a Fragment from Qumran" (Hebrew), *Leshonenu* 55 (1990): 75.

10. The form זֹאתָה from Jer 26:6 is excluded.

11. The second passage reads כי ארץ זו הגברת "for you strengthened this land."

12. Note also the spelling זת in a phylactery (XHev/Se 5 2, 4, 5 at Exod 13:5, 10, 14). The spelling זאת is, overall, the most common spelling, though זואת in the nonbiblical scrolls is more common than זאת. The spelling זאות is less common in both the biblical and nonbiblical scrolls.

(11Q1 [11QpaleoLev[a]] at Lev 18:27; 4Q33 [4QDeut[f]] at Deut 7:22; 4Q38a [4QDeut[k2]] at Deut 19:11).

Personal Pronouns

As many summaries of DSS Hebrew note, the orthographic representation of the independent personal pronouns and pronominal suffixes and/or their phonetic realization are distinct from those of the MT. The independent pronouns are described by both Qimron and Abegg, so I limit my comments to the most important features. The references to relative frequencies concern the nonbiblical manuscripts (unless otherwise indicated), since biblical manuscripts tend to mimic the biblical text. The pronunciation of the suffixes with MT-like short forms and alternative long forms ending with a *heh mater* are discussed together at the end of this section, in the subsection titled "General Comments."

First Person

The first-person singular independent pronoun is usually אני; where אנוכי and אנכי occur in nonbiblical texts the antecedent is God.[13] The plural pronouns אנו and אנחנו occur with about the same frequency, though the occurrences of the latter are concentrated in 4QMMT. The suffixed versions of these pronouns are as they occur in the MT, with at least one exception for the plural: אבתינא (4Q381 46a + b, 4), which is similar to the Aramaic pronominal suffix.

Second Person

The second-person masculine singular independent pronoun is almost always אתה, while the 2fs is not attested among the nonbiblical scrolls and appears as את among the biblical scrolls and אתי in 1QIsa[a] (at Isa 51:9, 10, 12). The form אתי occurs, as Kutscher notes, in some passages of the MT, as a *kethib*, and is more common in Aramaic.[14] The 2mp in the scrolls is אתם and אתמה, the former occurring slightly more often than the latter

13. See Qimron, *HDSS*, 57 and Abegg, "Hebrew of the Dead Sea Scrolls," 330.

14. Kutscher, *Isaiah*, 208. For a listing of the forms of the 2fs pronoun with the *kethib* form אַתְּי, see GKC §32h.

in both the biblical and nonbiblical scrolls. The two pronouns occur in the same texts (e.g., 1QM XVII, 2 and 8; 4Q185 1–2 i, 9 and 1–2 ii, 7).

As mentioned above in "*Plene* Orthography" (§3.2), the 2ms pronominal suffix is often written with a *heh mater* (כה-).[15] In some instances, however, the suffix appears without the *heh*, even where preceding forms have the *heh*, as in 1QM XIX, 3: תן ידכה בעורף אויביך "set your hand on the neck of your enemies."[16] Qimron argues that the spelling of certain singular forms with a *yodh mater* between the noun and suffix indicates that the suffix was usually articulated with penultimate accent.[17] Many of the examples are debateable, as perhaps reflecting plural forms (e.g., מותריכה "your excess" or "your excesses" 4Q417 2 i, 17) or dittography (בעוזביכה "when you abandon" in 4Q460 9 i, 8, right before אלוהיכה "your God"). Nevertheless, some forms certainly reflect singulars, as with רעיכה "your friend" (4Q417 2 ii + 23, 7; 4Q525 14 ii, 21; 4Q129 [4QPhyl B] at Deut 5:20, for MT רֵעֶךָ) and the alternative spellings of the singular ריעיכה (11Q19 LIV, 20), רעיך (4Q41 [4QDeut^{n}] and 4Q134 [4QPhyl G] at Deut 5:20). In other words, it seems that the standard form for "your friend" in the DSS-SP9 texts was similar to (if not identical with) the pausal form found in the MT רֵעֶךָ (Deut 5:21). Note also the same spelling in 4Q41, which is DSS-NSP. It stands to reason that many of the 2ms pronouns (especially in DSS-SP9 texts) were articulated in a similar way (perhaps sometimes as *-akā* for prepositions, compare pausal אִתָּכָה in MT at Exod 29:35) even if this is not always revealed in the spelling of words.[18] This does not imply, however, that the 2ms pronoun could not be articulated as *-əkā*, especially for the scribes writing/reading the DSS-NSP texts. Notice also that the 2ms suffix on *qal* imperfect verbs tends to follow the pattern *yqṭwlkh* (rather than *yqwṭlkh*), suggesting the absence of a vowel under the last root consonant.

The 2fs suffix is often simply (ך-), like the simple form of the masculine suffix. In around thirty instances, however, the suffix is כי-, akin to

15. On the history of the suffix, see Richard C. Steiner, "From Proto-Hebrew to Mishnaic Hebrew: The History of ךָ- and הָ-," *HAR* 3 (1979): 157–74.

16. Note that although this passage seems to echo some of the language of Gen 49:8 where the suffix is spelled without *heh*, the inconsistency in spelling of the suffix is not always connected with a biblical text: e.g., מידכה versus ממשלותך in 4Q369 3, 3–4 and מדבריך vs. בבריתכה in 3Q382 104, 1.

17. Qimron, "Studies in the Hebrew of the Dead Sea Scrolls," 79–92.

18. Ibid., 88.

the corresponding Aramaic suffix, attested in Imperial and DSS Aramaic.[19] That the pronunciation of the suffix when spelled כי- was something similar to that preserved in Biblical Aramaic (-*ēkī*) is implied in the spellings וגאליכי *wəgō'ălēkī* "and your redeemer" (4Q176 8–11, 7) and מאתיכי *mē'ittēkī* "from you" (4Q176 8–11, 12). Since the suffix (or at least the consonants corresponding to it) is also found in the Hebrew portions of the MT (2 Kgs 4:3, 7, Jer 11:15, Ps 103:4–7 [six times], 116:7 [twice], 19, 137:6), it might be argued that this represents an early form of the Hebrew suffix and this is possible, since etymologically the Hebrew suffix was -*ki*.[20] All the same, the occurrences in the MT come primarily from later texts, when Aramaic was in ascendancy, and it is conceivable that they are due to Aramaic influence too. Some of the occurrences of the suffix in the DSS might be attributable to the presence of the suffix in the common (original?) Hebrew text; for example, the suffix כי- appears in 4Q84 (4QPs[b]) at Ps 116:19 in the same place where it occurs in the MT ([בתוכ]כי "in your midst" for MT בְּתוֹכֵכִי). This cannot explain, however, the concentration of occurrences of this suffix in 1QIsa[a] (twenty-one occurrences); together with other factors, this concentration points to Aramaic influence.[21]

The second-person plural pronominal suffix is restricted to the masculine and is either כם- or כמה-, the latter appearing most commonly in 11Q19 and 11Q20. Again, there is variation from one line to the next; the form without *heh* appears once in 1QM X, 3 and the form with *heh* appears twice in the very next line. Abegg lists variant forms as כהם- and יכהמה- (on masculine plural nouns), though these are probably just due to scribal mistake.[22] The first one appears in 4Q427 7 ii, 16; the scribe wrote רחמיכה "your mercy" and then added a final *mem* and cancellation dots to indicate רחמים. The second example occurs in 11Q19 XLVIII, 10 in אלוהיכהמה "your God," where the scribe seems to have become confused between the forms אלוהיכה in line 7 and אלוהיכמה in line 8.

19. See Muraoka, *GQA*, 43–44. The Aramaic suffix, according to Muraoka, was, in the era of the DSS, "in a state of transition" and was losing this final vowel and is attested a few times written simply ך- (*GQA*, 43).

20. See *HGhS*, 255 k'.

21. Kutscher, *Isaiah*, 210–12 and Abegg, "Linguistic Profile," 41.

22. See Abegg, "Hebrew of the Dead Sea Scrolls," 333.

Third Person

The third-person masculine and feminine singular independent pronouns have the forms they do in the MT, הוא and היא; they also occur with a final *heh mater* הואה, היאה. The forms with a final *heh* are less frequent than the forms without *heh* and seem to be concentrated in certain texts, most prominently 1QS. Here again, there is much variation within individual texts, even from line to line (e.g., 4Q266 6 i, 8 and 11). The *qere perpetuum* of the 3fs suffix הִוא, attested in the Torah books of the MT, is also presumed in the editions of two DSS and one slightly later text from Masada: Mas1b (MasLev[b]) at Lev 10:17 and 11:6; 4Q26 (4QLev[d]) at Lev 17:11; and 8Q3 (8QPhyl) at Deut 11:10 (in each case where the MT has the *qere perpetuum*). Of these, only the word in Mas1b at Lev 10:17 is clearly legible in the photograph, though it is written interlinearly and is, thus, smaller than the other words. This scroll is particularly close to the textual tradition evidenced in the MT, but the reading of the pronoun is still suspect. The cause of this *qere perpetuum* in the MT is, according to Joüon-Muraoka, "a certain late recension of the Pentateuch," the scribes of which, unable to distinguish the *waw* from a *yodh*, copied the pronoun as though it were (almost) always *waw*.[23] Given the similarity between *waws* and *yodhs* in Mas1b, one wonders if we are justified in seeing here the earliest evidence of this *qere perpetuum* phenomenon.

The plural independent pronouns are as they appear in the MT, with the masculine showing two possible forms: הם, המה and the feminine just one הנה. For the masculine, the forms with *heh* are slightly more frequent than the forms without, but both occur together in individual texts (e.g., 1QH[a] X, 25 and 31). The feminine occurs extremely rarely.

The third-person pronominal suffixes are also attested with some regularity. For the 3ms, the forms follow, more or less, the paradigms found in the MT, where the suffix is ו- on singular nouns except etymological III-*waw*/*yodh* words where the suffix is הו- (שדהו "his field" 4Q158 10–12,

23. Joüon-Muraoka §39Ac. They note that in the MT there are eleven exceptions where the 3fs pronoun is spelled with a *yodh*. For another opinion, that הִוא in the MT Pentateuch reflects either *hū* or *hīw*, see Steven E. Fassberg, "The *Kethiv/Qere* הִוא, Diachrony, and Dialectology," in *Diachrony in Biblical Hebrew* (ed. Cynthia L. Miller-Naudé and Ziony Zevit; LSAWS 8; Winona Lake, Ind.: Eisenbaruns, 2012), 171–80.

7 and passim).[24] If the word מעש׳הו "his deed" in 1QIsa[a] at Isa 5:19 (for MT מַעֲשֵׂהוּ) is read correctly, then this suggests a pronunciation of the suffix akin to that of the MT, *-ēhū*.[25] On plural nouns the suffix is usually יו-, though occasionally it is written defectively, מעשו "his works" (1QS VI, 17) and מצוותו "his commandments" (4Q266 2 i, 4), as observed above in "Diphthongs and Triphthongs" (§4.10), where we have postulated the contraction *-āw* > *-ō* in many of these forms. In that same section, we have also addressed the shift *-īhū* > *-īyū* associated with the 3ms suffix on short nouns like אב, אח, פה.

In some relatively rare cases the 3ms pronominal suffix on plural nouns appears as it does in Aramaic, והי-. The exact number of instances and where they occur is debated. Qimron, along with many other scholars, sees the Aramaic והי- suffix in certain Hebrew words among the nonbiblical scrolls (e.g., ועינוהי "and his eyes" 1QS V, 5; עלוהי "over him" 1QpHab XII, 11); nevertheless, Abegg, as well as some earlier scholars, read these as יהו- (ועיניהו; עליהו).[26] Abegg, however, does recognize this Aramaic suffix as occurring some sixteen times in 1QIsa[a] (e.g., מעשוהי "his works" at Isa 10:12 for MT מַעֲשֵׂהוּ).[27]

A similar kind of ambiguity pertains to the spelling ה- for the 3ms suffix on singular nouns in various passages like בה בדרשה "by him when he examines" (4Q266 8 i, 2, for an expected בו בדרשו which occurs in CD XV, 11).[28] It is conceivable that the *heh* represents the old Hebrew

---

24. Note, however, the exceptional form שדו "his field" in 4Q396 (4QMMT) 1–2, iv, 7 and עושו "his maker" (4Q299 3a ii–b, 7 and 8).

25. Note the apparent anomaly of משניו "his second" (4Q405 11, 3) for what would be in the MT מִשְׁנֵהוּ.

26. Qimron, *HDSS*, 61. Qimron notes that this Aramaic suffix also occurs once in the MT תַּגְמוּלוֹהִי (Ps 116:12). In addition, e.g., Qimron and Charlesworth ("Rule of the Community," passim) mostly follow Qimron, as does *DSSSE* and Joosten ("Hebrew, Aramaic, Greek," 359). Abegg, "Hebrew of the Dead Sea Scrolls," 332–33.

27. Abegg, "Linguistic Profile," 41; Kutscher, *Isaiah*, 211.

28. See Joseph M. Baumgarten, *Qumran Cave 4.XIII: The Damascus Document (4Q266–273)* (DJD 18; Oxford: Clarendon, 1996), 30, who lists several cases. Gregory L. Doudna evaluates these and considers the words above to exhibit examples of the 3ms suffix, together with אפה (4Q266 2 ii, 21) and דעתה (8 i, 6); the case of לחללה (5 ii, 6) is ambiguous (*4Q Pesher Nahum: A Critical Edition* [JSPSup 35; London: Sheffield Academic, 2001], 133 n. 163). Doudna finds other possible examples of this suffix in חירה "its hole" (4Q169 3–4 i, 6 in a quotation of Nah 2:13), [ח]ילה (3–4 iii, 10), and [מ]לחמתה (3–4 iii, 11) (ibid., 134–35, 524–25). The form of טרפה in 4Q169 3–4 i, 6 and 9 less likely contains the 3ms suffix (ibid., 154–55).

suffix -*ō*, seen approximately fifty times in the MT, but it is also possible it represents the Aramaic 3ms suffix -*ēh*. Cases like בוה (4Q128 [4QPhylA] at Exod 12:43, 44; in 4Q140 [4QPhyl M] at Exod 13:3) for MT בּוֹ "in it," in addition to cases like [רע]ה (4Q22 [4QpaleoExod^{m}] at Exod 32:17) for MT רֵעֹה "his friend" and כלה (1QIsa[a] at Isa 15:3; 1Q8 [1QIsa[b]] at Isa 16:7) for MT כֻּלֹּה "all of it" suggest that the ה- suffix in nonbiblical scrolls reflects Hebrew -*ō*.[29]

The 3fs pronoun is usually, as in the MT, represented by a single *heh*, as in בה "in it" (1QS IV, 6 = MT בָּהּ) and כמוה "like it" (1QM I, 12 = MT כָּמוֹהָ). Occasionally, however, the 3fs suffix is represented by an initial *heh* and a following *mater* (either *heh* or *aleph*) when the corresponding form of the MT pronoun presupposes -*hā*, as in כמוהה "like it" (1QM XVIII, 10); חטותיהא "her sins" (4Q176 1–2 i, 6), quoting Isa 40:2, for MT חַטֹּאותֶיהָ; ומאצילהא "and from its sides" (4Q176 1–2 i, 10), quoting Isa 41:9, for MT וּמֵאֲצִילֶיהָ; יתנהה "he will (not) give her" (4Q271 3, 9, compare וְאֶתְּנֶהָ 1 Kgs 14:8); עליהא (1QIsa[a] at Isa 34:11, and passim).[30] In rare cases, the combination הא- is used in 1QIsa[a] even where we would expect, based on the paradigm in the MT, just ה- (= -*āh*), as in כיתבהא "write it" (1QIsa[a] at Isa 30:8) for MT כָּתְבָהּ; and בהא "in it" (at Isa 34:10, 11, 62:4, 66:10) for MT בָּהּ. This is presumably related to the use of הא- to mark word-final /ā/ in this text (היהא 1QIsa[a] at Isa 5:1, 12:2 for MT הָיָה and וַיְהִי, respectively), as well as very rarely in a few other texts, like דעהא "knowledge" (1QS VII, 4 = MT דֵּעָה); עתהא "now" (4Q175 11, quoting Num 24:17, for MT עַתָּה); חופהא "canopy" (4Q321a V, 7 = MT חֻפָּה).[31] Alternatively, the suffix in 1QIsa[a] could be due to analogy with the Aramaic 3fs suffix -*ahā*

29. Note also רעה (4Q258 II, 2 and perhaps 3) for *רעהו (found in lines 4 and 5); דוקוה (4Q321a V, 5) for *דוקו (found in IV, 8 and V, 8); לוה (4Q138 [4QPhyl K] at Deut 10:18) for MT לוֹ; עלמה (4Q52 [4QSam[b]] at 1 Sam 20:38) for MT הַנַּעַר, but reflecting a tradition also found in certain Septuagint texts which contain παιδαρίου αὐτοῦ (see Ulrich et al., *Biblical Qumran Scrolls*, 280); אותוה (1QIsa[a] at Isa 36:21) for MT אֹתוֹ; חיקוה (1QIsa[a] at Isa 40:11) for MT חֵיקוֹ; כוחוה (1QIsa[a] at Isa 63:1) for MT כֹּחוֹ. A similar use of וא- as a digraph to mark /ō/ is found occasionally, as in לוא (1QIsa[a] at Isa 57:18) for MT לוֹ and עמוא (1QIsa[a] at Isa 63:11) for MT עַמּוֹ; see §3.5, "Digraphs." See also Ian Young, "Observations on the Third Masculine Singular Pronominal Suffix -*h* in Hebrew Biblical Texts," *HS* 42 (2001): 225–42.

30. Note the reverse sequence of letters in עליאה "upon it" (4Q369 1 ii, 3) due to metathesis.

31. See Kutscher, *Isaiah*, 185; and "Digraphs" above (§3.5). Note also the examples of והיאה (1QIsa[a] at Isa 65:10) and היאה (2Q13 [2QJer] at Jer 48:27) in each case

(as in Onkelos) or due to the retention of a historical vowel between the noun and suffix.[32]

The third-person masculine plural pronominal suffixes are either ם- or מה- on verbs and singular nouns, while הם- and המה- appear on plural nouns. Both sets of pronouns appear on monosyllabic and bisyllabic prepositions. In each case, the form with a final *heh mater* is less common than its partner form. Again, both forms occur in individual texts (בם and במה in 4Q265 4 i, 8 and 4 i, 10, respectively; להם and להמה in 1QM VIII, 2 and IX, 6, respectively).[33] On plural nouns that bear an *-ōt* ending in the DSS, the suffixes without initial *heh* (ם-, מה-) seem to alternate with suffixes with initial *heh* (יהם-, יהמה-), just as in the MT, with certain words and/or texts showing an affinity for one set of pronouns over another.[34]

---

for MT הָיָה, which suggests an analogous use of אה- (if the letters היאה do not represent the 3fs independent pronoun).

32. See Qimron, "Studies in the Hebrew of the Dead Sea Scrolls," 83–85 for other possible examples of words that retain a historical vowel.

33. Qimron points out that on verbal forms that end in a high vowel (/i/ or /u/; e.g., קטלתי and קטלו), only the short form of the suffix is found; he asserts "such consistency implies that our texts reflect a living language" ("History of Early Hebrew," 355). There are, e.g., fourteen examples of the 1cs perfect verb with the 3mp suffix and twenty-two cases of the 3cp perfect with the 3mp suffix. Although Qimron is right that there are no exceptions to this rule, it should be remembered that of the around 450 instances where the 3mp suffix occurs on all finite verbs (i.e., not only 1cs and 3cp), the long form (מה-) occurs only ten times: 1QH[a] V, 27 and 29; 4Q174 4, 6; 4Q292 2, 3; 4Q416 2 iii, 17; 11Q13 II, 6; 11Q19 XXVI, 12; LV, 21; LXIV, 11 (corrected) and 14. Thus, it would seem that the short form is dominant on all finite verb forms, no matter the final vowel.

34. Steiner suggests that for Tiberian Hebrew the suffixed pronouns had allomorphs, one for words ending in a vowel *-hū*, *-hā*, … *-hem*, etc., and one used for words ending in a consonant, *-āh* … *-ām*, etc. ("Ancient Hebrew," 153–54). The same held for plural nouns. But, at some point (presumably in the Iron Age) the suffix *-ēhem* (made up of the resolved diphthong from the earlier oblique dual ending, *-ē-*, plus the 3mp *-hem*) was "reanalyzed" as a complete suffix and thus was used on certain words that ended in a consonant, like the word for daughters בְּנוֹתֵיהֶם. This happened only with some nouns; the word for fathers, e.g., still took the *-ām* suffix (i.e., אֲבֹתָם). For the alternation in the form of the suffixes, note, e.g., מחשבותם (1QH[a] V, 26; X, 19; XII, 15, 20; 4Q430 1, 2 [partially preserved]; Jer 6:19, Ps 56:6, Lam 3:60, 61) but מחשבותיהמ(ה) (1QIsa[a] and MT at Isa 59:7, 65:2, 66:18); עצמותמ(ה) (1Q34bis 3 i, 3; 11Q19 LI, 4; Ezek 32:27, Mic 3:2) but עצמותיהם (Num 24:8, 1 Sam 31:13, Mic 3:3). For more on the variation in these pronouns on feminine plural nouns, see Moshe Bar-Asher, "The Language of Qumran: Between Biblical and Mishnaic Hebrew (A Study

According to Qimron, the same *-ām* suffix occurs with *waw* as ום-, but his examples are ambiguous.[35] If these are cases of the 3mp suffix, it is possible to interpret the *waw* as caused by the following *mem*, akin to the *waw* that appears in other words where MT forms have only a *qamets*. The spelling עליהום in 4Q176 20, 3 is probably due to Aramaic influence, as is [על]יהן "over them" (4Q277 1 ii, 7) and אביהן "their father" (4Q17 [4QExod–Lev^f] at Exod 40:15).[36]

That the pronunciation of these suffixes is similar to that in the MT is suggested occasionally by the *plene* orthography in certain words: שביא[ם] "their captivity" (4Q385a 18 i a–b, 7), the *aleph* marking a preceding /ā/, for what would be in the MT *שְׁבְיָם; and ויחביאים "he hid them" (4Q382 1, 2 in a quotation or allusion to 1 Kgs 18:4 וַיַּחְבִּיאֵם).

The 3fp suffix occurs rarely, usually as הן-, though some four times as ן-.[37] It occurs once as הון- in ועליהון (1QS III, 25), corresponding to the masculine Aramaic-influenced form עליהום (note the similar mistake in Aramaic of בינהון "between them" 11Q10 XXXVI, 2, corrected to בינהן). In several cases, the 3fp suffix has the form of the 3mp suffix.

General Comments

As demonstrated above, the various second- and third-person pronouns almost all occur with and without a final *heh mater*. One question pertaining to the forms, especially אתמה/אתם, הואה/הוא, היאה/היא, then, concerns whether they reflect a common underlying pronunciation with final *-ā*, sometimes represented graphically, sometimes not, or whether they represent two different pronunciations, one with final *-ā*, and one without. There is no definitive answer to this, but two factors suggest the existence of alternative pronunciations. First, the fact that one can find

---

in Morphology)," *Meghillot* 2 (2004): 137–49 and idem, "Qumran Hebrew Between Biblical and Mishnaic Hebrew: A Morphological Study," in *The Dynamics of Language and Exegesis at Qumran* (ed. Devorah Dimant and Reinhard G. Kratz; FAT^2 35; Tübingen: Mohr Siebeck, 2009), 3–17.

35. See the discussion in "*Waw* Marking /u/ Class Vowel in Nouns Where MT Has No /u/ Class Vowel" (§5.4). According to Qimron, these occur in רוחום (1QS IX, 14); הונ(ו)ם (1QS V, 20); בואום (1QSa I, 4).

36. The Aramaic of the DSS attests both the older form of the suffix with *mem*, מנהם "some of them" (4Q112 [4QDan^a] at Dan 2:41) for MT מִנְּהֵון, as well as the more recent form with *nun*, עמהון "with them" (1Q20 XXII, 1).

37. Abegg, "Hebrew of the Dead Sea Scrolls," 334.

varying realizations of pronouns in the MT (e.g., פִּיהוּ and פִּיו in Exod 4:15 and הֵם and הֵמָּה in Gen 42:35), which reflect different pronunciations, suggests that the DSS could also have preserved a similar variation in pronouns.[38] A similar assumption is made by Muraoka for similar Aramaic pronouns that exhibit long and short forms.[39] Second, one finds the 3ms independent pronoun spelled הו (3Q15 [Copper Scroll] XI, 9 and 4Q266 11, 9), which implies a pronunciation without a final *-ā*.[40]

Another question pertains to the historicity of the forms. Do they represent true Hebrew forms, that is, forms derived from earlier Semitic bases? Do they represent Aramaic influences? Or, are they entirely artificial? Morgenstern has recently written on the independent pronouns and concludes that there are clear historical bases for the long forms peculiar to the Hebrew DSS (and the Samaritan Hebrew oral tradition).[41] Nevertheless, others have suggested that they are the result of archaizing analogy; that is, the endings of historically legitimate forms like the pronoun *ʾattā*, the nominal suffix *-kā*, and the verbal suffix *-tā* were used as the model for other pronouns.[42] It is hard to be sure which explanation is right. Possibly, both are correct; that is, some forms are due to historical preservation (e.g., הואה), while others are the result of analogy (e.g., the suffixed המה-).

Aramaic influence on the pronouns is implied in aberrant forms like אבתינא "our fathers" (4Q381 46a + b, 4); עליהום "over them" (4Q176 20, 3);

38. Morgenstern, on the other hand, suggests that they could have been pronounced the same ("The System of Independent Pronouns at Qumran and the History of Hebrew in the Second Temple Period" [Hebrew], in *Shaʿarey Lashon: Studies in Hebrew, Aramaic and Jewish Languages Presented to Moshe Bar Asher, vol. 2: Mishnaic Hebrew and Aramaic* [ed. A. Maman et al.; Jerusalem: Mosad Bialik, 2007], 50, 53).

39. He writes: "When faced with mixed data in a single author, even in a single document, one needs to remember that a living language allows coexistence of alternative forms, particularly when a given feature is in a state of fluidity or transition, in the process of changing from an old form to a new alternative" (*GQA*, 43). Much the same must be true of certain dead languages, as the alternative forms of פֶּה from the MT cited above demonstrate.

40. Muraoka makes a similar point, citing הו in Mur 42 4 ("Hebrew," 1:342).

41. Morgenstern, "System of Independent Pronouns," 51, 53.

42. See, e.g., Frank Moore Cross, "Some Notes on a Generation of Qumran Studies," in vol. 1 of *The Madrid Qumran Congress, Proceedings of the International Congress on the Dead Sea Scrolls, Madrid 18–21 March 1991* (ed. Julio Trebolle Barrera and Luis Vegas Montaner; STDJ 11; 2 vols.; Leiden: Brill, 1992), 4; Fassberg, "Preference for Lengthened Forms," 229–31 and 234–36.

[על]יהן "over them" (4Q277 1 ii, 7); אביהן "their father" (4Q17 [4QExod–Lev^f] at Exod 40:15); the 2fs suffix כי- (in 1QIsa^a); the 3ms suffix on plural nouns והי- (in 1QIsa^a). Ambiguity surrounds some other cases of והי- in the nonbiblical scrolls. All things considered, therefore, the conclusion to be drawn is that Aramaic did occasionally influence the pronominal suffixes, though this is a relatively rare phenomenon. These occur in both the DSS-SP9 texts and in at least one DSS-NSP text (4Q381).

5.3. Nouns

Lexicon

Qimron's *HDSS* contains lists of nouns categorized according to whether they occur in LBH, RH, or in no other Hebrew tradition. His *Grammar* contains lists of nominal bases and the words that correspond to them. Additional nouns, not found in Qimron's lists, that appear in the scrolls include ארּרה "curse" (4Q410 1, 4 and passim); בקיע "fissure" (4Q385 6, 4); גדפן "blasphemer" (4Q387 2 ii, 8 and passim); גשר "bridge" (4Q521 7 + 5 ii, 12); דון "misery" (4Q385 4, 1); הגוי "meditation" (4Q417 1 i, 16 and passim), זידה "insolence" (1Q29 13, 4); חלמה "cement" (4Q277 1 ii, 4); חרבן "desolation" (4Q390 1, 8); יוד "*yodh*" as reference to יהוה (4Q511 10, 12);[43] מאפלה "darkness" (4Q216 V, 10); מגע "(unclean) touching" (4Q274 1 i, 8 and passim); משיכה "drawing" (4Q251 1–2, 4); נצפה "caper-bush" (4Q386 1 ii, 5); עור "chaff" (4Q433 1, 3);[44] עילול "child" (4Q169 3-4 iv, 2);[45] עכשו "now" (4Q225 2 ii, 7); צער "pain" (4Q491c 11 i, 16); קשות "cucumber" (4Q274 3 i, 9); רחש "worm" (4Q266 6 i, 8 and in a parallel

43. Unless this is due to metathesis and one should read ידו "his hand" (*DSSSE*); see Baillet, DJD 7:227.

44. See Kister, "Three Unknown Hebrew Words," 36–37.

45. The noun is also found in 4Q169 3–4 iv, 4; 1QH^a XV, 24; 1QIsa^a at Isa 13:16 (see Kutscher, *Isaiah*, 381). This word is actually in Qimron's list, but Strugnell ("Notes en marge," 208) and, more recently, Stegemann, Schuller, Newsom (DJD 40:207 n. 7) read as though these were attestations of the MT word עֹולָל, where the *qamets* has shifted to /o/ due to the following *lamedh*. However, as Qimron observes ("Waw and Yod," 110), the initial reading of Allegro (עילוליה and עילוליו) seems more likely. The base of the noun (**qīṭul*/**qīṭāl* [?]) is found in Biblical Hebrew words from II-*waw*/*yodh* and geminate roots like נִיחוֹחַ "appeasement" (from נוח) and נִיצוֹץ "spark" (from נצץ) and even with strong roots as in קִיטוֹר "fog" or "smoke." These words are usually spelled with a *yodh mater* and a *waw mater* in the DSS, as they often are in the MT

passage 4Q272 1 i, 16); רעדודיה "trembling" or "its trembling" (4Q377 2 ii, 9); שטמה "animosity" (1QM XIV, 9); שדך "ease" (4Q386 1 ii, 7).[46] These words are otherwise unknown from earlier Hebrew, but related to other nouns and/or verbs in the MT (מְאֵרָה/אָרַר "to curse"/"curse"; דָּוָה/דְּוַי "be sick"/"illness"; זָדוֹן/זֵד "insolent"/"insolence"; חָרְבָּה/ חֹרֶב "desolation"; מַאְפֵּלְיָה "darkness"), in RH (בְּקִיעַ "fissure"; גדפן "blasphemer," גֶּשֶׁר "bridge"; חלמה "cement"; יוד "yodh"; מַגָּע "touching"; מְשִׁיכָה "drawing"; נִצְפָּה "caperbush"; עַכְשָׁיו "now"; קִישׁוּת "cucumber"), and/or in Aramaic (גשר "beam" [*TAD* A2.2, 15 and passim]; דוונא "misery" [*Tg. Neb.* Jerm 8:18]; חרבן "desolation" [4Q210 1 ii, 14 and 4Q531 18,2]; עוּר "chaff" [MT at Dan 2:35]; צער "pain" [4Q530 1 i, 2]; רְחֵשׁ "worm" [*Tg. Onq.* Exod 16:20]; שְׁדַךְ "to be at ease" [*Tg. Neb.* Isa 14:7]). In other cases, the definition of the word is more conjectural or previously unknown: אוט (4Q416 2 ii, 12 and passim); בדני (1QM V, 9 and passim); דוק "new moon" or "full moon" (4Q321 II, 3 and passim); מלוש (4Q439 1 i + 2, 2); פענה (4Q381 31, 7); and תזיז (4Q386 1 ii, 5).[47]

In some cases, it is hard to decide whether a word is a previously unknown noun or an infinitive construct of a known verb used in a nominal manner, as in לוז "turning aside" (4Q424 1, 8).[48] In other cases, the relationship between an apparently new word and a previously known word is unclear. For example, פארה seems to mean "glory" in several passages (e.g., 1QH[a] XVI, 23 and passim) and is presumably connected to the word for "headdress" in the MT and RH פְּאֵר, but is commonly assumed to

---

(something unusual given the tendency in the MT for just one word-internal *mater* per word, as noted above).

46. More examples can be found in *DCH*, many of them only conjectural.

47. On the word אוט, see Tzvi Novick, "The Meaning and Etymology of אוט," *JBL* 127 (2008): 339–43 and *ThWQ*, cols. 1:84–86; on בדני, see *ThWQ*, cols. 1:366–70; on דוק, see *ThWQ*, cols. 1:659–65; on מלוש, see M. Weinfeld and D. Seely, "Lament of a Leader," in DJD 29:340 and Kister, "Three Unknown Hebrew Words," 35–36; on תזיז, see Dimant, DJD 30:64. For more recent lexical studies, see Bar-Asher, "Qumran Hebrew and Mishnaic Hebrew," 287–317; "Grammatical and Lexical Phenomena in a Dead Sea Scroll (4Q374)" (Hebrew), *Meghillot* 4 (2006): 153–67; and Kister, "Some Observations," 137–65; idem, "Lexical and Linguistic Gleanings from the Dead Sea Scrolls" (Hebrew), *Leshonenu* 67 (2004): 27–44; idem, "Some Lexical Features of the Writings from Qumran" (Hebrew) in *Qumran Scrolls and Their World*, 2:561–69.

48. Note, e.g., נוח in the phrase קול נוח (in 1QM VIII, 7 and 14). Is this the same word that appears in 2 Chr 6:41 (לְנוּחֶךָ), the parallel passage to which in Psalms (132:8) contains לִמְנוּחָתֶךָ?

be otherwise unknown. All the same, there is a graphically identical word פארה "branch" (= MT פֹּארָה) that occurs in the DSS and the MT. Could "glory" and "branch" actually be two meanings for the same word, the sense "glory" deriving metaphorically from the sense "branch," similar to how words associated with height can connote pride and/or majesty (e.g., גַּאֲוָה "majesty, pride" [compare גָּאָה to rise up] and גָּבֹהַּ "high, exalted, proud"), and similar to how tree imagery can connote pride, as with "cedars" and "oaks" in Isa 2:13?[49] Note also אשיש "man, adult" in 1QpHab VI, 11 and the ten (or more) times in 4Q502, what is labeled a "Ritual of Marriage." In both texts the word occurs in the context of נערים "youth," and in 1QpHab in the context of זקנים "elders" and נשים "women." It is undeniable that this word indicates a human person in the DSS. But, the existence of the word in the MT does not seem as well established. A word graphically identical to the DSS word, אֲשִׁישֵׁי, occurs in Isa 16:7; although *HALOT* defines it as the plural construct of the word "man," the NRSV, JPS and others translate it with the more traditional "raisin cakes of."

In still other cases, it is hard to know if a word with a clear Aramaic parallel should be considered an accidental slip of the scribe/writer or a reflection of a genuine Hebrew usage. In addition to some of the words listed above, note הטללים "the shadows" (4Q107 [4Qcant[b]] at Song 2:17) for MT הַצְּלָלִים; כידן "javelin" (e.g., 1QM V, 7); מוזנים "scales" (e.g., 4Q415 9, 11); מתקל "stumbling" (4Q525 14 ii, 26).

Etymological Bases

General features related to etymological bases and their variety in the DSS are brought up in the next few paragraphs. Further analysis of nouns and their bases are brought up in the following sections, especially as these relate to words containing a /u/ vowel: "*Waw* Marking /u/ Class Vowel in Nouns Where MT Has No /u/ Class Vowel" (§5.4) and "**quṭl* Nouns" (§5.5).

The DSS evidence nominal bases not present in the MT or only rarely found there, for example: פרוש "interpretation" (**qiṭṭūl*), כלל "all" (**qəṭāl*),

---

49. Note how the two words seem to occur in similar contexts: "the planting (מטע) of their trees is according to the level of the sun … to the bough (פארת) of honor" (1QH[a] XVI, 22–23) vs. "for all times his majesty, his glory (פארתו), belongs to the eternal plantation (מטעת)" (4Q418 81 + 81a, 13).

אלוהות "divinity" (*qiṭālūt).[50] Additional examples of these nominal patterns proposed by different scholars include *qiṭṭūl: גבול "creating" (1QS X, 25);[51] גדול "greatness" (4Q427 7 i, 15), הגוי "meditation" (4Q417 1 i, 17),[52] זמון "designation" (4Q371 7, 4); *qəṭāl: זמן "time" (4Q282b 1, 2); words ending in -ūt: ארמלות "widowhood" (4Q176 8–11, 6), הכרות "look of" (1QIsa[a] at Isa 3:9) for MT הַכָּרַת. It goes without saying that the identification of most of these forms is difficult and ambiguous, the etymology being determined in part through other Hebrew traditions (MT: זְמָן, כְּלָל; RH: גִּדּוּל, זִמּוּן, פֵּרוּשׁ) if not also Aramaic (אַרְמְלוּת, זְמָן, כְּלָל).

In many cases, a word of one base pattern in the DSS corresponds to a word of the same root, but of a different base pattern in the MT. Many examples of this will be cited in the discussion of words that appear to have a *quṭl base in the DSS, but a *qaṭl or *qiṭl base in the MT (see the discussion in §5.4, "*Waw* Marking /u/ Class Vowel in Nouns Where MT Has No /u/ Class Vowel"). In addition, there are cases of what is a *qiṭl noun in the MT appearing as either a *qaṭīl noun or a *qaṭūl noun, like נגיעים "blemishes, plagues" (1QH[a] XVI, 28) and נגועים (4Q422 III, 6) versus MT נְגָעִים.[53]

Sometimes the differences between an MT and DSS word can be subtle, as in the example of the apparent gentilic ending on עועיים *ʿiwʿīyīm* "distortion" (1QIsa[a] at Isa 19:14; 1QH[a] XIV, 26; XV, 8) for MT עִוְעִים.[54] In addition, as noted below, the word עילול "child" is found in the nonbiblical DSS more regularly (1QH[a] XV, 24; 4Q169 3–4 iv, 2 and 4) than the corresponding MT words עֹלָל/עוֹלֵל "child" (e.g., 4Q385a 17a–e ii, 8).[55] Furthermore, one finds מבנית "structure" in the DSS (occurring at least twelve times in the nonbiblical scrolls), where one might have expected מבנה "structure" (occurring three times in the nonbiblical scrolls), בנין "structure" (once), or בניה "structure" (four times), which correspond respectively to MT מִבְנֶה,

50. Qimron, *HDSS*, 65–66 and idem, *Grammar*, 263 (*qəṭāl), 267 (*qiṭṭūl), 275 (*qaṭlūt and other forms with the -ūt ending). Note also nouns of the *qaṭīlat base, like משיחה "anointing" (1QM IX, 8 and 4Q375 1 i, 9) and רחיצה "washing" (4Q262 1, 3). On DSS nouns with *qiṭṭūl and *qaṭīlat bases, see Moshe Bar-Asher, "Qumran Hebrew and Mishnaic Hebrew" (Hebrew), *Meghillot* 8–9 (2010): 299–310.

51. Kister, "Some Observations," 157.

52. See Strugnell and Harrington, DJD 34:165.

53. For these examples, see Qimron, *HDSS*, 66.

54. See Kister, "Some Observations," 161.

55. In the biblical scrolls, עילול occurs in 1QIsa[a] at Isa 13:16, though עלל occurs in the other attestations (4Q56 [4QIsa[b]] at Isa 13:16; 11Q5 [11QPs[a]] at Ps 137:9; note too Mur88 at Mic 2:9 and Nah 3:10).

בִּנְיָן, or בְּנִיָּה. In other cases, the new word occurs in the DSS more rarely than the etymologically related words also found in the MT; thus, מבינה "understanding" (occurring five times in the nonbiblical scrolls [four of which are in 4QInstruction: 4Q417 and 4Q418]), where one might expect בינה "understanding" (in at least eighty clear cases among the nonbiblical scrolls) or תבונה "understanding" (five times), which correspond to MT בִּינָה or תְּבוּנָה. The coexistence of so many synonyms sometimes seems to have led to confusion. Thus, in 4Q286 1 ii, 6 the scribe first wrote מבינה, then erased the *mem* (this mistake may also have been caused by dittography, the preceding and following words being מקור "source").[56]

The existence of *heh*-preformative nouns in the DSS is suggested by the word הנף, "waving," which occurs repeatedly in two calendrical texts, 4Q320 and 4Q321, as well as in 4Q513 3–4, 2 and 11Q19 XI, 10. In every case it is followed by the word "sheaf" (עמר or עומר). The word presumably derives from the *hiphil* infinitive absolute of נוף "to wave," which, although it does not occur in the MT, is reminiscent of the infinitive construct in Lev 23:12 הֲנִיפְכֶם אֶת־הָעֹמֶר "your waving of the sheaf." The consistent spelling of the DSS word without *mater* suggests an /e/ vowel after the *nun*, instead of an /i/ vowel, and thus understanding the word as derived from the infinitive absolute, not the construct, something also suggested by the vocalization of the word הָנֵף in RH, which according to Jastrow, refers to the waving ceremony on the second day of Passover. The synonym הניפה in the phrase ביום הניפת העומר "in the day of the waving of the sheaf" (11Q19 XVIII, 10) is best construed as an independent word, in this case, derived from the *hiphil* infinitive construct. Other cases of what seem to be nouns with a *heh*-preformative are best construed as infinitives construct used as nouns; examples of such infinitives are described

---

56. Note too possible confusion with מבנה since תבנית occurs three words before. In other cases the combination of the *min* preposition plus the word בינה could conceivably be construed as the word מבינה, as in 1QH[a] XXIII, 12: [למ]שמיע ליצר* מבינתו "to declare to creature(s) his understanding," instead of "to declare to creature(s) from his understanding." That the latter translation is the intended meaning seems clear from the context of the Hodayot where understanding or knowledge is often the means through which something is done (as in 1QH[a] VII, 25: ואני ידעתי בבינתך). That some of this was intentional seems implied by the word play elsewhere among the scrolls, even in the way a common word like "children," בנים, can be "misread" as a plural participle, "those who know," as seems reflected in ... ועתה מבין "Now, maven..." (4Q525 14 ii, 18, alluding to Prov 5:7) (see Kister, "Some Observations," 158).

in "Verbs" (§5.6). The words הקרב "offering of" (in 11Q19 XLIII, 10) and החרם "the destruction" (1QM IX, 7) are listed by Qimron as independent *heh*-preformative words, but these have other possible explanations (e.g., a defective spelling of the *hiphil* infinitive construct and the definite form of the noun "destruction," found in the MT חֵרֶם).[57]

Gender and Number

Some words that have a feminine form in the MT sometimes have a masculine form in the DSS, words like this being concentrated in the Songs of the Sabbath Sacrifice.[58] Thus, the word ברך corresponds to the word ברכה "blessing" in the other DSS and to בְּרָכָה in the MT; the masculine formed word occurs at least nine times in the scrolls of the Songs of the Sabbath Sacrifice (4Q403, 4Q404, 4Q405). These nouns are more rarely found in other scrolls; note, for example, the masculine plural מפלגיו "its divisions" in 4Q405 23 i, 7 (compare MT מִפְלַגּוֹת 2 Chr 35:12), as well as with different suffixes in 1QS (IV, 15 and 16), 1QM (X, 12), and 1QH^a (XVI, 22 and XX, 26); the singular occurs as מפלג in 4Q503 1–6 iii, 7 and 15–16, 11. By contrast, the occurrence of feminine by-forms to masculine nouns from the MT occurs regularly throughout the scrolls.[59] These generally correspond to feminine words or forms in RH: לחה "moisture" (e.g., 4Q274 3 ii, 5 and 4Q394 [4QMMT] 8 iv, 8 and passim; RH לֵחָה versus MT לֵחַ), מטעת "planting" (1QS VIII, 5 and passim; RH מַטַּעַת versus MT מַטָּע). At the same time, the masculine words corresponding to those in the MT also occur, sometimes with less frequency than the feminine words (e.g., מטע at least seven times in the nonbiblical scrolls versus מטעת at least eleven times; and לח at least three times in the nonbiblical scrolls versus לחה at least five times).

The actual gender of specific nouns is generally the same as it is in the MT. Even in cases where the gender of a noun varies in the MT, this variation is also usually found in the DSS. For example, עצם "bone" is identifiable as masculine and feminine in different passages in the MT and DSS (based on agreement with verb forms, adjectives, and pronouns); רוח "spirit" in both the MT and DSS is usually feminine and only sometimes

---

57. Qimron, *HDSS*, 107. The alternative interpretations are found, e.g., in Accordance.

58. Qimron, *HDSS*, 68–69.

59. Ibid., 69.

masculine. In rare cases there is a slight discrepancy in the distribution; although דרך "path" is more often masculine in the MT, it seems to be more often feminine in the DSS.[60]

The DSS sometimes attest to alternative plural forms not evidenced in the MT. Qimron cites the masculine plural form of רוח "spirit," which occurs only in the construct and with pronominal suffixes (רוחיו, רוחי).[61] Note also the plurals for the word "lip" שפה: ספות (1QM V, 12), שפות (11Q8 [11QPs[d]] at Ps 81:6), and שפאותיכה (1QIsa[a] at Isa 37:29).[62]

Although in the preceding pages distinctions between the pronunciation/morphology in the DSS and that in the MT has been emphasized, it bears mentioning that the words in the DSS sometimes exhibit forms quite close to what we find in the MT. Interestingly, the spelling of certain DSS segholate nouns that contain *aleph* suggests a pronunciation and morphology akin to that found in the MT, even though this pronunciation/morphology is sometimes unexpected from an etymological point of view. Thus, we find חטא "sin" written חט in 11Q19 LVII, 10 and חט^א in 11Q19 LXIV, 9, reflecting presumably a pronunciation like that in MT, חֵטְא. Similarly, שו "emptiness" in 1QH[a] XV, 37 reflects the pronunciation of MT שָׁוְא and גי "valley of" (4Q371 1a–b, 4 and passim) reflects MT גֵּיא. In addition, as I have already mentioned, the spelling of many other words in the DSS suggests similar correspondences with MT words: פתאים "simple" and פְּתָאִים; חטתיכמ "your sins" and חַטֹּאתֵיכֶם. Such examples should remind us that the forms of words in the DSS are not always terribly far from those in the MT.

5.4. *Waw* Marking /u/ Class Vowel in Nouns Where MT Has No /u/ Class Vowel

Among the DSS, there are numerous instances of words that are attested (sometimes once, sometimes multiple times) with a *waw mater* where the

60. The feminine gender of the singular דרך is implied by a feminine verb (1QS VIII, 25; XI, 17; 1QH[a] XII, 32), a pronoun (1QH[a] XII, 19; 11Q19 LVI, 18), an accompanying numeral (4Q473 2, 3); only once is the plural feminine (4Q381 31, 3). The masculine gender of the singular is evidenced only when it is followed by a participle or asyndetic relative clause (1QH[a] VII, 31; 11Q19 XXXI, 6); the plural appears as masculine with a following verb twice (1QS III, 6; 1QH[a] XV, 34).

61. Qimron, *HDSS*, 67.

62. See the note on this word in "*Aleph* < *Waw* and *Waw* < *Aleph*" (§4.5).

corresponding MT word has no /o/ or /u/ class vowel. The reasons for such *waw maters* could be many. Some of the likelier phonetic and morphological causes that have been proposed include: (1) words from the same root, but with a different base pattern (e.g., a word has a **quṭl* pattern in the DSS and a **qaṭl* pattern in the MT); (2) assimilation to consonants, that is, the surrounding consonants cause an /i/ or /a/ vowel to be pronounced as an /o/ or /u/ vowel; (3) the preservation of a historical /u/ vowel that had shifted to /i/ in the MT tradition; (4) vowel assimilation. In addition, the *waw* may reflect an /ō/ vowel derived from a Proto-Semitic /ā/ (through the "Canaanite Shift" /ā/ > /ō/), the /ā/ in the corresponding MT word having been preserved in the Tiberian tradition often due to influence from Aramaic (in which language Proto-Semitic /ā/ does not shift to /ō/). It seems less likely, as explained in the section "/å/ < /ā/ < Proto-Semitic /a/" (§4.9), that Proto-Semitic /a/ had universally shifted to /å/ or /o/ in the Hebrew of the DSS. As should be apparent from the examples below, it is often difficult to be certain which of the causes to prefer in the case of individual words.

Different Bases

Kutscher helpfully observes that a variation between **quṭl* and **qaṭl*/**qiṭl* bases is evidenced not only between the Tiberian and Babylonian vocalization traditions (e.g., Tiberian *ḥesed* versus Babylonian *ḥōsad*), but even within the MT (e.g., חֹסֶר "lack" versus חֶסֶר and סֹבֶל "burden" versus סֵבֶל).[63] That we should find this same variation between the Tiberian tradition and the DSS should not surprise us. The following words, drawn from Qimron's lists in *HDSS*, appear to be of (or incorporate) the **quṭl* pattern, though the corresponding MT words are (or do) not: לוהב "blade" (1QM V, 7 and passim) versus MT לַהַב (**qaṭl*); שלהובת "blade" (1QM VI, 3) versus MT שַׁלְהֶבֶת (**šaqṭalt*); פותי "simple" (1QSa I, 19 and passim) versus MT פְּתִי (**qaṭl*/**qiṭl*); תוחת "under" (1QS VII, 13) and תחות (1QIsa[a] at Isa 3:24 [twice]) versus MT תַּחַת (**qaṭl*); מועל "treachery" (4Q270 6 iv, 18 and passim) versus MT מַעַל (**qaṭl*); בורכים "knees" (4Q491 8–10 i, 4 and 1QIsa[a] at Isa 45:23, 66:12) versus MT בֶּרֶךְ (**qiṭl*).[64] Additional exam-

63. Kutscher, *Isaiah*, 460. He cites numerous other traditions that evidence a similar variation.

64. See Qimron, *HDSS*, 65, and Qimron's lists of words where he implies by his vocalization that these nouns have a **quṭl* base (ibid., 98–115). He also lists with a

ples include the proper names חופר and החופרי (4Q27 [4QNum[b]] at Num 26:32) for MT חֵפֶר and הַחֶפְרִי; פושתים "linen" (11Q2 [11QLev[b]] at Lev 13:59) for MT הַפִּשְׁתִּים; קושי "stubbornness" (1QS IV, 11; 1QM XIV, 7 and the parallel passage in 4Q491 8–10 i, 5), which corresponds to RH קוֹשִׁי and the *qaṭl base noun in the MT, קְשִׁי.[65] Examples of feminine-marked nouns spelled with a *waw* and thus presumably from a *quṭlat base, though the corresponding MT words come from a *qiṭlat (or other) base, include רוקמה "embroidered work" (e.g., 1QM V, 6 and passim) versus MT רִקְמָה; עושרות "tens (of soldiers)" (1QM II, 17 and passim) versus MT עֲשָׂרֹת (*qiṭalāt); תופלה "unseemliness" (4Q230 1, 2 and 4Q525 14 ii, 28) versus MT תִּפְלָה (*qiṭlat).

One might also include some examples from 1QIsa[a], though they only occur there, like גופן "vine" (at Isa 34:4) for MT גֶּפֶן (*qaṭl); לוחיי "jaws of" (Isa 30:28) for MT לְחָיֵי (sing. לְחִי, *qaṭl); קוברך "your grave" (at Isa 14:19) for MT קִבְרְךָ; רוגע "moment" (at Isa 54:7) for MT רֶגַע (perhaps *qaṭl); שׁ׳ובי "captivity" (at Isa 49:25) for MT שְׁבִי (*qaṭl/*qiṭl).[66] Kutscher also points to words from other bases that diverge from corresponding words in the MT, like מור "bitter" (at Isa 38:15) for MT מַר (*qall); אוט "gently" (at Isa 8:6) for MT אַט (*qall);[67] איקדח "jewel" (at Isa 54:12) for MT אֶקְדָּח

---

question mark "arranging" עורך in 1QM VII, 3, though this is parsed by Accordance as a *qal* participle; and also with a question mark "uncircumcision" ערול in 1QH[a] X, 20. In other cases, the readings he follows are debated; he reads, e.g., ולקול[יה]מה in 4Q491 8–10 i, 9, though Baillet (DJD 7:21) and others (e.g., *DSSSE*) read ולקיל־תמה; Qimron reads פחוז "wantonness" in 4Q184 1, 2, though others read פחין "traps" (Strugnell, "Notes en marge," 264; *DSSSE*). The reverse relationship also exists. Words that are of the *quṭl base in the MT appear to be of different bases in the DSS, as in MT חֹמֶר versus חמר in 1QS XI, 22 and passim (presumably akin to RH חֵמָר).

65. Confusingly, 1QS VI, 26 and 4Q393 (4QMMT) 1 ii – 2, 4 attest the phrase בקשי עורף (partially preserved in 4QMMT), where the word קשי might correspond to the MT *qaṭl base noun (קְשִׁי), the *quṭl base noun קושי spelled defectively, or the adjective קשה spelled with a final *yodh mater* instead of a *heh mater* (like the first word in the phrase מעני לשון 4Q171 3–10 iv, 27, which is in the singular; see §3.2, "*Plene* Orthography"). Given the well-known MT expression עַם־קְשֵׁה־עֹרֶף (Exod 32:9 and passim), the last interpretation seems the likeliest.

66. According to Kutscher, the /o/ or /u/ vowel in קוברך and שׁ׳ובי is due to a following *beth* or *resh* (*Isaiah*, 496–98). The /o/ or /u/ vowel presumed in לוחיי is perhaps due to the preceding *lamedh*, though Kutscher sees the form as reflective of Aramaic influence where the cognate word is לוֹעַ (*Isaiah*, 250).

67. Though, one wonders if this is related to another word, אוט, which is found in 4QInstruction (4Q415 18, 2 and passim in that work).

(*ʾaqṭal); רונה "cry" (at Isa 14:7 and passim) for MT רִנָּה (*qillat);[68] as well as the proper name חוזקיה (at Isa 36:15 and passim) for MT חִזְקִיָּהוּ.[69]

In general, the words that attest a *waw mater* (and that often appear to be of a *quṭl or *qull base) are found in DSS-SP9 and DSS-SP1c texts.[70] The corresponding words from DSS-NSP texts often are written in a manner akin to how they appear in the MT. However, it bears mentioning that within the DSS-SP9 and DSS-SP1c texts, there is not uniformity; a word like "simple" is sometimes spelled with a *waw* and sometimes without, even in the same scroll (פותאים in 1QHª V, 13 and פתיים in 1QHª X, 11); this word is found without a *mater* in many DSS-SP9 (1Q14, 4Q266) and DSS-SP1c (4Q169, 4Q424) texts. Since alternative forms of certain words appear in the MT within individual texts (see the examples cited below like מַחְמָד versus מַחְמוֹד "treasure" in Lamentations), I assume that alternative spellings in the DSS also reflect different pronunciations for the same basic word. The defective spelling in DSS-NSP texts reflects the lack of a /u/ or /o/ vowel, something inferred from the *plene* spelling of *quṭl nouns in this same group of texts.

In the DSS, words with *maqṭal bases seem to have variants with *maqṭul or *maqṭāl bases. Such variation is also found in the MT (e.g., מִבְחַר "choice" in Isa 37:24 versus מִבְחוֹר "choice" in the parallel to this verse at 2 Kgs 19:23).[71] Examples from the DSS include: מחמודינו "our desirable (places)" (1QIsaª at Isa 64:10) for MT מַחֲמַדֵּינוּ;[72] משלוח "act (lit.,

---

68. Kutscher notes, however, that it is not uncommon for words with a masculine *qull base to have a semantically similar feminine form of the *qillat type, the /i/ vowel being due to attenuation or dissimilation; he lists the examples of אֹמֶר and אִמְרָה, בֹּץ and בִּצָּה, זֹקֶן and זִקְנָה, יֹשֶׁר and יִשְׁרָה (*Isaiah*, 458). Since the root רנן attests a *qull base noun רֹן in the MT, it is conceivable that the more etymologically true form of the feminine is actually preserved in 1QIsaª as רונה.

69. Kutscher, *Isaiah*, 477–78. He notes that some examples, like נוגע in Isa 53:8 for MT נֶגַע might be due to different words, e.g., a participle. Another example of what seems to be a different word is צור (in 1QIsaª at Isa 5:28) for MT צַר.

70. For instance, פותי appears only in DSS-SP9 (1QSa, 1QHª, 4Q418, 4Q301, 11Q5) and DSS-SP1c texts (4Q439).

71. In the MT, note also מַחְמָד "treasure" (twelve times, at least two of which are in Lamentations [1:10, 2:4]) vs. מַחְמוֹד "treasure" (at least once in Lamentations [1:7]); מִשְׁקָל "weight" (many times, twice in Ezekiel [4:16, 5:1]) vs. מִשְׁקוֹל "weight" (once in Ezekiel [1:7]), מִכְלָל "perfection" (once in Proverbs) vs. מִכְלוֹל "perfection" (twice in Ezekiel).

72. Kutscher, *Isaiah*, 378.

outstretching of [hand])" (1QM I, 1; 4Q260 I, 1; 4Q418 87, 13; 89, 2; 159 i, 5) though elsewhere משלח appears (1QS IX, 23; X, 13; 4Q403 1 i, 36); ממוד "post, standing" (4Q266 10 i, 12) appears for *מעמוד, which is presumably equivalent to MT מַעֲמָד; מסחורכה "your merchandise" (4Q418 103 ii, 6 and three other times in the same scroll) for what would be (without suffix) in the MT *מִסְחָר; מדרוך "space" (4Q223–224 1 i, 2) appears in an apparent allusion to Deut 2:5, where the MT has the construct form מִדְרַךְ;[73] as well as the geminate noun משוסה "plunder" (11Q19 LIX, 8 and 1QIsa^a^ at Isa 42:22) for MT מְשִׁסָּה. Note also the possible variation between **muqṭal* and **muqṭāl* bases in מרדוף "chase" (1QM IX, 6) and מרדף (1QM III, 2, 9; VII, 13), presumably equivalent to the MT *hapax* מֻרְדָּף, unless the MT form is to be construed as an error and מרדף/מרדוף in 1QM should be considered as another example of the variation between **maqṭal* and **maqṭul*/**maqṭāl* bases. In some cases, the variants in the MT (מִשְׁלוֹחַ/מִשְׁלַח) have slightly different meanings, according to the dictionaries ("act, undertaking" for מִשְׁלַח versus "contribution, jurisdiction" for מִשְׁלוֹחַ), though the corresponding variants in the DSS do not seem to have different meanings (משלוח/משלח both usually followed by "hand" [כף/יד] = "act").

Assimilation to Consonants

The development of an /o/ or /u/ vowel might have been triggered by surrounding consonants. Kutscher lists instances from 1QIsa^a^ in which he believes a following bilabial (/b/, /m/, /p/) or *resh* causes the shift from an /i/, /e/, or /a/ vowel to an /o/ or /u/ vowel. In addition to the nouns, קוברך, רוגע, שיבי, listed above as examples of different nominal bases, note שובנא "Shebna" (at Isa 36:3, 11 [with interlinear *waw*], 22, 37:2) for MT שֶׁבְנָא; מהורסיך "those tearing you down" (at Isa 49:17) for MT מְהָרְסַיִךְ, *piel* participle from הרס; כורכובות "camels" (at Isa 66:20) for MT כִּרְכָּרוֹת; and the place name הוררט (at Isa 37:38) for MT אֲרָרָט.[74] Other possible examples

73. Note the spelling without a *mater* in 4Q392 2, 4: מדרך.

74. Kutscher, *Isaiah*, 496. He lists other words more tentatively, like הנומה at Isa 41:27 for MT הִנָּם (*hinnē* + 3mp suffix). He also lists as a single possible example of a preceding bilabial affecting the following vowel מיכמר at Isa 51:20 for MT מִכְמָר, though he notes the LXX reads the Hebrew as a *hophal* participle (ibid., 478). See also Kutscher's discussion of ניכחה (at Isa 57:2) for MT נְכֹחָה (ibid., 476). Note a second occurrence of הוררט in 4Q252 I, 10.

are משואם *miššōm* "from there" (6Q4 [6QpapKgs] at 2 Kgs 7:8) for MT מִשָּׁם; זלעופות "rages" (1QHª XIII, 32 and 4Q501 1, 6 for what would be in the MT זִלְעָפוֹת); חורטומים "magicians" (4Q365 2, 3 for what would be in the MT חַרְטֻמִּים).[75] A similar shift is evidenced in the MT with a preceding or following guttural or *qoph*.[76]

Qimron suggests that this shift is triggered not only by the bilabials and *resh*, but also by *lamedh* and *nun*.[77] As he mentions, most of the examples are ambiguous and allow for varying explanations.[78] He lists words that have a *waw mater* where a *qamets* appears in the MT. The best examples are the words אגונות "bowls," (4Q158 4, 5), rather than as in the MT אַגָּנוֹת;[79] and חנום "for nothing" (11Q5 [11QPsª] at Ps 119:161) for MT חִנָּם.[80] More uncertain is the supposed 3mp pronominal suffix spelled ום- for what would be in the MT ָם- in several words. In the end, I think it is unlikely that these should be interpreted as 3mp suffixes. For example, the suffix on "spirit" רוחום (1QS IX, 14) is parsed (I think correctly) as 3ms by Accordance (the *mem* being a 3mp pronoun added as a correction); this

75. It is less likely that the letters משואם might represent "their burden" *massāwām* for what would be in the MT *מַשָּׂאָם (as in Num 4:27); in the context, such a reading would lead to the translation: "they bore their burden" or "they uttered their oracle."

76. GKC (§10h) list all kinds of words from the MT where *hatef-qamets* appears before (and sometimes after) a guttural or an emphatic consonant (especially *qoph*), אֶשְׁקֳוטָה (Isa 18:4), even in places that never exhibited an etymological /u/ vowel, לֻקֳחָה (Gen 2:23); הֶחֳדַלְתִּי (Jud 9:9, 11, 13); נִבֳהָל (Prov 28:22); אֲלַקֳטָה (Ruth 2:2). See *HGhS*, 208t, which lists אֶשֳּׁקָה־ (1 Kgs 19:20) and אֶפְשֳׂעָה (Isa 27:4) though these are not attested in the Leningrad Codex, as well as *HGhS*, 357v, which lists יְתָאֳרֵהוּ (Isa 44:13). See also Bergsträsser, *Hebräische Grammatik*, 1:126. Other possible examples have other explanations, like נְגֹאֲלוּ (Isa 59:3 and Lam 4:14), which might be attributable to a confusion between *pual* and *niphal* stems (see *HGhS*, 356v). Furthermore, Bauer and Leander (*HGhS*, 211j) note that after the consonants /m/, /n/, /l/, /r/, the sibilants (/z/, /ṣ/, /s/, /š/), and /q/ a vocal shewa is sometimes found where one would expect a silent shewa (e.g., הַצְּפִינוֹ [Exod 2:3]); rarely the simple shewa is replaced by a *hatef-qamets* (לֻקֳחָה [Gen 2:23]).

77. Qimron, *HDSS*, 40.

78. Ibid. and the references cited there.

79. Alternatively, the spelling in the DSS could reflect a different base; cf. Arabic *ʾijjānat* (*HALOT*).

80. Though here one wonders if the DSS spelling is affected by the alternative adverbial ending *-ōm*, found on MT words like הֲלֹם and עֵירֹם. Note also שומה "destruction" (11Q19 LIX, 4 = MT שַׁמָּה); חורגול "cricket" (11Q19 XLVIII, 3 = MT חַרְגֹּל); יורדן "Jordan" (4Q379 12, 6 = MT יַרְדֵּן) (Qimron, *HDSS*, 39).

parallels the more obvious רצונו "his will" in the next line. In addition, the parsing as a 3ms suffix matches Qimron's own understanding of the same form רוחום "his spirit" earlier in the same text (1QS V, 21).[81] Perhaps a better example is provided by לדברים "to speak them" (4Q267 9 v, 12) where the parallel term in the next line is [כ]משפטם "[according] to their rule" and the corresponding CD text has לדברם (CD A, XIV, 8). Even here, however, there is the possibility that this is a mistake on the part of the corrector (as though the corrector thought it should read "for *him* to speak" and did not supply cancellation dots or marks around the *mem*).[82]

Other examples are also ambiguous. The word עולום (1QH[a] XIX, 30 for what would be in the MT עוֹלָם "forever") may be due to dittography, since the word that immediately precedes it is שלום; note the similar case of dittography between adjacent words: זהב טהוב (4Q365a 2 ii, 7) for *זהב טהור "pure gold."[83]

In other examples in which a *waw* appears where the corresponding Tiberian word has a *patach* or *qamets*, the bilabial or *nun* occurs before the relevant vowel: "the nettle" הסרפוד (1QIsa[a] at Isa 55:13) for MT הַסִּרְפַּד; and the names "Ephah" עיפו and "Sheba" שבאו (both in 1QIsa[a] at Isa 60:6) for MT עֵיפָה and שְׁבָא;[84] as well as תמנו (4Q522 9 i + 10, 13) for MT תְּמְנָה.

Examples where Proto-Semitic /a/ seems to have developed into a /u/ class vowel before an etymological *aleph* are perhaps due to a similar shift, or due to other causes. The words נו "raw" in 4Q11 (4QpaleoGen–Exod[l]) at Exod 12:9 (= MT נָא) and תו "chamber" (4Q365a 2 i, 10, twice) (= MT תָּא) perhaps developed as hypercorrect pronunciations in analogy to the negative particle לא, as if the scribes assumed that since the negative particle was written לא (*lā*) in Aramaic and ל(ו)א (*lō*) in Hebrew, then, נא (*nā*) should be pronounced *nō* and תא (*tā*) should be changed *tō*.[85] Cases

---

81. Ibid., 27. Furthermore, the word בבואום (1QSa I, 4) is read בבואים (as a mistake for בבואם) by *DSSSE* and Accordance. The remaining example with the 3mp pronoun that Qimron lists is הונום (1QS V, 20) corrected to הונם, though the erased *waw* is hard to perceive in the photograph (see James H. Charlesworth, *The Dead Sea Scrolls, Rule of the Community: Photographic Multi-Language Edition* [Philadelphia: American Interfaith Institute, 1996]).

82. Note the corrector's imprecision in correcting another word in the same line: ההיגי for *ההגיי.

83. See "Scribal Mistakes" (§3.1).

84. Kutscher suggests possible influence from Nabatean where a *waw* often follows Arabic names (*Isaiah*, 123).

85. The word "chamber" is written also תא (4Q365a 3, 5), תאו (11Q19 XXXVIII,

like the construct plural רואשי (1QSa I, 14), ראושי (4Q286 17a, 2) and the plural with suffix רואשיהמה (1QIsa[a] at Isa 51:11 for MT רֹאשָׁם), for what would ordinarily be in the MT, respectively, רָאשֵׁי and רָאשֵׁיהֶם, are presumably attributable to the influence of the vowel of the singular form, as seems likely to be the case in the MT at Isa 15:2 רֹאשָׁיו.[86]

Given the ambiguity of most of the examples, one hesitates to say with certainty whether or not the sound shift /a/ > /o/ (or /u/) in the vicinity of bilabials, *lamedh*, *nun*, *resh* really affected specific words. Nevertheless, it should be recognized that a similar phenomenon affects /a/ vowels in Aramaic of various kinds, in Rabbinic Hebrew, and even in the Palestinian pronunciation evidenced by Jerome.[87] As explained in the section "/å/ < /ā/ < Proto-Semitic /a/" (§4.9), it seems less likely that all /a/ vowels had shifted to /å/ or /o/. It is preferable to isolate such a shift to the environment of bilabials and /l/, /n/, and /r/.

The examples that Qimron cites and those from the above paragraphs are from DSS-SP9 texts, with two exceptions (4Q379, 4Q381 = DSS-NSP texts). This implies that if /a/ vowels did indeed shift in some phonetic contexts, this was a feature isolated primarily to some of these texts and the dialect(s) of their scribes.

Preservation of a Historical /u/ Vowel

Kutscher notes also that the expected development of /u/ > /i/ did not take place in some words from 1QIsa[a] of the **quṭṭūl* base pattern (perhaps,

---

15, twice; XL, 10), and in the plural תאים (11Q19 XXXVIII, 15). Alternatively, these are words with different bases: נו *nāw* (akin to שוא/שו *šāw*; the root is ניא, according to *HALOT*); תו *tāw* (note Aramaic תַּוָּא in Tg. Ezek 40:7; תַּוַּיָּא in 40:12). Qimron suggests תאו/תו represents *ta*^{w}*u* or something similar, from an earlier diphthong *au* (*HDSS*, 34). In a more recent article, he suggests that the word may be derived from a root תאי (Elisha Qimron, "Studies in the Hebrew of the Dead Sea Scrolls" [Hebrew], *Hebrew Linguistics* 33–35 [1992]: 83; this is the English title offered in the English contents page, though the actual Hebrew title to the article might be translated: "Accentuation in the Hebrew of the Dead Sea Scrolls"). Conceivably too the defective spelling תָּאָו "its chambers" four times in the MT of Ezekiel has influenced the spelling in the scrolls.

86. Qimron, *Grammar*, 257 n. 45. Contrast these with יומי "days of" in 1QS II, 19; III, 5; י֯ימי (1QIsa[a] at Isa 38:10) for an intended ימי; and בי֯ימי "in days of" (1QIsa[a] at Isa 1:1), which likely reflect Aramaic influence (see Abegg, "Linguistic Profile," 41).

87. See Kutscher, *Isaiah*, 496–97, and the references he cites. There is little evidence for historical /i/ vowels developing into /u/ or /o/ vowels.

quṭṭāl*). Words of this base shifted to **qiṭṭūl* in the Tiberian tradition, as in עִזּוּז "strong" and לִמּוּד "taught."[88] In 1QIsa[a], the /u/ is retained in only four words: עוזוז (at Isa 43:17) for MT עִזּוּז; גודפים (at Isa 43:28) for MT גִּדּוּפִים "revilings"; רוקחיך (at Isa 57:9) for MT רִקֻּחָיִךְ "your perfumes"; קובציך (at Isa 57:13) for MT קִבּוּצַיִךְ "your collections"; in other cases, the orthography presumes a pronunciation parallel to that of the Tiberian tradition: שלומים "vengeance" (at Isa 34:8), as well as five others.[89] The only other possible example I am aware of is עוּבורתמה "their pregnancy" (4Q418 211, 3).[90] In all likelihood the preservation (or secondary development) of a /u/ vowel in **quṭṭūl*/quṭṭāl* base patterns is primarily a feature of 1QIsa[a]. Alternatively, these examples might be explained as due to vowel assimilation.

Vowel Assimilation

A /u/ vowel is sometimes responsible for the appearance of another /u/ class vowel where none existed before. This might be a contributing factor in the MT form לֻֽקֳחָה "was taken" (Gen 2:23) from an earlier **luqaḥā*, as well as in סֻבֳּלוֹ "his burden" (Isa 9:3 and passim), a **qutl* base noun, from an earlier **sublō*.[91] The same tendency is evidenced in *hophal* forms of I-guttural roots: הָחֳרָבָה "it is laid waste" (Ezek 26:2, in pause), יָחֳרַם "will be forfeited" (Ezra 10:8), מָאֳחָזִים "fastened" (2 Chr 9:18), as well as in certain spellings of names in the LXX בֹּעַז = Βοοζ and מֹלֶךְ = Μολοχ. In these cases, it is an initial /u/ or /o/ vowel that occasions the appearance in the

88. See *HGhS*, 480–81.

89. Kutscher, *Isaiah*, 475. Kutscher (*Isaiah*, 474, 477) also suggests that the *waw* in the word "desert" ישומון in 1QIsa[a] at Isa 43:19, 20 (MT יְשִׁימוֹן) may reflect a similar shift, as may the *waw* in "cry" רונה at Isa 14:7 (MT רִנָּה), and eight other times. The word "desert" is spelled in its only other occurrence with a *yodh* in 4Q88 (4QPs[f]) at Ps 107:4, and "cry" is otherwise written defectively with no *mater* (see the discussion of this word in the subsection "Different Bases" [§5.4]). Kutscher also mentions other examples, like שולח for MT שְׁלַח, though the etymologies of these words are less clear evidence for this phenomenon since their etymologies are more obscure.

90. Strugnell and Harrington, DJD 34:430–31. The corresponding word in RH is masculine, עִבּוּר. The words listed in Qimron's *Grammar* under this base (**quṭṭūl*) do not occur with the *waw* after the initial consonant; for example, גדוף is found in four passages among the nonbiblical scrolls.

91. See GKC §10h for further examples, though some of these, like וְּסֳעָדָה (1 Kgs 13:7), are not found in the Leningrad Codex.

next syllable of another (nonetymological) /u/ or /o/ vowel. Usually a guttural separates both vowels, but not always. That something similar takes place in words from the DSS seems likely. For example, in **quṭl* base nouns one sometimes encounters a *waw mater* between the second and third radicals in construct forms, as in ישור "uprightness of" in 1QS XI, 2 for what would be in the MT יֹשֶׁר. As explained below in "**quṭl* Nouns" (§5.5), the assumption for these kinds of nouns is of a development through epenthesis *quṭl* > *qoṭl* > *qŏṭol*.

In other cases, a /u/ class vowel appears in the DSS where the MT vowel is shewa and the following vowel is a /u/ class vowel. Such a development is found in certain MT Hebrew forms which contained an initial etymological /u/ vowel (e.g., קָרָבְכֶם "[as] you approach" [Deut 20:2] from **qurbukumu* or **qurubkumu*); as well as in noun and verbal forms where the initial /u/ class vowel is clearly not etymological: יָחְנְךָ "he will favor you" (Gen 43:29, Isa 30:19; versus וִיחֻנֶּךָּ in Num 6:25 which is closer to the etymological *yaḥunnakā*).[92] Qimron has noted some examples of DSS nouns of the **quṭulat* base where, although the etymological first /u/ was lost, another /u/ class vowel in this initial syllable emerged due to the presence of a guttural followed by a /u/ class vowel: אוחזת "possession of" (1QS XI, 7); כוהונו[ת] "priesthoods" (4Q400 1 ii, 19); כוהנתנו "our priesthood" (4Q400 2, 6); בפיעלת "deeds of" (4Q426 1 ii, 4); פועלתי "my work" (1QIsa[a] at Isa 49:4); פועלתמה "their work" (1QIsa[a] at Isa 65:7), corresponding respectively to the MT nouns אֲחֻזָּה, כְּהֻנָּה, פְּעֻלָּה.[93] The development might be characterized as **puʿulā* > **pəʿulā* > **pəʿullā* > *puʿullā*. One reason that these are best interpreted as reflecting the secondary development of another /u/ class vowel and not the misplacement of a *mater* due to the quiescence of the middle guttural consonant (that is, **pəʿullā* > **pullā*) is that such displacement of the *mater* is extremely rare and restricted to places where there is no preceding vowel, even in cases where the guttural is *aleph* and the preceding vowel shewa.[94] The development of a secondary /u/ class vowel seems to be concentrated in DSS-SP9 and DSS-SP1c texts.

---

92. Note also LXX Σόδομα for סְדֹם and Σολομών for שְׁלֹמֹה.

93. Qimron, "Work Concerning Divine Providence," 199. Alternatively, it may be that these words in the DSS derive from a different base, e.g., **quṭlat*.

94. See "Digraphs" (§3.5).

Canaanite Shift: /ā/ > /ō/

DSS words occasionally attest the Canaanite Shift (/ā/ > /ō/) where the MT does not. This is possibly the case for the word רחמון "merciful" (4Q381 10–11, 3 and 47, 1 instead of MT רַחֲמָנִי), though the vowel represented by the *waw* may also be explained as due to the *nun*.[95] Note three other examples perhaps reflecting the same Canaanite Shift: אנושי "men of" (1QSa I, 2 and passim, and 1QH[a] XXII, 27) for what would be in the MT presumably אַנְשֵׁי;[96] שובועי "weeks of" (4Q403 1 i, 27 and passim in the Songs of the Sabbath Sacrifice) for what might be in the MT שָׁבוּעֵי;[97] and אבירום

95. The Biblical Hebrew word is probably an Aramaic loanword. There are very few other words in Biblical Hebrew that attest this /-ān/, whereas most have /-ōn/ (see *HGhS*, 498–500).

96. The plural for "man" in the MT (אִישׁ) is typically אֲנָשִׁים in the absolute, which is probably connected to the Aramaic word for "man," vocalized in Biblical Aramaic in the MT אֱנָשׁ in the singular and אֲנָשִׁים in the plural (in which case the final *mem* is due to Hebrew influence), and vocalized in Syriac *ʾnāšā* in the singular and *ʾnāšīn* in the plural (in both cases the *aleph* is silent). I.e., the plural form of "man" in Hebrew is perhaps borrowed from Aramaic where the Proto-Semitic /ā/ vowel has not shifted to /ō/ (through the Canaanite Shift). Hebrew, of course, preserves its own word from Proto-Semitic **ʾunāš*, אֱנוֹשׁ, which, however, does not have an explicitly marked plural form. Qimron's assertions that the word in question should be read אנישי in the DSS is not followed by most editions (see Qimron, *HDSS*, 66; idem, "Waw and Yod," 106; versus *DSSSE*, Accordance, Charlesworth and Stuckenbruck ["Rule of the Congregation," 110], and Stegemann, Schuller, Newsom [DJD 40:274]). Stegemann and Schuller assert that the word in question is not the plural of Hebrew אֱנוֹשׁ, but a by-form of the plural construct of "man," אַנְשֵׁי, which is rendered in Job 34:10 (in the MT) אַנְשֵׁי (Stegemann, Schuller, Newsom, DJD 40:274). One suspects in 1QS and 1QH[a] a phonetic play with the passive participle אנוש "sickened," which also appears in 1QS VII, 12 and 1QH[a] XIII, 30 and XVI, 29, among other places.

97. The construct form of the masculine plural form does not occur in the MT, but both the masculine and feminine absolute forms occur with a *qamets*, שָׁבֻעֹת, שָׁבֻעִים, as does a suffixed feminine plural form, שָׁבֻעֹתֵיכֶם. That these contain examples of what was perceived to be an etymological Proto-Semitic /ā/ is suggested by the fact that this *qamets* does not reduce in the MT in the plural forms as well as by the Aramaic cognate in the plural: שָׁבוּעִין and שָׁבוּעַיָּא (see Jastrow, s.v.). This is most likely not a true etymological /ā/, but one that developed to distinguish the word "weeks" from the word "oath," which in Hebrew (and Aramaic) has an initial shewa: sing. שְׁבֻעָה, pl. שְׁבֻעֹת; Aram. sing. שְׁבוּעָה. Alternatively, as Newsom observes, the first *waw* of שובועי might represent the assimilation of the following /u/ vowel (DJD 11:266). Still another possibility is the emergence of an /o/ or /u/ vowel due to the influence of the following *beth*.

(4Q27 [4QNum^b] at Num 16:1) for MT אֲבִירָם "Abiram." By contrast, some words that appear to have an /ō/ vowel from the Canaanite Shift in the MT are rendered without a *waw mater* in the DSS and, thus, presuppose a possible retention of the Proto-Semitic /ā/ or influence from Aramaic, as in כידן "javelin" (attested five times only in 1QM) versus MT כִּידוֹן (written *plene* seven times and defective once).[98]

There are many other proper nouns that exhibit a *waw mater* in 1QIsa^a which can be explained by one or more of the above phonetic phenomena, if not by still other causes. The names include סודם (at Isa 1:9 and passim) for MT סְדֹם; רומליהו (at Isa 7:1 and passim) for MT רְמַלְיָהוּ; השולח (at Isa 8:6) for MT הַשִּׁלֹחַ; עורערו (at Isa 17:2) for MT עֲרֹעֵר; תורתן (at Isa 20:1) for MT תַּרְתָּן; דודנים (at Isa 21:13) for MT דְּדָנִים; קור (at Isa 22:6) for MT קִיר; ארואל (at Isa 29:1) for MT אֲרִיאֵל; שראוצר (at Isa 37:38) for MT שַׂרְאֶצֶר; אסרחודן (at Isa 37:38) for MT אֵסַר־חַדֹּן.[99] Additional examples are ותורצה (4Q27 [4QNum^b] at Num 27:1) for MT וְתִרְצָה and העודו[למי] (4Q364 9a–b, 10) for MT הָעֲדֻלָּמִי. In relation to these names, note the similar examples of names with /u/ and /o/ vowels in the LXX where the MT has a muttered vowel or *patach* (and no etymological /u/ and /o/ vowel): Ὀχοζίας for אֲחַזְיָה, Ὀρνα for אֲרַוְנָה, Γοδολίας for גְּדַלְיָה, Μοολι for מַחְלִי, Μερόβ for מֵרַב, Ὀδολλαμίτου for הָעֲדֻלָּמִי, Γοθολία for עֲתַלְיָה, Σοφονίας for צְפַנְיָה, Τοχός for תַּחַשׁ, and θολμαΐ/ for תַּלְמַי.[100]

5.5. *QUṬL NOUNS

As Kutscher describes in relation to 1QIsa^a, **quṭl* base nouns (like MT קֹדֶשׁ "holiness, sanctuary") may appear in one of three orthographic forms in the DSS: (1) as they typically do in the MT, either defective קטל or *plene* קוטל; (2) as they typically do in Biblical Aramaic, with a *waw mater* after the second root consonant קטול (e.g., Biblical Aramaic קְשֹׁט); (3) with a *waw mater* after the first and second root consonants קוטול.[101] He writes that these forms presume three possible pronunciations, *qoṭel*, *qəṭol*, and *qoṭol*, though the last one, he feels, is perhaps the more common, his opin-

98. See Qimron, *Grammar*, 47–48.

99. Kutscher, *Isaiah*, 96–122.

100. Clemens Könnecke, *Die Behandlung der hebräischen Namen in der Septuaginta* (Programm des Koeniglichen und Groening'schen Gymnasiums zu Stargard in Pommern 124; Stargard: Gymnasium, 1885), 20, 25.

101. Kutscher, *Isaiah*, 502. On the Aramaic forms, see ibid., 201–3.

ion being informed by transliterations of names in the LXX, like Μολοχ for MT מֹלֶךְ (as in 2 Kgs 23:10).[102] Qimron seems more confident that this type of noun was consistently pronounced *qoṭol* in the absolute and *qŏṭol* in the construct; the slightly different pronunciation for the construct is based on his observation that absolute nouns only exhibit the קוטל pattern, while construct nouns are spelled in all three ways.[103]

Although I think Qimron's thesis is right (even for the writing/reading register of the scribes and writers), the evidence is not as transparent as one might initially think. First, in many cases, the nouns that are listed by him as being **quṭl* nouns with a *waw mater* after the second radical may, in fact, not be **quṭl* nouns. For example, Qimron notes that there are six examples of the **quṭl* noun גֹּדֶל "greatness" spelled גדול in the construct state.[104] He does not list the exact passages, but one of them surely is in 1QH^a VI, 34 where we find the phrase כגדול כוחך "according to the greatness of your strength."[105] Due to the orthography, however, one might understand the first word as the adjective גָּדוֹל "great" used as a substantive, similar to its use in Exod 15:16: בִּגְדֹל זְרוֹעֲךָ "by the power of your arm."[106] Since this seems to be the only time in the MT that גָּדוֹל is used in this particular way, perhaps we should consider such a usage in the DSS unlikely.[107] Nevertheless, several factors might encourage the reading of the letters as the adjective in 1QH^a VI, 34. First, the passage from Exodus must have been known to the writers of the DSS and could have influenced their use of the adjective. Second, the consonants גדול seem to suggest a similar abstract meaning in another Hodayot text from Cave 4, הבו גדול לאלנו "ascribe greatness to our God" (4Q427 7 i, 15).[108] Third, the word

102. Ibid., 502.

103. Qimron, *HDSS*, 37.

104. Ibid., 38.

105. Indeed, the first word is parsed according to Stegemann, Schuller, Newsom as the abstract noun (גֹּדֶל) in construct (DJD 40:338).

106. This is the understanding of the word גדול in 1QH^a VI, 34 as reflected in the *Dead Sea Scrolls Concordance* (see 1:171, listed under 1QH^a VI, 23).

107. Qimron seems to imply that such forms as גְּדֹל in Exod 15:16 are also examples of this same phenomenon, that is, the construct state of an abstract noun (in the case of Exod 15:16, גֹּדֶל). He writes "This kind of differentiation of the construct state from the absolute … is attested in the Tiberian tradition as well, e.g., … קֹדֶשׁ / קְדֹשׁ" (*HDSS*, 37). Nevertheless, as far as I know, in the MT קְדֹשׁ is usually parsed as the construct form of the adjective קָדוֹשׁ, not the noun קֹדֶשׁ.

108. The word in 4Q427 is interpreted as the abstract noun גְּדוּל by Schuller (DJD

גדול occurs as an adjective in construct with an abstract noun at the end of the very same line, in the phrase גדול / [החס]דים "(the Lord) … full of mercies" (1QHa VI, 34-35).[109] It seems conceivable, at the least, that the writers and scribes of 1QHa had the adjective in mind in the phrase כגדול כוחך and perhaps also in similar phrases.

Analogous ambiguities exist with other words. Sometimes the morphological ambiguity is connected to a question of orthography. For example, in 1QS IV, 11, a word for "heaviness" is transliterated either as כובוד or כיבוד.[110] Do the letters reflect a *quṭl noun כֹּבֶד or a *qiṭṭūl noun כִּיבּוּד (like that found in RH)?[111]

Nevertheless, the rare instances of nouns with two *waw mater*s make explicit that words of the *quṭl base pattern at least sometimes have an epenthetic /u/ class vowel, in addition to the /u/ class vowel they usually carry. Qimron's proposal for the pronunciation of the absolute/construct as *qoṭol*/*qŏṭol* (at least for some scribes and writers of the DSS-SP9 texts) seems very sensible.

The nouns easiest to interpret as *quṭl nouns (in construct) with a *waw mater* between second and third radicals are: אמוץ "strength of" (1QM XIV, 7; 1QHa X,10); ארוך "length of" (1QM VI, 15; 4Q416 2 iii, 19); חזוק "strength of" (1QS X, 26; 1QM XIV, 6; 1QHa X, 9; XVI, 36); חסור "lack

---

29:104), though the corresponding word in RH (גִּידּוּל) has a different connotation (Jastrow: "rearing, growth"). Note also that it is conceivable that phrases from the Bible like גְּדָול־כֹּחַ in Nah 1:3 influenced the writer of 1QHa; in this biblical text the adjective is used as a substantive referring to God, "one great (in) power," though such a usage does not seem likely for the passage from 1QHa.

109. This expression is similar to גְּדָול־כֹּחַ in Nah 1:3, cited in the preceding footnote, and וּגְדָל־חָסֶד "one (i.e., God) full of mercy" in Ps 145:8.

110. See, e.g., Wernberg-Møller, *Manual of Discipline*, 81 and Henoch Yalon, *Studies in the Dead Sea Scrolls: Philological Essays* (Hebrew; Jerusalem: Shrine of the Book and Kiryat Sepher, 1971), 73.

111. The difficulty of interpreting this word is still reflected in contemporary resources. As with גדול in 1QHa VI, 34, the *Dead Sea Scrolls Concordance* parses as the adjective (כבוד) (as do Qimron and Charlesworth, "Rule of the Community," 16), while Accordance reads it as the RH noun (כיבוד). The latter noun is not found in other DSS in an unbroken context (cf. [כי]בוד in 4Q487 24, 20) and this reading is further complicated by the fact that the initial /i/ vowel in these kinds of words is almost never written with a *mater* in the DSS (though, see HazGab 24 and Bar-Asher's comment on קיטוט ["*Vision of Gabriel*," 509–15]). A similar problem exists with חזוק "strength" (1QS X, 26 and passim) since there also occurs a RH word חִיזּוּק. The easiest interpretation of the word in 1QS IV, 11 is as כֹּבֶד, as Kutscher suggests (*Isaiah*, 502).

of" (11Q19 LIX, 3); יישור "uprightness of" (1QS XI, 2); כבוד "heaviness of" (4Q169 3–4 ii, 4, but not 1QIsa[a] at 21:15 where the word could easily be interpreted as "glory of"); כפור "ransom of" (4Q414 8, 4); להוב "blade (of)" (1QH[a] X, 28; XI, 31; 4Q169 3–4 ii, 3); עצום "might of" (1QM XI, 5); ערול "uncircumcised of" (1QH[a] X, 20); קדוש "holiness of" (4Q418 81 + 81a, 4); קצור "shortness of" (1QS IV, 10); רחוב "breadth (of)" (1QS IV, 9; 1QH[a] XVII, 27; 4Q365 12b iii, 9; 4Q487 15, 3; 11Q19 XXXVIII, 12); שחוד "bribe" (1QIsa[a] at Isa 5:23, 33:15); שפול "lowness of" (1QS IV, 9); תחות "under" (1QIsa[a] at Isa 3:24).[112] Those examples where two *waw maters* appear include אוהיול "tent of" (1QIsa[a] at Isa 16:5); יושור "uprightness of" (1QH[a] XIV, 13, following Qimron); כובוד "heaviness of" (1QS IV, 11); פועול "work of" (1QIsa[a] at Isa 59:6); שוחוד "bribe" (1QIsa[a] at Isa 45:13).[113] All these forms with *waw* after the second root consonant occur in DSS-SP9 and DSS-SP1c texts, suggesting a common orthographic tendency, if not also a common pronunciation, for the writers/scribes of these texts.

---

112. Many of the examples come from Qimron, *HDSS*, 38. The word כפור in the fragmentary 4Q414 8,4, is more likely כֹּפֶר than כִּפּוּר given the relative frequency of the former and rarity of the latter (especially as a singular noun). Of the nouns listed above, the *waw* appears after the first root consonant only in the following distributions (sometimes where the word bears a pronominal suffix): אומץ occurs four times in the biblical and nonbiblical scrolls (e.g., 4Q298 3–4 ii, 6; 4Q491 8–10 i, 4); אורך over ten times (e.g., 4Q426 1 i, 1; 4Q461 4, 3); חוזק seven times (e.g., 4Q301 2b, 3; 4Q491 8–10 i, 4); יושר five times (e.g., 1QS III, 8; 4Q184 1, 17); כופר at least three times (e.g., 1QH[a] VII, 37; 4Q219 II, 20); לוהב three times (1QM V, 7 and 10; VI, 2); עוצם once (4Q169 3–4 iii, 11); קודש many times (throughout the scrolls); קוצר once (1QS VI, 26); רוחב around eighteen times (e.g., 1QM V, 13; 4Q254a 1–2, 3); שוחד at least eight times (e.g., 1QH[a] VI, 31; 4Q437 9, 1); תוחת once (1QS VII, 13). The instances of these words with *waw* after the first root consonant are primarily, but not exclusively, in texts of the DSS-SP9 group.

113. The readings of these five words are not universally agreed upon. Note the disagreement over כובוד in footnote 110, above. Accordance reads אוהליו, though Ulrich et al. read as Kutscher did אוהיול (*Biblical Qumran Scrolls*, 361). Stegemann, Schuller, Newsom read יושיר (DJD 40:182). As for the words with interlinear *waws*, although the non-erasure or non-dotting of the other *waw* may be a case of scribal lapse or inattention, I assume that the scribes intended to write two *waw maters* to indicate two separate vowels (see Tov, *Scribal Practices*, 221). Of the nouns with two *waw maters* and not listed in the preceding footnote, the *waw* appears after the first root consonant only in the following distributions (sometimes where the word bears a pronominal suffix): אוהל seven times (e.g., 11Q19 XVII, 9); פועל five times (e.g., 1QIsa[a] at Isa 41:24; 11Q5 [11QPs[a]] at Ps 143:5).

The forms with a *waw* after the second root consonant (including those with a *waw* after the first consonant) are, as Qimron points out, almost always in the construct state and hardly ever found with a following possessive suffix. The only words to occur in the absolute are להוב (1QH[a] XI, 31; 4Q169 3–4 ii, 3) and שוחוד/שחוד in 1QIsa[a] (at Isa 5:23, 33:15, 45:13).[114] The only word to occur with a suffix is רחובו (4Q365 12b iii, 9). The presence of the *waw* in these forms is due to the guttural which is so weak it is not pronounced, thus an earlier **lohob* has become *lōb* and the *mater* could just as easily be placed before the *heh*.[115] That this is the case for roots with a middle *ḥeth* seems less likely given that *ḥeth* is the least weak of the gutturals; nevertheless, it is conceivable that in the dialect of the 1QIsa[a] scribes, it was so weak as to elide. All the same, שחוד/שוחוד and רחובו may also be due to scribal mistakes and/or influence from Aramaic orthography/pronunciation (the latter especially relevant to שחוד in 1QIsa[a], where Aramaic influence is seen in numerous ways).[116]

**quṭl* nouns probably also had a /u/ class epenthetic vowel in DSS Aramaic, where spellings such as קשט, קושט, קשוט, קושוט "truth" reflect, presumably, the presence of two vowels, though the exact phonetic realization, as in Hebrew, is not explicit (that is, *quṭul*, *quṭol*, *qoṭol*, and *qoṭul*).[117] This seems to be a halfway point in the Aramaic development of **quṭl* nouns, which would lead to pronunciations like **qəṭol* in Biblical Aramaic and other Aramaic dialects. Muraoka notes that there were no hard and fast rules for writing such nouns in Aramaic texts, with the result that in the same text a single word is not uncommonly spelled in two different ways, often in the same state (e.g., קשוט in 1Q20 III, 13 and קושט in 1Q20 II, 18).[118] That is, there is no distinction in spelling between nouns in the absolute and construct states. Muraoka adds that the realization of **quṭl* nouns in the Hebrew of the DSS is "more likely influenced by a contemporary Aramaic idiom rather than the other way round."[119]

The Hebrew II-*aleph* word מאד "much" deserves special attention. Based on its Akkadian cognates (*maʾdû* and *muʾdû*), it would seem to be

114. Qimron, *HDSS*, 37.

115. Ibid., 26.

116. Although it seems unlikely that a scribe would indicate a single vowel with two *maters*, as in **šōd*, note the spelling נואום in 1QIsa[a] at Isa 37:34.

117. Muraoka, *GQA*, 69. He admits the evidence for this is tenuous.

118. Ibid., 67.

119. Ibid., 69, n. 290.

of the *qaṭl or *quṭl pattern. In the MT, however, it is vocalized as מְאֹד; in the scrolls it appears in a wide variety of ways: מאד, מאדה, מאוד, מאודה, מואדה, מוד, מודה.[120] The forms without an *aleph* suggest that this word (at least sometimes) had a single vowel (that is, no epenthetic vowel), presumably due to the quiescence of the *aleph*. In these cases the word might have been pronounced *mōd* (its development being analogous to ראש *rōš* "head"). The MT form of the word is best explained as a late, secondary form, one based on the Aramaic form of **quṭl* nouns in the Common Era (that is, **mu'd* or **ma'd* > **mōd* > *mə'ōd*). This would parallel, therefore, Blau's supposition for the development of the MT word בְּאֵר "well" from an earlier **bi'r* (that is, **bi'r* > **bēr* > *bə'ēr*).[121] That such a development is likely for מאד is bolstered by the fact that in other cases where the *aleph* precedes an /o/ or /u/ class vowel and is preceded itself by a full vowel or shewa (that is, in the sequence -V'ō-), the *aleph* is usually preserved (שאול *šə'ōl* "Sheol"; מאור *mā'ōr* "light") and, where there is a *waw mater*, it almost never comes before the *aleph*.[122] Thus, if the word had been pronounced regularly *mə'ōd*, we would not expect it to be written מואד. This implies that the word was probably pronounced *mōd*, the *aleph* being (as in the case of ראש) a historical spelling where it appears.

In a similar way, the word "utterance" was likely pronounced among those writing and reading the DSS like a noun of the **quṭl* base. It most often occurs among the biblical DSS, where it is written נאם over twenty-five times (some examples are difficult to read); however, it occurs sixteen times as נואם, primarily in 1QIsa[a], but also in other DSS-SP9 texts like 2Q13 (2QJer) and 4Q27 (4QNum[b]). In addition, it occurs with this spell-

---

120. The unusual spellings derive mostly from DSS-SP9 and DSS-SP1c texts. The forms with a *waw* before the *aleph* (nonbiblical 9; biblical 21) are overall more common than those with *waw* after the *aleph* (8/2). Perhaps due to the conservatism associated with biblical texts, there are no examples of the word lacking an *aleph* in the biblical texts; there are twelve examples of the word without *aleph* in the nonbiblical scrolls.

121. Blau, *Phonology and Morphology*, 55. The relevant passage is quoted above in the subsection "Quiescence of *Aleph*" in §4.3, "Weakening of Gutturals." The word מאד in the MT has a slightly different morphology than other II-*aleph* *quṭl nouns like בְּאשׁ "stench"; when suffixes attach to מאד, the word retains its secondary vowels (מְאֹדוֹ, מְאֹדֶךָ), while באש reflects its etymological vowels (בָּאְשָׁם, בָּאְשׁוֹ). The dominance of the secondary vowels in מאד is due presumably to the word's frequency as an unsuffixed adverb with these same vowels. See *HGhS*, 580r.

122. For examples, see the discussion in "Digraphs" (§3.5).

ing in two nonbiblical scrolls (4Q175 10 and 4Q177 10–11, 2). It is only rarely spelled with a *waw* between the second and third root consonants: נאום (4Q175 9; 1QIsa[a] at Isa 1:24, 41:14) for MT נְאֻם and נואום (1QIsa[a] at Isa 37:34) for MT נְאֻם. Where it is spelled with *waw* in this position it is, as it always is, in construct with a following word; this makes it parallel to other **quṭl* base nouns that also exhibit fluctuation and variation in the number and placement of *waw maters* (see the discussion above). The word seems to have been understood in the MT tradition as a *qal* passive participle or as a **quṭūl*/**qiṭūl* base noun (akin to MT כְּרוּב "cherub" and לְבוּשׁ "clothing"). As with מאד "much," if the word "utterance" was pronounced *nəʾum* or *nəʾūm*, we would not expect it to be spelled so frequently נואם. Thus, it seems likeliest that this word was pronounced as *nūm* among the scribes of the DSS-SP9 texts.

Another word deserving comment is the noun תאר "form." Although the etymology of the word is not agreed upon, the form of the word in the MT (תֹּאַר) and among many DSS (תאר, תואר, תאור) suggests it was understood as a **quṭl* noun.[123] The word, like מאד, was sometimes spelled without an *aleph*, תור and תר, which suggests that in these cases the word was spoken without an epenthetic vowel: *tōr*.[124] Here too the pronunciation *tōr* may have been on analogy to ראש (*rōš*), if not also to other similar words like תור "turn, row" (= MT תּוֹר) and תור "turtle dove" (= MT תּוֹר), not to mention תורה "law" (= MT תּוֹרָה).[125]

The presence of an epenthetic vowel for **quṭl* nouns suggests the existence of an epenthetic vowel (presumably /a/ or /e/) for the other segholate bases (**qaṭl*/**qiṭl*), though the orthography does not usually help us ascertain this. Note, however, למעאן "so that" in 4Q175 4 (for what would be in the MT לְמַעַן), in which *aleph* may mark a preceding /a/ epenthetic vowel

---

123. Joüon-Muraoka characterize it as from ראה (§88Lv), while *HALOT* suggest perhaps it is from the verb תאר "to sketch," which itself may be related to תור "to spy."

124. The spelling תאר or תואר occurs in 4Q525 2 iii, 4; 14 i, 12; 11Q19 LXIII, 11; 1QIsa[a] at Isa 52:14, 53:2 (תאור); 1Q8 (1QIsa[b]) at Isa 53:2; 4Q9 (4QGen[j]) at Gen 41:18; 5Q6 (5QLam[a]) at Lam 4:8; the spelling תור in 4Q426 1 i, 9; 11Q5 (11QPs[a]) XXVIII, 9; and תר in 11Q5 (11QPs[a]) XXI, 11; 1Q8 (1QIsa[b]) at Isa 52:14. Note the spelling תור in the Masada text to Sir 43:18 (Mas 1h VI, 12).

125. In 11Q5 (11QPs[a]) XXI, 11 (= Sir 51:14) the word has a 3fs pronominal suffix, making it (presumably) identical in sound to the word "Torah" (Reymond, *New Idioms within Old*, 31 and references there). In relation to these nouns, note also נאוד (= MT נאד "skin-bottle") in 4Q89 (4QPs[g]) at Ps 119:83 and 11Q5 (11QPs[a]) at Ps 119:83; צאן (4Q251 10, 6), צואן (4Q177 5–6, 15), צאון (11Q19 XLIII, 15), and צון (4Q266 11, 13).

(though caution is in order since this text exhibits many unusual spellings related to *aleph*).

5.6. Verbs

Lexicon

It sometimes happens that a verb unattested in the MT is found in the DSS. The number of verbs not found in the MT seems smaller than the number of nouns. An example is the verb תלש "to tear" (4Q238 1), which is attested rather frequently in RH. In some cases, there is a shift in distribution, as with the verb צנע "to be humble" which appears once in the MT (Mic 6:8), though at least twelve times in the nonbiblical scrolls. A similar pattern is attested for חרת "to engrave." In BDB, it is suggested that the single occurrence of the passive participle of this verb (חָרוּת in Exod 32:16) may be a scribal mistake (due to influence from Aramaic חרת "to engrave" which is cognate with Hebrew חרשׁ "to engrave, plow"). Nevertheless, there are at least fifteen occurrences of חרת "to engrave" in the nonbiblical scrolls, often as a passive participle, but also as a finite verb (1QM XII, 3 and 4Q400 1 i, 15). (The Hebrew realization of this etymological root, חרשׁ, also occurs in the nonbiblical scrolls, though it is always used in the sense of "to plow"; the related noun חרש "engraver" occurs six times.)[126]

Some words from LBH are attested more commonly than those from SBH. For example, זעק "to cry out" occurs once in the Pentateuch but six times in Nehemiah and 1–2 Chronicles and exclusively in the nonbiblical scrolls (at least fourteen times); the synonymous צעק "to cry out" occurs over fifteen times in the Pentateuch, but only twice in Nehemiah and 1–2 Chronicles and never in the nonbiblical scrolls.[127] Even where a MT text attests צעק, the DSS corresponding to it might attest זעק, as throughout 1QIsa[a] at Isa 33:7, 42:2, 46:7, 65:14 (but not at Isa 19:20 where both the MT and the scroll have צעק) and in 4Q365 6a i, 4 at Exod 14:15 and 6a ii + 6c, 10 at Exod 15:25.

Sometimes, as in the MT, there exist pairs of roots that express the same idea. For example, both בוז and בזה mean "to despise"; both דכא and דכה mean "to crush"; both חקה and חקק mean "to engrave." The DSS pre-

126. For more on this word and its cognates, see *ThWQ*, cols. 1:1077–79.

127. See Kutscher, *Isaiah*, 34.

sume other pairs not found in the MT, like הפך "to turn, change" and אפך; although the latter root is not attested clearly it can be assumed based on forms like יופך (4Q422 III, 7) and ויופכו (4Q501 1, 4) since the imperfect of הפך ordinarily takes an /a/ vowel with the prefix in the MT and presumably also in the DSS (e.g., יהפכו), while the root אפך in the Mishnah takes an /o/ vowel with the prefix.[128]

Lack of Confusion between III-*Waw/Yodh* and III-*Aleph* Verbs

Most classes of verbs have a morphology identical to that found in the MT. This applies, also, to III-*waw/yodh* and III-*aleph* verbs. Although a confusion between these verb (and root) types is common in Aramaic, such is not found in the Hebrew of the scrolls.[129] To judge from the orthography, the two root types are almost always distinguished in verbs. Notice, for example, that in the approximately fifty easily readable 3cp perfect verb forms that are from III-*aleph* roots in the nonbiblical scrolls listed by Accordance, only one has a form reminiscent of a III-*waw/yodh* root (מלו "they fulfilled" in 4Q401 22, 2). By contrast, in the three clear examples of the 3mp perfect of III-*aleph* roots in the Aramaic DSS, two have patterns characteristic of III-*waw/yodh* roots (אטמיו in 4Q531 1, 1 and חטו in 4Q550 5 + 5a, 2). Cases like מלו reflect quiescence of *aleph*, not confusion of verb types: *millǝʾū* > *millū*. Although the quiescence of *aleph* makes these forms look like analogous forms from III-*waw/yodh* roots, the same is not true for second person verb forms like ברתנו "you created us" (4Q504 1–2 Riii, 4), which is distinct from עשיתם "you made them" (4Q504 1–2 Rii, 18). Even in 1QIsa[a], where we might expect to see the confusion of verb types (given the Aramaic influence on other words and forms), III-*aleph* and III-*waw/yodh* verbs are usually distinct. This might not be obvious at first blush since III-*waw/yodh* verb forms that end with a vowel are sometimes marked with a final *aleph mater* (ונלוא "he will join" 1QIsa[a] at Isa 14:1 for MT וְנִלְוָה; הטא "stretch" at Isa 37:17 for MT הַטֵּה) and III-*aleph* verb forms are sometimes marked with a final *heh mater* (חוטה "who sins" at Isa 1:4 for MT חֹטֵא; יקרה "he is called" at Isa 54:5 for MT יִקָּרֵא).[130] Nevertheless, where these verb types are clearly distinguishable through the

128. Note also מפאכת and מאפכת (1QIsa[a] at Isa 1:7 and 13:19 for MT מַהְפֵּכַת "overthrown by") (ibid., 506).

129. See Muraoka, *GQA*, 23–24.

130. Note also: יקרה "he is called" (1QIsa[a] at Isa 56:7) for MT יִקָּרֵא; ימלה "he will

orthography, there is little evidence of confusion: קראתי "I called" (1QIsa[a] at Isa 30:7) and with elision of *aleph* וקרתי "I will call" (at Isa 22:20 for MT וְקָרָאתִי; see also Isa 42:6 and 51:2), but never *קריתי. Similarly, III-*waw/yodh* verbs are written normally (e.g., עשיתי at Isa 10:11) and not like III-*aleph* verbs (*עשאתי or *עשתי).[131] In other places where there appears to be confusion between root types, the spelling really reflects a similar (if not identical) pronunciation, also reflected in the MT tradition: תנשינה "they will be lifted" (at Isa 66:12 for MT תִּנָּשֶׂאנָה; cf. 1Q8 [1QIsa[b]] at Isa 60:4); נמציתי "I was found" (1QIsa[a] at Isa 65:1) for MT נִמְצֵאתִי; והוציתי "I will bring forth" (at Isa 65:9) for MT וְהוֹצֵאתִי.[132] These same tendencies are found throughout the Hebrew scrolls and this knowledge helps the reconstruction of some verbs: the reading [פ]דיתנו (*DSSSE*) seems more likely than [ב]ריתנו (Accordance) in 1QM XIII, 9.[133]

Conjugations

To the degree that the consonantal text allows us to determine it, the scrolls evidence the stems we typically associate with Tiberian Hebrew (including those associated with weak roots like the *polel*, *polal*, *hithpolel*, *pilpel*, and *hithpalpel*). Most of the rarer stems (e.g., the "*nithpael*" as in וְנִכַּפֵּר "it will be absolved" of Deut 21:8) are not attested in the nonbiblical DSS, though at least one may be. The DSS perhaps evidence a stem associated with

---

(not) fulfill" (at Isa 65:20) for MT יְמַלֵּא; ונטא "he will stretch" (at Isa 34:11) for MT וְנָטָה; ויבנא "he built" (at Isa 5:2) for MT וַיִּבֶן.

131. Kutscher (*Isaiah*, 164) remarks on the spelling להפלה (1QIsa[a] at Isa 29:14) for MT הַפְלִיא; if the III-*aleph* verbs were really patterning themselves after III-*waw/yodh*, then we would have expected to see *להפלות.

132. There are two cases that potentially do reflect confusion with III-*waw/yodh* roots in 1QIsa[a], ימחוא "they will clap" 1QIsa[a] at Isa 55:12 for MT יִמְחֲאוּ and תקרוא "you (mp) will be called" at Isa 61:6 for MT תִּקָּרֵאוּ. But, these can also be explained, respectively, as quiescence of *aleph* after a muttered vowel and assimilation of *aleph* to a following /u/ vowel (see §3.5, "Digraphs").

133. Other mistakes involving III-*aleph* verbs do not reflect confusion between roots, but reflect the phonetic development of /ʾ/ > /y/, as in ישייכה (1QIsa[a] at Isa 37:10); see "*Aleph* < *Yodh* and *Yodh* < *Aleph*" (§4.4). Still other misspellings of III-*aleph* verbs can be explained as due to haplography: יוצי איש (4Q159 2–4, 8; see *DSSSE* and cf. Allegro's reading יוצו in DJD 5:8) for *יוציא איש; הוצי את (4Q408 3+3a, 7) for *הוציא את. Thus, שנאתה[in 4Q462 1, 18 is better read not as "she was hated" = *ni*]*snātā* (a III-*yodh* pausal form) but as שנאתה "she changed" = *šānātā*.

LBH and RH called the *nuphal*. The stem's presence in LBH is remarked on tersely by Joüon-Muraoka in relation to נוּלְּדוּ "were born" (1 Chr 3:5, 20:8).[134] In RH, it appears, apparently, in more verbs.[135] That DSS Hebrew contained something similar hinges on the reading of two different words: לניכנעים "to those humbled" as a *niphal* (1QS X, 26) versus לנוכנעים as a *nuphal* and ונ'קפו "they will be cut down" as a *niphal* (4Q161 8–10, 6) versus וניקפו as a *nuphal*.[136]

The *qal* passive was probably long forgotten by the time of the late Second Temple period, though it is attested, as it is in the MT, with verbs that appear to be *pual* or *hophal* but which do not occur in the corresponding active stems (*piel* or *hiphil*) and which have meanings that seem to be simply the passive of the *qal* stem. In the MT, the common examples for this conjugation in the perfect are לֻקַּח "to be taken" and יֻלַּד "to be born" and in the imperfect יֻקַּח and יֻתַּן "it will be given."[137] In the DSS, the orthography of certain words suggests that some words were pronounced as *qal* passives/*puals*/*hophals*. For example, one finds, in the biblical scrolls, the perfect: יולד "he was born" (1QIsa^{a} at Isa 9:5 for MT יֻלַּד); לוקח "he was taken" (1QIsa^{a} at Isa 52:5 and 53:8 for MT לֻקַּח and לֻקָּח); the imperfect: תושד "you will be destroyed" (1QIsa^{a} at Isa 33:1 for MT תּוּשַּׁד); and the participle מורט "was made smooth" (4Q56 [4QIsa^{b}] at Isa 18:7 for MT מוֹרָט); note also יתץ "it will be broken" (Mas 1b [Mas Lev^{b}] at Lev 11:35 for MT יֻתָּץ); [י]תן "it will be given" (Mas 1b [Mas Lev^{b}] at Lev 11:38 for MT יֻתַּן). In the nonbiblical scrolls, one finds only the imperfect יושדו "(which) will be destroyed" (1QH^{a} XXV, 8).

---

134. Joüon-Muraoka §60h.

135. See Henoch (Hanoch) Yalon, *Introduction to the Vocalization of the Mishna* (Jerusalem: Bialik, 1964), 152–59; and Menahem Moreshet, "On the Nuf'al Stem in Post-Biblical Hebrew" (Hebrew), in *Studies in Hebrew and Semitic Languages Dedicated to the Memory of Prof. Eduard Yechezkel Kutscher* (ed. Gad B. Sarfatti et al.; Ramat-Gan: Bar-Ilan University, 1980), 126–39.

136. See "*Plene* Orthography" (§3.2) and also Qimron, *Grammar*, 53–54 and 177.

137. The original pronounciation of these forms would have been **quṭil* and **yuqṭal* (the /i/ of the perfect shifting to /a/ to match the imperfect and/or on analogy to the other passive stems with /a/ vowels like the *pual* and *hophal*); these forms experienced spontaneous gemination of the middle root consonant in order to preserve the distinctive short /u/ vowel in the initial syllable, leading to the perfect looking and sounding identical to the *pual* perfect and the imperfect looking and sounding like the *hophal* imperfect (see Joüon-Muraoka §58a; Waltke and O'Connor, *Introduction to Biblical Hebrew Syntax*, 373–76; Bauer and Leander, *HGhS*, 285–88).

The status of some verbs in the MT is debated, and subsequently also for the DSS, for example, יכתו "they will be crushed" (1QM XVIII, 2 for what would be in the MT יֻכַּתּוּ, as in Jer 46:5 and Mic 1:7) and similarly יוכת (1QIsa[a] at Isa 24:12 for MT יֻכַּת).[138] Due to the unpredictable orthography of some scrolls, in particular 1QIsa[a], where short /u/ vowels are sometimes represented by *waw mater* and sometimes not, one is left to wonder about the pronunciation of some words. For example, note זרו "they were (not) pressed out" (1QIsa[a] at Isa 1:6) for MT זֹרוּ; תאכלו "you will be eaten" (1QIsa[a] at Isa 1:20) for MT תְּאֻכְּלוּ.[139]

The fact that the *qal* passive was no longer understood as such is reflected in various alterations in the biblical scrolls, especially 1QIsa[a]. For example, the third-person plural form of the verb sometimes replaces the singular *qal* passive; presumably the plural is indicating an impersonal construction, as is common in Aramaic: עבדו "(which) was done (lit., they did = MT עָבְדוּ)" (1QIsa[a] at Isa 14:3) for MT עֻבַּד;[140] יקחו "can it be taken (lit., can they take)" (1QIsa[a] at Isa 49:24) for MT יֻקַּח.[141] Sometimes the 3ms is used with an impersonal sense: ישיר "it will be sung (lit., he will sing)" (1QIsa[a] at Isa 26:1) for MT יוּשַׁר. Alternatively, the passive was turned into an active: ילדה "she bore" (4Q1 [4QGen–Exod[a]] at Gen 35:26) for MT יֻלַּד "was born." In other cases the spelling suggests a *niphal*, as in ילקח "it will be taken" (1QIsa[a] at Isa 49:25) for MT יֻקָּח, or makes explicit a *pual* conjugation, as in ממורט and ממרט "was made smooth" (1QIsa[a] at Isa 18:2 and 7, respectively), for MT מוֹרָט.[142]

The peculiar distribution of some MT verbs in certain stems is sometimes reflected (at least partially) in the DSS. So, for example, the verb בין in the MT means "to understand" in both the *qal* and *hiphil*, and is used with and without direct objects in both stems with this meaning. In the DSS, the verb also occurs in both stems with the meaning "to understand," though with this meaning it almost always takes the *beth* prepo-

138. Note also the possible example of תוגע "do (not) be touched" (4Q417 1 i, 23) (as suggested by Qimron, cited in Strugnell and Harrington, DJD 34:167).

139. See also אסרו (1QIsa[a] at Isa 22:3), הרג (at Isa 27:7), עזב (at Isa 32:14).

140. The verb in the scroll has the sense "to do" as in Aramaic. See Kutscher, *Isaiah*, 401–2.

141. This shift is seen consistently with MT קֹרָא "it is called" in 1QIsa[a], where it is realized as יקראו (at Isa 48:8), וקראו (at Isa 58:12, 61:3, and 62:2); only once is it found קרא (at Isa 65:1). Kutscher notes a similar shift from the *niphal* of קרא to the *qal* 3mp (*Isaiah*, 402).

142. See ibid., 344 and 364.

sition (whether *qal* or *hiphil*), while in the *hiphil* where it takes a direct object it typically means "to teach." The exceptions to this rule (that is, where the verb means "to understand" and takes a direct object) are from DSS-SP1c (4Q424 3, 2) and DSS-NSP (4Q372 3, 3) texts. As in the MT, the morphology of the imperfect forms of the verb (e.g., יבין) does not allow us to decide whether they were construed as *qal* or *hiphil*.

Some verbs attest stems in the DSS that are not attested for these same verbs in the MT. Often, these are easiest to identify when the verbal stem has an extra consonant that makes its identification clear, as in the *hithpael* stem. In the DSS the following verbs occur in the *hithpael* (though in the MT they do not): אחר "to delay" (1QS I, 14 and passim); בהל "to rush, be dismayed" (4Q215 1–3, 5); יסר "to chasten" (1QS III, 6 and passim); רשע "to be evil" (4Q491 8–10 i, 7); שלם "to complete" (4Q385 2, 3 and passim). In many cases, these verbs in the *hithpael* have a passive meaning and, as Qimron notes, there seems little distinction from the *niphal*.[143] In a similar way, Qimron and Menahem Moreshet have both noted instances where what is often attested in SBH in the MT as a *qal* (e.g., זנח "to reject," לעג "to mock") appears in LBH, Ben Sira, the DSS (and often RH) as a *hiphil* (הזנחתני "you did [not] reject me" 1QH^a XVII, 7; ילעיגו "they will mock" 1QpHab IV, 2).[144] In these examples, the later *hiphil* form has the same meaning as the earlier *qal*. In other cases, a verb appears in the *hiphil* for the first time in the DSS, with a causative sense, distinct from the sense conveyed by the *qal*: for example, עשה occurs in the MT only in the *qal* and *niphal* (and once, perhaps, in the *pual*), but appears in the *hiphil* "to cause to do" in the DSS (4Q440 3 i, 21 and 4Q470 1, 4), as it does in RH.[145] Another case is perhaps found in הוגירני "he made me fear" (4Q111 [4QLam^a] at Lam 1:12) for MT הוֹגָה "he made suffer"; the verb יגר occurs only in the *qal* in the MT.[146] The same happens with the *niphal*:

143. Qimron, *HDSS*, 49. Note, however, the apparent variation between the two stems with the root חבא "to hide" in Gen 3:8 and 10. See Joel Baden, "Hithpael and Niphal in Biblical Hebrew: Semantic and Morphological Overlap," *VT* 60 (2010): 36.

144. Qimron, *HDSS*, 49, and M. Moreshet, "The Hiphil in Mishnaic Hebrew as Equivalent to the Qal" (Hebrew), *Bar-Ilan* 13 (1976): 253–57.

145. See Moshe Bar-Asher, "Two Phenomena in Qumran Hebrew," 176–180; idem, "Qumran Hebrew and Mishnaic Hebrew," 292–93. In other cases, a verb might have a slightly different nuance: שטם "to have animosity toward" occurs only in the *qal* in the MT, but in both the *qal* (4Q174 4, 4) and *hiphil* "to accuse" (4Q225 2 i, 10) in the DSS.

146. See Cross, DJD 16:235.

פשט appears in the MT most commonly in the *qal* and *hiphil* meaning usually "to strip off (something)" or, in the *qal*, "to raid," but in the DSS it occurs (together with the *qal* and *hiphil*) in the *niphal* meaning "to be spread out" (1QM VIII, 6; XVII, 10), a stem and meaning that also occur in RH. In other cases, the lack of a prefix or *mater* suggests a different stem. For example, יללו "they wailed" (4Q387 A, 4 and 4Q422 G, 1) seems to suggest a *piel* form for the root ילל, as is found in RH (parallel to Aramaic in the D-stem), instead of the MT *hiphil*.

In some cases, a given expression in the MT will exhibit one stem and the equivalent expression in the DSS will exhibit a different stem; Fassberg notes in relation to the *pual* participle in מגולי אוזן *məgullē ʾozon* "those with uncovered ears" (1QM X, 11) that one might have expected the *qal*, *גלויי אזן, given the similar expression גְלוּי עֵינָיִם "one with uncovered eye" in Num 24:4 and 16.[147]

Two texts, 1QS and 1QIsa^a^, exhibit features in the *hiphil* that reflect influence from Aramaic. As noted above (in the subsection "Quiescence of *Heh*" in §4.3, "Weakening of Gutturals"), these texts attest verbal forms in which an *aleph* appears for the *heh* of the *hiphil* prefix and this is thought to parallel the alternation in Aramaic between *haphel* and *aphel* stems (both of which are causative stems). Alone, the presence of an *aleph* for *heh* could easily be interpreted as a phonetic confusion. However, both texts exhibit other verbal forms that seem closer to Aramaic causative stems than Hebrew. Specifically, some *hiphil* imperfects and participles bear a prefixed *heh* just as in Aramaic: ויהכין "and he will establish" (1QS III, 9); ואהסתר "and I hid" (1QIsa^{a} at Isa 57:17) for MT הַסְתֵּר "hiding"; מהסיר "is removing" (1QIsa^{a} at Isa 3:1) for MT מֵסִיר; מהניף "waving" (1QIsa^{a} at Isa 19:16) for MT מֵנִיף.[148] That similar forms are almost unknown from other texts suggests this is a feature peculiar to 1QS and 1QIsa^{a} and underlines well the peculiar Aramaic influence found in some DSS.[149]

147. Steven E. Fassberg, "The Movement from *Qal* to *Piʿʿel* in Hebrew and the Disappearance of the *Qal* Internal Passive," *HS* 42 (2001): 243–55.

148. See Kutscher, *Isaiah*, 198. Some readings are disputed: יהבינהו "he will teach him" (1QS VI, 15) is often read now והבינהו; note also יהודיע "will make me know" (1QIsa^{a} in an addition to Isa 38:20) or והודיע.

149. I know of only יהסירך "he will remove you" (4Q60 [4QIsa^{f}] at Isa 22:19) for MT יֶהֶרְסֶךָּ "he will destroy you."

Perfect and *Waw*-Consecutive Perfect

Apart from the characteristic *plene* spelling of second-person masculine singular/plural perfect forms, the perfect forms for most verbs are identical to their counterparts in the MT. As mentioned above (in §3.2, "*Plene* Orthography"), the 2ms perfect is characterized by a *heh mater* in most cases in the DSS-SP9 and DSS-SP1c texts, though only infrequently in the DSS-NSP texts. The 2fs perfect ends with תי- instead of the expected ת- in 1QIsa[a] (eighteen times), in 1QIsa[b] (once), and in 4Q72 (4QJer[c]) (once), though no other time.[150] This ending is also preserved in some *kethib* forms of the 2fs perfect in the MT (similar to the preservation of *kethib* versions of the 2fs independent pronoun אַתְּי), as well as in Samaritan Hebrew.[151] Although it is possible, as Ben-Ḥayyim argues, that these forms in the MT and in Samaritan Hebrew are derived from the etymological forms of the 2fs perfect, it is likeliest that, as Kutscher argues, the forms in 1QIsa[a] are attributable to Aramaic influence, as well as the forms in the MT (since they occur in later books).[152]

The 2mp perfect occurs approximately eighty times in the nonbiblical scrolls and around 275 times in the biblical scrolls. It is marked תמה- in approximately 60 percent of its occurrences in the nonbiblical scrolls and in 20 percent of the biblical scrolls (and תם- in the other cases). Most texts seem consistent in using one or the other form (11Q19 and 11Q20 contain at least twenty instances of the long form and no instances of the short), though the two types do occur in close proximity to each other in two texts: 4Q365 32, 8 and 4Q418 55, 8. The 2fp occurs once marked in the biblical scrolls תן- and once תנה-; it does not occur in the nonbiblical scrolls.

As in the MT, one sometimes finds anomalous forms for the 3fs perfect: זנת "(who) acted the prostitute" (4Q394 [4QMMT] 3–7 i, 12) and וקברת "it will be buried" (4Q418 127, 2).[153] In these two cases, one sus-

150. Abegg, "Linguistic Profile," 31.

151. For a listing of the forms of the 2fs perfect with the *kethib* ending תְּי-, see GKC §44h.

152. Ben-Ḥayyim, *Grammar of Samaritan Hebrew*, 104; Kutscher, *Isaiah*, 188–90; and Abegg, "Linguistic Profile," 41. Ben-Ḥayyim also observes that for Samaritan Hebrew the preservation of this ending is due to the identical ending (תי-) on 2fs perfects in Aramaic (ibid.).

153. It is, of course, possible to interpret these words in other ways, but these seem likely cases of the 3fs perfect. The form זנת might be the feminine singular par-

pects influence from Aramaic. Some forms that are relatively rare in the MT are more common in the DSS and/or show a different distribution. For example, the *hiphil* second- and first-person perfect forms of בוא often bear an *ō* connecting vowel in the DSS, as in הביאותה "you brought" (1QH[a] XIV, 15) (versus הבאתי "I brought" 4Q389 2, 6), though in the Bible it is more common not to find the connecting vowel for this verb (e.g., הֵבֵאתִי Gen 31:39) and where it appears it is on a verb form that also bears an object suffix (e.g., וַהֲבִיאוֹתִיךָ Ezek 38:16).[154] In the DSS, the forms with the connecting vowel do not generally have an object suffix. A similar distribution of second-/first-person forms occurs between the MT and the DSS with the *hiphil* perfect of נוף, which always appears (four times, only in the second-person) in the DSS with an /ō/ connecting vowel (e.g., הניפותה "you waved" in 1QH[a] XV, 10), while the same verb appears without the connecting vowel in five of its six occurrences (in the second- and first-person) in the MT (e.g., הֵנַפְתָּ in Exod 20:25).

Imperfect and *Waw*-Consecutive Imperfect

The following paragraphs address the prefix-conjugations as found in the DSS. For comments on the form of the *qal* imperfect and imperative with suffix, see the following sections: "*Qal* Imperfect + Suffix" and "*Qal* Imperative + Suffix." In the former, the tendency for plural imperfects to exhibit a theme vowel is addressed.

---

ticiple, like פֹּרָת (from פרה) in Gen 49:22. The form קברת might also be a participle (see Strugnell and Harrington, DJD 34:359).

154. The forms where a *mater* clearly marks the /ō/ connecting vowel appear in 1QH[a] XIV, 15; XXI, 10; 4Q438 3, 3; 11Q19 XVIII, 13; LIX, 11; LXIII, 12; 1QIsa[a] at Isa 37:26 for MT הֲבֵאתִיהָ, 43:23 for MT הֵבֵאתָ, 48:15 for MT הֲבִיאֹתִיו, 56:7 for MT הֲבִיאֹתִים; 1Q8 (1QIsa[b]) at Isa 43:23 for MT הֵבֵאתָ; 4Q11 (4QpaleoGen–Exod[l]) at Exod 26:33 for MT הֵבֵאתָ. Forms with defective orthography and/or with no /ō/ connecting vowel appear in 4Q176 15, 2; 4Q389 2, 6; as well as commonly among the biblical scrolls: 1Q8 (1QIsa[b]) at Isa 56:7; 4Q1 (4QGen–Exod[a]) at Gen 39:17, Exod 6:8; 4Q22 (4QpaleoExod[m]) at Exod 26:11; 4Q24 (4QLev[b]) at Lev 23:10; 4Q26c (4QLev[i] = XLev[c]) at Lev 26:36; 4Q58 (4QIsa[d]) at Isa 48:15; 4Q61 (4QIsa[g]) at Isa 43:23; 11Q1 (11QpaleoLev[a]) at Lev 26:25. Note also Mas 1d at Ezek 36:24 and 37:12; Mur 1 at Exod 6:8; Mur 88 at Joel 4:5 and at Hag 1:8, 9. In the MT, the forms with an /ō/ connecting vowel occur sixteen times, while the forms without the connecting vowel number sixty-two.

The theme vowel of certain verbs in the imperfect (and imperative) is /a/ in the MT but an /o/ or /u/ class vowel in 1QIsa[a] (e.g., תזריענו "you will plant it" at Isa 17:10; אפעולה "I will do" at Isa 43:13; ישכובו "they will lie down" at Isa 43:17; יואכולם "he will eat them" at Isa 51:8 and passim).[155] Outside of 1QIsa[a], this phenomenon is found more rarely: ישכוב "he will lie down" (1QS VII, 10, but otherwise without a *waw mater*); ישחוקו "they will laugh" (1QpHab IV, 6) corrected to ישחקו (perhaps reflecting misplacement of the final *mater*; see §3.1, "Scribal Mistakes").[156] That the unexpected forms are mostly restricted to 1QIsa[a] suggests this is a feature especially of this scroll's scribes, perhaps related to influence from Aramaic, where the cognates to some of these verbs (that is, אכל, בחר, זרע, פעל, שכב) often take an /o/ or /u/ theme vowel.[157]

As in the MT, some stative verbs show an /o/ or /u/ theme vowel, as with תשכון "she will dwell" (4Q184 1, 7 and passim [always with a *waw mater* in the nonbiblical scrolls], = MT תִּשְׁכּוֹן Jer 33:16) and יבול "it withers" (1QH[a] XVI, 27 and passim, for what would be in the MT יִבּוֹל). At least some verbs that show both /a/ and an /o/ theme vowel in the MT, on the other hand, do not exhibit such alternation, presumably, in the DSS (specifically in the DSS-SP9 and DSS-SP1c texts; see יחפץ, יבגוד, and §4.7, "Accent or Stress").

Abegg, in his "Hebrew of the Dead Sea Scrolls" article, offers specifics for the number of verbal forms with and without *maters*; although these give the general sense of the distribution, they do not precisely reflect the evidence and should be used with caution. For example, he writes that the *qal* 2mp imperfect of strong verbs attests only the so-called pausal

155. For the full list, see Kutscher, *Isaiah*, 341–42; other verbs include חרב, נגש, שפל, חפר, בחר.

156. Abegg, "Hebrew of the Dead Sea Scrolls," 340 and 350. He also lists a biblical precedent: *qere* אֶסְלַח and *kethib* אסלוח in Jer 5:7. The reading of [יש]מועו in 4Q491 1–3, 13, also listed by Abegg, is read [יש]מיעו by Accordance.

157. An /o/ theme vowel is found for אכל, זרע, פעל in Palestinian Aramaic (שכב has an /a/ vowel), and for all the same verbs in Syriac (where שכב also sometimes takes an /a/ vowel). The verbs חפר and שפל do not take an /o/ or /u/ vowel. Of course, other reasons can be found for the appearance of the /o/ or /u/ theme vowel for some of these verbs. E.g., אכל apparently originally took a /u/ theme vowel in the imperfect of the basic stem and developed its /a/ vowel based on dissimilation (or, analogy to other I-*aleph* verbs); Kutscher takes the spelling of אכל above as evidence for the lack of dissimilation in the idiolect of the scribe of 1QIsa[a] (*Isaiah*, 476–77).

form.[158] This expresses the dominance of the pausal form among DSS-SP9 and DSS-SP1c texts, but not the fact that in DSS-NSP texts the plural imperfect forms do not appear with *maters*: [תש]רפון "you will burn" and [תש]מרו "you will keep" (4Q368 2, 5 and 9, respectively); ירמסו "they will trample" (4Q381 46a + b, 8). Curiously, among the DSS-SP9 and DSS-SP1c texts, the pausal forms for 3mp imperfects are not as ubiquitous as the 2mp forms, but still represent the majority of forms.[159] For more on what appear to be pausal forms of the plural imperfect in the DSS, see the sections "Accent or Stress" (§4.7) and "*Qal* Imperfect + Suffix" (§5.7).

Abegg's counting of *waw*-consecutive imperfects in his corpus suggests that this construction is approximately half as common in the DSS as it is in the MT; conversely, the perfect verb form is used much more commonly than in the MT.[160] Verb types and conjugations that attest a short form in the *waw*-consecutive imperfect in the MT (that is, especially II-*waw*/*yodh*, III-*waw*/*yodh*, and *hiphil* verbs) generally show a similar shortened form in the DSS (for specifics, see below). That the short (that is, etymological jussive/preterite) forms dominated the *waw*-consecutive paradigm is revealed by an analysis of the verb forms from II-*yodh* and III-*waw*/*yodh* roots as well as *hiphil* verbs. The II-*yodh* and *hiphil* forms very rarely attest a *yodh mater* (and when they do it is often influenced by other factors, like a word-final *aleph*: ויוציא "he brought forth" in 11Q5 [11QPs^{a}] at Ps 136:11 for MT וַיּוֹצֵא), though the corresponding imperfect forms do. III-*waw*/*yodh* verbs exhibit a similar consistency between short *waw*-consecutive imperfect forms and long (non-*waw*-consecutive) imperfects; where there are exceptions, these are isolated to specific texts like the very brief 1Q7 (1QSam) which exhibits the long form of the imperfect three times (ויכה at 2 Sam 23:10, 12 for MT וַיַּךְ and ויע[ש]ה at 23:10 for MT וַיַּעַשׂ) and 1QIsa^{a} which frequently (but not always) shows the long form of the imperfect for common roots, like ויבנא (at Isa 5:2) for MT וַיִּבֶן, ויעשה (at Isa 5:2) for MT וַיַּעַשׂ, and ותהיה (at Isa 29:11, 13) for MT וַתְּהִי. The *waw mater* attested in II-*waw waw*-consecutive imperfect forms probably represents a short /o/, as explained above in §3.4, "Etymological Short /u/ Marked with *Waw*."

Another characteristic feature of the imperfect in the DSS is the frequency of the pseudo-cohortative forms, where the final ה ָ- ending typi-

158. Abegg, "Hebrew of the Dead Sea Scrolls," 339.

159. Ibid.

160. Ibid., 338.

cal of the first-person volitive forms is used in contexts in which a volitive notion does not seem likely. Such forms are also present in LBH in great numbers. The pseudo-cohortative appears to function as a regular imperfect (ואשלחה "and I will send" 4Q216 II, 12), and also as a *waw*-consecutive imperfect (ואשחקה "I laughed" 11Q5 [11QPs[a]] XXI, 15); the regular first common imperfect forms are used throughout the scrolls with just about as much regularity as the cohortative and pseudo-cohortative forms.[161] It is interesting to observe that with the increasing use of the cohortative form as a *waw*-consecutive imperfect, the *waw*-consecutive imperfect paradigm begins to look uniformly volitive in form (in other words, it is marked by forms that have the same shape as jussives and true cohortatives). In relation to this, as well as other observations, Qimron asserts that the *waw*-consecutive paradigm "was repatterned after the cohortative-jussive paradigm."[162] This pseudo-cohortative is dominant in DSS-SP9 texts, but appears also in DSS-NSP texts (e.g., 4Q258 IX, 7, 9).

Abegg counts only eight short (non-*waw*-consecutive) imperfect forms (for the II-*waw*/*yodh* roots, III-*waw*/*yodh* roots, and *hiphil* forms) out of a total of 600 (not including those preceded by a regular *waw* conjunction or the negative אל): for example, יעל "will go up" (1QH[a] XVI, 26).[163] He notes that these do not seem to carry a jussive or volitional sense (not to mention a preterite sense). Together with the fact that some long forms do carry a volitional sense, he argues that the short forms may have "lost the sense of command in Q[umran] H[ebrew]."[164] It should be pointed out, however, that the short form is regular after the negative particle אל; and this construction does sometimes carry a sense of command (in effect the negative form of the imperative), something especially evident in the context of a wisdom instruction, as in אל תתאו "do not desire" (4Q416 2 iii, 8 = 4Q418 9 + 9a–c, 7); אל תשת "do not drink" (4Q417 2 ii + 23, 24); [אל] תאמר "do not reject (or, exchange [?])" (4Q418 8, 6);[165] אל תחשך "do not darken/obscure" (4Q418 95, 3); אל תמשל *ʾal tamšēl* "do not let rule" (4Q424 1, 10); אל תשלט *ʾal tašlēṭ* "do not give power to" (11Q5 [11QPs[a]]

161. For specific statistics, see Abegg, "Linguistic Profile," 32 and "Hebrew of the Dead Sea Scrolls," 336–37.

162. Qimron, *HDSS*, 46.

163. Abegg, "Hebrew of the Dead Sea Scrolls," 336.

164. Ibid.

165. See the discussion in "*Aleph* as Internal *Mater*" (§3.3).

XIX, 15).[166] Thus, although the short form ceased to be used to express a positive jussive notion, it was used by convention with the negative אל; in only some cases, however, can the construction be construed as a negative command.[167] Abegg also notes that short imperfects after *waw* may, in a significant minority of instances (20 percent), represent the simple imperfect.[168] He cites as an example ותעש "and you will make" (1QM XI, 9).[169] These, together with examples like יעל "will go up" (1QH[a] XVI, 26) and ואשלחה "and I will send" (4Q216 II, 12), cited just above, suggest that there was a significant amount of confusion among the scribes regarding the proper forms to be used.

The forms of the *qal* imperfect of I-*aleph* verbs are generally the same as the forms attested in the MT. Thus, the forms of אכל "to eat," אמר "to say," אבד "to perish" often attest a *waw mater* after the prefix element, probably reflecting /ō/.[170] In not a few instances, the *aleph* is dropped from the spelling not only in the 1cs (as in the MT), but also in the other forms of the imperfect (e.g., יובדו "they will perish" in 4Q88 X, 12). As in the MT, the same vowel is attested in some other verbs occasionally: ותוסף "it is gathered" (1QH[a] XIII, 16, spelled without *aleph* as is also found in the MT at Ps 104:29); ויוחז "he will seize" (1QIsa[a] at Isa 5:29) corrected to ויא͏חז for MT וְיֹאחֵז. In some cases, I-*aleph* verbs that never attest a *holem* after the *aleph* in the MT attest a *waw mater* after, or in place of, the *aleph*, reflecting presumably an /o/ or /u/ vowel. For example, יורבו "they lie in wait" (1QH[a] XIII, 12) derives from ארב and is similar (in the loss of the *aleph*) to the spelling of the same verb in the MT, וַיָּרֶב (1 Sam 15:5).[171] In other cases, in 1QIsa[a], verbs that regularly take such an initial /o/ vowel, attest forms

---

166. Abegg notes that the short form of the imperfect occurs after אל in 70 percent of the examples from his corpus ("Hebrew of the Dead Sea Scrolls," 336).

167. Qimron describes the use of the short imperfect form with אל as a "'fossilized' use"; see Elisha Qimron, "Consecutive and Conjunctive Imperfect: The Form of the Imperfect with *Waw* in Biblical Hebrew," *JQR* 76 (1986–1987), 150 n. 4.

168. Abegg, "Hebrew of the Dead Sea Scrolls," 338.

169. Other examples include ישמע ויעש (11Q19 LVI, 8) and ישמור ויעש (11Q19 LIX, 16).

170. The verb אבה implies the quiescence of *aleph* but does not give an indication of its vowel in תבה (11Q1 [11QpaleoLev[a]] at Lev 26:21). The verb אפה is not attested in the *qal* imperfect with a *waw mater* or where *aleph* is elided.

171. Stegemann, Schuller, Newsom, DJD 40:171. See also ויופכו "they overturned" (4Q501 1, 4) from the root אפך, a by-form of הפך. See the discussion of this verb in the subsection "Quiescence of *Heh*" in §4.3, "Weakening of Gutturals."

that presume an initial /e/ or /a/ vowel: תאכולנו "it will eat him" (1QIsa[a] at Isa 31:8).[172]

As mentioned above in "Phonemic Inventory" (§4.1), I-*nun* verbs sometimes do not attest assimilation of their first consonant.

The singular *waw*-consecutive imperfect forms for II-*waw* roots often have a *waw mater* (e.g., ויקום "he arose" in 4Q160 1, 3), as mentioned above in "Etymological Short /u/ Marked with *Waw*" (§3.4). It is assumed that these are cases where the *waw* is marking what would be a *qamets hatuf* in the MT. That is, it is assumed these are not cases of the regular imperfect (*וַיָּקוּם). This assumption is bolstered by the fact that other *waw*-consecutive imperfect forms have the form of volitives (e.g., ואשחקה "I laughed" 11Q5 [11QPs[a]] XXI, 15) as well as by the fact that the II-*yodh* verbs and *hiphil* verbs (without suffix) are almost always written defectively (e.g., ותשם "you set" in 1QH[a] IX, 30; ותצל *wattaṣṣēl* "you delivered" 1QH[a] XIII, 15); they hardly ever occur with a corresponding *yodh mater* where they occur as *waw*-consecutives.[173] If all the middle weak roots had simple imperfect forms, we would expect *waw maters* on the II-*waw* roots and *yodh maters* on the II-*yodh* roots.

The pronunciation of 3fp/2fp imperfects of II-*waw/yodh* roots corresponds to that of the MT, as implied by the spelling תבואינה (4Q268 1, 1 and similarly 4Q381 31, 3 [-נא] = MT תְּבוֹאֶינָה). Where the alternative forms for II-*waw/yodh* roots occur in the MT, like תָּבֹאנָה and תָּשֹׁבְנָה, the corresponding biblical scrolls are fragmentary or (in 1QIsa[a]) have the form תבואינה (e.g., 1QIsa[a] at Isa 47:9). There is only one exception: תבאנה (1Q8 [1QIsa[b]] at Isa 47:9).

---

172. According to Kutscher, the root in 1QIsa[a] is like אחז in the MT where it appears as either יאחז or יֶאֱחֹז (*Isaiah*, 467–77). Note, however, יואכולם "he will eat them" at Isa 51:8, cited above.

173. Out of the eleven occurrences of שׂים (parsed as a singular *waw*-consecutive verb form by Accordance) among the nonbiblical scrolls, none occurred with a *yodh mater*; of the twelve examples of the same verb in the biblical scrolls, only one had a *yodh* (ות]שים]) in 4Q13 [4QExod[b]] at Exod 2:3 for MT וַתָּשֶׂם), where, not surprisingly, the text does not closely follow the MT version. Similar distributions are found for other II-*yodh* verbs like בין, as well as *hiphil waw*-consecutives for roots like קום and כון. The regular imperfects (according to Accordance) preceded by *waw* are, in fact, rare (only two clear examples); in one instance the form may just as likely be a *waw*-consecutive וישם (4Q464 5 ii, 2).

The forms of III-*aleph* verbs are generally similar to those of the MT, as described in the preceding subsection "Lack of Confusion between III-*Waw*/*Yodh* and III-*Aleph* Verbs" (§5.6).

Geminate verbs in the *qal* and other stems generally appear as they do in the MT, with some slight distinctions. Thus, for the *qal*, the geminates usually seem to have the theme vowel associated with the same verb in the MT. For example, one finds ירועו "they will break" (1QH[a] XII, 34; 4Q511 3, 7; and 20 ii, 3), as one would expect from MT יָרֹעַ. Often, DSS-NSP texts exhibit forms without the *waw mater* (יזמו "they will devise" in 4Q381 45a + b, 2; יחן "he will [not] pity" in 4Q386 1 iii, 1), while DSS-SP9 texts exhibit forms with the *mater* (יזומו in 4Q171 1–2 ii, 14; ותחון in 4Q504 1–2R v, 11). The pronunciation of the singular forms was probably the same in both corpora and analogous to that of the MT (יָחֹן Deut 28:50); the pronunciation of the plural forms in the DSS-SP9 seems to follow the historical form of the verbs (*יָזֹמּוּ, analogous to יָסֹבּוּ), while the defective writing in the DSS-NSP texts is ambiguous and could alternatively represent forms where the gemination has been lost and the etymological /u/ theme vowel has reduced, as is sometimes evidenced in the MT (e.g., יָזְמוּ Gen 11:6).[174] Occasionally, one finds verbs that seem to evidence an /a/ theme vowel, based on defective orthography, where the MT verb has /o/ or /u/. Thus, one finds ויחגו "and they will totter" (4Q418b 1, 4), quoting Ps 107:27 for MT יָחוֹגּוּ; and נחגה "let us celebrate" (4Q504 5 ii, 4).[175] In other cases, the form of a geminate verb in a DSS-SP9 text may be influenced from the model of the MT: ישלוכה *yəšollūkā* "they will plunder you" (1QpHab VIII, 15 and IX, 3) appears in a quote of Hab 2:8 (for MT יְשָׁלּוּךָ) instead of *ישולוכה.

The paragogic *nun*, according to Accordance, appears clearly on around twenty-five imperfect plural forms, both third- and second-person, among the nonbiblical scrolls.[176] Note that in some biblical scrolls, where the MT has a paragogic *nun*, the DSS does not (e.g., ישברו "they will be

174. The form יָזְמוּ derives from *יָזֹמּוּ (see GKC §67dd).

175. Note that 4Q504 is a DSS-SP9 text and we would expect a *plene* writing, admitting again, that there are occasional examples of defective writing for *qal* imperfect verbs that take an /o/ or /u/ theme vowel. On the passage from 4Q418b, see Strugnell and Harrington, DJD 34:499. Note that 4Q88 (4QPs[f]) at Ps 107:27 attests יחיגו.

176. Abegg's statistics for this form are low ("Hebrew of the Dead Sea Scrolls," 336).

drunk" in 1QIsaᵃ at Isa 49:26) and vice versa (e.g., יבשרון "they will tell" in 1Q8 [1QIsaᵇ] at Isa 60:6). The same suffix is found four times on the 2fs imperfect among the biblical scrolls.

The energic *nun*, which appears between the verbal form and object suffix, occurs rather frequently, as evidenced by the examples in "Qal Imperfect + Suffix" (§5.7). At least twice the energic *nun* does not assimilate to the following suffixal consonant among the biblical scrolls: יכבדנני "he will honor me" (4Q85 [4QPsᶜ] at Ps 50:23) for MT יְכַבְּדָ֑נְנִי and ונכנהו "and let us strike him" (4Q70 [4QJerᵃ] at Jer 18:18) for MT וְנַכֵּ֣הוּ.

Imperatives

As with imperfects, the imperatives in the *qal* often exhibit forms akin to the pausal forms in the MT, though these are not always in places we would expect pause to occur.[177] So, for example, we find the masculine plural occasionally written *plene*: עמודו "stand" in 4Q491c 11 ii, 13, which is like MT pausal עֲמֹ֑דוּ (Nah 2:9) and unlike contextual עִמְד֛וּ (also Nah 2:9). The feminine singular is much more uncommon and is found written *plene* only in the biblical scrolls: עבורי "cross" (4Q57 [4QIsaᶜ] at Isa 23:10) for MT עִבְרִ֣י.[178] Note too the spelling of the mp imperative "possess" ראשו (4Q364 26a ii, 3 at Deut 9:23 for MT רְשׁ֖וּ), where the *aleph* is explicitly indicating the unreduced pausal /ā/ vowel of the imperative seen in Deut 2:24 and 31 רָ֑שׁ (= ראש in 4Q364 24a–c, 4) (see §3.3, "*Aleph* as Internal Mater"). For examples of the *qal* imperative with suffixes, see §5.8, "Qal Imperative + Suffix."

In the *hiphil*, the imperative, as in the MT, does not typically have a *mater* (העמד "make stand" 4Q160 3–4 ii, 3), unless it has an ending (either a plural morpheme, a paragogic *heh*, or an object suffix): הוסיפו "increase" 4Q298 3–4 ii, 6; הקשיבה "pay attention" 4Q177 14, 4; הודיענו "make us know" 4Q266 1a–b, 19).

The long imperative (that is, the form with paragogic *heh*) in the MT is often used in contexts where the person uttering the imperative expects the

---

177. Ibid., 339.

178. In only one instance, the *mater* is after the first root consonant: עוברי (1QIsaᵃ at Isa 23:6) for MT עָבְר֑וּ. Other examples include: עבורי (4Q57 [4QIsaᶜ] at Isa 23:10) for MT עִבְרִ֣י; idem (at 23:12) for MT עֲבֹרִ֔י; אמורי (1QIsaᵃ at Isa 40:9) for MT אִמְרִי֙; עבורי (at Isa 47:2) for MT עִבְרִ֣י; חשופי (at Isa 47:2) for MT חֶשְׂפִּי; עמודי (at Isa 47:12) for MT עִמְדִי; שכוני (2Q13 [2QJer] at Jer 48:28) for MT שִׁכְנוּ.

action of the verb to be directed towards him or her; the long imperative in the DSS is not used as consistently in this way.[179] For example, one finds קומה גבור "arise, hero" (1QM XII, 10).[180] In some cases, the long imperative seems to be associated with certain passages, as in the many cases of שמעה ישראל "hear, Israel" in versions of Deut 5:1 (4Q41 [4QDeut^n], 4Q42 [4QDeut^o], 4Q134 [4QPhyl G], 4Q137 [4Q Phyl J], XQ3 [XQPhyl 3], for MT שְׁמַע יִשְׂרָאֵל), but in only one version of Deut 6:4 (4Q135 [4QPhyl H]).[181] The vocalization of the long imperative is not known, but certain forms written *plene* suggest that these were often vocalized akin to MT pausal forms: זכורה *zəkōrā* "remember" (4Q508 2, 2) and thus implying שמחה *səmāḥā* "rejoice" (4Q416 4, 3, compare סְלָחָה in the MT at Dan 9:19). On the other hand, the confused form [ע]ומודה *ʿomdā* or *ʿămōdā* "stand" (4Q137 [4QPhyl J] at Deut 5:31) suggests that the contextual form may have been known too.

Infinitives

In the *qal*, the infinitive construct for most strong roots is written with a *waw mater* after the second root consonant, unless it bears a suffix, in which case the *waw mater* appears after the first consonant (in line with the vocalization in the MT). In a select few cases where the infinitive construct has a suffix, the *waw mater* appears after the second consonant (e.g., לתפושם "to seize them" 1QpHab IV, 7).[182] This variation presumes a distinction between *quṭl/*qoṭl- and *qəṭul-/*qəṭol- pronunciations. Although a similar syllabic variation occurs with infinitives in the MT, there the syl-

179. For this tendency in the MT, see Steven E. Fassberg, "The Lengthened Imperative קָטְלָה in Biblical Hebrew," *HS* 40 (1999): 7–13.

180. This passage echoes Judg 5:12 (in the MT קום ברק ושבה שביך). See also 4Q88 X, 7–8 (שמחה יהודה ... שמחה שמחתכה וגילה גילך); 4Q416 4, 3 (ואתה מבין שמחה בנחלת אמת); 4Q508 2, 2 (זכורה ... מועד רחמיך). Fassberg suggests that where the long imperative appears, but where it does not indicate an action directed toward the speaker, this often (especially in Psalms) involves an action directed towards the speaker and his people (ibid., 13). Such an interpretation is also possible in many passages from the DSS.

181. Note also שמעה ישראל in 1QM X, 3. Notice that these include both DSS-SP9 and DSS-NSP texts.

182. Abegg, "Hebrew of the Dead Sea Scrolls," 339. I count five instances of this in the DSS: לתפושם (1QpHab IV, 7); ללכודני (4Q437 2 i, 2); לפקודכה (4Q504 1–2R v, 16); כקרובכמה (11Q19 LXI, 14);]נתושם[(4Q70 [4QJer^a] at Jer 12:14).

lable containing the historic /u/ vowel is always followed by two consonants (e.g., אָכְלָם "their eating" in Lev 22:16; אֲכָלְךָ "your eating" in Gen 2:17). In the examples from the DSS, where an /o/ or /u/ vowel occurs after the second root consonant, sometimes only one consonant follows the /o/ or /u/ vowel, as with לתפושם. This suggests a variation in the place of the vowel for the *qal* infinitive construct + suffix similar to that found in the *qal* imperfect + suffix and the *qal* imperative + suffix, as discussed below.

Although certain verbs in the MT are written with an /a/ vowel in the infinitive construct (the primary example being שְׁכַב "to lie down"), where the vowel matches the theme vowel of the imperfect, the same infinitives construct in the DSS usually attest a *waw mater*, which implies an /o/ or /u/ vowel: שכוב (4Q160 7, 4; 4Q223–224 2 v, 3; 4Q51 [4QSam^{a}] at 2 Sam 11:11). Note also שלוח in 1QIsa^{a} at Isa 58:9 for MT שְׁלַח.

The final *-ā* on *qal* infinitives is relatively rare among the nonbiblical scrolls. Thus, one does find יראה "to fear" (4Q158 6, 5 and 4Q364 28a–b, 7) and אהבתכה "your loving" (4Q504 1–2R ii, 9) but one does not find a clear example of *קראה "to call," *קרבה "to approach," *שנאה "to hate."[183] Instead, one finds forms like לאהוב "to love" (1QS I, 9). The feminine *-t* ending, however, is rather common, as in the MT, especially on certain III-*aleph* verbs (קראת "to call), on some I-*yodh* verbs (e.g., דעת "to know," צאת "to go forth," and so on), as well as on some I-*nun* verbs (e.g., גשת "to draw near").

For I-*nun* verbs, the loss of a *nun* in the infinitive construct is regularly found in most places where it is found in the MT; where a particular verb preserves a *nun* in the MT, it preserves it in the DSS (e.g., the *qal* infinitives construct of נגע "to touch" and נפל "to fall").

A number of what are apparently *qal* infinitives occur with a preformative *mem*, making them look like Aramaic infinitives. Accordance parses the following as infinitives construct: משוב (1QS III, 1; 1QM I, 13; III, 6; 4Q403 1 i, 23); משיב (4Q257 III, 2); מתיר (1QS III, 3; 4Q521 2 ii + 4, 8); מוכיחו (1QpHab V, 1); ממוד (4Q266 10 i, 12). Different readings are found for some of these, like משוב for משיב and מתור for מתיר. Based on the presence of other features of the language that seem close to Aramaic in 1QS (e.g., the *aleph* marking the causative stem), one might want simply to explain these as due to Aramaic influence. Nevertheless, the real situation may be more complex. The MT evidences some exam-

183. For examples from the MT, see GKC §45d.

ples of *mem*-preformative nouns that function like infinitives (that is, verbal nouns), for example the word מַשָּׂא "bearing" (in Num 4:24, 2 Chr 20:25).[184] It is perhaps easier to understand such forms not as infinitives *per se* (that is, productive forms derived from the verb based on Aramaic morphology), but rather as *mem*-preformative nouns that have developed a verbal notion. Although perhaps such forms are loosely based on Aramaic influence, they are not simply mistakes for true Hebrew forms (as though the scribe wrote משא but intended שאת); nor do they represent a genuine way of creating an infinitive construct in Hebrew. The words from the DSS can be construed similarly. Thus, the word ממוד I have listed above as an example of a noun "post, standing" with a **maqṭul* base in the DSS and a **maqṭal* base in the MT.[185] The word משוב "return" is morphologically analogous to מבוא and perhaps so is מתור "going around." The word מוכיחו is perhaps a *mem*-preformative noun, analogous to תוכחה, though I think it is easier to interpret this as a participle: "you have formed him for his rebuker (1QpHab V, 1, quoting Hab 1:12 = MT לְהוֹכִיחַ)."[186]

The infinitive construct forms of the III-*aleph* verb מלא "to fill" are peculiar: מלא (4Q491 1–3, 15), מלוא (1QSa I, 12; 4Q383 B, 1 and passim); מילאת (1QS VI, 17); מולאת (1QS VI, 18, 21 [twice]; VIII, 26); מילואת (1QSa I, 10; partially preserved in 4Q512 21–22, 2; 27,1); מליאות (4Q284 2 i, 3); and מולות (4Q511 63–64 iii, 2). Based on orthography alone, these might represent a combination of *qal*, *piel*, and *pual* infinitives. In the MT, the *qal* infinitive construct of this verb occurs as מְלֹאת and מְלאות; the forms from the DSS like מלואת (1QS VII, 20, 22), מלאות (4Q258 VII, 2; 4Q259 II, 3, 5; 4Q367 1a–b, 6, 8; 11Q1 [11QpaleoLev[a]] at Lev 25:30), and מלות (KhQ1 8) correspond to these MT forms, the placement of the *waw* varying (as we would expect) due to the quiescence of the *aleph* and the lack of a preceding vowel.[187] The instances of the infinitive construct

---

184. Grammars and dictionaries categorize משא differently. Thus, e.g., BDB describes it as a "n. verb," while Joüon-Muraoka describe it as an "infinitive" (§49e). The distinction is misleading since the infinitive really is a verbal noun.

185. See "*Waw* Marking /u/ Class Vowel in Nouns Where MT Has No /u/ Class Vowel" (§5.4).

186. Cf. "How will he hold up before the one reproving him (מוכיח בו)" (1QH[a] XX, 31). Note also the substitution of a noun for an MT infinitive in 1QIsa[a] at Isa 38:9 (Kutscher, *Isaiah*, 321).

187. See "Digraphs" (§3.5) and the subsection "Quiescence of *Aleph*" in §4.3, "Weakening of Gutturals."

like מלא and מלוא are also easily explained as *qal*, due to analogy to the strong root; in fact, this is the form we would expect based on the etymology of the word (like בְּרֹא "to create" in Gen 5:1). The form from 4Q284, מליאות, is likely *piel malləyōt*, its *yodh* developing due to a phonetic process similar to the one that results in תתיאמרו in 1QIsa[a] at Isa 61:6 for MT תִּתְיַמָּרוּ "you will boast," and לביותיו in 4Q169 3–4 i, 4 at Nah 2:13 for MT לְבִאֹתָיו "its lionesses."[188] The other forms (מילאת, מולאת, מולות) have various explanations. They could be *piel*, the /o/ vowel presumed by the *waw* being due to influence of a following /o/ or /u/ vowel or the *lamedh*; they could be *qal*, by analogy to other *qal* infinitives construct (of intransitive verbs) where, when a feminine suffix is added, an /o/ vowel appears under the first root consonant (e.g., MT לְטָמְאָה "to be unclean," לְקָרְבָה "to approach").[189] Alternatively, they could be *pual*.[190] The form

188. See the discussion of these and similar forms in "*Aleph* < *Yodh* and *Yodh* < *Aleph*" (§4.4). In 4Q284 2 i, 3, the *piel* fits perfectly, with the meaning of completing an amount of time (as in the MT at Gen 29:27, 2 Chr 36:21, and elsewhere): "when (he) completes for himself seven [days]." See BDB, s.v., *piel*, def. 3. In this case, the *lamedh* prepositional phrase לו expresses a dative of interest. The use of the *lamedh* here is akin to its appearance in Lev 25:30.

189. Earlier scholars proposed reading these as מילאת and מילואת and interpreting the *yodh* as replacing a shewa (see Qimron, "Waw and Yod," 108). By contrast, Qimron (*HDSS*, 110 and 117) and Yeivin (*Hebrew Language Tradition*, 669–70) suggest that these are akin to the pronunciation of the infinitive construct of this word in the Babylonian tradition, though its pronunciation with a /u/ vowel there is also anomalous and perhaps is to be explained on analogy to forms like the infinitive of טמא: *ṭumʾå^h* and *ṭumʾat* (see Yeivin, *Hebrew Language Tradition*, 670). Qimron, more recently, characterizes the notion of this and related forms (ו[י]ענות 4Q437 2 i, 7; ברובות 1QSa I, 19; כגולו[ת] 4Q300 3, 5) as intransitive ("עֲנוֹת and Its Kindred Forms" [Hebrew], *Leshonenu* 67 [2004]: 21–26.).

190. Although the *pual* of this root is only attested once in the MT, for which BDB offers the definition "filled, i.e. *set* with jewels," a passive notion of the *piel* "to complete [an amount of time]" does not seem impossible for the DSS passages. Thus, e.g., the relevant part of 1QS VII, 20–21 can be translated "when two years (of) days have been completed by him…," the *lamedh* indicating the agent of the verb. Although these phrases from the Community Rule (and even 4Q284) seem to be based on Lev 25:30 (or a similar text), where the infinitive is in the *qal* (עַד־מְלֹאת לוֹ שָׁנָה תְמִימָה), the phrase in the MT is confusing due to the ambiguous role of the *lamedh* phrase. Does the pronoun refer back to "dwelling-house" ("until a year elapses for it"), or is it referring to the generic "person" of the preceding verse ("until a year elapses for him")? Notice that in 1QS and 1QSa the forms of מלא that are not followed by the prepositional phrase לו are easily interpreted as *qal*; it is only when they are followed by the

מילואת is better read מולואת (as Licht and Charlesworth and Stuckenbruck do in 1QSa I, 10).[191] In this case, it can be construed as another example like מולאת.

In the *hiphil*, the infinitive construct sometimes does not have a *yodh mater*, especially after the negative particle אין and after the *lamedh* preposition, even with II-*waw*/*yodh* roots (e.g., להוכח "to reprove" 4Q302 3 ii, 7; להשב "to bring back" 4Q368 10 ii, 5; בהושע "when he delivered" 6Q15 3, 2).[192] This is in contrast to the tendency in the MT for such defective orthography to appear on forms with a suffix. As mentioned above in "*Plene* Orthography" (§3.2), this means that the infinitives construct in the DSS sometimes look like infinitives absolute. Given the occasional tendency for the infinitives construct not to have a *mater* in the MT, it is easiest to understand these forms in the DSS as infinitives construct. Nevertheless, there is ambiguity; van Peursen interprets three similarly defective *hiphil* infinitives in Ben Sira manuscripts as infinitives absolute.[193]

As in the MT, there are also occasional examples of infinitives construct of derived stems in the DSS that exhibit Aramaic-like forms. In Biblical Aramaic, the causative stem infinitives often have a form like הַקְטָלָה; such forms for the infinitive are found very rarely in DSS Hebrew in words that function nominally in their respective contexts: הוריה "teaching" (4Q491c 11 i, 16); ה[ז]יה "sprinkling" (4Q512 1–6, 6).[194] Similarly, as in the MT, there are examples of infinitives from derived stems in the DSS that

lamedh preposition that they have unexpected forms. This might suggest that their form (with *waw*) is reflective of some variable other than simple phonology. Perhaps, the writers of 1QS were not totally familiar with the idiom of Lev 25:30 and used a different stem (*pual*) for the verb in order to create what was for them a more sensible text, while also preserving the allusion to the biblical verse.

191. Jacob Licht, *The Rule Scroll: A Scroll from the Wilderness of Judaea, 1QS, 1QSa, 1QSb, Text, Introduction and Commentary* (Jerusalem: Bialik, 1965), 257; Charlesworth and Stuckenbruck, "Rule of the Congregation," 112.

192. Abegg, "Hebrew of the Dead Sea Scrolls," 341, 349. He estimates that for his more limited corpus, 86 percent of strong roots have *plene* forms and 90 percent of II-*waw*/*yodh* roots. Of course, note that the *plene* form also occurs very frequently with the *lamedh* preposition (Qimron, *HDSS*, 47).

193. See van Peursen, *Verbal System*, 278–79.

194. Three out of the four Aramaic-influenced infinitives in the MT (e.g., הֲנָחָה in Est 2:18) also function nominally (see Joüon-Muraoka §88Lb).

exhibit the final -*ūt* ending, as in להערי[בו]ת "to the setting of" (4Q394 [4QMMT] 3–7 i, 18); ההשתחוות "the prostrating" (4Q271 5 i, 15).[195]

Participles

The feminine singular participle in some derived stems is marked by the ה- morpheme more often than it is in the MT (excluding from consideration III-*waw*/*yodh* verbs, where this is the expected morpheme). For example, in the *piel*, the fem. sing. participle appears four times with the ה- morpheme (twice with the verb שׁכל "to be bereaved" משכלה) in 4Q169 3–4 ii, 3; 4Q285 8, 8; 4Q405 23 i, 7; 11Q14 1 ii, 11. In the MT, only two *piel* fem. sing. participles appear with this morpheme (in Exod 22:17 and 23:26). In the *niphal*, the fem. sing. participles in the DSS seem to show a greater preference for this same ending (ה-) rather than the alternative (ת-) (excluding III-*waw*/*yodh* roots and II-*waw*/*yodh* roots); according to my count of the Accordance search of nonbiblical scrolls, there are thirty clear examples of the fem. sing. *niphal* participle with the ה- ending (e.g., נשברה 1QS VIII, 3) and fourteen with the ת- ending (e.g., נשברת 1QH[a] XV, 5). By contrast, in the MT from Genesis through Deuteronomy, there are no examples of the participle with the ה- ending and eleven with the ת- ending, while in the book of Isaiah there are two examples with the ה- ending and thirteen with the ת- ending. In the *hiphil*, however, the ת- ending is dominant both in the DSS and in the MT.

5.7. *Qal* Imperfect + Suffix

Among the DSS (specifically among the DSS-SP9 and DSS-SP1c texts), one often finds *qal* verbal forms that appear to have the /o/ or /u/ theme vowel preserved, though in the Tiberian tradition such theme vowels are preserved only in pause. Thus, we find יכתובו *yiktōbū* "they will write" (1QM IV, 13) where we might otherwise expect יכתבו *yiktəbū*.[196] These *qal* imperfect forms are often referred to as "so-called pausal forms" due

195. The two MT examples are לְהַשְׁמָעוּת Ezek 24:26 and הִתְחַבְּרוּת Dan 11:23 (see Joüon-Muraoka §88Mj).

196. The presence of a *waw mater* to mark an /o/ or /u/ vowel in these verbal forms is similar to the use of *waw* in other nominal and verbal forms in the DSS where corresponding forms in the MT usually have no *mater* (e.g., חוק vs. MT חֹק is similar to יכתובו vs. pausal יִכְתֹּבוּ). Texts of the DSS-NSP category sometimes do not exhibit

to the fact that they look like MT pausal forms but do not always occur in places we would expect pausal forms to appear. The reason for the *waw mater* (and the associated vowel) is hard to know. Scholars have proposed that it is due to the penultimate accent in this dialect of Hebrew;[197] due to the presence of a shewa colored by the original vowel (in essence a *hatef-qamets*, similar to the vowel one often sees in the MT in the first syllable of the plural form of חֳדָשִׁים "months" as well as in some verbal forms like אֶשְׁקֳוטָה "I will be quiet" [Isa 18:4]);[198] due to a tendency to use archaic forms;[199] the result of a preservation of the etymological unaccented /o/ or /u/ vowel as in the Babylonian tradition;[200] or the result of writing what was perceived to be the correct verbal form.[201] For me, the last two opin-

---

this *mater*, even where the verb form occurs in pause (e.g., ישפוטו 1Q8 [1QIsa^b] at Isa 51:5 for MT יִשְׁפֹּטוּ).

197. Qimron offers a slightly different summary of the scholarship in *HDSS*, 50–51. The explanation for penultimate stress is often associated with Ben-Ḥayyim ("Traditions in the Hebrew Language," 202–3; and "Tradition of the Samaritans," 225–26); see also Kutscher, *Isaiah*, 330–40 and references there as well as Morag, "Qumran Hebrew," 155.

198. Kutscher (*Isaiah*, 335 n. 2, 339–40) cites other forms from the MT like וָאֶשְׁקֳולָה (Ezra 8:25), as well as forms with what seems to be a long vowel יִשְׁפּוּטוּ (Exod 18:26), תַּעֲבוּרִי (Ruth 2:8) and other evidence (e.g., the Secunda's ιεφφολου [for MT יִפְּלוּ Ps 18:39] and ουιεροyου [for MT וְיַחְרְגוּ Ps 18:46]). He believes that forms with a *hatef* vowel may be regarded as "remnants of an early stage" in the development of these forms, though for 1QIsa^a the *waw* probably does not represent a *hatef* vowel, but rather an accented short /o/. See also Goshen-Gottstein, "Linguistic Structure," 123–24 and the references there.

199. Steven E. Fassberg suggests the possibility that the long forms of the imperfect are due to the scribes' preference for archaic, literary forms ("The Preference for Lengthened Forms in Qumran Hebrew" [Hebrew], *Meghillot* 1 [2003]: 235).

200. Israel Yeivin sees the DSS verbal forms as akin to Babylonian verbal forms that preserve the /o/ or /u/ theme vowel and are accented on the last syllable ("The Verbal Forms יקטולנו, יקוטלנו in DSS in Comparison to the Babylonian Vocalization" [Hebrew], in *Bible and Jewish History: Studies in Bible and Jewish History Dedicated to the Memory of Jacob Liver* [ed. Benjamin Uffenheimer; Tel-Aviv: Tel-Aviv University, 1971], 256–76). Qimron sees them as older verbal forms ("Nature of DSS Hebrew," 243).

201. Einar Brønno argues that the writing of the verbal forms with a *waw* after the second root consonant is reflective of what the scribes *thought* they were speaking (i.e., *yiqṭōlū*), when in reality they were saying something more abbreviated (i.e., *yiqṭəlū*), as in English we might write "I will" but pronounce the words "I'll" ("The Isaiah Scroll DSIa and the Greek Transliterations of Hebrew," *ZDMG* 106 [1956]: 255). Skehan and

ions seem most convincing. But whatever the cause, the phenomenon seems to be quite well-attested in DSS-SP9 and DSS-SP1c texts, though it is not found in all texts or in all *qal* verbal forms (e.g., ידרשו "they will seek" 4Q418 103 ii, 5). Further illustrations of the preference among the DSS for pausal forms in verbal and nominal morphology are offered in "Accent or Stress" (§4.7).

The "pausal" forms of the *qal* imperfect verb are attested in the DSS even where corresponding verbal forms in pause in the MT do not usually evidence a theme vowel (again almost exclusively in DSS-SP9 and DSS-SP1c texts). For example, the *qal* 2ms imperfect with pronominal object suffix appears with a *waw mater*: תעזובני "you do [not] abandon me" (1QH[a] XXII, 37) versus MT pausal תַּעַזְבֵנִי (Ps 71:9).[202] Scholars have applied to these forms the same or similar explanations as those listed above for יכתובו.[203] Again, the most convincing explanation is that these forms preserve the etymological theme vowel and/or represent what the scribes thought they were speaking.

In other cases, a *mater* does not appear between the second and third root consonants, but rather, between the first and second root consonants: ידורשהו "he will examine him" (1QS VI:14). These forms are more or less peculiar to DSS Hebrew. *Qal* verbal forms with a *mater* in this position only occur with object suffixes.[204] These forms have also elicited the attention of scholars who have explained them as reflecting a helping vowel,

---

Ulrich, for their part, note simply: "the imperfect verbal forms such as ידרושו... are interpreted as orthographic" ("Isaiah," in DJD 15:46).

202. Very rarely one finds in the MT a *qal* imperfect + suffix where the /o/ or /u/ vowel is preserved in pause: יֶהְדֳּפֶנּוּ (Num 35:20 for an intended *יֶהְדְּפֶנּוּ, as in Jos 23:5), אֶצֳּרֶנָּה (Isa 27:3, versus תִּנְצְרֵנִי in Ps 140:2); יִקֳּבֶנָּה (Isa 62:2); תִּשְׁמוּרֵם (Prov 14:3, versus יִשְׁמְרֵנִי in Job 29:2); see Kutscher, *Isaiah*, 335 n. 2, 339–40. On the other hand, one regularly finds an /o/ vowel after the second root consonant in these kinds of verbs in the Babylonian tradition (see Yeivin, *Hebrew Language Tradition*, 451, 469–71).

203. Scholars often note in relation to these forms the preservation of a similar vowel in verbs from the Secunda and Jerome, as well as Babylonian Hebrew. For example, Kutscher cites εμωσημ (for MT אֶמְחָצֵם Ps 18:39) and εσοκημ (for MT אֶשְׁחָקֵם Ps 18:43), as well as one example from Jerome: *iesbuleni* for MT יִזְבְּלֵנִי at Gen 30:20 (*Isaiah*, 336 n. 3). Note, however, the verbs that exhibit an /o/ vowel in the Secunda have an /a/ theme vowel in the imperfect in the MT, while the verbs with a corresponding vowel in the imperfect in the DSS overwhelmingly have an /o/ or /u/ theme vowel in the MT.

204. The form יהופכו in 4Q432 4, 1 is parsed as *qal* in Accordance, presumably

akin to the /i/ and /å/ vowels that occur in similar (but not identical) Babylonian and Samaritan forms (e.g., Babylonian: *tišimʿū* versus MT תִּשְׁמְעוּ "you will hear," and Samaritan: *yērå̄ṣṣū* versus MT יִרְחֲצוּ "they will wash"), as well as the /e/ vowel in two forms from the Secunda (ουειεσαμου [for MT וְיִשְׂמְחוּ "and they will rejoice" Ps 35:27] and ιχερσου [for MT יִקְרְצוּ "they will wink" Ps 35:19]), and an /o/ vowel at least once in the MT (הַיְחָבְרְךָ "will he join you?" Ps 94:20).[205] Alternatively, these forms may be explained as the result of vowel assimilation (similar to how פעולה "work" becomes פועלה).[206] Or, the two different forms, *yqṭwl* + suffix and *yqwṭl* + suffix, can be understood simply as alternative forms to each other, similar to how there are alternative forms for *qal* imperative + suffix and *qal* infinitive construct + suffix in the DSS (שומרני *šomrēnī* "guard me" 11Q5 [11QPs[a]] at Ps 140:5 for MT שָׁמְרֵנִי versus שמורני *šəmorēnī* "guard me" 11Q5 [11QPs[a]] at Ps 141:9 for MT שָׁמְרֵנִי and למושחני *ləmošḥēnī* "to

---

based on the parallel word in 1QH[a] X, 19 יהפוכו; the *waw* in יהופכו is due to confusion with the root (found in RH) אפך (see the subsection "Lexicon" in §5.6, "Verbs").

205. Ben-Ḥayyim notes the parallel to the Babylonian tradition ("Studies in the Traditions," 87–88) and the Samaritan forms (*Grammar of Samaritan Hebrew*, 109, 128); the Samaritan transcription should have a macron over the /å/ vowel. See also Kutscher, *Isaiah*, 336–37. On the forms from the Secunda, see Einar Brønno, *Studien über hebräische Morphologie und Vokalismus auf Grundlage der mercatischen Fragmente der zweiten Kolumn der Hexapla des Origenes* (Leipzig: Deutsche Morgenländische Gessellschaft / Brockhaus, 1943), 32–35 and Janssens, *Studies in Hebrew*, 1982), 159. On the form יְחָבְרְךָ from Ps 94:20, see Yeivin, "Verbal Forms," 261. In addition, the forms תָעָבְדֵם (Ex 20:5, 23:24, Deut 5:9, all in pause) and נָעָבְדֵם (Deut 13:3, in pause), which in their context cannot be construed as *hophal*s, may also evidence this /o/ vowel between the first and second root consonants, as if they should have been *תְּעָבְדֵם and *נְעָבְדֵם. According to this explanation, the unexpected /o/ vowel after the prefix in these biblical forms (-תָ and -נָ) may be an auxiliary vowel, similar to the analysis of the initial /o/ vowel as auxiliary (though from an etymological /u/) in infinitive forms like קָרָבְכֶם "(as) you approach" (Deut 20:2) and מָאָסְכֶם "(because of) your rejecting" (Isa 30:12) (Yeivin, "Verbal Forms," 265; Joüon-Muraoka §63b and §65c). One sees a similar movement of an /o/ vowel toward the prefix of an imperfect verb in the contextual MT form יָחְנְךָ "he will show you favor" (Gen 43:29 and Isa 30:19); cf. וִיחֻנֶּךָּ (Num 6:25) (see GKC §67n).

206. Kutscher seems to imply that the /o/ or /u/ vowel in the DSS forms (e.g., ידורשהו) is due to assimilation when he compares the vowel in *yqwṭl* + suffix to the initial vowel of עומרה (*Isaiah*, 337 n. 2 [top note]). Thus, the forms like *yqwṭl* + suffix may have emerged through assimilation, *yiqṭolēnī* > *yəqoṭolēnī* > *yəqoṭlēnī*. On פועלה, see "*Waw* Marking /u/ Class Vowel in Nouns Where MT Has No /u/ Class Vowel" (§5.4).

anoint me" 11Q5 [11QPs^a] XXVIII, 8 versus ללכודני *lilkōdēnī* "to capture me" 4Q437 2 i, 2). A similar alternation of vowel placement in the imperative appears in the Babylonian tradition (*wəduqreni* "pierce me" 1 Sam 31:4 [for what would be in the MT *וְדָקְרֵנִי, though the MT has a *waw*-consec. perfect here] versus *məšokeni* "pull me" Song 1:4 [compare MT מָשְׁכֵנִי]).[207] Alternation of vowel placement in the infinitive occurs in both the Babylonian and Tiberian traditions (*lišmorəkå* and לִשְׁמָרְךָ "to guard you" Ps 91:11 versus *šukbəkå* and בְּשָׁכְבְּךָ "when you lie down" Deut 6:7).

In the following list, I summarize the variety of possible *qal* imperfect verb forms with suffix that diverge from the Tiberian model. Excluded from consideration are those forms whose first root consonant is not attested and/or those whose suffix is not attested.

1. *Mater* between second and third root consonant
    - 1.1. imperfect (stem) forms that end in consonant
    - 1.2. *waw*-consec. imperfect (stem) forms that end in consonant
    - 1.3. imperfect (stem) forms that end in vowel (defective and *plene* 3mp morpheme)
    - 1.4. *waw*-consec. imperfect (stem) forms that end in vowel (defective and *plene* 3mp morpheme)

2. *Mater* between first and second root consonant
    - 2.1. imperfect (stem) forms that end in consonant
    - 2.2. *waw*-consec. imperfect (stem) forms that end in consonant
    - 2.3. imperfect (stem) forms that end in vowel (defective and *plene* 3mp morpheme)

---

207. Yeivin, "Verbal Forms," 274–75. He notices that other Hebrew traditions do not use an /o/ or /u/ helping vowel in verbs and the fact that the *waw* after the first root consonant in the imperfect appears only in *qal* forms with suffixes. See also Qimron, *HDSS*, 52–53. More examples of *qal* ms imperative + suffix in the DSS are found in "*Qal* Imperative + Suffix" (§5.8). Most examples of *qal* infinitives + suffix in the DSS have the *waw mater* after the first root consonant; I could find only five examples where the *waw* follows the second root consonant; see the subsection "Infinitives" in §5.6, "Verbs." The examples from the Babylonian tradition are drawn from Yeivin, *Hebrew Language Tradition*, 480 and 489.

2.4. *waw*-consec. imperfect (stem) forms that end in vowel (defective and *plene* 3mp morpheme)

1. *Mater* between second and third root consonant
   1.1. imperfect (stem) forms that end in consonant
      וישמורכה"he will guard you" (1QS II, 3)
      תעזובנו "do (not) abandon us" (1QH[a] XXII, 37)
      אעזובכה "I will (not) abandon you" (4Q382 9, 7)
      תטושני "do (not) forsake us" (4Q504 7, 10)
      יטושנה "he will (not) forsake it" (4Q525 2 ii + 3, 5) (+ energic *nun*)
      תזריענו "you will plant it" (1QIsa[a] at Isa 17:10) (+ energic *nun*) for MT תִּזְרָעֶנּוּ
      אצורנה "I will guard it" (1QIsa[a] at Isa 27:3) (+ energic *nun*) for MT אֶצֳּרֶנָּה
      תאכולנו "you will eat it" (1QIsa[a] at Isa 31:8) (+ energic *nun*) for MT תֹּאכְלֶנּוּ
      אעזובם "I will abandon them" (1QIsa[a] at Isa 41:17) for MT אֶעֶזְבֵם
      ואצורכה "I will guard you" (1QIsa[a] at Isa 42:6) for MT וְאֶצָּרְךָ
      ויערוכהה "he will arrange it" (1QIsa[a] at Isa 44:7) for MT וְיַעְרְכֶהָ
      ויצורהו "he formed him" (1QIsa[a] at Isa 44:12) for MT יִצְּרֵהוּ
      ואצורכה "I will guard you" (1QIsa[a] at Isa 49:8) for MT וְאֶצָּרְךָ
      יאכולם "he will eat them" (1QIsa[a] at Isa 50:9) for MT יֹאכְלֵם
      יקובנו "he will indicate it" (1QIsa[a] at Isa 62:2) (+ energic *nun*) for MT יִקֳּבֶנּוּ
      יצנופך "he will turn you round" (4Q60 [4QIsa[f]] at Isa 22:18) for MT יִצְנָפְךָ
      [ו]אצורך "I will guard you" (4Q62 [4QIsa[h]] at Isa 42:6) for MT וְאֶצָּרְךָ
      תעזובני "you will (not) abandon me" (4Q83 [4QPs[a]] at Ps 38:22) for MT תַּעַזְבֵנִי

1.2. *waw*-consec. imperfect (stem) forms that end in consonant
וישמורהו "he will guard him" (1QH[a] XXI, 27)
וילכודה "he captured it" (1QIsa[a] at Isa 20:1) for MT וַיִּלְכְּדָהּ
ויתפושם "he seized them" (1QIsa[a] at Isa 36:1) for MT וַיִּתְפְּשֵׂם
ויפרושה "he spread it out" (1QIsa[a] at Isa 37:14) for MT וַיִּפְרְשֵׂהוּ
[ויר]מוסהו "he trampled it" (4Q113 [4QDan[b]] at Dan 8:7), damaged, for MT וַיִּרְמְסֵהוּ
ויכת[ו]בם "he wrote them" (4Q135 [4QPhyl H] at Deut 5:22), extremely damaged for MT וַיִּכְתְּבֵם

1.3. imperfect (stem) forms that end in vowel (defective and *plene* 3mp morpheme)[208]
ידרושהו "they will examine him" (1QS VI, 17)
יפקודהו "they will appoint him" (1QS VI, 21)
יכתובהו "they will write him" (1QS VI, 22)
יחשובוני "they consider me" (1QH[a] XI, 7)
יעבודוכי "they will serve you" (1QIsa[a] at Isa 60:12) for MT יַעַבְדוּךְ
יאכולוהי "they will eat it" (1QIsa[a] at Isa 62:9) for MT יֹאכְלוּהוּ
יזכורוכה "they will remember you" (1QIsa[a] at Isa 64:4) for MT יִזְכְּרוּךָ

1.4. *waw*-consec. imperfect (stem) forms that end in vowel (defective and *plene* 3mp morpheme)
None.

2. *Mater* between first and second root consonant

2.1. imperfect (stem) forms that end in consonant
ידורשהו "he will examine him" (1QS VI, 14)
ישופטני "he will judge me" (1QS X, 13)
[ת]דורשהו "you will examine him" (1QSb III, 20)
ישופטנו "he will judge him" (1QpHab XII, 5) (+ energic *nun*)

---

208. Note the similar forms with paragogic *nun*: תכרותון "you will cut down" 11Q19 II, 7; תעבודון "you will serve" 11Q19 LIV, 14.

אדורשכה "I will seek you" (1QH^{a} XII, 7)
יעוברנה "he will (not) cross it" (1QH^{a} XIV, 24) (+ energic *nun*)
יעושקנו "he will oppress him" (1Q27 1 i, 10) (+ energic *nun*)
יסומכנו "he will (not) support him" (4Q161 8–10, 18) (+ energic *nun*)
[ת]שוטפני "it will wash me away" (4Q437 2 i, 10) (+ energic *nun*)
אחורתם "I will engrave them" (4Q511 63–64 ii, 3)
יעוזבנה "he will (not) abandon it" (4Q525 2 ii + 3, 5) (+ energic *nun*)
אדורשנה "I will seek it" (11Q5 [11QPs^{a}] XXI, 12) (+ energic *nun*)
תשופכנו "you will pour it out" (11Q19 LII, 12) (+ energic *nun*)
תשופכנו "you will pour it out" (11Q19 LIII, 5) (+ energic *nun*)
אדורשנו "I will seek it" (11Q19 LIII, 11) (+ energic *nun*)
תקוברמה "you will bury them" (11Q19 LXIV, 11)
יעיבורנה "he will not cross it" (1QIsa^{a} at Isa 35:8) (+ energic *nun*) for MT יַעַבְרֶנּוּ [209]
יעוטך "he will hold you" (1QIsa^{a} at Isa 22:17) for MT וְעֹטְךָ (*qal* ptc.)[210]
תעובדם "you will (not) serve them" (1Q13 [1QPhyl] and 4Q41 [4QDeut^{n}] at Deut 5:9) for MT תָעָבְדֵם[211]
תעובדמה "you will (not) serve them" (4Q129 [4QPhyl B] and 4Q137 [4QPhyl J] at Deut 5:9) for MT תָעָבְדֵם

209. I assume that only one *mater* was intended in this form; i.e., this is a partially corrected form. Kutscher notes that the interlinear *mater* seems to have been written by another scribe (*Isaiah*, 340).

210. Burrows first read a *waw* as the initial letter, while Accordance and Ulrich et al. (*Biblical Qumran Scrolls*, 370) see a *yodh*. There are no other examples of an /o/ vowel between first and second root consonants of III-*waw*/*yodh* verbs.

211. Although the parsing of the MT form is debateable, it seems at least possible that the forms in the MT are examples of the *yqwṭl* + suffix form. See Joüon-Muraoka §63b and §65c.

ישומרכה "he will protect you" (11Q5 [11QPs[a]] at Ps 121:7) for MT יִשְׁמָרְךָ

2.2. *waw*-consec. imperfect (stem) forms that end in consonant

ויכותבם "he wrote them" (4Q41 [4QDeut[n]] at Deut 5:22) for MT וַיִּכְתְּבֵם

ותחושבהו "you have thought of them" (11Q5 [11QPs[a]] at Ps 144:3) for MT וַתְּחַשְּׁבֵהוּ

2.3. imperfect (stem) forms that end in vowel

יעובדוכה "they will serve you" (1QSb V, 28)

ויעובדוני "they will serve me" (4Q365 2, 7 at Exod 8:16) for MT וְיַעַבְדֻנִי

ויסוקלוני "they will stone me" (4Q365 7 i, 3 at Exod 17:4) for MT וּסְקָלֻנִי

ידורשוהו "they will (not) seek him" (4Q423 9, 2)

ידורשום "they will (not) seek them" (4Q475 1, 2)

יעוזבוהו "they will abandon him" (11Q19 LVII, 7)

ידורשוה "they will seek it" (11Q5 [11QPs[a]] at Ps 119:2) for MT יִדְרְשׁוּהוּ

יעוזרני "they will help me" (11Q5 [11QPs[a]] at Ps 119:175) for MT יַעֲזְרֻנִי (not the expected *יַעְזְרֻנִי)

2.4. *waw*-consec. imperfect (stem) forms that end in vowel (defective and *plene* 3mp morpheme)

וישומעוני "they heard me" (1QH[a] XII, 25)

There are eight conclusions to draw. First, most of the verb forms (both *yqṭwl* + suffix and *yqwṭl* + suffix) derive from DSS-SP9 texts. For *yqwṭl* + suffix this is not surprising since this feature is one that marks the texts as DSS-SP9; the dominance of DSS-SP9 texts in the *yqṭwl* + suffix category may partially reflect the tendency for *plene* spelling in these texts (note the many examples from biblical scrolls where a *waw* appears for a MT *qamets-hatuf* or *hatef-qamets*). The examples of *yqwṭl* + suffix that come from DSS-NSP texts (that is, 1Q13, 4Q41) parallel the verbal forms attested in the MT with a *qamets-hatuf* between first and second root consonants (e.g., תָּעָבְדֵם Deut 5:9). Such distribution suggests that the MT forms like תָּעָבְדֵם are not related to the *yqwṭl* + suffix forms and have another explanation (that is, the *qamets* under the *ʿayin* represents a secondary vowel, like that after *heh* in צָהֳרַיִם "noon" Isa 58:10 and 59:10, spelled *plene* צהורים in

1QIsa[a]).[212] Second, the total number of *yqṭwl* + suffix forms is thirty-one, while the number of *yqwṭl* + suffix forms is thirty-four (including the four examples from Deut 5:9). In other words, all things being equal, it seems just as likely that a verb would have a *mater* after the first root consonant as after the second. These may be contrasted with the approximately sixty-five *qal* verbal forms from strong, I-*nun*, and I-guttural roots with an /o/ or /u/ theme vowel that attest a suffix and which have no *mater* marking their theme vowel in the DSS.[213] Many of these are the same verbs that attest *waw maters*, like ידרשוכה (1QH[a] XII, 16), ישפטנו (1QpHab X, 5), and יעזבם (4Q171 1–2 ii, 14). These may represent defective spellings of either the *yqṭwl* + suffix or *yqwṭl* + suffix patterns or yet another pattern with a muttered vowel under the second root consonant, parallel to the common pronunciation in the MT. Third, almost all the examples are of verbs from strong roots, I-*nun* roots (only for *yqṭwl* + suffix), and I-guttural roots.[214] The main exception for *yqṭwl* + suffix forms is תזריענו (1QIsa[a] at Isa 17:10), which is best understood in light of other III-guttural verbs which take an /o/ or /u/ theme vowel in 1QIsa[a].[215] The main exceptions for *yqwṭl* + suffix forms are the III-guttural verb attested in 1QH[a] XII, 25 וישומעוני and the apparent III-*waw*/*yodh* verb attested in 1QIsa[a] at Isa 22:17 יעוטך. It seems

212. It seems less likely that the MT has inherited such verbal forms from a tradition like that exhibited by the DSS-SP9 texts. But, is it conceivable that the biblical תעבדם was so well-known that it influenced the DSS forms?

213. Tigchelaar, without mentioning specifics, suggests that the various *qal* imperfect + suffix forms occur in roughly equal distribution. He writes: "The *yiqṭolu* forms (or spellings?) are extremely common in 1QIsa[a], though there are a few *yiqṭ[e]lu* ones, but in other texts the cases of either form/spelling are rare, but more or less equally distributed. The same goes for the *yiqṭ[e]leni*/*y[e]quṭleni* form" ("Assessing Emanuel Tov's 'Qumran Scribal Practice,'" in *The Dead Sea Scrolls: Transmission of Traditions and Production of Texts* [ed. Sarianna Metso, et al; STDJ 92; Leiden: Brill, 2010], 193).

214. I-*yodh*, II-guttural, III-guttural, etymological III-*waw*/*yodh* roots are not attested with a *waw mater*. As a sample, note the following verbs that take object suffixes without a *waw mater* in biblical and nonbiblical scrolls: בחר, בלע, גאל, זבח, זרע, ידע, טבע, לקח, נחל, נצח, משח, פרע, שנא, שאל, שכח, שלח, שמע. Geminate roots are, of course, excluded from consideration since a /u/ class vowel after the first root consonant is characteristic of the *qal* geminate paradigm and, therefore, the appearance of *waw maters* in these forms is not surprising. Note finally that no other conjugation except for the *pual* regularly evidences a *waw mater* between the first and second root consonants.

215. See, Kutscher, *Isaiah*, 341–42, though he does not list this specific form. See also the subsection "Imperfect and *Waw*-Consecutive Imperfect" in §5.6, "Verbs."

possible that the verb form וישומעוני is due to its being conceived (here at least) as a *yiqṭōl* imperfect.[216] With regard to יעוטך, the easiest explanation is a confusion between an initial *waw* and *yodh*, exacerbated, perhaps, by variant traditions (e.g., although the MT has a participle, וְעֹטְךָ, the scrolls 1Q8 [1QIsa^b] and 4Q56 [4QIsa^b] have what seems to be a *waw* + imperfect: ויע[טך] and ויעטך, respectively); in other words, יעוטך might be a mixture of the imperfect and participle forms. The consistency with which one sees *yiqṭōl* imperfects suggests the *waw mater* in *yqwṭl* + suffix forms is related to the theme vowel. Fourth, the presence or absence of an energic *nun* does not seem to affect the form. The energic *nun* occurs on most verb types with suffixes. Fifth, the presence of a long vowel at the end of the verbal form (like the 3mp affix -*ū*) does not affect the form. Sixth, any type of suffix (3ms, 3fs, and so on) seems capable of being used with any verb form.[217] Seventh, there seems to be no connection between the type of consonant (aside from gutturals and *waws*/*yodhs*) that appears in the middle of the word and the preference for the form of the verb; that is, the middle consonant might be a labial, a liquid, or a dental. Finally, since there is no good evidence for imperfect + suffix forms spelled with *waw maters* after both first and second root consonants (as is found, for example, with some **quṭl* nouns), it is likeliest that there was only one vowel between the root consonants (that is, *yiqṭōlēnī* and *yəqoṭlēnī*). This finds support in the form יְחָבְרְךָ from Ps 94:20, as well as in other evidence from the MT and Babylonian tradition for *yqṭwl* + suffix forms.

Based on the above analysis, some statements by previous scholars should be reevaluated. Tov's listing of thirty-four instances of "*y^{e}quṭlenu*" is the same as my own; his specific listings are more puzzling, however.[218]

---

216. Note the possible reading of [יש]מועו in 4Q491 1–3, 13, though Accordance reads [יש]מיעו.

217. Note, however, there are seven instances of *yqṭwlkh* forms, while only two (likely) instances of *yqwṭlkh* (אדורשכה 1QH^a XII, 7; ישומרכה 11Q5 [11QPs^a] at Ps 121:7). One wonders if the frequency of *yqṭwlkh* forms is related to the tendency, found in the MT, for the 2ms suffix to have no connecting vowel between the verb form and the suffix (except primarily in pause): יִשְׁמָרְךָ (Ps 121:7, pronounced *yišmorkā*) as opposed to pausal יִשְׁמְרֶךָ (Num 6:24). Arguing against this interpretation, of course, is the fact that ישומרכה from 11Q5 [11QPs^a] at Ps 121:7 is not in pause and, in fact, one would expect a *waw mater* between the second and third root consonants, based on the MT form יִשְׁמָרְךָ. Furthermore, as stated earlier, the *qal* verb forms in the DSS seem to prefer pausal forms.

218. Tov, *Scribal Practices*, 339–343.

He finds thirteen instances of *yqwṭl* + suffix in 1QIsa[a], but I find only one.[219] The statement by Morag that the "most usual of all patterns" for the *qal* imperfect + suffix is *yqwṭl* + suffix must be revised.[220]

Although Yeivin and Qimron's comparison to the alternation seen in *qal* imperatives + suffixes and infinitives construct + suffix in the DSS and other traditions is correct, it should be qualified slightly.[221] For example, the DSS seems to be the only tradition that sees so much variation. Variation in *qal* imperatives + suffix takes place very rarely in the MT (involving "long imperatives" in the *kethib* like מָלְוֹכָה "rule" in Judg 9:8 and צָרְופָה "refine" in Ps 26:2), though it is more common in the Babylonian tradition (*wəduqreni* versus *məšokeni*, cited above).[222] Alternative forms for infinitives + suffix in the MT are restricted by certain phonological principles (an /o/ vowel appears after the second root consonant only when there is no vowel that comes between the verbal root and the suffix, for example, בְּשָׁפְכְּךָ *bəšofkəkā* "when you pour out" Ezek 9:8 versus אֲמָרְךָ *ʾămorkā* "you said" Ezek 35:10).[223] A similar pattern holds for infinitives + suffix in the Babylonian tradition.[224] In the Samaritan tradition, the alternate forms of the infinitive + suffix are based, in part, on the presence or absence of

219. Note that Kutscher, in commenting on the form יעׄבורנו from 1QIsa[a] at Is 35:8, says that such forms as *yqwṭl* for MT *yqṭl* are "not found in the Isa. Scr., but do appear in other Qumran scrolls" (*Isaiah*, 340). Similarly, Abegg says the form above with two *waws* is the only one that contains a *waw* between the first and second consonants ("Linguistic Profile," 32). E. Tigchelaar in his review of Tov's book ("Review of Emanuel Tov, *Scribal Practices and Approaches Reflected in the Texts Found in the Judean Desert*," *DSD* 14 [2007]: 368–372) does not mention the discrepancy in Tov's chart.

220. Morag, "Qumran Hebrew," 155.

221. Qimron (*HDSS*, 52) writes: "DSS Hebrew, like other Hebrew traditions, has two possibilities for the infinitive and imperative with suffixes: קוטלני alongside קטולני (imperative), and לקוטלני alongside לקטולני (infinitive).… The corresponding doublets in the imperfect with suffixes (יקטולני /יקוטלני) are an analogical extension of this behavior."

222. On the imperative with suffix, see §5.8, "*Qal* Imperative + Suffix."

223. See Muraoka, "Hebrew," 1:343.

224. In the Babylonian tradition an /o/ vowel typically occurs after the second consonant in *qal* infinitives with a second-person suffix, with a muttered vowel (sometimes) appearing after the third root consonant: *lirdopəkå* in 1 Sam 25:29 (= MT לִרְדָפְךָ) (see Yeivin, *Hebrew Language Tradition*, 489). By contrast, a vowel typically occurs after the first root consonant with other suffixes (e.g., *bəzukrenu* in Ps 137:1 [= MT בְּזָכְרֵנוּ; ibid., 488).

an affixed preposition.[225] Criticisms like these do not make one question the validity of Qimron's general observation on the possible interrelatedness of the forms in DSS Hebrew, but it does make one wonder about the precise relationships of these forms to those in the other traditions.

Kutscher's suggestion of vowel assimilation may be possible, though in the other cases where a /u/ develops in front of another /u/ vowel, the /u/ that develops secondarily stands at the beginning of the word (e.g., פועלה "work"), where another vowel once stood. By contrast, there is no etymological vowel after the first root consonant in *qal* imperfects.[226]

The suggestion that the /o/ vowel in *yqwṭl* + suffix forms is a helping vowel seems the weakest to me, though perhaps this too is possible. Note יעוזרני (11Q5 [11QPs[a]] at Ps 119:175) for MT יַעֲזְרֻנִי, though this verb is ordinarily pronounced without a helping vowel in the MT, יַעְזְרוּנִי (2 Chr 28:23) and יַעְזְרֻכֶם (Deut 32:38).

Another explanation for the *yqwṭl* + suffix forms may be that they are based on analogy to the pausal form of geminate verbs with suffixes, where one sometimes finds an /o/ or /u/ vowel between the first and second root consonants: יחונכה "he will favor you" (1QS II, 3 and passim), corresponding to MT pausal וִיחֻנֶּךָּ (Num 6:25), וִיחָנֵנוּ (Mal 1:9), and similar forms like יְחָנַּנִי (2 Sam 12:22); יסובוכ[ה] "they will surround you" (4Q460 7, 8), corresponding to similar MT forms like יְסֻבּוּהוּ (Job 40:22) and יְסוּבֵּנִי (Ps 49:6).[227] Conceivably, the development of *yqwṭl* + suffix forms was due to several simultaneous factors, including one or more of the above explanations.

5.8. *Qal* Imperative + Suffix

The distribution of the *qal* imperative + suffix is somewhat similar to that of the *qal* imperfect + suffix. As mentioned above, the forms seem, at least

---

225. See Ben-Ḥayyim, *Grammar of Samaritan Hebrew*, 207–8. In general, however, it is hard for me to get a sense of the distribution of the forms based on Ben-Ḥayyim's descriptions.

226. In a similar way, where the theme vowel shifts forward in geminate and other verbs to the prefix, it replaces a historical vowel: יָחְנְךָ (Gen 43:29, Isa 30:19) derives from a form akin to the pausal יְחֻנֶּךָּ; and וַיְּשְׁרֵם "he directed them" (2 Chr 32:30) from *וַיְיַשְּׁרֵם.

227. The /o/ or /u/ vowel between first and second root consonants in geminate verbs is also found in cases where there is no suffix: יזומו (4Q171 1–2 ii, 14); ישוגו (4Q266 9 iii, 4 and 4Q418 188, 7); ירועו (1QH[a] XII, 34; 4Q511 3, 7; and 20 ii, 3).

superficially, to be related to each other. Just as in the case of the imperfect, when suffixes are attached to the *qal* imperative, a *waw* sometimes appears after the second root consonant (three times), sometimes after the first (five times). This distribution presumes two different pronunciations: *qoṭlēnī* and *qəṭōlēnī*, paralleling the two different pronunciations for the imperfect + suffix.

Qal ms imperatives with suffix

נקובני "designate me" (4Q364 4b–e ii, 5)
עובדם "serve them" (4Q416 2 iii, 17)
דורשם "seek them" (4Q418 103 ii, 4)
זכורני "remember me" (11Q5 XXIV, 10)
כיתבהא "write it" (1QIsa[a] at Isa 30:8) for MT כָּתְבָהּ
עוזרני "aid me" (11Q5 [11QPs[a]] at Ps 119:86) for MT עָזְרֵנִי
שומרני "guard me" (11Q5 [11QPs[a]] at Ps 140:5) for MT שָׁמְרֵנִי
שמורני "guard me" (11Q5 [11QPs[a]] at Ps 141:9) for MT שָׁמְרֵנִי

Note that we are again concerned with roots that are strong, I-*nun* or I-guttural. All the verbs have *yiqṭol* imperfects. The MT contains very rare comparable examples of the *qṭwl* + suffix pattern (mentioned above, of the *kethib* מָלְוּכָה and צָרְופָה), though the Babylonian tradition attests more examples.[228] However, the DSS and Babylonian traditions are not identical in relation to these forms. The *qal* imperative + suffix in the Babylonian tradition has an /o/ or /u/ vowel after the second root consonant regularly, and has a similar vowel after the first root consonant only where the form is accented penultimately (e.g., *wəduqrenīʸ* 1 Sam 31:4 [= MT וְדָקְרֵנִי "pierce me"]).[229] The DSS forms listed above do not attest this same limitation (e.g., עובדם *ʿobdēm*). The variation in the DSS forms is exemplified in the exact same verb form exhibiting a *waw* after the first root consonant in one passage of a scroll and a *waw* after the second root consonant in another passage from the same scroll (שומרני versus שמורני).

The *qal* feminine singular imperatives do not occur with suffixes. Similarly, there are no clear instances of the *qal* masculine plural imperative + suffix; the closest we come is דורש[והו] "examine him" in 1QSa II, 10,

228. See Yeivin, *Hebrew Language Tradition*, 480.
229. Ibid.

though others reconstruct [דורש[יהו].[230] All the texts listed above are DSS-SP9 texts, except one that is DSS-SP1c (4Q508).

5.9. Adverbial *Heh*

As many have observed, what is often called the directional *heh* in Biblical Hebrew appears on words in the DSS, in which the *heh* does not necessarily imply a direction. In truth, even in the MT the *heh* does not always imply a direction, as in Jer 52:23, where the *heh* of רוּחָה implies where the pomegranates are, not a motion associated with them: "The pomegranates were ninety-six on (its [the Bronze Sea's]) side(s) (רוּחָה)."[231] In at least one case, there is not even a locational sense קוּמָה עֶזְרָתָה לָּנוּ "rise up as a help to us" (Ps 44:27); and, in another passage, it is used on what appears to be a compound preposition, לְמַעְלָה ראשׁ "beyond (the) top" (Ezra 9:6).[232]

The *heh* in the DSS functions in a way akin to its use in these biblical examples, in what might be called simply an adverbial way, as in 1QM XII, 13: "Zion, rejoice much (מאדה)" and in 11Q5 (11QPs[a]) XXII, 12 "above all the world" (מעלה לכול תבל)." As in the MT, in the DSS the *heh* is often affixed to adverbs or to substantives used as adverbs (מאדה "much," מעלה "above," סביבה "around"), but the number of substantives to which it attaches is fewer than in LBH or SBH.[233] At the same time, these adverbial words with the *heh* occur quite frequently in the DSS. Since "long forms" of the adverbs (like מאדה) are one defining feature of DSS-SP9 texts, it is not surprising that the occurrences of such adverbs are predominantly among these texts, though there are exceptions (e.g.,

230. See Charlesworth and Stuckenbruck "Rule of the Congregation," 116.

231. Although the consonants could be interpreted as the word "side" plus the 3fs suffix, the MT clearly has this as the so-called directive *heh*. Despite BHS's comment on this word "crrp", the versions suggest that the best interpretation of this *heh* is not as a pronominal suffix, but as the directive *heh* used in its locative sense. Another example is from Jer 13:7 "from where (שָׁמָּה) I hid it." A metaphorical sense of location is found in Ps 120:1: בַּצָּרָתָה לִּי "in my distress."

232. See GKC §90h. Note also the use of the *heh* in one repeated temporal phrase: מִיָּמִים יָמִימָה "from year to year (lit., days to days)." It also occurs with other common nouns, but these are sometimes the subjects of their phrases (see Judg 14:18 בְּטֶרֶם יָבוֹא הַחַרְסָה "before the sun came up") or part of prepositional phrases (GKC §90f–g). Muraoka notes that in the Aramaic of the DSS the analogous ending is not simply locative, but more broadly "adverbial" (*GQA* 92, n. 542).

233. Joosten, "Hebrew, Aramaic, Greek," 357.

מאדה in 4Q22 [4QpaleoExod^{m}] at Exod 12:38). Joosten has observed that the way the *heh* in the DSS functions suggests a development from its use in BH and LBH.[234]

234. Ibid.

Conclusions

The preceding analysis has documented a number of characteristics of the DSS, both among the nonbiblical scrolls, as well as among the biblical scrolls. If one were to extract a general observation from the many phenomena found in the diverse texts described above (which also reflect an equally diverse range of dialects and idiolects), it may be a tendency reflected in DSS-SP9 and DSS-SP1c texts to write and pronounce the writing/reading register of Hebrew in a manner that would better reflect its characteristic vowels and syllabic contours, both through natural linguistic developments (like a preference for verbal and nominal forms that retain etymological vowels יקטולו and the use of *aleph* as an epenthetic consonant), as well as more artificial means (like *plene* orthography, *aleph* as a word-internal *mater* for /ā/, the graphic duplication of a consonantal *yodh* or *waw*). Running counter to this tendency (and presumably something that partially precipitated it) are phenomena that threatened to obscure the etymological vowels and consonants of the language, the most pedestrian being scribal error, but which also include natural shifts in the language like the assimilation of /ʾ/ to /y/ or /w/; diphthong and triphthong contraction (especially, *-āw* > *-ō* and *-īhū* > *-īyū* in the 3ms suffix); the inherent weakness of the gutturals and their confusion or near disappearance in certain dialects; and vowel reduction. In addition, the language's historical shape was also affected by occasional influence from Aramaic in its lexicon and morphology, as well as by a limited tendency toward (perceived) archaism in its orthography (e.g., ביא, מיא).

Many of the characteristics of the scrolls (especially as relates to the phonology, but also the orthography and morphology) are shared with the Hebrew of the MT, though they are found in the DSS much more often than in the Hebrew Bible. In particular, students who are encountering the Hebrew of the DSS for the first time should pay attention to the following traits in order to better make sense of the Hebrew text:

(1) Scribal mistakes occur in numerous texts and one should be watchful for cases of dittography, haplography, and metathesis, as well as the occasional confusion between similar looking or similar sounding consonants.

(2) *Aleph* is used as a *mater* in at least two ways atypical of the MT: as a word-internal *mater* for /ā/ (e.g., דאוה for MT דָּוָה) and as part of a digraph (with *waw* or *yodh*) to mark a preceding /ō/, /ū/, or /ī/ (e.g., כיא for MT כִּי). In its use as an internal *mater*, it frequently appears before or after a consonantal *waw* or *yodh*.

(3) *Aleph* representing a glottal stop sometimes develops from an etymological *yodh*, usually in the sequence /īyī/ (e.g., כתיאים for MT כִּתִּיִּים) or the sequence /āy/, /ōy/, and even once /ūy/ (e.g., אואב for MT אֹיֵב). In rare cases, the opposite shift takes place, /ʾ/ shifts to /y/ where *aleph* might have quiesced (e.g., לביותיו for MT לְבָאוֹתָיו).

(4) On the other hand, etymological *aleph* is not written (reflecting the loss of the glottal stop) in positions where the glottal stop seems to have quiesced in corresponding MT forms and words (e.g., at the end of a syllable, ברתה and MT בָּרָאתָ; after a consonant שו and MT שָׁוְא; and after a shewa שרית and MT שְׁרִית, compare שְׁאֵרִית), as well as within words of the **qaṭl*/**qiṭl*/**quṭl* base patterns (e.g., רוש for MT רֹאשׁ and מוד for MT מְאֹד).

(5) *Heh* as a *mater* marks word-final /ā/ in places that the MT usually has simply a *qamets* (e.g., קטלתה for MT קָטַלְתָּ).

(6) A *heh* that constitutes a morphological affix (like the definite article, the *heh* that begins the *niphal* infinitive construct and the *hiphil* perfect and infinitive construct) can sometimes elide, as in the MT. The elision in the DSS, however, is more frequent than in the MT and together with other factors, suggests the quiescence of *heh* in the dialects of some writers/scribes. In some texts (notably 1QIsa[a] and 1QS) it can be replaced by *aleph*. Rarely, it seems that *heh* assimilates to a neighboring vowel (as in תהוו *tōwū*).

(7) *Waw* as a *mater* marks all manner of /u/ and /o/ vowels. The unexpected presence of *waw mater* in a word (i.e., the presence of a *waw* where the corresponding MT word does not have a /u/ or /o/ vowel) is often attributable to a base pattern for a noun unlike the one found in the MT (e.g., **quṭl* instead of MT **qaṭl*); due to a neighboring bilabial, *lamedh*, *nun*, or *resh*; due to a distinct morphology (i.e., pausal forms *yqṭwlw* and *qṭwlw*, as well as imperfect + suffix forms *yqṭwl* + suffix and *yqwṭl* + suffix).

(8) *Ḥeth* seems to represent a clearly articulated and distinct phoneme. It is sometimes confused with *heh* due to the two letters' similar shape and the similarity in their place of articulation.

(9) *Yodh* as a *mater* is rarely used to mark word-internal /ē/ or short /i/ where the corresponding MT words do not contain a *mater*. In addition, two *yodhs* (and more rarely two *waws*) can mark the presence of a single consonantal *yodh* (or *waw*) (e.g., יהייה for MT יִהְיֶה) or the presence of two contiguous *yodhs* (or *waws*) (e.g., ענייה for MT עֲנִיָּה). Sometimes /y/ shifts to /ʾ/ where *aleph* might quiesce (see point 3 above).

(10) *ʿAyin*'s quiescence is found only occasionally; it is worth noting again that no word with etymological *ʿayin* is misspelled consistently among the scrolls. Nevertheless, certain texts (especially those associated with the sect 1QS, 1QH[a], 1QIsa[a]) seem to exhibit a particular tendency to drop this letter and presumably its associated sound.

(11) *Resh* is presumably articulated in the back of the mouth, as it was in later Masoretic times. Such a pronunciation seems to have made it easy for scribes to miss it in copying and writing.

(12) *Samekh* is often written for etymological *śin* and vice versa, both letters representing the sound /s/.

(13) The morphology of pronouns will generally be clear to the student who knows Biblical Hebrew, but one should note the frequent ה- ending to most independent and suffixed pronouns. Note also the apparent collapse of the diphthong /āw/ to /ō/ in the 3ms suffix on plural nouns, the result of which is that where one would expect יו-, one sometimes finds just ו-; furthermore, in 1QIsa[a] where one would expect ו-, one sometimes finds יו-.

(14) The morphology of nouns is characterized, as stated just above, by a variation in the base pattern for certain nouns (e.g., **quṭl* instead of MT **qaṭl* as well as **maqṭul* or **maqṭāl* instead of MT **maqṭal*); by the emergence of new base patterns or the growing prominence of rare patterns (e.g., **qiṭṭūl:* פרוש); by the emergence of new by-forms for otherwise well-attested words (e.g., מבינה instead of MT בִּינָה), especially where this concerns the emergence of a masculine by-form of a feminine MT word (e.g., ברך for MT בְּרָכָה) or a feminine by-form of a masculine MT word (e.g., מטעת for MT מַטָּע). Also, **quṭl* nouns in construct can have an optional Aramaic-like form (e.g., קטול).

(15) The morphology of verbs will also usually be clear to the student familiar with Biblical Hebrew, especially if one keeps in mind the orthographic and phonological tendencies noted above (e.g., loss of *aleph*, marking of short /o/ with *waw mater*, and so on). In addition to the emergence of entirely new verbs, one should note the use of common verbs in different stems and with somewhat different nuances. One will also note the tendency for pausal forms in the *qal* plural imperfect and imperative

(*yqṭwlw* and *qṭwlw*), as well as the peculiar morphology of the *qal* imperfect + suffix, *yqwṭl* + suffix, which seems to alternate with the so-called pausal form, *yqṭwl* + suffix, and with the defective form *yqṭl* + suffix. Some features, like the use of the pseudo-cohortative for the 1cs/p *waw*-consecutive imperfect will be familiar to students who have read texts dominated by LBH. But, the use of short forms of III-*yodh* roots in places one would expect the long form will seem unusual.

Further conclusions relate to specific points that may not be essential for the intermediate student to master, but which contribute to our understanding of the language as it is manifested in the DSS.

First, the plethora of scribal errors in the scrolls should give caution to anyone attempting to draw significant linguistic information from a single misspelling of a word. Furthermore, the study illustrates that despite a tendency for *plene* orthography among the DSS-SP9 texts, there is still a great deal of variation in the spelling of words.

The study confirms that historical short /u/ vowels were often marked with a *waw mater*, though only erratically for **quṭlat* nouns like חכמה "wisdom." In part, this might have been to distinguish between otherwise orthographically and phonetically similar forms like *עורמה **ʿormāh* (*"her cleverness") and ערמה *ʿormā* ("cleverness"). In other cases, the short /u/ vowel is marked by a *waw mater*, though corresponding words (or verb forms) from the MT do not bear a /u/ class vowel. Many examples are adduced for this phenomenon, but since each word usually admits of at least two explanations, it is difficult to be sure which explanation to trust. Ambiguity also inheres in the identification of some **quṭl* nouns in the construct state; such nouns may be spelled in their construct form with a *waw mater* between second and third root consonants, which makes them look like adjectives (e.g., גדול might be the construct form of the abstract noun גדל "greatness" or the adjective גדול "great").

The sequence *aleph* + *waw mater* alternates with *waw mater* + *aleph* in cases where there is no preceding vowel (ראוש "head" versus רואש, both = *rōš*). Where there is a preceding vowel (including a muttered vowel [that is, vocal shewa]), and the *aleph* has not been lost due to quiescence or, as rarely happens, due to assimilation to a preceding or following vowel, the *waw mater* almost always follows the *aleph* (e.g., מאור "light"). This suggests that the *aleph* was pronounced as a glottal stop (*māʾōr*, const. *məʾōr*).

The study demonstrates the reality of the practice of writing two *yodh*s or *waw*s for a single consonantal *yodh* or *waw* (or, more rarely, for two contiguous *yodh*s or *waw*s with no intervening vowel). Other instances of juxtaposed *yodhs* in the orthography can best be explained not as indicating a single vowel, but rather as cases of a consonantal *yodh* followed by an /i/ vowel (ייראו "they will fear"), of dittography (בייד "in the hand"), of orthographic practices shared with the MT (יי to represent *-īyī-* as in עִבְרִיִּים "Hebrews" or *-īyē-* as in נשיי "leaders of" [reflecting the shift **nəsī'ē > nəsīyē*]).

In relation specifically to phonology, the study has demonstrated that although some guttural consonants could sometimes be confused with each other due to their imprecise articulation, not all gutturals were equally liable to such imprecision, nor were the gutturals equally likely to be confused for each other. *Aleph* is lost with some frequency word-internally at the end of a syllable and when preceded by a consonant or muttered vowel, though, it seems to be retained when preceded by a full vowel (although rarely in these cases it assimilates to a preceding or following vowel). *Aleph* sometimes replaces etymological *heh* and, more rarely, etymological *'ayin*, suggesting the relative weakness of the phonemes associated with these letters (especially in DSS-SP9 texts). More often than in the MT, the *heh* is lost word-internally when it would have been preceded by a muttered vowel. The *'ayin* is more rarely lost word-internally than either *aleph* or *heh*, and is not repeatedly dropped from specific words in the DSS. The quiescence of the *'ayin* phoneme is most frequent in 1QS, 1QH[a], as well as 1QIsa[a]. Although *ḥeth* was sometimes lost from the end of syllables, this is quite uncommon; and, misspellings of *kaph* for *ḥeth* suggest that this guttural was not "weakened" as other gutturals sometimes were.

The study has shown that although *aleph* and *yodh* can alternate with each other, the environments where such shifts typically take place are rather predictable. The shift of *yodh > aleph* occurs somewhat frequently, especially between /ī/ vowels (*-īyī- > -ī'ī-*, as in כתיאים "Kittim") and where a diphthong (*-āy-* or *-ōy-*) might have formed between the preceding vowel and the *yodh* consonant (*-āyī- > -ā'ī-*, as in פתאים "simple"; *-ōyī- > -ō'ī-*, as in גואים "peoples"). In these cases, *aleph* seems to function as a means of separating vowels or a consonant + vowel combination and thus as a means of preserving the syllabic structure of words. The shift *aleph > yodh*, on the other hand, is attested infrequently, primarily where an /ī/ vowel directly precedes the *aleph* and another (non-/i/ vowel) follows (*-ī'ă- > -īyə-* or *-īye-*, as in ישייכה "he will deceive you"; *-ī'ā- > -īyā-*, as in אליב "Eliab"; *-ī'ē- > -īyē-*, as in דניל "Daniel"; *-ī'ū- > -īyū-*, as in החטיום "they made them sin"). In some cases the shift *aleph > yodh* may also help preserve the syllabic structure of a word; this is attested where the *aleph* was liable to quiesce (e.g., לביותיו in 4Q169 3–4 i, 4 in a quotation of Nah 2:13 for MT לְבְאוֹתָיו "its lionesses"). Similar shifts involving *aleph* and *waw* are found in the DSS for similar reasons.

Of the remaining phonological shifts evidenced in the scrolls, the most important are *-īhū* > *-īyū* and *-āw* > *-ō*, both of which involve the 3ms pronominal suffix. Although these shifts are suspected to be real features of some idiolects, they are not always represented through the orthography. Instead, the 3ms suffix on singular short words like אב "father" is most often הו- (i.e., אביהו) and the 3ms suffix on plural words and certain prepositions (like על) is יו- (i.e., עליו). At least in some texts, these spellings probably represent a pronunciation closer to that in the MT (e.g., *ʾābīhū*, *ʿālāw*). The writing of a *yodh* in the 3ms suffix on plural words (יו-) seems to be an orthographic way of distinguishing plural nouns. Often, in plural feminine nouns ending in *-ōt*, where the 3ms suffix has no *yodh*, the feminine plural morpheme has a *waw mater* (ותו-), and where this *mater* is missing, the suffix is usually spelled with a *yodh* (תיו-).

The place of the accent or stress is not known, but the DSS do attest a consistent preference for forms that correspond to MT pausal forms. This occurs with some noun + suffix forms (e.g., רעיכה), but applies most frequently to verbs. For example, *qal* plural imperfects attest a *mater* to mark the theme vowel (יקטולו); an /o/ or /u/ vowel appears between first and second root consonants in *qal* geminate verbs (יחונכה and יזומו). Furthermore, DSS verbs whose MT analogs show alternate theme vowels (one for context and one for pause) consistently evidence in the DSS a preference for the vowel they exhibit in their MT pausal forms. Specifically, the verb בגד attests an /o/ or /u/ theme vowel, but חפץ and טרף attest an /a/ vowel; an /a/ vowel also occurs in the imperative of ירש.

In relation to morphology, the study has demonstrated that there is little real evidence for the *qere perpetuum* phenomenon of the 3fs independent pronoun (הוא = *hīʾ*) in the DSS. The alternation one finds in this and other independent pronouns between the basic form and the form with a final *heh mater* are probably reflective of distinct pronunciations (הוא = *hūʾ* and הואה = *hūʾā*).

Verb forms and certain orthographic practices that are rare in the MT are more common in the DSS and vice versa. This applies not only to the well known *plene* spelling of the 2ms perfect verbs (קטלתה) and apparent pausal forms (יקטולו), but also to forms like the *hiphil* second- and first-person perfect forms of בוא "to come" which often bear an *ō* connecting vowel in the DSS, as in הביאותה "you brought," though not in the MT, where such a connecting vowel appears primarily where object suffixes are attached to the verb. In a similar way, although the *hiphil* infinitives construct in the MT are written defectively primarily when suffixes are attached, in the DSS the *hiphil* infinitives construct appear defective after אין "not" and after the *lamedh* preposition. Finally, the *niphal* and *piel* feminine singular participles are marked by the ה- morpheme more often than in the MT, where the ת- morpheme predominates.

Almost all examples of *yqwṭl* + suffix involve verbs with an /o/ or /u/ theme vowel. This makes it likely that the *waw mater* between first and second root consonants is prompted by the theme vowel (e.g., ידורשהו "they will examine him" 1QS VI, 14). Variation between *yqṭwl* + suffix and *yqwṭl* + suffix is paralleled by similar variation among the DSS in *qal* imperative + suffix and the rarer variation in the *qal* infinitive construct + suffix. The variations found in these three groups are similar but not identical to the variations in other Hebrew traditions.

With the exception of 1QIsa[a], 1QS, and a few other shorter texts (like 4Q107 [4QCant[b]]), the influence from Aramaic seems marginal. Nevertheless, one still gets a hint of Aramaic influence in a wide variety of ways in a wide variety of texts, including in some DSS-NSP texts (e.g., 4Q229, 4Q381, 4Q448). In terms of orthography, the use of *aleph* as an internal *mater* for /ā/ may be related to the same, more widespread orthographic practice in Aramaic. In relation to morphology, note the Aramaic-like pronoun זן or זך "this" (4Q371 1a–b, 8, compare Aramaic דֵּן or דֵּךְ) and the following examples of pronominal suffixes: the numerous cases of the 3ms והי- attested in 1QIsa[a] (e.g., מעשוהי "his works" 1QIsa[a] at Isa 10:12); the 3mp עליהום "over them" (4Q176 20, 3), אביהן "their father" (4Q17 [4QExod–Lev[f]] at Exod 40:15), [על]יהן "over them" (4Q277 1 ii, 7); 3fp עליהון "over them" (1QS III, 25); 2fs (in 1QIsa[a], as in לבכי "your heart" at Isa 47:7 for MT לִבֵּךְ); and 1cp אבתינא "our fathers" (4Q381 46a+b, 4). Note also the alternation between *aleph* and *heh* in the prefix of the causative stem in 1QS for example, באופיע "when [they] shine" 1QS X, 2) and in 1QIsa[a] (e.g., אודו "give thanks" 1QIsa[a] at Isa 12:4) as well as the presence of *heh* prefixes in some imperfect and participial forms (ויהכין "and he will establish" 1QS III, 9; מהסיר "is removing" 1QIsa[a] at Isa 3:1 for MT מֵסִיר); the תי- ending of 2fs perfect verbs in 1QIsa[a] (eighteen times); the /o/ or /u/ theme vowel in the *qal* imperfect to אכל, בחר, זרע, פעל, שכב (again in 1QIsa[a]); *heh*-preformative verbal nouns הוריה "teaching" (4Q491c 11 i, 16); ה[ז]יה "sprinkling" (4Q512 1–6, 6); and the final *nun* on plural forms: ימין "days" (11Q20 XII, 5) corrected to ימים, פחין "traps" (4Q184 1, 2),

בשמין "spices" (4Q107 [4QCant[b]] at Song 4:10). In addition, the spelling of the construct form of **quṭl* nouns with a *waw mater* between second and third root consonants (i.e., קדוש) may reflect Aramaic influence. Lexical items that presumably show Aramaic influence (whether or not they were interpreted by speakers as genuine Hebrew words) include some of the words listed above in the section "Nouns" (§5.3), including הטללים "the shadows"; כידן "javelin"; מוזנים "scales"; מתקל "stumbling." Note too the verbs: כנף"to gather" or "to be gathered" (1QIsa[a] at Isa 30:20); [י]סתגון "they will increase" (4Q523 3, 1), as well as the interjections: היכה "how?" (1QIsa[a] at Isa 1:21); הכן "indeed" (1QIsa[a] at Isa 40:7). Also of relevance are the various plural spellings of the word "day" with a *waw mater*, which suggests Aramaic influence: יומי "days of" (1QS II, 19; III, 5); ויומי "my days" (1QIsa[a] at Isa 38:10) for an intended יומי; and ביומי "in days of" (1QIsa[a] at Isa 1:1). Some words that seem borrowed from Aramaic are also found in the MT, like קצת "end." Other features that may reflect Aramaic influence include the independent form of the preposition *min* instead of prefixing to a following word (e.g., מן טהרת "from the purity of" 1QS VII, 3); the spelling and associated pronunciation (reflecting /wū/ > /ū/) of the 3mp imperfect of הוה: יהו *yəhū* "may they be" (4Q448 II, 7). In other matters, the Hebrew of the DSS seems to parallel phenomena in Aramaic: the shift /ā/ > /ō/ in proximity to bilabials, *lamedh*, *nun*, *resh*; the shifts /y/ > /ʾ/ and /ʾ/ > /y/; the apparent penultimate accent on some verbal forms ending in a vowel.

It should also be stated that although some texts, like 1QIsa[a], do attest numerous phenomena and words apparently due to Aramaic influence, it is also the case that certain features of Aramaic are not attested. For example, the blurring of distinctions between III-*waw*/*yodh* and III-*aleph* verbs is found perhaps only two times in 1QIsa[a], though the same blurring is widespread in DSS Aramaic.

One conclusion that can be drawn from the above list is that the Aramaic influence on Hebrew was not pervasive. It seems to affect the idiolects of certain scribes or writers, and specific features within these idiolects. Given the influence of Hebrew on DSS Aramaic, one can conclude that the Aramaisms found in the scrolls are at least in part due to some scribes/writers being bilingual, if not multilingual.[1]

---

1. On the Hebraisms in DSS Aramaic, see Muraoka, *GQA*, passim (e.g., for loanwords, 78–81). That scribes were bi- or multilingual seems to be the consensus. See Willem F. Smelik, *The Targum of Judges* (OTS 36; Leiden: Brill, 1995), 8; Steven E.

Some of the features documented in this book are common to all groups of texts, while some are peculiar to DSS-SP9 only or to DSS-SP9 and DSS-SP1c texts. Those features that seem to be widespread and are attested in all text groups include: scribal mistakes; marking etymological short /u/ with *waw* (though this is not found typically in the biblical scrolls of the DSS-NSP group); preservation of the sequence *aleph* + *waw mater* when the *aleph* is present and when a vowel (sometimes even shewa) immediately precedes the *aleph*; the use of וא-, או-, יא-, אי- to mark final vowels; spirantization; elision of *aleph* (and quiescence of the glottal stop); elision of *heh* (and quiescence of the glottal fricative); writing of *aleph* for etymological *yodh* in gentilic nouns, II-*yodh*, and III-*yodh* nouns; writing of *yodh* for etymological *aleph*; occasional elision of *resh*; writing *samekh* for *śin* and *śin* for *samekh*; writing the 3ms pronominal suffix הו- on short words (like פה "mouth"); use of the pseudo-cohortative; lack of short jussive forms.

Most of these features, it should be mentioned, have parallels in the MT and suggest a shared heritage between the Hebrew of the MT (especially LBH) and that of the DSS. The relative frequency of some of these features in the DSS as compared to the MT may suggest a diachronic development: for example, elision of *aleph* and *heh*, the variation between *aleph* and *yodh*, and confusion between *samekh* and *śin*, not to mention the use of the pseudo-cohortative.

Those features that seem to be most common or peculiar to the DSS-SP9 and DSS-SP1c texts include: **quṭl* bases for MT **qaṭl*/**qiṭl* bases; development of an /o/ or /u/ vowel due to a neighboring bilabial (/b/, /m/, /p/), *lamedh*, *nun* or *resh* or due to another /o/ or /u/ vowel; **quṭl* nouns in construct exhibiting a *waw mater* between second and third root consonants; *qal* imperfect + suffix with a *waw mater* between first and second root consonants (*yqwṭl* + suffix); ראש "head" spelled with a *waw mater* with or without the *aleph*; writing two *yodh*s for a consonantal *yodh* and two *waw*s for a consonantal *waw*; occasional elision of *ʿayin* (i.e., quiescence of voiced pharyngeal fricative); writing *waw* for etymological *aleph*; writing *aleph* for etymological *waw*; the contractions -*īhū* > -*īyū* and -*āw* > -*ō* in the 3ms pronominal suffix on plural nouns; increased use of prothetic *aleph*; spelling the 2ms/p pronominal suffix with a final *heh mater*; spell-

---

Fassberg, "Which Semitic Language Did Jesus and Other Contemporary Jews Speak?" *CBQ* 74 (2012), 277; Joosten, "Hebrew, Aramaic, Greek," 359.

ing the 3mp pronominal suffix with a final *heh mater*; spelling the 2mp independent pronoun with a final *heh mater* (אתמה); spelling the 3m/fs independent pronouns with a final *heh mater* (הואה, היאה); the Aramaic 3ms suffix on plural nouns, והי-; spelling the 2ms/p perfect forms with a final *heh mater*; adverbial *heh* on words like מאדה "much."

Some of the above features of DSS-SP9 and DSS-SP1c texts are to be attributed to a specific dialect or tradition belonging to those writing the majority of the DSS. Note especially the **quṭl* bases, the development of /o/ or /u/ vowels, occasional elision of *ʿayin*, the phonologic shifts *-īhū* > *-īyū* and *-āw* > *-ō*, the pronunciation of various pronouns with an optional *-ā* ending, the adverbial *heh* on adverbs like מאדה. The consistency with which one sees these features suggests they were not only part of the spoken vernacular of the scribes, but also part of the language with which they used to write and read (some) texts.[2] This presumes, of course, that the Hebrew of these texts is not entirely artificial or merely archaizing, but rather reflects in some muted ways, unique dialects of Hebrew.

2. This does not mean, however, that such scribes were necessarily ignorant of alternate orthographies, phonologies, and morphologies.

Bibliography

Abegg, Martin G. "The Hebrew of the Dead Sea Scrolls." Pages 325–58 in vol. 1 of *The Dead Sea Scrolls after Fifty Years: A Comprehensive Assessment*. Edited by Peter W. Flint and James C. VanderKam. 2 vols. Leiden: Brill, 1998–1999.

———. "Linguistic Profile of the Isaiah Scrolls." Pages 25–41 in *Qumran Cave 1, II: The Isaiah Scrolls, Part 2: Introductions, Commentary, and Textual Variants*. Edited by Eugene Ulrich and Peter W. Flint. DJD 32. Oxford: Clarendon, 2010.

———. "Qumran Text and Tagging." In Accordance 9.5. Altamonte Springs, Florida: OakTree Software, 1999–2009.

Abegg, Martin G., James E. Bowley, Edward M. Cook, and Casey Towes. "Grammatical Tagging of Dead Sea Scrolls Biblical Corpus." In Accordance 9.5. Altamonte Springs, Florida: OakTree Software, 2009.

Abegg, Martin G., James E. Bowley, Edward M. Cook, Emanuel Tov. *The Dead Sea Scrolls Concordance*. 3 vols. Leiden: Brill, 2003–.

Accordance 9.5. Altamonte Springs, Florida: OakTree Software, 2011.

Alexander, P. and G. Vermes. *Qumran Cave 4.XIX: 4QSerekh Ha-Yaḥad and Two Related Texts*. DJD 26. Oxford: Clarendon, 1998.

Allegro, John M. *Qumran Cave 4.I (4Q158–186)*. DJD 5. Oxford: Clarendon, 1968.

Andersen, Francis I. and A. Dean Forbes. *Spelling in the Hebrew Bible: Dahood Memorial Lecture*. BO 14. Rome: Pontifical Biblical Institute, 1986.

———. *The Vocabulary of the Old Testament*. Rome: Pontifical Biblical Institute, 1992.

Baden, Joel. "Hithpael and Niphal in Biblical Hebrew: Semantic and Morphological Overlap." *VT* 60 (2010): 33–44.

Baillet, Maurice. *Qumran Grotte 4.III (4Q482–4Q520)*. DJD 7. Oxford: Clarendon, 1982.

———. "Textes des Grottes 2Q, 3Q, 6Q, 7Q à 10Q." Pages 45–166 in vol. 1 of *Les 'Petites Grottes' de Qumrân*." Edited by Maurice Baillet, J. T. Milik, R. de Vaux. 2 vols. DJD 3. Oxford: Clarendon, 1962.

Bar-Asher, Moshe. "A Few Remarks on Mishnaic Hebrew and Aramaic in Qumran Hebrew." Pages 115–30 in *Diggers at the Well: Proceedings of a Third International Symposium on the Hebrew of the Dead Sea Scrolls and Ben Sira*. Edited by T. Muraoka and John F. Elwolde. STDJ 36. Leiden: Brill, 2000.

———. "Grammatical and Lexical Phenomena in a Dead Sea Scroll (4Q374)" (Hebrew). *Meghillot* 4 (2006): 153–67.

———. "המן (= מן) in a Fragment from Qumran" (Hebrew). *Leshonenu* 55 (1990): 75.

———. "The Language of Qumran: Between Biblical and Mishnaic Hebrew (A Study in Morphology)" (Hebrew). *Meghillot* 2 (2004): 137–49.

———. "On the Language of '*The Vision of Gabriel*.'" *RevQ* 23 (2008): 491–524.

———. "On the Language of the 'Vision of Gabriel'" (Hebrew). *Meghillot* 7 (2009): 193–226.

———. "Qumran Hebrew between Biblical and Mishnaic Hebrew: A Morphological Study." Pages 3–17 in *The Dynamics of Language and Exegesis at Qumran*. Edited by Devorah Dimant and Reinhard G. Kratz. FAT 2/35. Tübingen: Mohr Siebeck, 2009.

———. "Qumran Hebrew and Mishnaic Hebrew" (Hebrew). *Meghillot* 8–9 (2010): 287–317.

———. "Some Unusual Spellings in the Qumran Scrolls" (Hebrew). *Meghillot* 3 (2005): 165–76.

———. "Two Phenomena in Qumran Hebrew: Synchronic and Diachronic Aspects" (Hebrew). *Meghillot* 1 (2003): 167–83.

Barr, James. *The Variable Spellings of the Hebrew Bible: The Schweich Lectures of the British Academy, 1986*. Oxford: Oxford University Press, 1989.

Bauer, Hans and Pontus Leander. *Historische Grammatik der Hebräischen Sprache des Alten Testamentes*. 2 vols. Halle: Niemeyer, 1922.

Baumgarten, Joseph M. "Damascus Document." Pages 1–185 in *The Dead Sea Scrolls, Hebrew, Aramaic, and Greek Texts with English Translations, Volume 3: Damascus Document II, Some Works of the Torah, and Related Documents*. Edited by James H. Charlesworth. Princeton Theological Seminary Dead Sea Scrolls Project 3. Tübingen: Mohr Siebeck, 2006.

———. *Qumran Cave 4.XIII: The Damascus Document (4Q266–273)*. DJD 18. Oxford: Clarendon, 1996.

Ben-Ḥayyim, Ze'ev. "The Forms of the Pronominal Suffixes, ךָ-, תְּ-, הּ- in the Different Masoretic Schools of the Hebrew Language" (Hebrew). Pages 66–99 in *Sefer Asaph qovets ma'amare meḥqar, mugash li-khevod ha-Rav prof. Simḥah Assaf, 'al yede yedidab, ḥaverab ve talmidab, li-melo't lo shishim shanah*. Edited by U. Cassuto, J. Klausner, and J. Gutman. Jerusalem: ha-Rav Quq, 1953.

———. *A Grammar of Samaritan Hebrew: Based on the Recitation of the Law in Comparison with the Tiberian and Other Jewish Traditions*. Jerusalem: Magnes, 2000.

———. *Studies in the Traditions of the Hebrew Language*. Madrid: Instituo Arias Montana, 1954.

———. "Traditions in the Hebrew Language, with Reference to the Dead Sea Scrolls." Pages 200–214 in *Aspects of the Dead Sea Scrolls*. Edited by Chaim Rabin and Yigael Yadin. Scripta Hierosolymitana 4. Jerusalem: Magnes, 1958.

———. "The Tradition of the Samaritans and its Relationship to the Linguistic Tradition of the Dead Sea Scrolls and Rabbinic Language" (Hebrew). *Leshonenu* 22 (1958): 223–45.

———. "ישנים גם חדשים מן צפוני מדבר יהודה" (Hebrew). *Leshonenu* 42 (1977–1978): 278–93.

Bergsträsser, G. *Hebräische Grammatik*. 2 vols. Leipzig: Vogel, 1918 (vol. 1 [phonology and morphology]); Leipzig: Hinrichs, 1926–1929 (vol. 2 [verb]).

Bernstein, Moshe J. and Aaron Koller. "The Aramaic Texts and the Hebrew and Aramaic Languages at Qumran: The North American Contribution." Pages 155–96 in *The Dead Sea Scrolls in Scholarly Perspective: A History of Research*. Edited by Devorah Dimant. STDJ 99. Leiden: Brill, 2012.

Beyer, Klaus. *Althebräische Grammatik*. Göttingen, Vandenhoeck & Ruprecht, 1969.

———. *Die Aramäischen Texte vom Toten Meer, samt den Inschriften aus Paläsina, dem Testament Levis aus der Kairoer Genisa, der Fastenrolle und den alten talmudischen Zitaten*. Göttingen: Vandenhoeck & Ruprecht, 1984.

Biber, Douglas. *Dimensions of Register Variation: A Cross-Linguistic Comparison*. Cambridge: Cambridge University, 1995.

Blau, Joshua. "A Conservative View of the Language of the Dead Sea Scrolls." Pages 20–25 in *Diggers at the Well: Proceedings of a Third International Symposium on the Hebrew of the Dead Sea Scrolls and Ben Sira*. Edited by T. Muraoka and John F. Elwolde. STDJ 36. Leiden: Brill, 2000.

———. "Non-Phonetic Conditioning of Sound Change and Biblical Hebrew." *HAR* 3 (1979): 7–15.

———. *On Polyphony in Biblical Hebrew*. Israel Academy of Sciences and Humanities Proceedings 6/2. Jerusalem: Israel Academy of Sciences and Humanities, 1982.

———. *On Pseudo-Corrections in Some Semitic Languages*. Jerusalem: Israel Academy of Sciences and Humanities, 1970.

———. *Phonology and Morphology of Biblical Hebrew: An Introduction*. LSAWS 2. Winona Lake, Ind.: Eisenbrauns, 2010. An earlier edition appeared in Hebrew as *Torat ha-hegeh veha-tsurot* (1972).

———. "Some Remarks on the Prehistory of Stress in Biblical Hebrew." *IOS* 9 (1979): 49–54.

Bloomfield, Leonard. *Language*. New York: Holt, Rinehard, and Winston, 1965.

Bolozky, Shmuel. "Israeli Hebrew Phonology." Pages 287–311 in vol. 1 of *Phonologies of Asia and Africa*. Edited by Alan S. Kaye. 2 vols. Winona Lake, Ind.: Eisenbrauns, 1997.

Breuer, Yohanan. "On the Hebrew Dialect of the *ʾĀmōrāʾīm* in the Babylonian Talmud." Pages 129–50 in *Studies in Mishnaic Hebrew*. Edited by Moshe Bar-Asher. ScrHier 37. Jerusalem: Magnes, 1998.

———. "Intervocalic *Alef*/*Yodh* Interchanges in Mishnaic Hebrew." *Revue des Études juives* 159 (2000): 63–78.

Brockelmann, C. *Grundriss der vergleichenden Grammatik der semitischen Sprachen*. 2 vols. Berlin: n.p., 1908–1913; reprinted Hildesheim: Georg Olms, 1961.

———. *Hebräische Syntax*. Neukirchener: Neukirchener Verlag, 1956; 2nd ed. 2004.

Brønno, Einar. "The Isaiah Scroll DSIa and the Greek Transliterations of Hebrew." *ZDMG* 106 (1956): 252–58.

———. *Studien über hebräische Morphologie und Vokalismus auf Grundlage der mercatischen Fragmente der zweiten Kolumn der Hexapla des Origenes*. Leipzig: Deutsche Morgenländische Gesellschaft / Brockhaus, 1943.

———. "Zu den Theorien Paul Kahles." *ZDMG* 100 (1951): 521–65.

Carmignac, J. "Compléments au texte des hymnes de Qumrân," *RevQ* 2 (1959–1960): 267–76, 449–558.

———. "Précisions apportées au vocabulaire de l'hébreu biblique par La Guerre des Fils de Lumière Contre les Fils de Ténèbres." *VT* 5 (1955): 345–65.

Charlesworth, James H. *The Dead Sea Scrolls, Rule of the Community: Photographic Multi-Language Edition*. Philadelphia: American Interfaith Institute, 1996.

———. *The Pesharim and Qumran History: Chaos or Consensus*. Grand Rapids: Eerdmans, 2002.

Charlesworth, James H. et al., eds. *The Dead Sea Scrolls, Hebrew, Aramaic, and Greek Texts with English Translations, Volume 1: Rule of the Community and Related Documents*. Princeton Theological Seminary Dead Sea Scrolls Project 1. Tübingen: Mohr Siebeck, 1994.

Charlesworth, James H. and Loren Stuckenbruck. "Rule of the Congregation." Pages 108–17 in *The Dead Sea Scrolls, Hebrew, Aramaic, and Greek Texts with English Translations, Volume 1: Rule of the Community and Related Documents*. Edited by James H. Charlesworth. Princeton Theological Seminary Dead Sea Scrolls Project 1. Tübingen: Mohr Siebeck, 1994.

———. "Blessings." Pages 119–31 in *The Dead Sea Scrolls, Hebrew, Aramaic, and Greek Texts with English Translations, Volume 1: Rule of the Community and Related Documents*. Edited by James H. Charlesworth. Princeton Theological Seminary Dead Sea Scrolls Project 1. Tübingen: Mohr Siebeck, 1994.

Ciancaglini, Claudia A. *Iranian Loanwords in Syriac*. BI 28. Wiesbaden: Reichert, 2008.

Collins, John J. *Beyond the Qumran Community: The Sectarian Movement of the Dead Sea Scrolls*. Grand Rapids: Eerdmans, 2010.

Cook, John A. "The Hebrew Verb: A Grammaticalization Approach." *ZAH* 14/2 (2001): 117–43.

———. "The Semantics of Verbal Pragmatics: Clarifying the Roles of Wayyiqtol and Weqatal in Biblical Hebrew Prose." *JSS* 49 (2004): 247–73.

Cross, Frank Moore. "Lamentations." Pages 229–37 in *Qumran Cave 4.XI: Psalms to Chronicles*. Edited by Eugene Ulrich et al. DJD 16. Oxford: Clarendon, 2000.

———. "Some Notes on a Generation of Qumran Studies." Pages 1–14 in vol. 1 of *The Madrid Qumran Congress, Proceedings of the International Congress on the Dead Sea Scrolls, Madrid 18–21 March 1991*. Edited by Julio Trebolle Barrera and Luis Vegas Montaner. 2 vols. STDJ 11. Leiden: Brill, 1992.

———. "Some Problems in Old Hebrew Orthography with Special Attention to the Third Person Masculine Singular Suffix on Plural Nouns [-âw]." *EI* 27 (2003): 18*–24*.

Cross, Frank Moore and E. Eshel. "1. KhQOstracon." Pages 497–507 in *Qumran Cave 4.XXVI: Cryptic Texts and Miscellanea, Part 1*. Edited by S. J. Pfann et al. DJD 36. Oxford: Clarendon, 2000.

Cross, Frank Moore, Donald W. Parry, Richard J. Saley, and Eugene Ulrich. *Qumran Cave 4.XII: 1–2 Samuel*. DJD 17. Oxford: Clarendon, 2005.

Delitzsch, Friedrich. *Die Lese- und Schreibfehler im Alten Testament*. Berlin/Leipzig: Walter de Gruyter, 1920.

Dimant, Devorah. "An Apocryphon of Jeremiah from Cave 4 (4Q385B = 4Q385 16)." Pages 11–30 in *New Qumran Texts and Studies: Proceedings of the First Meeting of the International Organization for Qumran Studies, Paris 1992*. Edited by George Brooke. STDJ 15. Leiden: Brill, 1994.

———. *Qumran Cave 4.XX: Parabiblical Texts, Part 4, Pseudo-Prophetic Texts*. DJD 30. Oxford: Clarendon, 2001.

———. "Two Discourses from the Apocryphon of Joshua and Their Context (4Q378 3 i–ii)." *RevQ* 23 (2007): 43–61.

Doudna, Gregory L. *4Q Pesher Nahum: A Critical Edition*. JSPSup 35. London: Sheffield Academic, 2001.

Driver, G. R. "Supposed Arabisms in the Old Testament." *JBL* 55 (1936): 101–20.

Elwolde, John F. "Developments in Hebrew Vocabulary between Bible and Mishnah." Pages 17–55 in *The Hebrew of the Dead Sea Scrolls and Ben Sira: Proceedings of a Symposium Held at Leiden University, 11–14 December, 1995*. Edited by T. Muraoka and John F. Elwolde. STDJ 26. Leiden: Brill, 1997.

———. "*RWQMH* in the Damascus Document and Ps 139:15." Pages 65–83 in *Diggers at the Well: Proceedings of a Third International Symposium on the Hebrew of the Dead Sea Scrolls and Ben Sira*. Edited by T. Muraoka and John F. Elwolde. STDJ 36. Leiden: Brill, 2000.

Enos, Gregory. "Phonological Considerations in the Study of Hebrew Phonetics: An Introductory Discussion." Pages 41–47 in *Linguistics and Biblical Hebrew*. Edited by W.R. Bodine. Winona Lake, Ind.: Eisenbrauns, 1992 [written in 1986].

Eshel, E. and H. Eshel. "Jericho papDeed of Sale ar." Pages 37–41 in *Miscellaneous Texts from the Judaean Desert*. Edited by James Charlesworth et al. DJD 38. Oxford: Clarendon, 2000.

Eskhult, Mats. "Some Aspects of the Verbal System in Qumran Hebrew." Pages 29–46 in *Conservatism and Innovation in the Hebrew Language of the Hellenistic Period: Proceedings of a Fourth International Symposium on the Hebrew of the Dead Sea Scrolls & Ben Sira*. STDJ 73. Leiden: Brill, 2008.

———. *Studies in Verbal Aspect and Narrative Technique in Biblical Hebrew Prose*. Studia Semitic Upsaliensia 12. Stockholm: Almqvist & Wiksell, 1990.

Farrar, Christopher and Yehiel Hayon. "The Perception of the Phoneme *Aleph* (/ʾ/) in Modern Hebrew." *HAR* 4 (1980): 53–78.

Fassberg, Steven E. "The Infinitive Absolute as Finite Verb and Standard Literary Hebrew of the Second Temple Period." Pages 47–60 in *Conservatism and Innovation in the Hebrew Language of the Hellenistic Period: Proceedings of a Fourth International Symposium on the Hebrew of the Dead Sea Scrolls and Ben Sira*. STDJ 73. Leiden: Brill, 2008.

———. "Israeli Research into Hebrew and Aramaic at Qumran." Pages 363–80 in *The Dead Sea Scrolls in Scholarly Perspective: A History of Research*. Edited by Devorah Dimant. STDJ 99. Leiden: Brill, 2012.

———. "The *Kethiv/Qere* הִוא, Diachrony, and Dialectology." Pages 171–80 in *Diachrony in Biblical Hebrew*. Edited by Cynthia L. Miller-Naudé and Ziony Zevit. LSAWS 8. Winona Lake, Ind.: Eisenbrauns, 2012.

———. "The Lengthened Imperative קָטְלָה in Biblical Hebrew." *HS* 40 (1999): 7–13.

———. "The Movement from *Qal* to *Piʿʿel* in Hebrew and the Disappearance of the Qal Internal Passive." *HS* 42 (2001): 243–55.

———. "The Preference for Lengthened Forms in Qumran Hebrew" (Hebrew). *Meghillot* 1 (2003): 227–40.

———. "The Syntax of the Biblical Documents from the Judean Desert as Reflected in a Comparison of Multiple Copies of Biblical Texts." Pages 94–109 in *Diggers at the Well: Proceedings of a Third International Symposium on the Hebrew of the Dead Sea Scrolls and Ben Sira*. Edited by T. Muraoka and John F. Elwolde. STDJ 36. Leiden: Brill, 2000.

———. "Which Semitic Language Did Jesus and Other Contemporary Jews Speak?" *CBQ* 74 (2012): 263–80.

Field, F. *Origenis Hexaplorum quae supersunt, sive, Veterum interpretum Graecorum in totum Vetus Testamentum fragmenta*. Oxford: Clarendon, 1875.

Fitzmyer, Joseph A. "Tobit." Pages 1–76 in *Qumran Cave 4.XIV: Para-Biblical Texts, Part 2*. Edited by M. Broshi et al. DJD 19. Oxford: Clarendon, 1998.

———. *A Wandering Aramean: Collected Aramaic Essays*. Missoula, Mont.: Scholars Press, 1979.

Freedman, D. N. "Chapter 1: The Evolution of Hebrew Orthography." Pages 3–17 in *Studies in Hebrew and Aramaic Orthography*. Edited by D. N. Freedman, A. Dean Forbes, and F. I. Andersen. Winona Lake, Ind.: Eisenbrauns, 1992.

García Martínez, Florentino. "Review of E. Qimron, *Hebrew of the Dead Sea Scrolls*." *JSJ* 19 (1988): 115–17.

Gavrilov, A. K. "Techniques of Reading in Classical Antiquity." *Classical Quarterly* 47 (1997): 56–73.

Goerwitz, Richard L. "Tiberian Hebrew Seghol: A Reappraisal." *ZAH* 3 (1990): 3–10.

Gogel, S. L. *A Grammar of Epigraphic Hebrew*. SBLRBS 23. Atlanta: Scholars Press, 1998.

Gordis, R. *The Biblical Text in the Making: A Study of the Kethib-Qere*. New York: Ktav, 1937.

Goshen-Gottstein, Moshe H. "Linguistic Structure and Tradition in the Qumran Documents." Pages 101–37 in *Aspects of the Dead Sea Scrolls*. Edited by Chaim Rabin and Yigael Yadin. *ScrHier* 4. Jerusalem: Magnes, 1958.

———. *Text and Language in Bible and Qumran*. Jerusalem: Orient Publishing House, 1960.

Greenstein, E. L. "An Introduction to a Generative Phonology of Biblical Hebrew." Pages 29–40 in *Linguistics and Biblical Hebrew*. Edited by W.R. Bodine. Winona Lake, Ind.: Eisenbrauns, 1992 [written in 1989].

Gumpertz, Y. F. *Mivṭa'e Śefatenu: Studies in Historical Phonetics of the Hebrew Language*. Jerusalem: Haraav Kook, 1953.

Gzella, Holger. *Tempus, Aspect, und Modalität im Reichsaramäischen*. Akademie der Wissenschaften und der Literatur: Mainz Veröffentlichungen der Orientalischen Kommission 48. Wiesbaden: Harrassowitz, 2004.

Hackett, Jo Ann. "Hebrew (Biblical and Epigraphic)." Pages 139–56 in *Beyond Babel: A Handbook for Biblical Hebrew and Related Languages*.

Edited by J. Kaltner and S. McKenzie. SBLRBS 42. Atlanta: Society of Biblical Literature, 2002.

Harviainen, Tapani. *On the Vocalism of the Closed Unstressed Syllables in Hebrew: A Study Based on Evidence Provided by the Transcriptions of St. Jerome and Palestinian Punctuations*. SO 48. Helsinki: Finish Oriental Society, 1977.

Hendel, Ronald S. "Sibilants and šibbōlet (Judges 12:6)." *BASOR* 301 (1996): 69–75.

Holmstedt, Robert D. "The Phonology of Classical Hebrew: A Linguistic Study of Long Vowels and Syllable Structure." *ZAH* 13 (2000): 145–55.

Huehnergard, John. "Afro-Asiatic." Pages 138–59 in *The Cambridge Encyclopedia of the World's Ancient Languages*. Edited by Roger D. Woodard. Cambridge: Cambridge University, 2004.

Hurvitz, Avi. "Was QH a 'Spoken' Language? On Some Recent Views and Positions: Comments." Pages 110–14 in *Diggers at the Well: Proceedings of a Third International Symposium on the Hebrew of the Dead Sea Scrolls and Ben Sira*. Edited by T. Muraoka and John F. Elwolde. STDJ 36. Leiden: Brill, 2000.

Isbell, C. D. "Initial *'Alef-Yod* Interchange and Selected Biblical Passages." *JNES* 37 (1978): 227–36.

Janssens, G. *Studies in Hebrew Historical Linguistics Based on Origen's Secunda*. Orientalia Gandensia 9. Leuven: Peeters, 1982.

Joosten, Jan. "Biblical Hebrew as Mirrored in the Septuagint: The Question of Influence from Spoken Hebrew." *Textus* 21 (2002): 1–19.

———. "The Disappearance of Iterative WEQATAL in the Biblical Hebrew Verbal System." Pages 135–47 in *Biblical Hebrew in Its Northwest Semitic Setting: Typological and Historical Perspectives*. Edited by S. E. Fassberg and A. Hurvitz. Winona Lake, Ind.: Eisenbrauns, 2006.

———. "The Function of the Semitic D Stem: Biblical Hebrew Materials for a Comparative-Historical Approach." *Orientalia* 67 (1998): 202–30.

———. "Hebrew, Aramaic, and Greek in the Qumran Scrolls." Pages 351–74 in *The Oxford Handbook of the Dead Sea Scrolls*. Edited by Timothy H. Lim and John J. Collins. Oxford: Oxford University, 2010.

———. "The Knowledge and Use of Hebrew in the Hellenistic Period." Pages 115–30 in *Diggers at the Well: Proceedings of a Third International Symposium on the Hebrew of the Dead Sea Scrolls and Ben Sira*. Edited by T. Muraoka and John F. Elwolde. STDJ 36. Leiden: Brill, 2000.

———. "Pseudo-Classicisms in Late Biblical Hebrew, in Ben Sira, and in Qumran Hebrew." Pages 146–59 in *Sirach, Scrolls, and Sages: Proceed-*

ings of a Second International Symposium on the Hebrew of the Dead Sea Scrolls, Ben Sira, and the Mishnah, held at Leiden University 15–17 December, 1997. Edited by T. Muraoka and J. F. Elwolde. STDJ 33. Leiden: Brill, 1999.

Joosten, Jan and Jean-Sébastien Rey, eds. *Conservatism and Innovation in the Hebrew Language of the Hellenistic Period; Proceedings of a Fourth International Symposium on the Hebrew of the Dead Sea Scrolls and Ben Sira*. STDJ 73. Leiden: Brill, 2008.

Kesterson, J. C. "Tense Usage and Verbal Syntax in Selected Qumran Documents." Ph.D. dissertation. Washington, D.C.: Catholic University of America, 1984.

Khan, Geoffrey. "The Historical Background of the Vowel *ṣere*." *BSOAS* 57 (1994): 133–44.

———. "The Pronunciation of the *resh* in the Tiberian Tradition of Biblical Hebrew." *HUCA* 66 (1995): 67–80.

———. "The Pronunciation of the Verbs *hyh* and *xyh* in the Tiberian Tradition of Biblical Hebrew." Pages 133–44 in *Semitic and Cushitic Studies*. Edited by G. Goldenberg and S. Raz. Wiesbaden: Harrassowitz, 1994.

———. "The Tiberian Pronunciation Tradition of Biblical Hebrew." *ZAH* 9 (1996): 1–23.

———. "Vowel Length and Syllable Structure in the Tiberian Tradition of Biblical Hebrew." *JSS* 32 (1987): 23–82.

Kim, Yoo-Ki. "The Origin of the Biblical Hebrew Infinitive Construct." *JSS* 57 (2012): 25–35.

Kister, Menahem. "Lexical and Linguistic Gleanings from the Dead Sea Scrolls" (Hebrew). *Leshonenu* 67 (2004): 27–44.

———. "Newly-Identified Fragments of the Book of Jubilees: Jub. 23:21–23, 30–31." *RevQ* 12 (1985–1987): 529–36.

———. "Some Lexical Features of the Writings from Qumran" (Hebrew). Pages 561–69 in *The Qumran Scrolls and Their World*. Volume 2. Edited by Menahem Kister. Jerusalem: Yad Ben-Zvi, 2009.

———. "Some Observations on Vocabulary and Style in the Dead Sea Scrolls." Pages 137–65 in *Diggers at the Well: Proceedings of a Third International Symposium on the Hebrew of the Dead Sea Scrolls and Ben Sira*. Edited by T. Muraoka and John F. Elwolde. STDJ 36. Leiden: Brill, 2000.

———. "Three Unknown Hebrew Words in Newly-Published Texts from Qumran" (Hebrew). *Leshonenu* 63 (2000–2001): 35–40.

Könnecke, Clemens. *Die Behandlung der hebräischen Namen in der Septuaginta*. Programm des Koeniglichen und Groening'schen Gymnasiums zu Stargard in Pommern 124. Stargard: Gymnasium, 1885.

Kutscher, E. Y. "Canaanite, Hebrew, Phoenician, Aramaic, Mishnaic Hebrew, Punic" (Hebrew). *Leshonenu* 33 (1969): 83–110.

———. "Hebrew Language: Dead Sea Scrolls." Cols. 1583–90 in vol. 16 of *Encyclopedia Judaica*. New York: MacMillan, 1971.

———. *A History of the Hebrew Language*. Edited by R. Kutscher. Jerusalem: Magnes, 1982.

———. *The Language and Linguistic Background of the Complete Isaiah Scroll*. STDJ 6. Leiden: Brill, 1974. Originally published in Hebrew as *Ha-Lashon ve-ha-Reqa' ha-Leshoni shel Megillat Yesha'yahu ha-Selema mi-Megillot Yam ha-Melaḥ*. Jerusalem: Magnes, 1959.

———. *Studies in Galilean Aramaic*. Translated by M. Sokoloff. Ramat-Gan: Bar Ilan University, 1976.

———. "Two 'Passive' Constructions in Aramaic in the Light of Persian." Pages 133–51 in *Proceedings of the International Conference on Semitic Studies, Jerusalem, 19–23 July 1965*. Edited by Z. Ben-Hayyim et al. Jerusalem: Israel Academy of Sciences and Humanities, 1969.

Licht, Jacob. *The Rule Scroll: A Scroll from the Wilderness of Judaea, 1QS, 1QSa, 1QSb, Text, Introduction and Commentary*. Jerusalem: Bialik, 1965.

Martin, Malachi. *Scribal Character of the Dead Sea Scrolls*. Louvain: Publications universitaires, 1958.

McCarter, P. Kyle. "Hebrew." Pages 319–64 in *The Cambridge Encyclopedia of the World's Ancient Languages*. Edited by Roger D. Woodard. Cambridge: Cambridge University, 2004.

Mercati, G. *Psalterii Hexapli Religuiqae, pars, prima, Codex rescriptus Bybliothecae Ambrosianae O. 39 SVP: Phototypice expressus et transcriptus*. Rome: Bybliotheca Vaticana, 1958.

Meyer, Rudolf. "Bemerkungen zu der hebräischen Aussprachetradition von Chirbet Qumrān." *ZAW* 70 (1958): 39–48.

———. *Hebräische Grammatik*. 3rd ed. 4 vols. Berlin: de Gruyter, 1966–1968.

———. "Das Problem der Dialektmischung in den hebräischen Texten von Chirbet Qumran." *VT* 7 (1957): 139–48.

Milik, J. T. "Textes Non Bibliques." Pages 77–149 in *Qumran Cave 1*. Edited by D. Barthélemy and J. T. Milik. DJD 1. Oxford: Clarendon, 1955.

Morag, Shelomo. "The Geminated Vowels" (Hebrew). *Tarbiz* 23 (1952): 236–39.
———. *The Hebrew Language Tradition of the Yemenite Jews*. Jerusalem: Academy of the Hebrew Language, 1963.
———. "On the Historical Validity of the Vocalization of the Hebrew Bible." *JAOS* 94 (1974): 307–15.
———. "Language and Style in *Miqṣat Ma'aśe ha-Torah*: Did *Moreh ha-Ṣedeq* Write This Document?" (Hebrew). *Tarbiz* 65 (1996): 209–23.
———. "Palestinian and Babylonian Features in the Oriental Traditions of Hebrew." Jerusalem: Institute of Asian and African Studies, Hebrew University of Jerusalem, n.d.
———. "Pronunciations of Hebrew." Cols. 547–62 in vol. 16 of *Encyclopedia Judaica*. 2nd ed. Detroit: MacMillan, 2007. First published in cols. 1120–45 of vol. 13. New York: MacMillan, 1972.
———. "Qumran Hebrew: Some Typological Observations." *VT* 38 (1988): 148–64.
———. "Review of E. Y. Kutscher, *The Language and Linguistic Background of the Isaiah Scroll*." *Kirjath Sepher* 36 (1960): 24–32.
———. *Studies on Biblical Hebrew* (Hebrew). Jerusalem: Magnes, 1995.
Moreshet, Menahem. "The Hiphil in Mishnaic Hebrew as Equivalent to the Qal." *Bar-Ilan* 13 (1976): 249–81.
———. "On the Nuf'al Stem in Post-Biblical Hebrew." Pages 126–39 in *Studies in Hebrew and Semitic Languages Dedicated to the Memory of Prof. Eduard Yechezkel Kutscher*. Edited by Gad B. Sarfatti et al. Ramat-Gan: Bar-Ilan University, 1980.
Morgenstern, Matthew (Moshe). "Notes on the Language of the Qumran Scrolls" (Hebrew). *Meghillot* 2 (2004): 157–68.
———. *Studies in Jewish Babylonian Aramaic Based upon Early Eastern Manuscripts*. HSS 62. Winona Lake, Ind.: Eisenbrauns, 2011.
———. "The System of Independent Pronouns at Qumran and the History of Hebrew in the Second Temple Period" (Hebrew). Pages 44–63 in *Sha'arey Lashon: Studies in Hebrew, Aramaic and Jewish Languages Presented to Moshe Bar Asher, vol. 2: Mishnaic Hebrew and Aramaic*. Edited by A. Maman et al. Jerusalem: Mosad Bialik Institute, 2007.
Muchiki, Yoshi. "Spirantization in Fifth-Century B.C. North-West Semitic." *JNES* 53 (1994): 125–30.
Muraoka, T. "An Approach to the Morphosyntax and Syntax of Qumran Hebrew." Pages 193–214 in *Diggers at the Well: Proceedings of a Third International Symposium on the Hebrew of the Dead Sea Scrolls and*

Ben Sira. Edited by T. Muraoka and John F. Elwolde. STDJ 36. Leiden: Brill, 2000.

———. *A Grammar of Qumran Aramaic*. ANES Supp 38. Leuven: Peeters, 2011.

———. "Hebrew." Pages 340–45 in vol. 1 of *Encyclopedia of the Dead Sea Scrolls*. 2 vols. Edited by Lawrence H. Schiffman and James C. VanderKam. New York: Oxford University, 2000.

———. "The Participle in Qumran Hebrew with Special Reference to Its Periphrastic Use." Pages 188–204 in *Sirach, Scrolls, and Sages: Proceedings of a Second International Symposium on the Hebrew of the Dead Sea Scrolls, Ben Sira, and the Mishnah, held at Leiden University 15–17 December, 1997*. Edited by T. Muraoka and John F. Elwolde. STDJ 33. Leiden: Brill, 1999.

———. "Verb Complementation in Qumran Hebrew." Pages 92–149 in *The Hebrew of the Dead Sea Scrolls and Ben Sira: Proceedings of a Symposium Held at Leiden University, 11–14 December 1995*. Edited by T. Muraoka and John F. Elwolde. STDJ 26. Leiden: Brill, 1997.

Murtonen, A. *Hebrew in Its West Semitic Setting: A Comparative Survey of Non-Masoretic Hebrew Dialects and Traditions*. Studies in Semitic Languages and Linguistics 13 [Part 1: A Comparative Lexicon], 16 [Part 2: Phonetics and Phonology. Part 3: Morphosyntactics]. 3 vols. Leiden: Brill, 1986–1990.

———. "A Historico-Philological Survey of the Main Dead Sea Scrolls and Related Documents." *Abr-Nahrain* 4 (1963–1964): 56–95.

Naudé, Jacobus A. "A Perspective on the Chronological Framework of Biblical Hebrew." *JNSL* 30 (2004): 87–102.

———. "The Transitions of Biblical Hebrew in the Perspective of Language Change and Diffusion." Pages 189–214 in *Biblical Hebrew: Studies in Chronology and Typology*. Edited by Ian Young. London: T&T Clark, 2003.

Newsom, Carol. "Admonition on the Flood." Pages 85–97 in *Qumran Cave 4.XIV: Para-Biblical Texts, Part 2*. Edited by M. Broshi et al. DJD 19. Oxford: Clarendon, 1998.

———. "Shirot 'Olat HaShabbat." Pages 173–401 in *Qumran Cave 4.VI: Poetical and Liturgical Texts, Part 1*. Edited by E. Eshel et al. DJD 11. Oxford: Clarendon, 1998.

Nitzan, B. "Curses." Pages 1–8 in *Qumran Cave 4.XX: Poetical and Liturgical Texts, Part 2*. Edited by E. Chazon et al. DJD 29. Oxford: Clarendon, 1999.

Nöldeke, Theodor. *Compendious Syriac Grammar*. Translated by James A. Crichton. London: Williams & Norgate, 1904. Repr. Winona Lake, Ind.: Eisenbrauns, 2001.

Norton, Jonathan. "The Question of Scribal Exegesis at Qumran." Pages 135–54 in *Northern Lights on the Dead Sea Scrolls: Proceedings of the Nordic Qumran Network 2003–2006*. Edited by Anders K. Petersen et al. STDJ 80. Leiden: Brill, 2009.

Novick, Tzvi. "The Meaning and Etymology of אוט." *JBL* 127 (2008): 339–43.

Ohala, J. J. "Sound Change." Pages 520–25 in vol. 11 of *Encyclopedia of Language and Linguistics*. Edited by Keith Brown. 2nd ed. 14 vols. Oxford: Elsevier, 2006.

Olyan, Saul. "ParaKings et al." Pages 363–416 in *Qumran Cave 4.VIII: Parabiblical Texts, Part 1*. Edited by H. Attridge et al. DJD 13. Oxford: Clarendon, 1994.

Pardee, D. "Canaanite Dialects." Pages 386–90 in *The Cambridge Encyclopedia of the World's Ancient Languages*. Edited by Roger D. Woodard. Cambridge: Cambridge University, 2004.

———. "Review of *Matres Lectionis in Ancient Hebrew Epigraphs* by Z. Zevit." *CBQ* 44 (1982): 503–4.

Pérez Fernández, Miguel. *An Introductory Grammar of Rabbinic Hebrew*. Leiden: Brill, 1999.

Peursen, Wido Th. van. *The Verbal System in the Hebrew Text of Ben Sira*. SSLL 41. Leiden: Brill, 2004.

Poirier, John C. "The Linguistic Situation in Jewish Palestine in Late Antiquity." *Journal of Greco-Roman Christianity and Judaism* 4 (2007): 55–134.

Polak, Frank. "Style is More than the Person: Sociolinguistics, Literary Culture, and the Distinction between Written and Oral Narrative." Pages 38–103 in *Biblical Hebrew: Studies in Chronology and Typology*. Edited by Ian Young. London: T&T Clark, 2003.

Puech, Émile. "Du bilinguisme à Qumrân?" Pages 171–89 in *Mosaïque de langues mosaïques culturelle: Le bilinguisme dans le Proche-Orient Ancien*. Paris: Maisonneuve, 1996.

———. *Qumran Grotte 4.XXVII: Textes araméens, deuxième partie: 4Q550–575a, 580–587 et appendices*. DJD 37. Oxford: Clarendon, 2009.

———. *Qumran Grotte 4.XVIII: Textes hébreux (4Q521–4Q528, 4Q576–4Q579)*. DJD 25. Oxford: Clarendon, 1998.

———. “Le Rouleau de Cuivre de la Grotte de Qumran (3Q15).” Pages 169–219 in *Le Rouleau de cuivre de la grotte 3 de Qumran (3Q15): Expertise—Restauration—Epigraphie* by Daniel Brizemeure, Noël Lacoudre, Emile Puech. 2 vols. STDJ 55. Leiden: Brill, 2006.

Qimron, Elisha. “Consecutive and Conjunctive Imperfect: The Form of the Imperfect with *Waw* in Biblical Hebrew.” *JQR* 76 (1986–1987): 149–61.

———. “Diphthongs and Glides in the Dead Sea Scrolls” (Hebrew). *Meḥqarim* 2–3 (1987): 259–78.

———. “The Distinction between Waw and Yod in the Qumran Scrolls” (Hebrew). *Beth Mikra* 52 (1972): 102–12.

———. *Grammar of the Hebrew Language of the Scrolls of the Judean Desert* (Hebrew). Jerusalem: Hebrew University, 1976.

———. *The Hebrew of the Dead Sea Scrolls*. HSS 29. Atlanta: Scholars Press, 1986.

———. *History of the Hebrew Language: The Classical Division. Unit 2: The Hebrew of the Second Temple Period* (Hebrew). Tel Aviv: The Open University of Israel, 2004.

———. “Initial *Alef* as a Vowel in Hebrew and Aramean Documents from Qumran Compared to Later Hebrew and Aramaic Sources” (Hebrew). *Leshonenu* 39 (1975): 133–46.

———. “The Language.” Pages 65–108 in *Qumran Cave 4.V: Miqsat Ma'ase ha-Torah*. Edited by Elisha Qimron and John Strugnell. DJD 10. Oxford: Clarendon, 1994.

———. “The Language and Linguistic Background of the Qumran Compositions.” Pages 551–60 in *The Qumran Scrolls and Their World*. Volume 2. Edited by Menahem Kister. Jerusalem: Yad Ben-Zvi, 2009.

———. “The Nature of DSS Hebrew and Its Relation to BH and MH.” Pages 232–44 in *Diggers at the Well: Proceedings of a Third International Symposium on the Hebrew of the Dead Sea Scrolls and Ben Sira*. Edited by T. Muraoka and John F. Elwolde. STDJ 36. Leiden: Brill, 2000.

———. “A New Approach to the Use of the Forms of the Imperfect without Personal Endings.” Pages 174–81 in *The Hebrew of the Dead Sea Scrolls and Ben Sira: Proceedings of a Symposium Held at Leiden University, 11–14 December, 1995*. Edited by T. Muraoka and John F. Elwolde. STDJ 26. Leiden: Brill, 1997.

———. “Observations on the History of Early Hebrew (1000 B.C.E. –200 C.E.) in the Light of the Dead Sea Documents.” Pages 349–62 in *The*

Dead Sea Scrolls: Forty Years of Research. Edited by Devorah Dimant and Uriel Rappoport. STDJ 10. Leiden: Brill, 1992.

———. "ראשׁ and Similar Words" (Hebrew). *Leshonenu* 65 (2003): 243–47.

———. "Studies in the Hebrew of the Dead Sea Scrolls" (Hebrew). *Hebrew Linguistics* 33–35 (1992): 79–92.

———. "*Waw* as Marker for a Glide" (Hebrew). Pages 362–75 in *Homage to Shmuel: Studies in the World of the Bible*. Edited by Zipora Talshir et al. Jerusalem: Bialik Institute, 2001.

———. "A Work Concerning Divine Providence." Pages 191–202 in *Solving Riddles and Untying Knots: Biblical, Epigraphic, and Semitic Studies in Honor of Jonas C. Greenfield*. Edited by S. Gitin et al. Winona Lake, Ind.: Eisenbrauns, 1995.

———. "עֲנָוֺת and Its Kindred Forms" (Hebrew). *Leshonenu* 67 (2004): 21–26.

Qimron, Elisha, and James H. Charlesworth. "Cave IV Fragments." Pages 53–103 in *The Dead Sea Scrolls, Hebrew, Aramaic, and Greek Texts with English Translations, Volume 1: Rule of the Community and Related Documents*. Edited by James H. Charlesworth et al. Princeton Theological Seminary Dead Sea Scrolls Project 1. Tübingen: Mohr Siebeck, 1994.

———. "Rule of the Community." Pages 1–51 in *The Dead Sea Scrolls, Hebrew, Aramaic, and Greek Texts with English Translations, Volume 1: Rule of the Community and Related Documents*. Edited by James H. Charlesworth et al. Princeton Theological Seminary Dead Sea Scrolls Project 1. Tübingen: Mohr Siebeck, 1994.

Qimron, Elisha, and John Strugnell. *Qumran Cave 4.V: Miqsat Ma'ase ha-Torah*. DJD 10. Oxford: Clarendon, 1994.

Qimron, Elisha and Alexey (Eliyahu) Yuditsky. "Notes on the So-Called *Gabriel Vision* Inscription." Pages 31–38 in *Hazon Gabriel: New Readings of the Gabriel Inscription*. Edited by Matthias Henze. SBLEJL 29. Atlanta: SBL, 2011.

Rabin, Chaim. "Historical Background of Qumran Hebrew." Pages 144–61 in *Aspects of the Dead Sea Scrolls*. Edited by Chaim Rabin and Yigael Yadin. *Scripta Hierosolymitana* 4. Jerusalem: Magnes, 1958.

———. *A Short History of the Hebrew Language*. Jerusalem: Publishing Department of the Jewish Agency, 1973.

Ravid, Dorit Diskin. *Spelling Morphology: The Psycholinguistics of Hebrew Spelling*. Literacy Studies 3. New York: Springer, 2012.

Rendsburg, Gary A. "Ancient Hebrew Morphology." Pages 85–105 in vol. 1 of *Morphologies of Asia and Africa*. Edited by Alan S. Kaye. Winona Lake, Ind.: Eisenbrauns, 2007.

———. "Ancient Hebrew Phonology." Pages 65–84 in *Phonologies of Asia and Africa*. Edited by A. S. Kaye. Winona Lake, Ind.: Eisenbrauns, 1997.

———. "The Galilean Background of Mishnaic Hebrew." Pages 225–40 in *The Galilee in Late Antiquity*. Edited by L.I. Levine. New York: Jewish Theological Seminary, 1992.

———. "*Hazon Gabriel*: A Grammatical Sketch." Pages 61–91 in *Hazon Gabriel: New Readings of the Gabriel Inscription*. Edited by Matthias Henze. SBLEJL 29. Atlanta: SBL, 2011.

———. *Israelian Hebrew in the Books of Kings*. Bethesda: CDL, 2002.

———. "Linguistic and Stylistic Notes to the Hazon Gabriel Inscription." *DSD* 16 (2009): 107–16.

———. *Linguistic Evidence for the Northern Origin of Selected Psalms*. SBLMS 43. Atlanta: Scholars Press, 1990.

———. "Qumran Hebrew (with a Trial Cut [1QS])." Pages 217–46 in *Dead Sea Scrolls at 60: Scholarly Contributions of New York University Faculty and Alumni*. STDJ 89. Leiden: Brill, 2010.

Revell, E. J. "Studies in the Palestinian vocalization of Hebrew." Pages 51–100 in *Essays on the Ancient Semitic World*. Edited by J.W. Wevers and D.B. Redford. Toronto: n.p., 1970.

———. *Hebrew Texts with Palestinian Vocalization*. Near and Middle East Series 7. Toronto: n.p., 1970.

Reymond, Eric D. *New Idioms within Old: Poetry and Parallelism in the Non-Masoretic Poems of 11Q5 (= 11QPsa)*. SBLEJL 31. Atlanta: SBL, 2011.

Sáenz-Badillos, Angel. "El Hebreo del S. II d. C a la Luz de las Transcripciones Griegas de Aquila, Simmaco, y Teodocion." *Sefarad* 35 (1975): 107–30.

———. *A History of the Hebrew Language*. Translated by J. Elwolde. Cambridge: Cambridge University, 1993. This is a slightly revised and expanded version of *Historia de la Lengua Hebrea*. Sabadell: Estrada Vilarrasa, 1988.

Sanderson, Judith E. "Ezekiel." Pages 209–20 in *Qumran Cave 4.XI: Psalms to Chronicles*. Edited by Eugene Ulrich et al. DJD 15. Oxford: Clarendon, 2000.

Schattner-Rieser, Ursula. *L'Araméen des manuscrits de la Mer Morte, I: Grammaire*. Instruments pour l'étude des langues de l'Orient ancien 5. Prahins, Switzerland: Zèbre, 2004.

Schiffman, Lawrence H. "Temple Scroll." Pages 1–173 in *The Dead Sea Scrolls, Hebrew, Aramaic, and Greek Texts with English Translations, Volume 7: Temple Scroll and Related Documents*. Edited by James H. Charlesworth. Princeton Theological Seminary Dead Sea Scrolls Project 7. Tübingen: Mohr Siebeck, 2011.

Schniedewind, William M. "Linguistic Ideology in Qumran Hebrew." Pages 245–55 in *Diggers at the Well: Proceedings of a Third International Symposium on the Hebrew of the Dead Sea Scrolls and Ben Sira*. Edited by T. Muraoka and John F. Elwolde. STDJ 36. Leiden: Brill, 2000.

———. "Qumran Hebrew as an Antilanguage." *JBL* 118 (1999): 235–52.

Schniedewind, William M. and D. Sivan. "The Elijah-Elisha Narratives: A Test Case for the Northern Dialect of Hebrew." *JQR* 87 (1997): 303–37.

Schoors, Antoon. "The Language of the Qumran Sapiential Works." Pages 61–95 in *The Wisdom Texts from Qumran*. Edited by C. Hempel et al. BETL 159. Leuven: Peeters, 2002.

Schorch, Stefan. "Spoken Hebrew of the Late Second Temple Period According to Oral and Written Samaritan Tradition." Pages 175–91 in *Conservatism and Innovation in the Hebrew Language of the Hellenistic Period; Proceedings of a Fourth International Symposium on the Hebrew of the Dead Sea Scrolls and Ben Sira*. Edited by Jan Joosten and Jean-Sébastien Rey. STDJ 73. Leiden: Brill, 2008.

Schuller, E. "Hodayot." Pages 69–254 in *Qumran Cave 4.XX: Poetical and Liturgical Texts, Part 2*. Edited by E. Chazon et al. DJD 29. Oxford: Clarendon, 1999.

———. "Non-Canonical Psalms. Pages 75–172 in *Qumran Cave 4.VI: Poetical and Liturgical Texts, Part 1*. Edited by E. Eshel et al. DJD 11. Oxford: Clarendon, 1998.

Segal, J. B. *Aramaic Texts from North Saqqâra with Some Fragments in Phoenician*. Texts from Excavations 6. London: Egypt Exploration Society, 1983.

Segal, M. H. *A Grammar of Mishnaic Hebrew*. Oxford: Clarendon, 1927.

Segal, M. Z. *Diqduq Leshon ha-Mishna* (Hebrew). Tel-Aviv: Devir, 1936.

Skehan, Patrick W. and Eugene Ulrich. "Isaiah." Pages 7–143 in *Qumran Cave 4.X: The Prophets*. Edited by Eugene Ulrich et al. DJD 15. Oxford: Clarendon, 1997.

Skehan, Patrick W., Eugene Ulrich, and Peter Flint. "Psalms." Pages 7–170 in *Qumran Cave 4.XI: Psalms to Chronicles*. Edited by Eugene Ulrich et al. DJD 16. Oxford: Clarendon, 2000.

Smelik, Willem F. *The Targum of Judges*. OTS 36. Leiden: Brill, 1995.

Smith, Mark S. "Converted and Unconverted Perfect and Imperfect Forms in the Literature of Qumran." *BASOR* 284 (1991): 1–16.

———. *The Origins and Development of the Waw-Consecutive*. HSS 39. Atlanta: Scholars Press, 1991.

———. "The Waw-Consecutive at Qumran." *ZAH* 3 (1991): 161–64.

Sperber, Alexander. "Hebrew Based Upon Biblical Passages in Parallel Transmission." *HUCA* 14 (1939): 153–249.

Stegemann, Hartmut, Eileen Schuller, Carol Newsom. *Qumran Cave 1.III: 1QHodayot*[a] *with Incorporation of 4QHodayot*[a–f] *and 1QHodayot*[b]. DJD 40. Oxford: Clarendon, 2009.

Steiner, Richard C. "Addenda to *The Case for Fricative-Laterals in Proto-Semitic*." Pages 1499–1513 in *Semitic Studies in Honor of Wolf Leslau*. Edited by A. S. Kaye; Wiesbaden: Harrassowitz, 1991.

———. "Ancient Hebrew." Pages 145–73 in *The Semitic Languages*. Edited by R. Hetzron. London: Routledge, 1997.

———. *The Case for Fricative-Laterals in Proto-Semitic*. AOS 59. New Haven: American Oriental Society, 1977.

———. "From Proto-Hebrew to Mishnaic Hebrew: The History of ךָ- and הָ-." *HAR* 3 (1979): 157–74.

———. "On the Dating of Hebrew Sound Changes (*ḫ > ḥ and Ġ > ʿ) and Greek Translations (2Esdras and Judith)." *JBL* 124 (2005): 229–67.

———. "Variation, Simplifying Assumptions, and the History of Spirantization in Aramaic and Hebrew." Pages *52–*65 in *Shaʿarei Lashon: Studies in Hebrew, Aramaic, and Jewish Languages Presented to Moshe Bar-Asher; Vol I: Biblical Hebrew, Masorah, and Medieval Hebrew*. Edited by A. Maman et al. Jerusalem: Bialik Institute, 2007.

Strugnell, John. "Notes en marge du volume V des 'Discoveries in the Judaean Desert of Jordan.'" *RevQ* 7 (1970): 163–276.

Strugnell, John, and Daniel J. Harrington. *Qumran Cave 4.XXIV: Sapiential Texts, Part 2, 4QInstruction (Mûsār Lĕ Mēvīn), 4Q415 ff.* DJD 34. Oxford: Clarendon, 1999.

Sukenik, E. L. *The Dead Sea Scrolls of the Hebrew University*. Jerusalem: Magnes, 1955.

Tigchelaar, E. "Assessing Emanuel Tov's 'Qumran Scribal Practice.'" Pages 173–208 in *The Dead Sea Scrolls: Transmission of Traditions and Pro-*

duction of Texts. Edited by Sarianna Metso et al. STDJ 92. Leiden: Brill, 2010.

———. "Review of Emanuel Tov, *Scribal Practices and Approaches Reflected in the Texts Found in the Judean Desert*." *DSD* 14 (2007): 368–72.

Tov, Emanuel. "Canticles." Pages 195–219 in *Qumran Cave 4.XI: Psalms to Chronicles*. Edited by Eugene Ulrich et al. DJD 16. Oxford: Clarendon, 2000.

———. "Correction Procedures in the Texts from the Judean Desert." Pages 232–63 in *The Provo International Conference on the Dead Sea Scrolls: Technological Innovations, New Texts, and Reformulated Issues*. Edited by Donald W. Parry and Eugene Ulrich. STDJ 30. Leiden: Brill, 1999.

———. "Jeremiah." Pages 145–207 in *Qumran Cave 4.XI: Psalms to Chronicles*. Edited by Eugene Ulrich et al. DJD 15. Oxford: Clarendon, 2000.

———. "Review of James Barr, *The Variable Spellings of the Hebrew Bible*." Pages 3–16 in *Hebrew Bible, Greek Bible, and Qumran: Collected Essays*. Emanuel Tov. TSAJ 121. Tübingen: Mohr Siebeck, 2008. Originally published in *JSS* 35 (1990): 303–16.

———. *Scribal Practices and Approaches Reflected in the Texts Found in the Judean Desert*. STDJ 54. Leiden: Brill, 2004.

———. *Textual Criticism of the Hebrew Bible*. 3rd revised ed. Minneapolis: Fortress, 2012.

Tov, Emanuel, ed. *Dead Sea Scrolls Electronic Library*. Provo, Utah: Brigham Young University, 2006.

Tov, Emanuel, and S. White. "365. Reworked Pentateuch." Pages 187–351 in *Qumran Cave 4.VIII: Parabiblical Texts, Part 1*. Edited by H. Attridge et al. DJD 13. Oxford: Clarendon, 1994.

Uffmann, Christian. "Intrusive [r] and Optimal Epenthetic Consonants." *Language Sciences* 29 (2007): 451–76.

Ulrich, Eugene. "24. 4QLev^{b}." Pages 177–87 in *Qumran Cave 4.VII: Genesis to Numbers*. Edited by Eugene Ulrich et al. DJD 12. Oxford: Clarendon, 1994.

Ulrich, Eugene et al., eds. *The Biblical Qumran Scrolls*. VTSup 134. Leiden: Brill, 2010.

Ulrich, Eugene et al. *Qumran Cave 4.XI: Psalms to Chronicles*. DJD 15. Oxford: Clarendon, 1997.

Ulrich, Eugene and Peter W. Flint. "Introduction to 1QIsa^{a}." Pages 59–95 in *Qumran Cave 1, II: The Isaiah Scrolls, Part 2: Introductions, Commentary, and Textual Variants*. Edited by Eugene Ulrich and Peter W. Flint. DJD 32. Oxford: Clarendon, 2010.

Ulrich, Eugene and Peter W. Flint, eds. *Qumran Cave 1, II: The Isaiah Scrolls, Part 2: Introductions, Commentary, and Textual Variants*. DJD 32. Oxford: Clarendon, 2010.

VanderKam, J. and J. T. Milik. "Jubilees." Pages 1–185 in *Qumran Cave 4.VIII: Parabiblical Texts, Part 1*. Edited by Harry Attridge et al. DJD 13. Oxford: Clarendon, 1994.

Vegas Montaner, Luis. "Some Features of the Hebrew Verbal Syntax in the Qumran *Hodayot*." Pages 273–86 in vol. 1 of *The Madrid Qumran Congress, Proceedings of the International Congress on the Dead Sea Scrolls, Madrid 18–21 March 1991*. Edited by Julio Trebolle Barrera and Luis Vegas Montaner. 2 vols. STDJ 11. Leiden: Brill, 1992.

Waltke, Bruce K. and M. O'Connor. *An Introduction to Biblical Hebrew Syntax*. Winona Lake, Ind.: Eisenbrauns, 1990.

Watson, Janet C. E. *The Phonology and Morphology of Arabic*. Oxford: Oxford, 2002.

Washburn, David L. *A Catalogue of Biblical Passages in the Dead Sea Scrolls*. Text Critical Studies 2. Atlanta: Society of Biblical Literature, 2002.

Weinfeld, M. and D. Seely. "Barkhi Nafshi." Pages 255–334 in *Qumran Cave 4.XX: Poetical and Liturgical Texts, Part 2*. Edited by E. Chazon et al. DJD 29. Oxford: Clarendon, 1999.

———. "Lament of a Leader." Pages 335–41 in *Qumran Cave 4.XX: Poetical and Liturgical Texts, Part 2*. Edited by E. Chazon et al. DJD 29. Oxford: Clarendon, 1999.

Weinreich, Uriel. "Is a Structural Dialectology Possible?" *Word: Journal of the Linguistic Circle of New York* 10 (1954): 388–400.

Weitzman, Steve. "Why Did the Qumran Community Write in Hebrew?" *JAOS* 119 (1999): 35–45.

Wernberg-Møller, P. *Manual of Discipline: Translated and Annotated with an Introduction*. STDJ 1. Leiden: Brill, 1957.

Wevers, J. W. "Heth in Classical Hebrew." Pages 110–12 in *Essays on the Ancient Semitic World*. Edited by J.W. Wevers and D.B. Redford. Toronto: University of Toronto, 1970.

Wright, W. *A Grammar of the Arabic Language*. 3rd ed. 2 vols. Cambridge: Cambridge University Press, 1896–1898.

Yadin, Yigael. *The Temple Scroll*. 3 vols. Jerusalem: Israel Exploration Society, 1983.

Yalon, Henoch (Hanoch). *Introduction to the Vocalization of the Mishna* (Hebrew). Jerusalem: Bialik, 1964.

———. *Studies in the Dead Sea Scrolls: Philological Essays* (Hebrew). Jerusalem: Shrine of the Book and Kiryat Sepher, 1971.

Yardeni, Ada and Binyamin Elizur. "A Hebrew Prophetic Text on Stone from the Early Herodian Period: A Preliminary Report." Pages 11–29 in *Hazon Gabriel: New Readings of the Gabriel Inscription*. Edited by Matthias Henze. SBLEJL 29. Atlanta: SBL, 2011.

Yeivin, Israel. *The Hebrew Language Tradition as Reflected in Babylonian Vocalization*. (Hebrew.) Text and Studies 12. 2 vols. Jerusalem: Academy of the Hebrew Language, 1985.

———. "The Verbal Forms יקטולנו, יקוטלנו in DSS in Comparison to the Babylonian Vocalization" (Hebrew). Pages 256–76 in *Bible and Jewish History: Studies in Bible and Jewish History Dedicated to the Memory of Jacob Liver*. Edited by Benjamin Uffenheimer. Tel-Aviv: Tel-Aviv University, 1971.

Young, Ian. *Diversity in Pre-Exilic Hebrew*. FAT 5. Tübingen: Mohr Siebeck, 1993.

———. "Observations on the Third Masculine Singular Pronominal Suffix -*h* in Hebrew Biblical Texts." *HS* 42 (2001): 225–42.

———. "Late Biblical Hebrew and the Qumran Pesher Habakkuk." *JHS* 8 (2008). http://www.arts.ualberta.ca/JHS/Articls/article_102.pdf.

Yuditsky, Alexey (Eliyahu). "The Weak Consonants in the Language of the Dead Sea Scrolls and in the Hexapla Transliterations." Pages 233–39 in *Conservatism and Innovation in the Hebrew Language of the Hellenistic Period; Proceedings of a Fourth International Symposium on the Hebrew of the Dead Sea Scrolls and Ben Sira*. Edited by Jan Joosten and Jean-Sébastien Rey. STDJ 73. Leiden: Brill, 2008.

Zevit, Z. *Matres Lectionis in Ancient Hebrew Epigraphs*. ASORMS 2. Cambridge, Mass.: ASOR, 1980.

Sources Index

Dead Sea Scrolls

Biblical Scrolls (Including Phylactery Texts)

1Q4 (1QDeut[a]) 7
Deut 13:4 79 n. 57

1Q7 (1QSam) 198
2 Sam 23:12 31

1QIsa[a] 7, 11, 17, 35, 46, 48, 72–77, 84, 98–99, 106, 111–13, 145–47, 157, 164, 174, 185, 186, 189, 194, 195, 197, 226, 227, 229, 231
Isa 1:1 34, 92, 177 n. 86, 232
Isa 1:4 189
Isa 1:6 192
Isa 1:7 189 n. 128
Isa 1:9 181
Isa 1:10 101
Isa 1:15 44, 133, 141
Isa 1:17 44
Isa 1:20 192
Isa 1:21 61, 105, 153, 232
Isa 1:23 44
Isa 1:24 2 n. 3, 105 n. 173, 147, 187
Isa 1:25 105
Isa 2:2 121 n. 227
Isa 2:3 47, 86
Isa 2:4 121 n. 227
Isa 2:6 120
Isa 3:1 194, 231
Isa 3:9 167
Isa 3:24 109, 171, 184
Isa 4:1 108
Isa 4:5 108 n. 186
Isa 5:1 59, 160
Isa 5:2 190 n. 130, 198
Isa 5:4 15, 23, 89
Isa 5:5 92, 104 n. 168
Isa 5:6 110
Isa 5:17 139
Isa 5:19 159
Isa 5:21 92
Isa 5:23 111, 184, 185
Isa 5:24 108 n. 186
Isa 5:25 146
Isa 5:26 121 n. 227
Isa 5:28 173 n. 69
Isa 5:29 200
Isa 6:9 94
Isa 6:13 61
Isa 7:1 181
Isa 7:14 132, 141
Isa 8:2 105
Isa 8:4 52
Isa 8:6 172, 181
Isa 8:7 134
Isa 8:9 101 n. 158
Isa 8:18 104 n. 168
Isa 8:23 121 n. 227
Isa 9:3 67
Isa 9:5 191
Isa 9:6 47
Isa 9:7 92
Isa 9:10 59
Isa 9:11 27, 146
Isa 9:12 96 n. 136
Isa 9:16 146

1QIsa[a] *(cont.)*
Isa 9:19 52 n. 128
Isa 9:20 146
Isa 10:4 146
Isa 10:7 121 n. 227
Isa 10:9 107 n. 179
Isa 10:11 190
Isa 10:12 159
Isa 10:31 231
Isa 11:1 51
Isa 11:10 121 n. 227
Isa 11:12 121 n. 227
Isa 11:14 120
Isa 11:15 61
Isa 11:16 61
Isa 12:2 59, 160
Isa 12:4 103, 231
Isa 13:4 121 n. 227
Isa 13:9 29
Isa 13:16 164 n. 45, 167 n. 55
Isa 13:19 87, 189 n. 128
Isa 13:22 130 n. 262
Isa 14:1 189
Isa 14:3 192
Isa 14:6 121 n. 227
Isa 14:7 173, 178 n. 89
Isa 14:9 121 n. 227
Isa 14:12 105
Isa 14:18 121 n. 227
Isa 14:19 172
Isa 14:26 121 n. 227
Isa 14:27 146
Isa 14:28 34
Isa 14:29 35
Isa 14:31 35
Isa 14:32 35
Isa 15:2 37 n. 67, 44
Isa 15:3 160
Isa 15:5 90
Isa 15:7 39
Isa 16:1 96
Isa 16:2 37
Isa 16:3 125, 129, 144
Isa 16:5 184
Isa 17:1 61
Isa 17:2 37, 181
Isa 17:4 92
Isa 17:9 61
Isa 17:10 197, 214, 218
Isa 18:2 192
Isa 18:7 192
Isa 19:6 30 n. 38
Isa 19:14 167
Isa 19:16 194
Isa 19:17 61
Isa 19:20 61, 188
Isa 20:1 181, 215
Isa 21:2 39
Isa 21:4 109
Isa 21:13 181
Isa 21:15 109, 184
Isa 22:1 134
Isa 22:3 192 n. 139
Isa 22:4 85 n. 76, 126
Isa 22:6 181
Isa 22:17 216, 218
Isa 22:20 190
Isa 23:1 103
Isa 23:2 94
Isa 23:3 121 n. 227
Isa 23:6 30 n. 38, 203 n. 178
Isa 24:12 192
Isa 25:1 92
Isa 25:3 130
Isa 25:7 121 n. 227
Isa 25:10 110
Isa 26:1 192
Isa 27:3 214
Isa 27:7 192 n. 139
Isa 27:9 132
Isa 28:4 61
Isa 28:7 58
Isa 28:15 89
Isa 28:20 89 n. 94
Isa 28:22 92
Isa 28:28 105
Isa 29:1 181
Isa 29:2 61
Isa 29:7 121 n. 227
Isa 29:8 121 n. 227, 146

Isa 29:9 90
Isa 29:11 198
Isa 29:13 198
Isa 29:14 190 n. 131, n. 133
Isa 29:16 30 n. 38
Isa 30:7 190
Isa 30:8 60, 160, 222
Isa 30:10 101
Isa 30:12 97
Isa 30:20 86, 232
Isa 30:21 47, 59
Isa 30:22 42
Isa 30:23 109
Isa 30:28 101, 107 n. 178, 121 n. 227, 172
Isa 30:31 46
Isa 30:33 110, 126, 132
Isa 31:3 134
Isa 31:8 201, 214
Isa 32:14 192 n. 139
Isa 33:1 27 n. 20, 191
Isa 33:7 134, 188
Isa 33:10 105
Isa 33:15 111, 184, 185
Isa 34:1 121 n. 227
Isa 34:2 121 n. 227
Isa 34:4 172
Isa 34:6 45
Isa 34:8 178
Isa 34:9 61
Isa 34:10 60, 160
Isa 34:11 60, 104, 160, 190 n. 130
Isa 34:13 61
Isa 34:15 134
Isa 35:6 44
Isa 35:8 34, 216, 220 n. 219
Isa 36:1 215
Isa 36:3 174
Isa 36:11 174
Isa 36:15 173
Isa 36:18 121 n. 227
Isa 36:21 126, 132, 160 n. 29
Isa 36:22 174
Isa 37:2 174
Isa 37:10 61, 126, 141, 190 n. 133
Isa 37:12 121 n. 227
Isa 37:13 101
Isa 37:14 215
Isa 37:17 189
Isa 37:20 103
Isa 37:26 101, 132, 196 n. 154
Isa 37:29 122, 133, 170
Isa 37:30 96
Isa 37:33 104
Isa 37:34 185 n. 116, 187
Isa 37:38 105, 146, 174, 181
Isa 38:9 206 n. 186
Isa 38:10 34, 177 n. 86, 232
Isa 38:15 172
Isa 38:20 194 n. 148
Isa 39:7 97
Isa 39:8 30 n. 38
Isa 40:7 105, 153, 232
Isa 40:9 36 n. 65, 203 n. 178
Isa 40:11 160 n. 29
Isa 40:12 84
Isa 40:14 89 n. 94
Isa 40:15 84, 121 n. 227
Isa 40:17 81 n. 63, 102, 121 n. 227, 144
Isa 40:21 87
Isa 40:24 33, 97
Isa 41:2 121 n. 227
Isa 41:5 41 n. 85, 44, 134
Isa 41:8 76 n. 48
Isa 41:14 187
Isa 41:17 214
Isa 41:18 121, 129, 141
Isa 41:24 184 n. 113
Isa 41:26 87
Isa 41:27 174 n. 74
Isa 42:1 121 n. 227
Isa 42:2 188
Isa 42:5 104
Isa 42:6 121 n. 227, 190, 214
Isa 42:13 77
Isa 42:14 103
Isa 42:16 109
Isa 42:19 25 n. 10, 47, 94
Isa 42:20 77, 97

1QIsa[a] *(cont.)*
Isa 42:22 174
Isa 42:25 48 n. 117
Isa 43:8 25 n. 10, 47
Isa 43:9 121 n. 227
Isa 43:13 197
Isa 43:17 178, 197
Isa 43:19 178 n. 89
Isa 43:20 178 n. 89
Isa 43:23 196 n. 154
Isa 43:28 178
Isa 45:1 121 n. 227
Isa 45:4 105
Isa 45:7 77
Isa 45:8 39, 61
Isa 45:12 104
Isa 45:13 184, 185
Isa 45:14 62 n. 166
Isa 45:20 121 n. 227
Isa 45:23 171
Isa 46:1 96 n. 140
Isa 46:7 188
Isa 47:2 203 n. 178
Isa 47:7 231
Isa 47:8 95 n. 128
Isa 47:9 201
Isa 47:12 203 n. 178
Isa 47:13 110
Isa 48:8 192 n. 141
Isa 48:11 41–42
Isa 48:14 89
Isa 48:15 196 n. 154
Isa 48:16 87
Isa 49:2 32 n. 50
Isa 49:4 48 n. 117, 90, 103 n. 162, 179
Isa 49:6 121 n. 227
Isa 49:8 214
Isa 49:9 121, 129
Isa 49:17 174
Isa 49:22 121 n. 227
Isa 49:23 27 n. 20
Isa 49:24 192
Isa 49:25 172, 192
Isa 49:26 203
Isa 50:6 77
Isa 50:9 214
Isa 50:11 61
Isa 51:2 190
Isa 51:4 103
Isa 51:6 32 n. 50
Isa 51:8 110, 197, 201 n. 172
Isa 51:9 109 n. 187, 110, 155
Isa 51:10 155
Isa 51:11 177
Isa 51:12 155
Isa 51:20 174 n. 74
Isa 52:5 191
Isa 52:10 121 n. 227
Isa 52:14 187 n. 124
Isa 52:15 121 n. 227
Isa 53:2 121, 187 n. 124
Isa 53:8 30 n. 38, 173 n. 69, 191
Isa 53:9 95
Isa 54:2 59, 103
Isa 54:3 52 n. 128, 121 n. 227
Isa 54:5 189
Isa 54:7 172
Isa 54:11 62, 96
Isa 54:15 30
Isa 55:5 32 n. 50
Isa 55:12 55, 172, 190 n. 132
Isa 55:13 104 n. 168, 176
Isa 56:2 15, 23
Isa 56:6 120 n. 220
Isa 56:7 189 n. 130, 196 n. 154
Isa 56:10 56 n. 135, 110
Isa 57:2 174 n. 74
Isa 57:9 178
Isa 57:13 178
Isa 57:15 101
Isa 57:17 194
Isa 57:18 160 n. 29
Isa 57:20 103
Isa 58:3 32
Isa 58:4 101
Isa 58:9 205
Isa 58:10 48, 217
Isa 58:11 107
Isa 58:12 192 n. 141

Isa 59:5 46
Isa 59:6 184
Isa 59:7 120 n. 223, 161 n. 34
Isa 59:10 48, 217
Isa 59:14 104 n. 168
Isa 59:17 146
Isa 59:19 130
Isa 60:3 121 n. 227
Isa 60:5 121 n. 227
Isa 60:6 67, 176
Isa 60:7 121, 141
Isa 60:11 121 n. 227
Isa 60:12 121 n. 227, 215
Isa 60:14 95
Isa 60:15 61
Isa 60:16 121 n. 227
Isa 61:3 192 n. 141
Isa 61:6 46, 55, 121 n. 227, 123, 124, 190 n. 132, 207
Isa 61:9 121 n. 227
Isa 61:11 121 n. 227
Isa 62:2 121 n. 227, 192 n. 141, 214
Isa 62:4 60, 160
Isa 62:8 130, 149
Isa 62:9 36 n. 66, 215
Isa 63:1 95 n. 130, 160 n. 29
Isa 63:7 44
Isa 63:8 30 n. 38
Isa 63:11 160 n. 29
Isa 63:13 32, 101
Isa 64:1 96, 121 n. 227
Isa 64:4 215
Isa 64:6 104
Isa 64:7 93, 95 n. 128
Isa 64:9 61
Isa 64:10 173
Isa 65:1 190, 192 n. 141
Isa 65:2 161 n. 34
Isa 65:3 77
Isa 65:7 48 n. 117, 90, 179
Isa 65:9 190
Isa 65:10 59 n. 152, 160 n. 31
Isa 65:14 188
Isa 65:20 190 n. 130
Isa 65:21 44
Isa 66:2 59
Isa 66:10 60, 104, 160
Isa 66:12 121 n. 227, 171, 190
Isa 66:18 121 n. 227, 161 n. 34
Isa 66:19 43 n. 96, 44, 55, 121 n. 227, 132
Isa 66:20 121 n. 227, 174

1Q8 (1QIsa[b]) 15 n. 7
Isa 16:2 37
Isa 16:7 160
Isa 17:2 37
Isa 26:2 52, 81 n. 61
Isa 41:8 76 n. 48
Isa 41:18 121
Isa 43:23 196 n. 154
Isa 47:9 201
Isa 48:20 126
Isa 51:5 210 n. 196
Isa 52:14 187 n. 124
Isa 53:2 187 n. 124
Isa 55:12 124, 141
Isa 55:13 30
Isa 56:7 196 n. 154
Isa 58:6 37
Isa 58:9 42, 62
Isa 60:4 190
Isa 60:6 203

1Q10 (1QPs[a])
Ps 119:32 36 n. 65

1Q16 (1QpPs) 9

2Q3 (2QExod[b]) 7, 7 n. 5
Exod 18:21 125 n. 242

2Q7 (2QNum[b]) 7

2Q12 (2QDeut[c]) 7

2Q13 (2QJer) 7, 186
Jer 48:27 59 n. 152, 160 n. 31
Jer 48:28 203 n. 178

2Q16 (2QRuth[a])
Ruth 2:22 145 n. 314

4Q1 (4QGen–Exod[a])
Gen 35:26 192
Gen 39:17 196 n. 154
Exod 6:8 196 n. 154

4Q5 (4QGen[e])
Gen 41:6 37

4Q7 (4QGen[g]) 133
Gen 1:9 132

4Q9 (4QGen[j])
Gen 41:18 187 n. 124

4Q11 (4QpaleoGen–Exod[l])
Exod 12:9 176
Exod 26:33 196 n. 154
Exod 28:40 153

4Q13 (4Q[Gen-]Exod[b]) 7
Exod 2:3 201 n. 173

4Q14 (4QExod[c])
Exod 17:7 69
Exod 17:8 29

4Q17 (4QExod–Lev[f])
Exod 40:15 66, 162, 164, 231
Exod 40:18 67
Exod 40:20 67
Exod 40:22 67

4Q22 (4QpaleoExod[m])
Exod 7:18 120 n. 222
Exod 12:38 224
Exod 25:27 37
Exod 26:11 196 n. 154
Exod 32:17 160

4Q23 (4QLev-Num[a])
Num 4:40 37

4Q24 (4QLev[b]) 98
Lev 2:16 80
Lev 22:23 94
Lev 23:10 196 n. 154

4Q26 (4QLev[d])
Lev 17:11 158

4Q26a (4QLev[e])
Lev 20:2 3 n. 4, 36 n. 66

4Q26c (4QLev[i] =XLev[c])
Lev 26:36 196 n. 154

4Q27 (4QNum[b]) 7, 186
Num 16:1 181
Num 19:1 31
Num 20:13 36 n. 65
Num 24:9 25
Num 26:32 172
Num 27:1 181
Num 31:54 125 n. 242

4Q31 (4QDeut[d])
Deut 3:18 37
Deut 3:19 36 n. 65
Deut 3:26 30

4Q32 (4QDeut[e])
Deut 8:2 145 n. 314

4Q33 (4QDeut[f]) 136 n. 286
Deut 7:22 155
Deut 8:9 108

4Q35 (4QDeut[h])
Deut 33:9 3 n. 4
Deut 33:10 28

4Q37 (4QDeut[j]) 7

4Q38 (4Q Deut[k1]) 7

4Q38a (4QDeut[k2]) 7
Deut 19:11 155

4Q40 (4QDeut[m]) 8

4Q41 (4QDeut[n])
Deut 5:1 204
Deut 5:9 216
Deut 5:20 156
Deut 5:22 217

4Q42 (4QDeut[o])
Deut 5:1 204

4Q44 (4QDeut[q])
Deut 32:42 26–27

4Q49 (4QJudg[a])
Judg 6:13 80 n. 59

4Q51 (4QSam[a])
1 Sam 2:29 127
1 Sam 31:3 76 n. 47
2 Sam 2:6 76 n. 47
2 Sam 6:2 32
2 Sam 6:3 76 n. 47
2 Sam 11:11 205
2 Sam 19:7 57
2Sam 24:16 121, 141
2Sam 22:44 121 n. 227

4Q52 (4QSam[b])
1 Sam 20:38 160 n. 29

4Q53 (4QSam[c]) 8
2 Sam 14:10 32
2 Sam 14:31 36 n. 65
2 Sam 15:3 33

4Q55 (4QIsa[a])
Isa 23:3 54 n. 131

4Q56 (4QIsa[b])
Isa 13:4 32
Isa 13:7 86
Isa 13:16 167 n. 55
Isa 18:7 191
Isa 19:18 110

4Q57 (4QIsa[c]) 8
Isa 9:6 59
Isa 23:10 203
Isa 23:12 203 n. 178
Isa 24:15 54
Isa 48:11 41

4Q58 (4QIsa[d])
Isa 48:11 59
Isa 48:15 196 n. 154
Isa 48:20 126
Isa 57:19 25

4Q59 (4QIsa[e])
Isa 8:6 109
Isa 8:8 95

4Q60 (4QIsa[f])
Isa 22:18 214
Isa 22:19 194 n. 149

4Q61 (4QIsa[g])
Isa 43:23 196 n. 154

4Q62 (4QIsa[h])
Isa 42:6 214
Isa 42:11 25

4Q68 (4QIsa[o]) 35

4Q70 (4QJer[a])
Jer 12:14 204 n. 182
Jer 14:10 121
Jer 15:19 126
Jer 18:21 3 n. 4
Jer 17:10 3 n. 4, 32
Jer 17:16 32
Jer 17:17 108
Jer 17:21 34
Jer 18:18 203
Jer 18:21 37

4Q72 (4QJer[c]) 195

4Q73 (4QEzek[a])
Ezek 23:44 81 n. 61, 52
Ezek 23:45 29

4Q74 (4QEzek[b])
Ezek 1:21 32

4Q76 (4QXII[a])
Mal 3:1 52, 81 n. 61

4Q77 (4QXII[b])
Zeph 2:13 32

4Q78 (4QXII[c]) 8
Joel 2:11 32

4Q79 (4QXII[d])
Hos 2:2 85

4Q80 (4QXII[e]) 8
Zech 4:2 87

4Q82 (4QXII[g]) 8
Hos 2:14 108
Hos 7:14 37 n. 67
Hos 12:8 92

4Q83 (4QPs[a])
Ps 38:22 214
Ps 69:4 117 n. 211

4Q84 (4QPs[b])
Ps 93:5 85 n. 78
Ps 102:16 130
Ps 103:10 27 n. 25
Ps 116:19 157

4Q85 (4QPs[c])
Ps 50:21 104
Ps 50:23 3 n. 4, 203
Ps 52:8 130

4Q86 (4QPs[d])
Ps 104:2 42
Ps 104:4 42

4Q87 (4QPs[e])
Ps ;126:2 121 n. 227

4Q88 (4QPs[f]) (non-Masoretic works listed under 4Q88 in "Nonbiblical Scrolls") xvii, 50 n. 122, 122
Ps 107:4 178 n. 89
Ps 107:27 49 n. 120, 202 n. 175
Ps 109:4 69
Ps 109:25 87

4Q89 (4QPs[g])
Ps 119:37 36 n. 65
Ps 119:43 36 n. 65
Ps 119:83 187 n. 125

4Q90 (4QPs[h])
Ps 119:13 69
Ps 119:14 56 n. 135, 133

4Q93 (4QPs[l])
Ps 104:4 42, 145 n. 314
Ps 104:5 69

4Q96 (4QPs[o]) 8
Ps 115:4 121 n. 227

4Q98 (4QPs[q])
Ps 112:1 145 n. 314

4Q98g (4QPs[x])
Ps 89:23 121, 141

4Q99 (4QJob[a])
Job 37:5 95

4Q104 (4QRuth[a])
Ruth 1:9 67 n. 7

4Q107 (4QCant[b]) 11, 37, 231
Song 2:13 60 n. 153
Song 2:17 166
Song 3:1 25
Song 2:13 26 n. 17
Song 4:10 66, 232

4Q109 (4QQoh[a]) 8
Qoh 5:15 154
Qoh 7:5 25
Qoh 7:7 95
Qoh 7:19 95 n. 132

4Q111 (4QLam) 8
Lam 1:12 193
Lam 1:15 30, 68
Lam 1:17 71, 110

4Q112 (4QDan[a])
Dan 2:41 162 n. 36

4Q113 (4QDan[b])
Dan 8:7 103 n. 163, 215
Dan 8:16 154

4Q114 (4QDan[c])
Dan 10:6 145 n. 314

4Q116 (4QDan[e])
Dan 9:12 35

4Q128 (4QPhyl A) 8
Exod 12:43 160
Exod 12:44 160
Deut 10:13 133, 145 n. 313

4Q129 (4QPhyl B) 8
Deut 5:10 133, 141
Deut 5:11 46
Deut 5:20 156
Deut 5:22 154
Deut 5:24 44
Deut 5:27 30
Deut 5:29 133

4Q130 (4QPhyl C)
Deut 11:13 133
Deut 11:21 36 n. 65

4Q134 (4QPhyl G) 8, 8 n. 6
Deut 5:1 204
Deut 5:20 156

4Q135 (4QPhyl H) 8, 8 n. 6
Deut 5:22 215
Deut 5:28 32
Deut 6:4 204

4Q136 (4QPhyl I) 8, 8 n. 6
Exod 12:44 69
Exod 12:48 69

4Q137 (4QPhyl J) 8, 8 n. 6
Deut 5:1 204
Deut 5:11 46
Deut 5:15 134
Deut 5:16 41 n. 85
Deut 5:29 133
Deut 5:31 204

4Q138 (4QPhyl K) 8, 8 n. 6
Deut 10:18 160 n. 29
Deut 11:1 145 n. 313
Deut 11:6 125, 141
Deut 11:9 36 n. 65

4Q139 (4QPhyl L) 8, 8 n. 6
Deut 5:11 46
Deut 5:15 134

4Q140 (4QPhyl M) 8, 8 n. 6
Exod 13:3 160
Deut 5:33 31
Deut 6:2 133, 145 n. 313

4Q141 (4QPhyl N) 8, 8 n. 6
Deut 32:17 132

4Q142 (4QPhyl O) 8

4Q143 (4QPhyl P) 8

4Q144 (4QPhyl Q) 8

5Q1 (5QDeut)
Deut 7:17 154

5Q6 (5QLam[a])
Lam 4:8 187 n. 124
Lam 5:2 120

6Q4 (6QpapKgs)
2 Kgs 7:8 175

6Q7 (6QpapDan)
Dan 10:12 81 n. 63, 125, 141

8Q3 (8QPhyl)
Deut 11:6 125
Deut 11:10 158

11Q1 (11QpaleoLev[a])
Lev 18:27 155
Lev 21:10 145 n. 314
Lev 25:30 52 n. 128, 206
Lev 25:32 107
Lev 26:18 80
Lev 26:19 31
Lev 26:21 200 n. 170
Lev 26:25 196 n. 154

11Q2 (11QLev[b])
Lev 13:58 30
Lev 13:59 172

11Q5 (11QPs[a]) (non-Masoretic works listed under 11Q5 in "Non-Biblical Scrolls") 8, 173 n. 70
Ps 93:1 29
Ps 104:24 49 n. 120
Ps 119:2 217
Ps 119:37 93 n. 117
Ps 119:40 32
Ps 119:42 80 n. 59
Ps 119:83 187 n. 125
Ps 119:86 222
Ps 119:117 92
Ps 119:161 175
Ps 119:175 217, 221
Ps 121:2 92
Ps 121:7 217, 219 n. 217
Ps 124:7 32
Ps 126:2 121 n. 227
Ps 126:6 145 n. 313
Ps 136:11 59 n. 146, 198
Ps 137:9 167 n. 55
Ps 139:17 80 n. 59
Ps 140:5 212, 222
Ps 141:7 151
Ps 141:9 212, 222
Ps 143:5 184 n. 113
Ps 144:3 217
Ps 149:7 121 n. 227

11Q6 (11QPs[b]) 8

11Q7 (11QPs[c]) 7 n. 5, 8
Ps 2:3 31

11Q8 (11QPs[d]) 8
Ps 81:6 133 n. 272, 170

XQ3 (XQPhyl 3)
Deut 5:1 204

Nonbiblical Scrolls

1Q14 (1QpMic) 8
8–10, 7 40 n. 81

1QpHab 8, 112, 146–147
I, 11 69
II, 6 57 n. 137
II, 12 120
III, 6 145 n. 313, 147
III, 7 145 n. 313
IV, 2 193
IV, 6 197
IV, 7 204
V, 1 205, 206
V, 5 145 n. 313
VI, 11 166
VII, 1 24
VIII, 3 136
VIII, 5 145 n. 311
VIII, 7 36, 142, 145 n. 311
VIII, 10 136

VIII, 15 202
IX, 3 202
IX, 9 62 n. 165
IX, 14 27, 45
X, 1 25
X, 2 42, 86
X, 5 218
X, 10 62, 146
X, 11 62, 101, 146
XI, 2 62
XI, 6 151
XI, 9 30
XII, 4 122, 141
XII, 5 215
XII, 11 159
XIII, 1 85

1Q18 (1QJub[b])
1–2, 2 147 n. 319
1–2, 3 147 n. 319

1Q20 (1QGenApocr)
II, 18 185
III, 13 185
XIV, 9 59 n. 150
XXI, 21 119
XXI, 34 143 n. 305
XXII, 1 162 n. 36

1Q22 (1QDibreMoshe) 8
1 ii, 10 40 n. 81

1Q26 (1QInstr) 8

1Q27 (1QMyst) 8
1 i, 3 49 n. 120
1 i, 10 216
1 i, 11 153

1QS (= 1Q28) 6, 8 ,10, 34, 52 n. 125, 99, 106, 112, 146, 147, 226, 227, 229, 231
I, 7 79 n. 57
I, 9 205
I, 14 193
I, 16 94
II, 3 135, 214, 221
II, 4 134
II, 19 34, 177 n. 86, 232
III, 1 205
III, 3 205
III, 5 34, 177 n. 86, 232
III, 6 170 n. 60, 193
III, 7 145 n. 313
III, 8 145 n. 313, 184 n. 112
III, 9 194, 231
III, 15 61, 109
III, 25 162, 231
IV, 4 96
IV, 6 160
IV, 9 153, 184
IV, 10 184
IV, 11 172, 183, 184
V, 2 94
V, 5 159
V, 10 100
V, 13 81 n. 61
V, 20 162, 176 n. 81
V, 21 176
V, 24 108
VI, 3 25
VI, 5 40 n. 81
VI, 6 40 n. 81
VI, 7 95
VI, 11 109
VI, 14 211, 215, 231
VI, 15 194 n. 148
VI, 17 145 n. 313, 159, 206, 215
VI, 18 206
VI, 20 94
VI, 21 206, 215
VI, 22 36, 50, 101 n. 158, 215
VI, 24 24
VI, 26 103, 172 n. 65, 184 n. 112
VI, 27 93
VII, 3 67, 70 n. 22, 94, 96, 232
VII, 4 59, 160
VII, 10 197
VII, 11 94 n. 126
VII, 12 180 n. 96
VII, 13 171, 184 n. 112

1QS (*cont.*)
VII, 14 94, 109
VII, 20 52 n. 128, 206
VII, 20–21 207 n. 190
VII, 22 52 n. 128, 206
VIII, 2 92
VIII, 3 209
VIII, 5 24, 169
VIII, 6 25, 40 n. 81
VIII, 8 51
VIII, 10 40 n. 81
VIII, 13 104
VIII, 25 31, 170 n. 60
VIII, 26 206
IX, 14 162 n. 35, 175
IX, 18–19 31 n. 48
IX, 20 154
IX, 23 174
X, 1 32
X, 2 103, 153, 231
X, 3 174
X, 6 105
X, 12 105
X, 13 215
X, 19 24
X, 25 167
X, 26 40, 183, 191
XI, 1 29
XI, 2 153, 179, 184
XI, 3 145 n. 313
XI, 7 32, 48 n. 117, 179
XI, 17 170 n. 60
XI, 21 107
XI, 22 172 n. 64

1QSa (= 1Q28a) 8, 52 n. 125, 112, 173 n. 70
I, 1 85
I, 2 180
I, 4 162 n. 35, 176 n. 81
I, 6 153
I, 10 206, 208
I, 11 32
I, 12 206
I, 14 177
I, 16 25
I, 18 145 n. 313
I, 19 171, 207 n. 189
I, 20 100
I, 22 145 n. 313
I, 27 85
II, 2 25
II, 10 40 n. 77, 222

1QSb (= 1Q28b) 8, 52 n. 125
III, 20 215
III, 27 27, 130 n. 262
V, 23 28 n. 26
V, 25 50
V, 27 29
V, 28 217

1Q29 (1QTongues Fire) 9
13, 4 164

1Q30 (1QLit Text? A) 9

1Q31 (1QLit Text? B) 9

1QM (= 1Q33) 6, 8, 10, 52 n. 125, 122, 181
I, 1 174
I, 4 120
I, 8 45 n. 103
I, 12 160
I, 13 205
II, 13 66
II, 17 51 n. 124, 172
III, 2 30, 174
III, 6 205
III, 9 174
III, 15 79 n. 57
III, 17 125 n. 242
IV, 1 79 n. 57
IV, 2 125 n. 242
IV, 9 101
IV, 13 209
V, 3 29, 91
V, 6 152, 172
V, 7 166, 171, 184 n. 112

V, 9 152 n. 6, 165
V, 10 24 n. 5, 184 n. 112
V, 12 24 n. 5, 133 n. 272, 170
V, 13 184 n. 112
VI, 1 56
VI, 2 184 n. 112
VI, 3 171
VI, 5 29, 91
VI, 10 29
VI, 15 183
VII, 3 172 n. 64
VII, 12 85
VII, 13 174
VII, 15 120
VIII, 2 161
VIII, 6 194
VIII, 7 165 n. 48
VIII, 14 165 n. 48
VIII, 15 100 n. 154
IX, 6 161, 174
IX, 7 169
IX, 8 167 n. 50
X, 3 157, 204 n. 181
X, 11 194
XI, 5 184
XI, 9 200
XII, 3 188
XII, 4 133, 141
XII, 10 204
XII, 13 223
XII, 14 141
XIII, 9 190
XIV, 6 183
XIV, 7 122, 149, 172, 183
XIV, 9 165
XV, 2 122
XVI, 7 120
XVII, 2 156
XVII, 8 156
XVII, 11 61
XVII, 10 194
XVIII, 2 192
XVIII, 10 160
XIX, 3 156

1QH[a] (= 1Q34)8, 35–36, 50 n. 22, 98–99, 112, 173 n. 70, 227, 229
II, 12 53
IV, 16 42
V, 13 121 n. 226, 173
V, 20 49 n. 120
V, 25 50
V, 26 161 n. 34
V, 27 161 n. 33
V, 29 161 n. 33
V, 30 58 n. 145
VI, 23 182 n. 106
VI, 31 184 n. 112
VI, 34 182
VI, 34–35 183
VII, 25 168 n. 56
VII, 27 153
VII, 31 170 n. 60
VII, 34 153, 183 n. 111
VII, 34–37 58 n. 142
VII, 37 184 n. 112
IX, 10 27
IX, 16 49 n. 120
IX, 17 35 n. 63
IX, 30 201
X, 9 42, 183
X, 10 183
X, 11 173
X, 19 161 n. 34, 212 n. 204
X, 20 172 n. 64, 184
X, 25 158
X, 28 30, 184
X, 30 79
X, 31 158
XI, 7 215
XI, 8 26
XI, 29 94, 94 n. 126
XI, 30 24
XI, 31 106, 184, 185
XI, 39 62
XII, 7 216, 219 n. 217
XII, 8 88 n. 89
XII, 14 58 n. 145
XII, 15 161 n. 34
XII, 16 218

1QH^a (cont.)
XII, 19 48 n. 117, 58 n. 145, 170 n. 60
XII, 20 161 n. 34
XII, 25 217, 218
XII, 30 154
XII, 32 170 n. 60
XII, 34 202, 221 n. 227
XII, 37 89 n. 93
XIII, 12 71, 200
XIII, 15 201
XIII, 16 80, 136, 200
XIII, 23 42 n. 89
XIII, 28 35 n. 63
XIII, 30 180 n. 96
XIII, 32 175
XIII, 36 148
XIII, 37 148
XIV, 11 79
XIV, 13 33, 184
XIV, 15 196
XIV, 24 57, 216
XIV, 26 167
XV, 5 24, 209
XV, 8 167
XV, 10 196
XV, 13 49, 137
XV, 14 24
XV, 15 24, 30
XV, 24 164 n. 45, 167
XV, 32 93 n. 117
XV, 34 170 n. 60
XV, 37 79, 91, 170
XVI, 8 26
XVI, 9 40 n. 78
XVI, 19 39
XVI, 22 169
XVI, 22–23 166 n. 49
XVI, 23 165
XVI, 26 199, 200
XVI, 28 167
XVI, 29 180 n. 96
XVI, 31 101
XVI, 36 183
XVI, 37 121, 141
XVII, 7 193
XVII, 23 32 n. 50
XVII, 27 56, 184
XVIII, 4 49 n. 120
XVIII, 8 25, 33
XIX, 30 28, 176
XIX, 31 91
XIX, 32 108
XIX, 35 88
XX, 10 91
XX, 12 58 n. 145
XX, 26 169
XX, 28 94
XX, 31 206 n. 186
XX, 35 154
XXI, 10 196 n. 154
XXI, 25 26
XXI, 27 215
XXII, 25 91
XXII, 27 180
XXII, 37 211, 214
XXIII, 12 168 n. 56
XXIII, 28 85
XXIV, 26 69
XXV, 8 191
XXVI, 27 79, 197

1Q34bis
3 i, 3 161 n. 34
3 i, 7 79

1QH^b (= 1Q35) 7 n. 5, 8

1Q36 (1QHymns) 7 n. 5, 8
25 ii, 3 30

3Q4 (3QpIsa) 9

3Q5 (3QJub) 9

3Q6 (3QHymn) 9

3Q9 (3QSectarian Text) 9

3Q15 (Copper Scroll) 6, 10–11, 67 n. 6, 98, 112
- I, 4 88
- III, 4 133
- VIII, 3 93
- IX, 2 89
- X, 3 132 n. 265
- XI, 4 91
- XI, 9 163
- XI, 10 89 n. 91
- XII, 1 89

4Q88 (4QPs[f]) (Psalms listed under 4Q88 in "Biblical Scrolls") xvii, 50 n. 122, 122
- VIII, 14 126 n. 248
- X, 7–8 204 n. 180
- X, 11 121, 129
- X, 12 200

4Q158 (4QRP[a]) 8
- 4, 5 175
- 4, 6 39
- 6, 5 205
- 9, 5 130 n. 262
- 10–12, 7 158–59
- 14 i, 8 41

4Q159 (4QOrdin) 8
- 1 ii, 5 142
- 2–4, 1 93 n. 117
- 2–4, 8 190 n. 133

4Q160 (4QVisSam) 8, 52 n. 125
- 1, 3: 201
- 3–4 ii, 3: 203
- 7, 4: 205

4Q161 (4QpIsa[a]) 8
- 8–10, 6 40, 191
- 8–10, 11 145 n. 311
- 8–10, 18 216

4Q162 (4QpIsa[b]) 9

4Q163 (4Qpap pIsa[c]) 8, 52 n. 125
- 23 i, 17 91

4Q164 (4QIsa[d]) 9

4Q165 (4QpIsa[e]) 8

4Q166 (4QpHos[a]) 8
- II, 18 67, 153

4Q167 (4QpHos[b]) 9

4Q168 (4QpMic?) 9

4Q169 (4QpNah) 9, 127, 173
- 3–4 i, 4 124, 141, 207, 230
- 3–4 i, 6 159 n. 28
- 3–4 i, 9 159 n. 28
- 3–4 ii, 3 106, 184, 185, 209
- 3–4 ii, 4 70, 184
- 3–4 iii, 2 93
- 3–4 iii, 4 93
- 3–4 iii, 5 122
- 3–4 iii, 10 159 n. 28
- 3–4 iii, 11 159 n. 28, 184 n. 112
- 3–4 iv, 2 164, 167
- 3–4 iv, 4 164 n. 45, 167

4Q171 (4QpPs[a]) 8
- 1–2 ii, 4 132, 141
- 1–2 ii, 14 135, 202, 218, 221 n. 227
- 1–2 ii, 23 152
- 1 + 3–4 iii, 5 80 n. 59
- 3–10 iv, 7 71
- 3–10 iv, 27 42, 172 n. 65

4Q172 (4QpUnidentified) 9

4Q174 (4QFlor) 8
- I, 6 57
- 1–2 i, 15 79
- 4, 4 193 n. 145
- 4, 6 161 n. 33

4Q175 (4QTest) 8, 11, 84
3 67
4 46, 100, 187
7 79
9 89 n. 94, 187
10 187
11 59, 129, 148, 160
15 102
16 91, 143
17 67
22 85, 127
23 103
28 79

4Q176 (4QTanḥ) 8
1–2 i, 6 60, 80, 160
1–2 i, 10 160
8–11, 7 157
8–11, 6 167
8–11, 12 157
15, 2 196 n. 154
20, 3 16 n. 10, 162, 163, 231
24, 2 26 n. 13

4Q176a (4QJub[i]?)
19–20, 3 48 n. 117, 50 n. 121

4Q177 (4QCatena A) 8
5–6, 15 187 n. 125
10–11, 2 187
10–11, 9 153
14, 4 203

4Q178 (Unclassified Fragments)
5, 2 40

4Q179 (4QApocrLam A)
1 i, 14 31, 49

4Q180 (4QAgesCreat A) 8

4Q181 (4QAgesCreat B) 8
2, 9 45 n. 103

4Q182 (4QCatena B) 9

4Q184 (4QWiles) 8
1, 2 66, 172 n. 64, 231
1, 7 197
1, 17 184 n. 112
2, 6 93 n. 118

4Q185 (4QSap Work) 9
1–2 I, 9 156
4 i, 3 49

4Q186 (4QHoros[c]) 8
1 i, 6 85

4Q197 (4QTob[b] ar)
4 i, 16 151 n. 4

4Q200 (4QTobit[e]) 8
2, 3 24
4, 6 80, 105 n. 173

4Q201 (En[a] ar)
3, 10 98

4Q204 (En[c] ar)
1 i, 26 62
4, 3 126 n. 246, 144 n. 309

4Q209 (Enastr[b] ar)
23, 4 98

4Q210 (Enastra[c] ar)
1 ii, 14 165

4Q215 (4QTNaph) 8
1–3, 5 193
1–3, 7 147 n. 319

4Q215a (4QTimes) 8

4Q216 (4QJub[a])
I, 4 79
II, 3 89
II, 12 199–200
V, 3 145 n. 314
V, 5–8 80 n. 59

V, 9 126, 145 n. 314
V, 10 164
VII, 10 27
VII, 15 32

4Q219 (4QJub[d]) 8
I, 12 62
II, 20 184 n. 112
II, 21 61
II, 26 61
II, 31 62
II, 32 102

4Q221 (4QJub[f]) 8, 146–47
3, 5 144, 145 n. 313
4, 9 144
5, 2 144
7, 10 145 n. 311
16, 5 136

4Q222 (4QJub[g]) 8
1, 2 147 n. 319
1, 4 95 n. 129

4Q223–224 (4QpapJub[h]) 8
1 i, 2 174
2 i, 45 43
2 ii, 4 43, 147
2 ii, 11 56
2 ii, 12 43, 147
2 iii, 12 43, 147
2 iv, 5 105 n. 173, 153
2 iv, 18 43, 147
2 v, 3 94, 205

4Q225 (4QPsJub[a]) 8
2 i, 4 143 n. 304
2 i, 6 111
2 i, 10 193 n. 145
2 ii, 4 142, 143 n. 304
2 ii, 7 164

4Q227 (4QPsJub[c]) 8

4Q230 (Catalogue of Spirits[a])
1, 2 172
1, 3 153

4Q238 (4QWords of Judgement)
1 188

4Q251 (4QHalakha A) 8
1–2, 4 164
8, 4 151
10, 6 187 n. 125

4Q252 (4QCommGen A) 63
I, 10 174 n. 74
I, 22 56
II, 6 61
IV, 1 147 n. 319
IV, 2 131 n. 262

4Q254 (4QComGen C) 8

4Q255 (4QpapS[a]) 9
2, 6 145 n. 313

4Q256 (4QS[b]) 8

4Q257 (4QpapS[c]) 8

4Q258 (4QS[d])
I, 2 101
II, 2 160 n. 29
II, 3 160 n. 29
VII, 2 52 n. 128, 206
VIII, 3 31 n. 48
IX, 7 199
IX, 9 199

4Q259 (4QS[e]) 8
II, 3 52 n. 128, 206
II, 5 52 n. 128, 206
III, 17–18 31

4Q260 (4QS[f]) 8
I, 1 174
II, 1 153

4Q261 (4QS[g]) 9
1a-b, 3 145 n. 313
5a-c, 3 91

4Q262 (4QS[h]) 9
B, 1 145 n. 313
B, 2 145 n. 313

4Q263 (4QS[i]) 9
3 26 n. 17, 60 n. 153

4Q264 (4QS[j]) 9

4Q265 (4QMisc Rules) 8
3, 2 136
4 i, 8 161
4, i, 10 161

4Q266 (4QDamascus Document[a]) 8, 147, 173
1a-b, 3 81 n. 61
1a-b, 19 203
1c-f, 4 81 n. 61
2 i, 4 145 n. 313, 159
2 ii, 2 145
2 ii, 4 145 n. 312
2 ii, 21 159 n. 28
5 i, 13 33
5 ii, 4 145 n. 313
5 ii, 6 159 n. 28
5 ii, 7 61 n. 158
6 i, 3 58 n. 145
6 i, 5 58 n. 145
6 i, 8 158, 164
6 i, 9 131 n. 262
6 i, 11 158
6 ii, 2 145 n. 311
6 ii, 4 81 n. 61
6 ii, 11 50
6 iii, 8 145 n. 313
8 i, 2 159
8 i, 3 120, 145 n. 311
8 i, 5 145 n. 311
8 i, 6 159 n. 28
8 i, 7 79, 81 n. 61
9 ii, 14 81 n. 61
9 iii, 4 221 n. 227
10 i, 2 174
10 i, 3 132, 141
10 i, 12 89, 205
11, 9 163
11, 13 188 n. 125

4Q267 (4QDamascus Document[b]) 8, 52 n. 125
9 v, 12 34, 176

4Q268 (4QDamascus Document[c]) 8
1, 1 201
1, 2 153
1, 3 79

4Q269 (4QDamascus Document[d]) 8

4Q270 (4QDamascus Document[e]) 9, 122, 147
6 ii, 7 145 n. 311
6 iv, 14 145 n. 313
6 iv, 18 171
6 iv, 19 145 n. 313
6 v, 15 145 n. 311
7 i, 18 111

4Q271 (4QDamascus Document[f]) 8
1, 2 69
3, 9 160
5 i, 3 153
5 i, 15 209

4Q272 (4QDamascus Document[g]) 9
1 i, 16 165

4Q273 (4QpapDamascus Document[h]) 8

4Q274 (4QToh A) 8
1 i, 8 164
2 i, 9 51
3 i, 9 164
3 ii, 5 169

4Q277 (4QToh B) 8
1 ii, 4 : 164
1 ii, 7 162, 164, 231
1 ii, 8 43

4Q280 (4QCurses) 8
3, 2 69

4Q282b (Unidentified Fragments B)
1, 2 167

4Q284 (4QPurification Liturgy)
2 i, 3 124, 141, 206, 207 n. 188

4Q284a (4QHarvesting)
2, 6 120

4Q285 (4QSefer ha-Milḥamah) 8
3, 2 120
8, 8 209

4Q286 (4QBer[a]) 8
1 ii, 3 32
1 ii, 6 168
5a-c, 2 62
17a, 2 177

4Q287 (4QBer[b]) 8

4Q289 (4QBer[d]) 8

4Q290 (4QBer[e]) 9

4Q292 (4QWork Cont. Prayers B) 8
2, 3 161 n. 33

4Q298 (4QCryptA Words of the Maskil)
3–4 ii, 6 184 n. 112, 203

4Q299 (4QMyst[a]) 8, 50 n. 122
3a ii – b, 5 49
3a ii – b, 7 145 n. 312, 159 n. 24
3a ii – b, 8 145 n. 312, 159 n. 24
3c, 6 145 n. 313
17 I, 2 49 n. 120

4Q300 (4QMyst[b]) 10, 50
1a ii – b, 4 49 n. 120
3, 3 49 n. 120
3, 5 207 n. 189

4Q301 (4QMyst[c]?) 8

4Q302 (papAdmonitory Parable)
3 ii, 7 40 n. 81, 208

4Q303 (4QMeditation on Creation A) 8
1, 5 102 n. 160

4Q304 (4QMeditation on Creation B) 9

4Q305 (4QMeditation on Creation C) 9

4Q306 (4QMen of People who Err) 9

4Q317 (4QCryptA Lunisolar Cal) 9

4Q320 (4QCal Doc/Mish A) 9, 168

4Q321 (4QCal Doc/Mish B) 9, 168
II, 3 165

4Q321a (4QCal Doc/Mish C)
IV, 8 160 n. 29
V, 5 160 n. 29
V, 7 59, 160
V, 8 160 n. 29

4Q322 (4QMish A) 9

4Q323 (4QMish B) 9

4Q324 (4QMish C) 9

4Q324a (4QMish D) 9

4Q324b (4QpapCal Doc A?) 9

4Q324c (4QMish E) 9

4Q325 (4QCal Doc/Mish D) 9

4Q328 (4QMish F) 9
1, 1 80 n. 59

4Q329 (4QMish G) 9

4Q329a (4QMish H) 9

4Q330 (4QMish I) 9

4Q337 (4QCal Doc E?) 9

4Q364 (4QRP[b]) 8, 52
3 ii, 7 43
4b-e ii, 5 222
9a-b, 10 181
9a-b, 11 153
11, 2 67
11, 3 26, 79 n. 58
17, 3 27, 30
21a-k, 3 143
22, 2 85
24a-c, 4 43, 136, 203
26a ii, 3 43, 136, 203
26c-d, 2 42
28a-b, 7 205
30, 5 62 n. 166

4Q365 (4QRP[c]) 8
1, 2 57, 59
2, 3 175
2, 7 217
6a i, 4 188
6a ii + 6c, 3 92
6b, 6 42 n. 90
7 i, 3 217
12a I, 4 42
12a-b ii, 2 96
12b iii, 5 145 n. 313
12b iii, 9 110, 184, 185
13, 1 45
23, 5 28
26a-b, 8 36, 145 n. 313
32, 8 195

4Q365a (4QT[a]?) 8
2 i, 10 176
2 ii, 7 24, 176
2 ii, 8 108
2 ii, 10 110
3, 5 176 n. 85

4Q366 (RP[d])
1, 2 151

4Q367 (4QRP[e])
1a-b, 6 52 n. 128
1a-b, 8 52 n. 128

4Q368 (4QapocrPent A)
2, 5 198
2, 9 198
10 ii, 5 40 n. 81, 208
10 ii, 7 102–3, 141, 144

4Q369 (4QPrayer Enosh) 8
1 ii, 3 104, 121 n. 228, 160 n. 30
2, 2 110
3, 3–4 156 n. 16

4Q370 (4QExhortation Based on the Flood)
1 i, 2 44

4Q371 (4QNarr and Poet Comp[a]) 9–10
1a-b, 4 170
1a-b, 8 154, 231
7, 4 167

4Q372 (4QNarr and Poet Comp[b]) 122
1, 11 47, 86
1, 15 47, 86
1, 20 143
3, 3 193
6, 4 122

4Q374 (4QExod/Conq. Trad.)
2 i, 4 85
2 ii, 8 145

4Q375 (4QapocrMos[a]) 8

4Q376 (4QapocrMos[b]?)
1 iii, 2 27 n. 23, 145 n. 314

4Q377 (4QapocPent B) 8
2 ii, 9 165

4Q378 (4QapocrJosh[a])
3 i, 5 49
3 ii + 4, 7 125 n. 242

4Q379 (4QapocrJosh[b]) 98, 99 n. 152, 177
12, 6 175 n. 80
22 ii, 13 96

4Q380 (4QNon-Canonical Psalms A)
2, 4 32 n. 50

4Q381 (4QNon-Canonical Psalms B) 32, 35, 52, 122, 164, 177, 231
1, 2 121, 141
1, 3 142
1, 5 105
10–11, 3 180
10–11, 47 180
15, 6 43 n. 94
31, 1 154
31, 3 170, 201
31, 6 105 n. 173
31, 7 165
33a-b + 35, 8 24
44, 2 154
45a + b, 2 135 n. 285, 202
46a + b, 4 155, 163, 231
46a + b, 5 37
46a + b, 8 198
50, 4 32, 86
69, 8 32
69, 9 143
76–77, 10 101
79, 5 56 n. 135
80, 1 101

4Q382 (4Qpap paraKgs) 8
1, 2 162
9, 6 41
9, 7 214
23, 1 26, 91
104, 1 156 n. 16

4Q384 (4Qpap apocr Jer B?) 8

4Q385 (4QpsEzek[a]) 52 n. 125
2, 3 105 n. 173, 193
2, 7 103
2, 9 153
4, 1 164
6, 4 164

4Q385a (4QapocrJer C[a])
17a-e ii, 8 167
18 i a-b, 3 121
18 i a-b, 7 43, 162
18 ii, 7 67

4Q386 (4QpsEzek[a])
1 ii, 4 79 n. 58, 154
1 ii, 5 164, 165
1 ii, 7 165
1 iii, 1 202

4Q387 (4QApocrJer C[b])
A, 4 194
2 ii, 8 164
3, 6 26, 47, 86

4Q388 (4QpsEzek[d])
7, 5 105 n. 173

4Q388a (4QapocrJer C[c])
7 ii, 4 145 n. 314
7 ii, 5 143

4Q390 (4QApcroJer C[e]) 10
1, 8 164

4Q392 (4QWorks) 10
1, 4 145 n. 312

4Q392 (*cont.*)
1, 5 145 n. 312
1, 9 145 n. 312
2, 4 174 n. 73
6–9, 5 153

4Q393 (4QComConf) 8

4QMMT 6, 10, 11, 18, 73

4Q394 (4QMMT[a]) 8
1–2 iv, 3 92
3–7 i, 5 39 n. 73, 153 n. 8
3–7 i, 8 32
3–7 i, 12 195
3–7 i, 15 143, 148
3–7 i, 18 209
3–7 i, 29 39 n. 73, 153 n. 8
3–7 ii, 1 143, 148–49
3–7 ii, 13 143, 148–49
3–7 ii, 14 39 n. 73, 153 n. 8
8 iv, 8 169

4Q396 (4QMMT[c]) 8
1–2 i, 3 39 n. 73, 153 n. 8
1–2 iv, 7 145 n. 312, 159 n. 24

4Q397 (4QMMT[d]) 8

4Q398 (4QpapMMT[e]) 8
11–13, 2 43, 132, 141
11–13, 3 132, 141
14–17 i, 7 145 n. 311
14–17 ii, 4 145 n. 312
14–17 ii, 7 145 n. 312

4Q399 (4QMMT[f]) 10

4Q400 (4QShirShabb[a]) 8
1 i, 15 188
1 ii, 6 106
1 ii, 19 48 n. 117, 179
2, 6 48 n. 117, 179

4Q401 (4QShirShabb[b]) 8
22, 2 189

4Q402 (4QShirShabb[c]) 8

4Q403 (4QShirShabb[d]) 8, 52 n. 125, 169
1 i, 1 79
1 i, 4 30
1 i, 19 32
1 i, 23 205
1 i, 27 32, 180
1 i, 31 29, 30
1 i, 36 174
1 i, 38 43 n. 94
1 i, 42 106
1 i, 43 145 n. 313
1 i, 45 55
1 ii, 24 32
1 ii, 26 106

4Q404 (4QShirShabb[e]) 10

4Q405 (4QShirShabb[f]) 8, 50 n. 125, 169
11, 3 159 n. 25
15 ii–16, 4 145
19, 4 106
19, 5 56
19, 7 24
20 ii-22, 7 145 n. 312
20 ii-22, 11 24, 68, 106
20 ii-22, 12 66
23 i, 7 169
23 i, 9 2 n. 3, 148
23 i, 13 145 n. 313
23 ii, 8 50
23 ii, 10 106

4Q407 (4QShirShabb[h]) 10

4Q408 (4QapocrMoses[c]?)
3+3a, 7 190 n. 133

4Q409 (4QLiturgical Work A) 10

4Q410 (4QVison Int) 8
1, 4 164

4Q412 (4QSap-Didactic Work A) 10

4Q413 (4QComp conc. Div. Provid.) 50 n. 122
1–2, 1 49 n. 120

4Q414 (RiPur A) 8
8, 4 184

4Q415 (4QInstr[a]) 8
9, 11 84, 166
18, 2 172 n. 67

4Q416 (4QInstr[b]) 8, 52 n. 125,
1, 16 143 n. 304
2 ii, 12 165
2 iii, 2 74 n. 43
2 iii, 8 199
2 iii, 16 31, 142, 143 n. 304
2 iii, 17 48 n. 117, 161 n. 33, 222
2 iii, 19 183
2 iv, 1 142, 143 n. 304
2 iv, 9 110
2 iv, 10 108 n. 185
4, 3 204

4Q417 (4QInstr[c]) 8, 146, 168
1 i, 16 24, 34 n. 57, 164
1 i, 17 34 n. 57, 167
1 i, 23 192 n. 138
2 i, 5 24
2 i, 10 108
2 i, 13 36 n. 65
2 i, 15 36 n. 65
2 i, 17 156
2 ii + 23, 7 136
2 ii + 23, 24 199
29 i, 7 145 n. 313, 156

4Q418 (4QInstr[d]) 8, 50 n. 122, 52 n. 125, 168, 173 n. 70
7b, 11 28
8, 6 44, 199
8, 11 44
9 + 9a-c, 7 199
55, 8 195
69 ii, 15 43 n. 94
81 + 81a, 4 48, 184
81 + 81a, 13 166 n. 49
87, 13 174
88, 5 26
89, 2 174
95, 3 199
103 ii, 4 222
103 ii, 5 211
103 ii, 6 174
126 ii, 5 49 n. 120
126 ii, 13 69
127, 2 195
127, 6 84
139, 2 49 n. 120
159 i, 5 174
167 a + b, 2 84
188, 7 221 n. 227
211, 3 178
223, 3 122 n. 233

4Q418a (4QInstr[e]) 8
14, 1 36 n. 65

4Q418b (Text with Quotation of Ps 107?)
1, 4 202

4Q418c (4QInstr[f]) 10

4Q419 (4QInstr-like Composition A) 8

4Q420 (4QWays[a]) 8

4Q421 (4QWays[b]) 8

4Q422 (4QParaGen-Exod) 8–9

4Q423 (4QInstr[g]) 9
6, 3 57
9, 2 217

4Q424 (4QInsruction-like Comp B) 10, 173
1, 8 165
1, 10 199
1, 13 121
3, 2 193

4Q425 (4QSap-Didactic Work B) 10
1+3, 6 25

4Q426 (4QSapiential Hymn Work A) 9
1 i, 1 184 n. 112
1 i, 4 91
1 i, 9 187 n. 124
1 ii, 4 179

4Q427 (4QH[a]) 9
7 i, 15 167, 182
7 ii, 16 157

4Q428 (4QH[b]) 9

4Q429 (4QH[c]) 9
2, 10 71
3, 7 148 n. 325

4Q430 (4QH[d]) 10
1, 2 161 n. 34

4Q431 (4QH[e]) 10

4Q432 (4QpapH[f]) 9
4, 1 102, 211 n. 204
5, 2 49 n. 120

4Q433 (4QHodayot-like Text A)
1, 3 164

4Q433a (4QpapHodayot-like Text B)7 n. 5, 9
2, 9 51

4Q434 (4QBarki Nafshi[a]) 10
1 i, 2 32
1 i, 3 31
1 i, 7 145 n. 313
7b, 3 92, 121, 129

4Q435 (4QBarki Nafshi[b]) 7 n. 5, 9

4Q436 (4QBarki Nafshi[c]) 9

4Q437 (4QBarki Nafshi[d]) 9
2 i, 2 204 n. 182, 213
2 i, 7 207 n. 189
2 i, 10 216
2 i, 16 153
9, 1 184 n. 112

4Q438 (4QBarki Nafshi[e]) 9
4 ii, 5 40 n. 78

4Q439 (4QLament) 10
1 i + 2, 2 165
1 i + 2, 7 121 n. 226

4Q440 (4QHodayot-like text C) 7 n. 5, 9
3 i, 21 193

4Q442 (4QIndiv Thanksgiving B) 10

4Q443 (4QPersonal Prayer) 9

4Q444 (4QIncant) 10

4Q448 (4QApocryphal Psalm and Prayer) 231
II, 2 34
II, 3 34
II, 7 142, 149, 232
II, 8 34

4Q453 (4QLament B)
1 105 n. 173, 153

4Q457b (4QEschat H) 10

4Q460 (4QNarrartive Work) 9
7, 8 221
9 i, 8 156

4Q461 (4QNarr B) 10
4, 3 184 n. 112

4Q462 (4QNarrative C) 9
1, 6 101 n. 158
1, 14 49
1, 18 190 n. 133
1, 19 31

4Q463 (4QNarr D) 10

4Q464 (4QExposition on the Patriarchs) 9
3 I, 6 31

4Q464a (4QNarr E) 10

4Q467 (4QText Mentioning 'Light of Jacob')
1+2, 3 153

4Q468b (4QUnidentified Fragments C)
1, 2 145 n. 314

4Q470 (4QText Mentioning Zedekiah)
1, 4 193

4Q471 (4QWar Scroll-like text B) 9

4Q471a (4QPol Text) 10

4Q471b (4QSelf-Glorifying Hymn);

4Q472 (4QEschatological Work B)
1, 4 145 n. 314

4Q473 (4QTwo Ways) 9
2, 3 170 n. 60

4Q474 (4QText Concerning Rachel and Joseph) 9

4Q475 (4QRenewEarth) 10
1, 2 217

4Q477 (4QRebukes Reported by Overseer) 9

4Q487 (4QpapSapB?) 10, 50 n. 122
2, 8 49 n. 120
5, 5 130
15, 3 184
24, 20 183 n. 111

4Q483 (papGen°)
1 40

4Q491 (4QM[a]) 9
1–3, 8 32 n. 50
1–3, 9 25, 47, 120 n. 221, 120 n. 224
1–3, 10 32, 32 n. 50, 125 n. 242
1–3, 13 197 n. 156, 219 n. 216
1–3, 15 206
1–3, 17 120 n. 221, 120 n. 224
8–10 i, 4 32, 171, 184 n. 112
8–10 i, 5 122, 148–49, 172
8–10 i, 7 193
8–10 i, 8 95
8–10 i, 15 15
8–10 ii, 13 28
8–10 ii, 17 32
13, 6 120

4Q491c (4Q491 11–12, 4QSelf-Glorification Hymn[b]) 11, 57
11 i, 8 32
11 i, 13 57
11 i, 16 164, 208, 231
11 i, 17 57
11 i, 18 57
11 i, 21 57
11 ii, 13 203

4Q492 (4QM[b]) 10

4Q493 (4QM[c]) 10

4Q494 (4QM[d]) 10

4Q495 (4QM[e]) 10
2, 1 79

4Q496 (4QpapM[f]) 9
13, 1 66

4Q498 (4QpapSap/Hymn) 10

4Q499 (4QpapHymn/Prayer) 10

4Q500 (4QpapBenediction) 10

4Q501 (4QapocrLam B) 9
1, 4 101, 189, 200 n. 171
1, 6 175

4Q502 (4QpapRitMar) 9, 166
1, 7 61

4Q503 (4QpapPrQuot) 9
1–6 iii, 7 169
15–16, 5 30
15–16, 11 169
21–22, 1 54
51–55, 8 29

4Q504 (4QDibHam[a]) 9
1–2R ii, 9 205
1–2R ii, 18 189
1–2R iii, 3 81 n. 63, 102, 141, 144
1–2R iii, 4 189
1–2R iii, 7 68
1–2R iv, 6 103
1–2R iv, 11 27 n. 23
1–2R v, 11 202
1–2R v, 16 204 n. 182
5 ii, 4 202
7, 6 29–30
7, 10 214

4Q505 (4QpapDibHam[b]?) 7 n. 5, 9

4Q506 (4QpapDibHam[c]) 9

4Q507 (4QPr Fêtes[b]) 10

4Q508 (4QpapPr Fêtes[b]) 10
2, 2 204

4Q509 (4QpapPrFêtes[c]) 9
7, 6 32, 59 n. 149

4Q510 (4QShir[a]) 10
1, 5 59

4Q511 (4QShir[b]) 9
3, 7 202, 221 n. 227
8, 5 121 n. 225
10, 11 43 n. 94
10, 12 164
20 ii, 3 202
30, 5 84
63 i, 4 45 n. 103
63–64 ii, 3 216, 221 n. 227
63–64 iii, 2 206
121, 2 62 n. 162, 121 n. 225

4Q512 (4QpapRitPur B) 9
1–6, 6 208, 231
21–22, 2 206
27, 1 206

4Q513 (4QOrd[b]) 9
3–4, 2 168

4Q514 (4QOrd[c]) 98
1 i, 6 111
1 i, 8 91

4Q521 (4QMessianic Apocalypse)
2 ii + 4, 8 205
2 ii + 4, 11 30
7 + 5 ii, 12 164

4Q522 (4QProph Josh) 9
8, 3 79
9 i-10, 13 176
9 i-10, 14 69
9 ii, 10 125, 141, 144
9 ii, 11 143

4Q523 (4QJonathan)
1–2, 2 103
3, 1 232

4Q524 (4QT[b]) 9

4Q525 (4QBeatitudes) 9
1, 1 49 n. 120
1, 2 49 n. 120
2 ii + 3, 5 214, 216
2 iii, 4 187 n. 124
5, 5 50
10, 6 37
14 i, 2 187
14 ii, 18 168 n. 56
14 ii, 21 156
14 ii, 26 166
14 ii, 28 172
23, 6 49 n. 120

4Q530 (EnGiants[b] ar)
1 i, 2 165

4Q531 (EnGiants[c] ar)
1, 1 189
18, 2 165

4Q542 (TQahat ar)
3 ii, 13 46

4Q550 (4QJews at the Persian Court ar)
1, 3 98
5 + 5a, 2 189

4Q552 (4QFour Kingdoms[a] ar)
1 i + 2, 7 98

4Q554 (NJ[a] ar)
1 i, 15 47

5Q10 (5QApocrMal [5QpMal?]) 10

5Q11 (5QS) 10

5Q12 (5QDamascus Document) 10

5Q13 (5QRule) 9

5Q15 (NJar)
1 ii, 7 47

6Q9 (6Qpap apocrSamKgs) 10
32, 1 120

6Q12 (6QApocr Proph) 10

6Q18 (6QpapHymn) 9

8Q4 (8QMez)
35 102

11Q5 (11QPs[a]) (Psalms passages listed under 11Q5 in “Biblical Scrolls”) 8
XVIII, 1 35 n. 65
XVIII, 3 49 n. 120
XIX, 15 63, 199–200
XXI, 11 187 n. 125
XXI, 12 216
XXI, 15 199, 201
XXII, 12 223
XXIV, 10 222
XXVII, 9 30
XXVIII, 8 213
XXVIII, 9 187 n. 124
XXVIII, 14 49 n. 120

11Q10 (tgJob)
VII, 5 98 n. 150
XXXV, 2 47
XXXVI, 2 162

11Q11 (11QApocPs) 9

11Q12 (11QJub + XQText A) 9
3, 2 56

11Q13 (11QMelch) 9
II, 6 161 n. 34
II, 11 62

11Q14 (11QSefer ha-Milḥamah) 9, 173
 1 ii, 11 209

11Q15 (11QHymns[a]) 10

11Q16 (11QHymns[b]) 9

11Q17 (11QShirShabb) 10
 IX, 7 106
 X, 5 145 n. 313
 X, 7–8 149

11Q18 (11QNJ ar)
 8, 3 143 n. 305
 9, 4 143 n. 305

11Q19 (11QT[a]) 9, 52, 157, 195
 II, 7 215 n. 208
 VIII, 10 153, 154
 XI, 10 168
 XVII, 9 184 n. 113
 XVII, 15 43 n. 94
 XVIII, 10 168
 XVIII, 13 196 n. 154
 XX, 16 151, 152
 XXVI, 12 161 n. 33
 XXIX, 9 126
 XXX, 9 153
 XXXI, 6 170 n. 60
 XXXIII, 13 133 n. 275
 XXXVI, 11 24 n. 5
 XXXVIII, 12 184
 XXXVIII, 14 24
 XXXVIII, 15 176–77 n. 85
 XL, 10 177 n. 85
 XL, 15 29
 XLII, 9 134
 XLII, 15 125 n. 242, 141
 XLII, 16 91
 XLIII, 10 169
 XLIII, 15 187 n. 125
 XLIV, 15 29
 XLVIII, 3 175 n. 80
 XLVIII, 10 157
 L, 14 30, 33
 LI, 4 161 n. 34
 LI, 5 30
 LI, 6 53 n. 130, 81, 132
 LII, 12 143 n. 304, 216
 LII, 16 29
 LIII, 5 216
 LIII, 11 216
 LIII, 20 25, 44 n. 97
 LIV, 14 215 n. 208
 LIV, 20 42, 156
 LV, 21 161 n. 33
 LVI, 8 200 n. 169
 LVI, 11 41 n. 85, 130
 LVI, 18 170 n. 60
 LVII, 4 125 n. 242
 LVII, 7 217
 LVII, 10 170
 LVII, 12 126, 129
 LVIII, 4 125 n. 242
 LVIII, 5 24
 LIX, 3 184
 LIX, 4 50, 175 n. 80
 LIX, 7 49
 LIX, 8 174
 LIX, 11 196 n. 154
 LIX, 16 200 n. 169
 LIX, 18 143
 LXI, 11 130
 LXI, 14 204 n. 182
 LXII, 5 53, 81, 132
 LXIII, 7 120 n. 223
 LXIII, 8 120 n. 223
 LXIII, 11 187 n. 124
 LXIII, 12 196 n. 154
 LXIV, 2 143 n. 304
 LXIV, 3 143 n. 304
 LXIV, 6 130
 LXIV, 9 170
 LXIV, 11 161 n. 33, 216
 LXIV, 14 161 n. 33
 LXV, 3 153
 LXV, 10 28
 LXVI, 13 25 n. 7
 LXVI, 9 79

11Q20 (11QT^b) 9, 157, 195
IV, 26 152
V, 3 152
XII, 5 66, 231
XII, 25 79 n. 58

11Q27 (11QUnidentified C) 9

11Q29 (11QFrg Rrelated to S) 10

PAM43686 9, 1 49 n. 120

PAM43692 85, 1 120

Mas 1b (MasLev^b)
Lev 10:17 158
Lev 11:35 191
Lev 11:38 191

Mas 1d (Ezekiel)
Ezek 36:24 196 n. 154
Ezek 36:35 154
Ezek 37:12 196 n. 154

Mas 1h (Ben Sira)
Sir 41:2 95 n. 129
Sir 42:4 84 n. 74
Sir 44:11 92 n. 112

Mas 1k (MasShirShabb) 9
i, 2 130 n. 262
ii, 23 30

Mas 1n (MasUnidentified Qumran-Type Frag.) 9

Hebrew Bible

Genesis

2:17 205
2:23 175 n. 76, 178
2:24 143 n. 304
3:8 193 n. 143
3:10 193 n. 143
5:1 207
9:22 142
10:3 30 n. 44
11:6 135, 202
13:9 47, 118 n. 215
15:4 97
17:6 97
22:7 143 n. 304
25:24 78 n. 53
26:29 76 n. 48
27:19 3 n. 4
29:27 207 n. 188
30:20 211 n. 203
31:39 196
38:21 153
38:27 78 n. 53
42:35 163
43:29 135, 179, 212 n. 205, 221 n. 226
45:23 79 n. 58
49:8 156 n. 16
49:22 196 n. 153
49:27 136 n. 286

Exodus

1:15 115
2:3 175 n. 76
3:18 116 n. 206
4:15 142, 163
6:24 123 n. 236
8:16 217
14:15 188
15:16 182, 182 n. 107
15:20 42 n. 90
15:25 188
17:4 217
18:26 135, 210 n. 198
20:25 196
22:17 209
29:35 156
30:35 106
32:9 172 n. 65
32:16 188
36:19 43 n. 94
36:35 42
39:17 45

Leviticus
11:14 123
22:16 205
23:12 168
25:30 207 n. 188, 207–08 n. 190
26:18 80 n. 59

Numbers
1:16 25 n. 12
4:24 206
4:27 175 n. 75
6:24 219 n. 217
6:25 135, 179, 212 n. 205, 221
9:7 41 n. 83
11:11 80
16:2 25 n. 12
24:4 194
24:8 161 n. 34
24:16 194
24:17 59, 160
26:9 25 n. 12
30:6 25 n. 11
32:24 118
35:20 135, 211 n. 202

Deuteronomy
1:21 136
1:45 85
2:5 174
2:24 203
2:31 43, 136, 203
3:24 36 n. 65
4:24 117
4:31 61
5:1 204
5:9 212 n. 205, 217–18
5:20 136
5:21 136, 156
6:4 204
6:7 213
7:24 41 n. 83
8:3 41 n. 83
9:23 43, 203
9:28 42
13:3 212 n. 205
13:12 130
14:13 123
15:12 115, 115 n. 202, 116 n. 206
17:13 130
19:20 130
20:2 179, 212 n. 205
21:8 190
21:18 143 n. 304
28:50 202
28:59 118
28:66 119
31:17 50 n. 121
32:38 221
32:46 62 n. 166
33:9 91 n. 106, 143 n. 304

Joshua
2:17 118
23:5 211 n. 202

Judges
4:4 117
4:21 45
5:12 204 n. 180
8:16 30 n. 42
9:8 220
9:9 175 n. 76
9:11 175 n. 76
9:13 175 n. 76
14:18 223 n. 232

1 Samuel
1:22 143 n. 303
2:10 145
4:7 151 n. 2
10:11 151 n. 2
14:21 151 n. 2
14:33 78 n. 53
15:5 80 n. 60, 200
16:1 66
16:7 143 n. 303
17:7 107 n. 178
19:7 151 n. 2
21:8 123
22:18 123

22:22 123
23:33 105 n. 171
25:18 134 n. 276
25:29 220 n. 224
31:3 76 n. 47
31:4 213, 222
31:13 161 n. 34

2 Samuel
2:18 117
3:25 28
5:2 151 n. 2
6:3 76 n. 47
6:9 104 n. 171
7:12 97
8:3 28 n. 28
11:24 119 n. 216
12:1 46
12:22 221
14:19 66
15:24 28 n. 28
16:11 97
19:14 80
20:8 145, 146
21:12 85, 119 n. 216
22:11 30 n. 44
22:40 82
22:43 92 n. 115
23:10 198
23:12 198
23:33 104 n. 171

1 Kings
1:18 76 n. 48
5:15 142
5:25 85 n. 79
9:9 150
11:17 116 n. 206
11:39 80 n. 59
12:4 76 n. 48
12:18 104 n. 171
13:7 178 n. 91
14:8 160
18:4 162
19:20 175 n. 76
21:7 76 n. 48

2 Kings
2:4 41
3:24 30 n. 42
4:3 157
4:7 157
8:28 116 n. 206
8:29 116 n. 206
11:4 123
11:9 123
11:10 123
11:15 123
13:6 80
19:23 173
19:25 78 n. 53
20:18 97
23:10 182

Isaiah
2:13 166
3:15 118 n. 214
3:16 134
9:3 178
10:13 78 n. 53
10:34 40
11:1 109 n. 187
15:2 177
16:7 166
18:4 175 n. 76, 210
23:12 116 n. 206
27:3 211 n. 202
27:4 175 n. 76
28:22 76 n. 48
30:12 212 n. 205
30:19 135, 179, 212 n. 205, 221 n. 226
30:21 118 n. 215
30:33 151 n. 2
37:20 76 n. 48
37:24 173
40:2 60, 80 n. 59, 160
40:11 118
40:28 45
41:9 45, 160

Isaiah (cont.)
44:13 175 n. 76
45:13 143 n. 303
48:8 136
48:20 126
50:4 121
51:19 118 n. 215
51:23 143 n. 303
59:3 175 n. 76
61:1 121
61:6 123
62:2 211 n. 202
63:15 36 n. 65

Jeremiah
2:10 115, 116 n. 206
2:34 118
3:2 117 n. 213
3:21 118 n. 213
5:7 197 n. 156
6:2 80
6:19 161 n. 34
11:15 157
12:11 108 n. 183
13:7 223 n. 231
13:25 45 n. 101
16:4 119
25:12 52 n. 128
26:6 154
30:10 43
32:31 151 n. 2
33:16 197
34:9 116 n. 206
38:11 118
38:12 118
46:5 192
46:27 43
52:23 223

Ezekiel
1:7 173 n. 71
4:16 173 n. 71
5:1 173 n. 71
9:8 220
14:14 123
14:20 123
19:2 124 n. 241
24:26 209
26:2 178
27:6 116 n. 206
28:3 123
32:21 43 n. 94
32:27 161 n. 34
33:11 135
34:8 50 n. 121
35:9 42
35:10 220
36:8 89 n. 94
38:16 196
43:11 28

Hosea
2:14 67
5:11 28 n. 28
14:6 51

Joel
4:9 121 n. 227
4:12 121 n. 227
4:19 120 n. 223

Amos
5:16 148
8:8 98 n. 151
9:6 145 n. 314
9:7 116 n. 206

Jonah
1:14 120 n. 223

Micah
1:7 192
2:8 151 n. 2
2:9 167 n. 55
3:2 161 n. 34
3:3 161 n. 34
6:8 188

Nahum
1:3 183 n. 108, 183 n. 109

2:9 203
2:13 124, 141, 159 n. 28, 207, 230
3:3 70
3:10 167 n. 55

Habakkuk
1:8 145 n. 313
1:12 206
2:5 145 n. 311
2:8 202
2:10 27 n. 24, 42, 86

Zephaniah
2:6 131

Haggai
1:8 196 n. 154
1:9 196 n. 154, 221

Malachi
1:9 135
2:10 136

Psalms
7:3 136 n. 286
8:8 118
9:16 154
9:17 121 n. 229
10:8 118 n. 215
10:10 118 n. 215
10:14 118 n. 215
13:3 153
18:11 30 n. 44
18:39 210 n. 198, 211 n. 203
18:40 82
18:43 92 n. 115, 211 n. 203
18:46 210 n. 198
19:14 31 n. 49, 42
26:2 220
35;19 121 n. 229, 212
35:27 212
37:9 132
44:27 223
49:6 221
52:2 123
55:16 58 n. 141
56:6 161 n. 34
58:8 86
71:9 211
73:2 27 n. 21
80:14 98
82:2 62
83:7 116
90:4 151 n. 2
90:10 109 n. 187
91:11 213
94:20 212, 219
103:4–7 157
104:12 118
104:29 80, 200
105:28 27
107:27 202
116:6 118
116:12 159 n. 26
119:130 117
120:1 223 n. 231
121:7 219 n. 217
137:1 220 n. 224
140:2 211 n. 202
141:5 58 n. 141
144:13 52 n. 125
145:8 183 n. 109
148:2 146

Job
6:27 42
7:5 86
13:3 135
13:51 80
15:22 148
15:31 80
24:12 42 n. 88
26:12 27
29:2 211 n. 202
31:22 151 n. 2
34:10 180 n. 96
38:13 98
38:15 98
40:19 145 n. 312
40:22 221

Job (*cont.*)
41:25 148

Proverbs
1:22 117
5:7 168 n. 56
7:11 118 n. 214
14:3 211 n. 202
16:27 146
20:21 109 n. 187
28:22 175 n. 76
31:21 118

Ruth
1:8 67 n. 7
1:9 67 n. 7
2:2 175 n. 76
2:8 135, 210 n. 198

Song of Songs
1:4 213
1:7 117
2:7 118
3:5 118
7:2 118

Qohelet
4:14 85
4:8 146
12:5 86 n. 82

Lamentations
1:4 108 n. 183
1:7 173 n. 71
1:10 173 n. 71
1:16 118 n. 214
2:4 173 n. 71
3:60 161 n. 34
3:61 161 n. 34
4:14 175 n. 76

Esther
1:14 27 n. 21
1:16 27 n. 21
1:21 27 n. 21

Daniel
2:35 165
3:8 119
3:12 119
8:26 76 n. 48
9:19 204
9:24 109 n. 187
10:17 105 n. 173
11:12 131
11:23 209 n. 195

Ezra
2:69 131
6:15 57 n. 139
8:2 123
8:25 135, 210 n. 198
9:6 223
10:8 178

Nehemiah
3:13 85
3:14 85
4:1 116
4:2 116
12:44 45 n. 101, 118
12:47 45 n. 101, 118
13:16 45

1 Chronicles
1:6 30 n. 44
2:13 66
3:1 129
3:5 191
4:43 82
5:10 116
5:19 116
5:20 116
6:8 123 n. 236
7:14 116 n. 206
10:3 76 n. 47
10:18 104 n. 171
11:35 104 n. 171
12:2 47, 118 n. 215
12:9 118
12:16 134

12:39 80, 82
13:7 76 n. 47
13:12 104 n. 171, 105 n. 173
17:24 76 n. 47
18:3 28 n. 28
20:8 191
22:9 123 n. 236
22:19 123 n. 236
25:4 123
25:27 123
28:9 76 n. 48

2 Chronicles
6:41 165 n. 48
9:18 178
17:11 116, 129
20:25 206
21:15 118
21:16 116
21:19 119
22:1 116
22:5 85
26:7 116, 131
28:23 221
29:22 43 n. 94
32:13 122
32:17 122
32:30 221 n. 226
33:7 28 n. 26
35:12 169
36:21 207 n. 188

Other Ancient Sources

ATNS 26, 6 149

Ben Sira (see also Mas 1h)
3:11 142 n. 302
3:16 142 n. 302
9:18 142 n. 302
14:1 142 n. 302
15:5 142 n. 302
37:24 142 n. 302
39:17 142 n. 302
39:31 142 n. 302
44:24 142 n. 302
48:12 142 n. 302

CD
II, 10 61 n. 158
XIV, 8 176
XV, 11 159

HazGab
64 109
68 102 n. 161
74 134

TAD
A2.2, 15 165

Other Texts from Dead Sea Region

Jer 3 ver, 1 98

KhQ 1
5 90
8 206

Mur 1
Exod 6:8 196 n. 154

Mur 42
4 151 n. 4

Mur 88 (XII)
Joel 4:5 196 n. 154
Amos 9:6 145 n. 314
Mic 2:9 167 n. 55
Nah 3:10 167 n. 55
Zeph 3:6 121 n. 227
Hag 1:8 196 n. 154
Hag 1:9 196 n. 154

5/6Ḥev 44 16 149 n. 332

XḤev/Se 5
2 (at Exod 13:5) 154 n. 12
4 (at Exod 13:10) 154 n. 12
5 (at Exod 13:14) 154 n. 12

Rabbinic Works

m. Ber.
6:1 62

m. Pe'ah
5:1 62

m. Soṭ.
4:3 62

m. Sanh.
1:6 62
8:4 62

m. Šebu.
3:11 62

t. ʿErub.
8:13 151 n. 4

t. Soṭ.
2:3 151 n. 4

b. B. Qam.
63a 151 n. 4

b. Bek.
7b 151

Word Index

Erroneously spelled words are listed under their proper spellings, except in rare cases.

Hebrew Words

אב, 31, 36 n. 65
אביו/אביהו, 19–20, 25 n. 7, 102, 142–50, 230
אבותו, 36, 145 n. 313
אבד (verb), 200
יאבד, 32 (יאב)
יובדו, 200
אבדן. *See* בדן
אביר, 30 (אביד)
אבית. *See* בית
אבן, 85 (הבנים)
אגן, 175 (אגונות)
אדס = הדס, 104 n. 168
אהב
אהוב (inf. cstr.), 205
אהבה, 101 n. 158
אֹהֶל, 54, 184 (אוהול)
אוב, 54
אוט, 165, 172 n. 67
אופן, 54
אוץ
תוצוו, 126
אוצר, 54
אור
האירותה, 56
יהיר, 105
מאירים, 56
אור, 54
אורה, 54
אורים, 54
אות, 54, 101
אזן
האזינו (imv.), 101 (אזינו)
אזן, 50 n. 123, 54
אזרוע. *See* זרוע
אח, 142, 145 n. 313, 145 n. 314
אחזה, 47 (אחוזה), 107 (אזתמ), 179 (אוחזת)
אחר (verb), 193
אוט/אט, 172
אֵי/אַי, 153
אִי, 130 n. 262 (אים < אם)
אויב/איב, 26–27 (איוב), 54, 119, 121, 129–30, 141, 149 (אוביך), 226
איה, 153
איכה, 153
איככה, 105, 153
אַיִל, 43
אַיָּל, 44 (איאל)
אִישׁ, 85 (הנשים ,היש), 104 (הנשי), 127 n. 251 (היש), 180 (אנושי)
אכזרי, 29 (אגזרי)
אכל (verb), 200
תאכולנו, 201, 214
יאכלו, 111 (< יאחלו), 197 (יואכולם), 215
אכול (inf. cstr.), 48 n. 117, 50 n. 121
אֹכֶל, 51 n. 123, 54
אכלה, 49, 54
אל (God), 24, 32 (א), 43, 95 (על), 95 n. 129 (עאל)
אל (these), 154
אל (to), 24, 33 (אל < על), 76, 93–95, 145 n. 311 (אלו)

אל (not), 94
אֵלֶה, 24, 154
אלוהות, 167
אלוהים, 24 (אלוהוהים), 36 n. 65, 102
  (אלויכה, אלוים)
אלף, 32
אִם, 34
אֹמֶץ, 183 (אמוץ)
אמר (verb), 200
  יואמר/ויואמר, 30, 30 n. 38, 44 (יומר),
    55, 80 (יומר)
  תואמרו, 44 (תמרו)
  תתאמרו/תתיאמרו, 46, 124
אמת, 31
אנה, 153
אנו, 155
אנוש, 48, 180 (אנושי)
אנחנו, 32, 155
אני, 155
אניה, 54
אנכי, 155
אסף
  תוסף, 80, 200
  הספם, 85
אפו, 57
אפך (verb), 189
  יופך, 189
  יופכו, 101–2, 189
אפס, 28 (אפץ), 30 (אכס)
אפר, 92
אקדח/אוקדח, 172
ארב
  יורו, 71
  יורבו, 71, 80 n. 60, 200
ארבע, 30 (אבעים)
ארך
  האריכי, 59
אֹרֶךְ, 51 n. 123, 54, 183 (ארוך)
ארמלות, 166
ארץ, 85 (הרץ, הרצות)
ארדה, 164
ארש
  יארש, 57
ישאש, 166
את/אתי, 155
אתה, 76, 92, 93, 95, 155
אתם/אתמה, 162–63, 234
אתמול. See תמול
אתנן, 67 (אתנם)
ב, 30 (כ), 57 (ביא)
באר, 79 n. 58 (בירות)
בבץ. See בוץ (<בצץ)
בגד
  יבגוד/תבגוד/נבגוד, 136
בדל
  הבדל (inf. cstr.), 101 (בדל)
בדן, 152 (אבדן), 165
בהל (verb), 189
בוא
  באו, 43 (באוו), 132 (בוו), 141
  יבוא, 52 (יבאו), 55, 79 (יבו), 81
  יבואו, 43 (יאבואו), 132 (יבאוו), 141
  תבואינה/תבאנה, 201
  הביאותה, 54, 81, 230–31
  הבאתי, 196
  הביא (inf. cstr.), 79 n. 57 (הבי)
  הביאו (imv.), 125 (הביו), 144
בוז (verb), 188
בוץ (<בצץ), 24
בזה (verb), 188
  בזה, 32 (בזא)
בחיר, 25, 27
בחר
  אבחר, 29, 105 (הבחרה)
  בחור, 37
בינה, 168
בית/אבית, 151–52
בכה
  יבכיון, 134
בכור, 47
בכר
  מבכריה, 26
במה, 44 (באמות)
בן, 3 n. 4
בנה
  בנוית, 134
בניה, 167
בנין, 167
בקיע, 164

בקשׁ
בשקתי, 25
ברא
ברתנו/בראתנו, 79, 189, 226
הבריך (inf. cstr. + suff.), 127
בריאה, 126 (בריה)
ברך
אברכנו, 105 (הברכנו)
מברכים, 24
הבריך, 40 n. 81 (הברך), 127
ברך (= ברכה), 169, 227
בורך/ברך, 171
בשׂם, 66 (בשמין), 232
בשׂר, 69 (בסר)
בתולים, 28
גאון, 53
גאות, 53
גבה (verb), 106
גֹּבַהּ, 51 n. 123, 106
גָּבֹהַּ, 107
גבול, 167
גבורה, 36 n. 65
גדול, 167, 182
גדוף, 178 (גודפים)
גדי, 134
גדל
יקדילו, 29
גֹּדֶל, 51 n. 123, 182 (גדול), 228
גדע, 93 n. 117
גדפן, 164
גוי, 38, 75, 82, 119, 121–22, 128–29, 141, 149, 229
גויה, 70
גור
גר, 30 (גד)
גזע
גיזע, 40 n. 78
גזע, 26, 40 n. 78
גיא, 170 (גי)
גלה
גלו (*qal* pass. part.), 148
מגולי, 194
גם, 34
גמל
גמל, 44 (גמלאם)
גער
תגער, 91
גופן/גפן, 172
גרן, 51 n. 123
גשׂר, 164
דאג
תדאיגי, 56
דאה
וידא, 30 n. 44 (וירא)
דבר
דבר (inf. cstr.), 176 (דברום)
דבר, 27 (דברוו)
דגל, 29 (דקלי)
דוה, 43 (דאוה), 226
דון, 164
דוק, 165
דור, 38
דושׁ
ידש, 30 n. 42 (ידע)
הדש (inf. abs.), 105
דיה, 134
דכא (verb), 188
דכה (verb), 188
דמע, 91
דעה, 59 (דעהא), 91
דֶּרֶךְ, 3 n. 4, 25, 36 n. 65, 170
דרשׁ
ידורשהו/ידרושהו, 211, 215–17, 231
דורשם, 222
-ה = -ו, 159–60
-הא (3fs suff), 60, 160
הֵא, 95 n. 129 (הע)
הגוי, 34 (הוגי), 164, 167
הדושׁ, 110 (חדוש)
הואה/הוא, 6, 15, 15 n. 7, 24, 132 (הוה), 141, 154, 158, 162–63, 230, 234
הוה
יהו, 142, 149, 232
הווה, 62
הוי, 27 n. 20
החרם, 169
היאה/היא, 58, 126 (היה), 154, 158, 162–63, 230, 234
היה
היה, 59 (היהא), 61 (הייה)

היה (*cont.*)
היית/הייתה, 61
יהייה, 61, 227
תהיה (= תהי), 198
נהייה, 61
תהיינה/תהינה, 3 n. 4, 37
היות, 61, 104 (איות)
נהיית, 61 n. 157
היכה, 153, 232
היככה (= MT איככה), 105, 153
הכן (= MT אכן), 105, 153, 232
הכרות, 167
הלזו/הלז, 154
הלך
נאלכה, 47, 86
התהלך (inf. cstr.), 100 (התלך)
-המה/-הם, 16, 16 n. 10, 161–62
המה, 154, 158
המן, 153
-הם = -הן, 162, 164, 231
הִנֵּה, 103 (אנה), 104 (אנה)
הניפה, 168
הנף, 168
הפך (verb), 189
יהופכו, 102
הקרב, 169
הרס
מהורסיך (= MT מהרסיך), 174
-יו = -ו, 142–50
-והי, 16 n. 10, 159, 164, 231, 234
זאת, 27–28 (זוות), 55
זה, 154
זהב, 24 n. 5
זו, 154
זור
האזורה, 46
זידה, 164
זך or זן, 154, 231
זכר
יזכורוכה, 215
זכורני, 222
זלעפה, 175 (זלעופות)
זמון, 167
זמם
יזומו/יזמו, 202, 221 n. 227, 230
זמן, 167
זנה
זנת (*qal* 3fs), 195
זנח
הזנחתני, 193
זעף
זאף, 93 n. 118
זעק (verb), 188
זעקה, 31
אזרוע/ זרוע, 151
זרע
תזרועני, 197, 214, 218
חביב, 109 (הביב?)
חגג
יחגו, 202
נחגה, 202
חגורה, 109 (הגורה)
חדר, 108
חובר, 110
חוה
השתחוות (inf. cstr.), 209
חול, 111 (< כול)
חרטם, 175 (חורטומים)
חזא
חוזא, 110
חזיון, 134
חזק
החזיקה, 108
החזיק (inf. cstr.), 104 (אחזיק)
חֹזֶק, 51 n. 123, 183 (חזוק)
חטא
חוטה/ חוטי/חטא (sing. part.), 42, 86, 189
החטיאום, 125, 141, 144, 229
חטא, 132 (חטאוו), 170 (חט)
חטאת, 36 n. 65, 53, 80, 170
חיד. *See* יחד
חיה
החיות, 101 (חיות)
חיה, 108
חכמה, 49–50 (חוכמה)
חליפה, 95 (על יפות)
חלל
איחל, 41, 59
חלמה, 164

חלץ
  חלוץ, 37
חמר, 30 n. 38 (חמ), 172 n. 64
חנינה, 108
חנם, 175 (חנום)
חנן
  יחן, 202
  יחונכה, 135, 221, 230
  תחון, 202
חֶסֶר, 183 (חסור)
חפה (< חפף), 59 (חופהא)
חפץ, 109 (הפץ)
חצוצרה, 30
חק (< חקק), 47
חקה (verb), 188
חקק (verb), 188
חרב
  וחרבו, 30 n. 38
חרב, 109 (הרב)
חרבה, 49
חרבן, 164
חרגל, 175 n. 80 (חורגול)
חרוץ, 28 (חרוש)
חרס, 110
חרשׁ (verb), 188
חרת (verb), 188
  אחורתם, 216
חשב
  תחושבהו, 217
  יחשובוני, 215
חשה
  החשיתי, 103 (אחשיתי)
חשק, 109 (השק)
טהוב. *See* טהור
טהור, 24, 106
טֹהַר, 24, 51 n. 123, 106
טהרה, 50 (טוהרה), 101 n. 158
טוב and טב, 24 n. 5,
טול
  הטל (inf. cstr.), 100–101 n. 154
טלל, 166, 232
טמא
  וטמיתם, 42
טמאה, 81, 132
טרף
  יטרפו, 136 n. 286
יבשׁ, 42 (יבישה)
יגה
  הוגו, 103 (אוגו)
יגע
  הוגיע (inf. cstr.), 101 (לוגיע)
יגר
  הוגירני, 193
יד, 61 (ייד)
ידה
  הודו (imv.), 103 (אודו), 231
ידע
  ידעתיכהו, 91
  יודיע, 77
-יו = -ו, 142–50, 230
יוד, 164
יום, 30 (מים > ים), 33, 34 (יומים), 66 (ימין), 131 n. 262 (הימים < המים), 231–32
יחד, 25
יטב
  יטב, 41 n. 85
  יטיב, 37
  תטיב, 37
יכח
  הוכיח, 40 n. 81 (הוכח), 108
יכל
  ייוכל, 61 n. 158
ילד
  יולד (*qal* pass.), 191
  ילדה, 192
ילל
  יללו (*piel?*), 194
  יליל, 37 n. 67
  ילילו, 37 n. 67
  הילילו (imv.), 103, (אילילו)
ים (< ימם), 62 (היים)
ימן
  תיאמינו, 47
יסד
  ישד, 69
יסף
  (ה)וסף, 40 n. 81
יסר (verb), 193

יעף, 137 (לעפים)
יפע
  הופיע (inf. cstr.), 103 (אופיע), 231
יצא
  [י]אצאו, 25, 47
  [ו]תצינה, 42 n. 90
  [הו]ציאתנ[ו], 42
  יוציא, 198
  תוציו/תוצוו, 126
יצג
  ויצק, 28 n. 28
יצר
  יצרת, 35 n. 63
ירא
  ירא, 32 (ירה), 86
  יראו, 41, 130, 229
  יראה (inf. cstr.), 205
ירה
  יור, 28
  יורו, 71
  הוריה (inf. cstr.), 208, 231
ירשׁ
  ייארש, 57, 59
  ראש/רש and ראשו/רשו, 43, 136
  תורישון, 31
ישׁב
  יישבו, 41
  תישבנה, 42
  שב, 41
ישׁימון, 178 n. 89 (ישומון)
ישׁע
  הושיענו, 103 (אושיענו)
  מושיא, 92
ישׁר/יושר/ישור, 33–34, 179, 184 (יושור)
יתום, 44 (יאתום)
כאר. *See* כאר/כער below
כבד
  יכבדנני, 3 n. 4, 203
  נכבד, 30
כִּבֵּד, 183, 184 (כובוד, כבוד)
כָּבוֹד, 30 (בוד)
כְּבוּד, 183
כבס
  וכבס, 30
כבשׁ
  כיבשו, 40
  כבושים, 139
כהנה, 48 n. 117 (כוהנה), 179 (כוהונות)
כול
  יכלכל, 32
כון
  הכינכה, 105
  יהכין, 194, 231
כורכובה, 174
כחשׁ
  יכחס, 70 n. 22, 96 n. 138
כי/כיא, 7, 15, 57, 225
כידן, 166, 181, 232
כל/כול, 27 (כוול), 27 n. 23 (כוול), 35
כלא, 24
כליה, 45 (כלאיות)
כלל, 166
כנע
  ניכנע/נוכנע, 40, 191
כנף (verb), 86, 232
כסא, 47 (כסיא), 59
כסף, 69 (כשפו)
כעס
  יכחס (?), 96
כאר/כער
  כארום, 93
  כאורה, 93
כִּפֶּר, 51 n. 123, 184 (כפור)
כרוב, 48
כרע, 25
כשׁל
  אכשיל. *See* שׂכל
כתב
  יכותב/יכתוב, 215, 217
  יכתובו, 36 (יכתובהו), 209
  כותבהא, 222
כתת
  יוכת (*qal* pass.?), 192
  יכתו (*qal* pass.?), 192
ל, 32 n. 50
לא, 32
לאום, 54
לבאה, 124 (לביותיו), 141, 207, 226, 230
להב/לוהב, 106 (להוב), 171, 184 (להוב)

לוה
נלוא, 189
לוז, 165
לחה = לח, 169
לוחי/לחי, 107 n. 178, 172
לחם
הלחם, 110 (חלחם)
לכד
ילכודה, 215
לכודני (inf. cstr.), 213
למעאן/למען, 46, 68, 100, 187–88
לעג
ילעיגו, 193
לקח
יקחו, 192
לוקח (*qal* pass.), 191
ילקח, 192
מוד(ה)/מואד(ה)/מאוד(ה)/מאד(ה), 54, 84, 185–86, 223–24, 234
מאה (מאיות/מאות), 122, 128, 141
מאור, 52–55, 81, 228
מוזנים/מאזנים, 84, 166, 232
מאס
מאשו, 69
מאפלה, 164
מבוא, 28 (מובאיו), 148–49 (מבואי)
מבינה, 168, 227
מבנה, 167
מבנית, 167
מגע, 164
מדבר, 25, 32
מדרוך/מדרך, 174
מה, 33, 35 (סה)
מהתלה, 101 (מתלות)
מוג
נמוג, 32, 35 (נסוג)
מוט
טמוט, 29
מוסד, 32
מוסדה, 31
מוסר, 31
מועד, 32 n. 50
מוצא, 28
מור
תמר, 44 (תאמר)
מחא
ימחאו, 55 (ימחוא), 124 (ימחיו), 141, 190 n. 132
מחה
מחיתה, 40 n. 78
מחמוד/מחמד, 173
מחשבה, 96, 109 (מהשבה)
מחשך, 109 (מהשוך)
מחתה, 40 n. 78 (מחיתה), 108
מטל
מטלים, 77
מטעת/מטע, 169, 227
מטר
המטר, 40 n. 81
מי, 57 (מיא), 60, 225
מכאוב, 31
מכה, 31
מכך
התמכך, 27 n. 20
מלא
מלו, 189
מלאות/מלואת (*qal* inf. cstr.), 52 n. 128, 55, 206–8
מלאות (*piel* inf. cstr.), 124 (מליאות), 141, 206–7
מלאכה, 26 n. 17 (מלכאה), 60 n. 153
מלוש, 165
מֶלֶךְ, 34 (מל)
ממלכה, 34
מן, 35 (-ם), 67
מסחור/מסחר, 174
מעה, 97
מועל/מעל, 171
מעלל, 32
ממוד/ מעמוד, 89, 174, 205
מַעֲנֶה, 42 (sing. מעני), 91
מְעֻנָּה, 91
מערב, 89
מערכה, 29, 91
מעשׂה, 27, 145 n. 313 (מעשו)
מפלג, 169
מצא
נמציתי, 190
מצוה, 36 n. 65, 38, 132–33 (מצאותי), 141, 145 n. 313 (מצותו)

מקדש, 32
מקנה, 36 n. 65
מור/מר, 172
מרדוף/מרדף, 174
מרה
תמר, 44 (תאמר)
וימרו, 44 (ויאמרו)
המרות, 103 (אמרות)
מרט
מורט (*qal* pass.), 191
ממורט, 192
מרר
תמר, 44 (תאמר)
משח
מושחני (inf. cstr.), 212–13
משיכה, 164
משלוח/משלח, 173–74
משוסה/משסה, 174
משפט, 36 n. 65
מתי, 153
מתקל, 166, 232
נא, 176 (נו)
נְאֻם, 54, 56 n. 135, 185 n. 116 (נואום), 186–87
נאן
מנעציך, 95
נאצה, 79 (נצה)
נבא
הנבא (*niphal* inf. cstr.), 103 (אנבא)
נביא, 58, 79 (נבי)
נגד
הגיד, 39 (היגד)
נגה (verb), 107
נֹגַה, 51 n. 123, 107
נגיע/ נגוע, 167
נגח
תנכח, 29
נגע
נגוע, 32
נדה, 110 (נדוח)
נהל
מנהל, 110 (מנחל)
נהר
יהיר, 105
נוא
יאנה, 25, 44 n. 97
הנא, 25, 25 n. 11, 44 n. 97
נום
נום (inf. cstr.), 56 n. 135
נוע
נעוו, 90
נוף
הניפותה, 196
הנפה (inf. cstr.), 101 (נפה)
מהניף, 194
נזה
הזיה, 208, 231
נזל
יזל, 39 (ייזל), 61
נחל
וינחיל, 32
נחשה, 31 (נחה)
נחשת, 108
נטה
נטויה/נטוי, 27 n. 21, 121 (נטואה), 134 (נטוה), 141
הטא, 189
נטש
תטושנו, 214
ניחוח, 111 (ניחוחכם)
נכה
יכה, 31, 46 (יאכה), 198 (= יך)
ויכו, 30 n. 42 (ויבו)
נכנהו, 203
נכה, 59 (נכאי)
נאכר/נכר, 47, 86
נכרי, 120 (נכריאים)
נפש, 36 n. 65
נצב
השיב, 28 n. 28
נצפה, 164
נצר
ינצר, 67
אצורנה, 214
נקב
יקובנו, 214
נקובני, 222
נקה
ינקו, 77

נקי, 119–20
נקף
נוקפו/ניקפו, 40, 191
נשׂא
אשא, 92
תשאו, 34 (תשוא), 39 (תישאו)
נושיאי[ם], 26, 79 n. 58
תנשינה, 190
הנשא (inf. cstr.), 105
נשׂג
תסיג/תשיג, 69
נשׂיא, 126 (נשיי), 128–29, 229
נשא
ישייכה, 61, 126, 129, 141, 229
נשף
נשׁף, 33, 97 (נעשף)
נתך
מתך, 26
נתן
יתן (*qal* pass.), 191
ינתן, 67
נתץ
יתץ (*qal* pass.), 191
סבב
יסובוכה, 221
סוג
אסיג, 104 n. 168
מסיג, 69
סור
יהסירך, 194 n. 149
מהסיר, 194, 231
סחר
סחורה, 96
סכות, 69
סלֶת, 51 n. 123
סמך
יסומכנו, 216
ספר
שפרתי, 69
ספרנו, 30
סקל
יסוקלוני, 217
סרפד, 30, 176 (סרפוד)
סתר
סתרת, 35 n. 63
אהסתר, 194
עבד
יעובדו/יעבודו, 215–16
עבוד (imv.), 48 n. 117, 222
יתעבד, 30
עֶבֶד, 32, 36 n. 65
עבורה, 178 (עובורתמה)
עבר
אברו, 94
יבור, 89
יאבורו, 94
יעובורנה, 33–34, 216
עבורי, 203
עד, 29 n. 35
עדה, 32, 91, 100
עדות, 27, 56 n. 135, 133
עואר. *See* עִוֵּר
עוד
העד (imv.), 105
ואתועדדה, 26, 91
עוה
יעוה, 95
נעוו, 90
נעוות, 36 n. 65
עויה, 63
עול, 62 (עוול)
עולם, 28 (עולום), 90 (לולם), 176 (עולום)
עון, 27 n. 25, 44 (עאון), 133, 141
עועי, 167
עואר/ עִוֵּר, 25 n. 10, 47, 94 (אואר)
עור, 164
עזב
יעוזב/ יעזוב, 211, 214, 216–17
עזוז, 48 (עוזז), 178 (עוזוז)
עזר
יעוזרני, 217
עוזרני, 222
עטה
יעוטך, 216, 218–19
עטה (sing. part.), 42 (עטי)
עילול, 164, 167
עילום, 28 n. 26
עים, 61
עין, 92
עיף, 121 (עאף)

עכשו, 164
על, 16 n. 10, 24, 76, 93–95
  עליו/עלו, 36, 142
עלה
  העלות, 91
עָלֶה, 96 (ההולה)
עלז
  תעלוז, 97
עִם, 24, 91, 92 (אם), 95 (> עת)
עם (> עמם), 24, 34
עמד
  יעמדו, 32
  עמודו (imv.), 203
עמוק, 47
עמס
  עמוס, 96
ענה
  ואענה, 80 n. 59
עניה, 62 (ענייה), 227
ענשׁ
  נאנש, 93 n. 117
עפר, 92
עץ, 25, 28 (עשים), 91
עצב, 32
עצה, 91, 92
עֹצֶם, 51 n. 123, 184 (עצום)
עצר and עוצר, 30 n. 38
ערב
  העריבות (inf. cstr.), 209
ערוה, 94
ערך
  יערוכהה, 214
עָרֵל, 184 (ערול)
ערמה, 49, 228
עֹרֶף, 51 n. 123
עשׂה
  עשיתי, 190
  עשיתם, 189
  עשו, 33
  ישה, 15–16, 23, 89
  יעשה, 15–16, 23, 198 (= יעש)
  עשה (sing. part.), 42 (עשי), 144 n. 312 (עושו)
עשׂרה/עשׂר, 51 n. 124, 88, 89, 92, 93, 172 (עושרות)
עשק
  יעושקנו, 216
  עשׂק (inf. cstr.), 92
עת, 29 n. 35, 95
עתה, 59 (עתהא), 76, 92, 93, 95
פארה, 165–166
פה (פיו / פיהו), 20, 142–50
פח, 66 (פחין), 172 n. 64, 231
פחוז, 172 n. 64
פטר
  נפטר, 29
פלא
  נפלאות, 32, 53, 81
  הפלא, 32 (הפלה)
פנים, 32, 145 (פנו)
פסח, 69 (פשח)
פעל
  אפעולה, 197
פֹּעַל, 184 (פועול)
פועלה/פעלה, 48 n. 117, 90, 179 (פועלת), 212
פענה, 165
פקד
  יפקודהו, 215
  פקוד, 37
פרושׁ, 166, 227
פרי, 44 (פריאם)
פרר
  הפר, 110 (> חפר)
פרשׂ
  יפרושה, 215
פשׁט (verb), 94
פושת/פשת, 172
פתואם, 39 (פיתואם)
פתח
  פתחו, 77, 97
פותי/פתי, 82, 119, 121–22, 129, 141, 170, 171, 173, 229
צבא, 53, 81, 132
צבע, 93 n. 117
צהרים, 48, 217–218
צוה
  צוה, 71 (צפה?), 131 n. 262 (> צה)
  יצווהו, 62
צחצחה, 107 (צצחות)

צחק, 28 n. 28
ציה, 62 (צייה), 121 (ציאה), 141
צנע (verb), 188
צנף
יצנופך, 214
צעק (verb), 188
צער, 164
צפה
צפה, 71
צפון, 24
קבוץ, 178 (קובציך)
קבר
תקוברמה, 216
קובר/קבר, 172
קדוש, 32, 106
קודש/קֹדֶשׁ, 30 (קודו, קוד, קד), 47–51, 106, 184 (קדוש)
קוה
יקוו, 132 (יקאו)
קוים, 132 (קואי), 141
קול, 32, 38
קום
קומה (imv.), 204
הקם, 40 n. 81
קפץ
יקופץ, 26
קצה
קצות (see also קצה (end) and קצת), 27
קצה (end), 27 n. 24, 44–45
קצר
יקצר, 29–30
קֹצֶר, 184 (קצור)
קצת, 27 n. 24, 44–45 (קצאוות), 232
קרא
קרתי, 190
קראו, 192 n. 141
קראו (inf. cstr.), 52, 55
יקרה, 189
יקראו, 192 n. 141
תקרוא, 190 n. 132
קרב
קרבת (*pual* 3fs), 195
קרוב, 25
קריא, 25, 25 n. 12
קשׁוה, 133 (קסאות)
קשב
הקשיבו (imv.), 103 (אקשיבו)
קשות, 164
קושי/קשי, 172
ראה
ראו, 43 n. 96 (ראוו), 132, 142 (ראו/ראואי), 148
ראויה, 79 (רויה)
נרעתה, 94
הראיתי, 39 (היראתי)
רוש/ראוש/רואש/ראש, 25, 52, 55, 74, 77–79, 81, 84, 177 (רואשי), 226, 228
ראשון, 56
ראשית, 74–75
רבו, 133 (רבואותם), 141
רֹבַע, 51 n. 123
רגם
ירגמהו , 3 n. 4, 36 n. 66
רגן
רוכנים, 29
רוגע/רגע, 172
רויה, 134
רוקמה, 51
רחב
נרחב, 109 (נרהב)
הרחיבו (imv.), 103 (ארחיבו)
רֹחַב, 184 (רחוב), 185 (רחובו)
רחוב, 110
רֹחַם, 51 n. 123
רחמון (= רחמן), 180
רחש, 164
רמס
ירמוסהו, 103 n. 163, 215
ירמסוויו, 102–3, 141, 144
רונה/רנה, 173
רע, 42 (ריע), 136 (רעיכה), 230
רעדודיה/ רעדוד, 165
רעיה, 61
רעע
ירועו, 202, 221 n. 227
רצין, 59 (רציאן)
רצץ
רצוץ, 37
רקוח, 178 (רוקחיך)

רוקמה/רקמה, 172
רשׁע (verb), 193
  מרישיעי, 26
רשׁעה, 96 (רשהה)
שׂבע
  שבו/שבאו, 89
שׂדה, 144 n. 312 (שדו), 158 (שדהו)
שׂחק
  ישחקו, 197 (ישחוקו <)
  אשחקה, 198
שׂחק, 28 n. 28
שׂטם (verb), 193 n. 145
  יסטמוני, 69
שׂטמה, 165
שׂכל,
  משכלה, 209
  אשכיל, 25, 33
  השכיל (inf. cstr.), 101 (שכיל)
שׂמח
  תשסח, 108
שׂנא
  [נ]שנאתה, 190 n. 133
שׂפה, 24, 122, 133 (שפאותיכה), 170
שׂרע
  שרוא, 94
שׁ-, 39 n. 73
שׁאה
  השאות (inf. cstr.), 101 (שׁאוות), 132
שׁאון, 53–54
שׁאר, 79 n. 58 (שר)
שׁארית, 79 (שרית), 81, 137, 226
שׁבה
  שבוי, 121 (שבאים)
שׁבוע, 180 (שובועי)
שׁבט, 32 n. 50
שׁובי/שׁבי, 43 (שביא[ם]), 172
שׁבעה/שׁבע, 30, 88
שׁבר
  נשברת/נשברה, 209
שׁגג
  ישוגו, 221 n. 227
שֵׁד, 59 (שדאים)
שׁדד
  תושד, 191
  יושדו, 191
שׁדך, 165
שׁדף
  שׁדוף, 37
שׁוא, 28 n. 28 (צו), 46 (לאשו), 62 (שוו),
  146, 170 (שו), 226
שׁוב
  השיב, 40 n. 81 (השב), 105
שׁוע
  תשויע, 42, 62
שׁועה, 31
שׁחיס, 96 (שעיס)
שֹׁחַד, 111 (שחוד), 184–85 (שוחוד)
שׁחת, 24
שׁטף
  תשוטפני, 216
שׁכב
  ישכוב, 197
  שכוב (inf. cstr.), 205
שׁכן
  תשכון, 197
שׁלהובת/שׁלהבת, 101 (שלבתה)
שׁלושׁ, 89
שׁלח
  אשלחה, 199
שׁלל
  ישלוכה, 202
שׁלם (verb), 193
שׁם, 175 (שואם)
שׁמה, 175 n. 80 (שומה)
שׁמים, 35 (שמי[ם])
שׁמם
  תשם, 108
שׁמע
  ישומעוני, 217–19
  שמעה (imv.), 204
  השמיע, 101 (שמיע)
שׁמע, 25
שׁמר
  ישומר/ישמור, 214–15, 217
  שמורני/שומרני, 222
שׁנה
  שנאתה, 190 n. 133
שׁנים, 32 (שים)
שׁעה
  אשא, 92

שׂען
נשנתי/נשענתי, 88
שׂער, 29
שׁפט
ישפוט, 215–16 (ישופטני)
ישפטו, 29 (ישפטתו)
שפוט (inf. cstr.), 48 n. 117
השפטו, 71
שׁפך
תשופכנו, 216
שֶׁפֶל, 184 (שפול)
שׁקוי, 148 n. 325
שׁקט
השקיט (inf. cstr.), 103 (אשקיט)
שׁרשׁ, 51, 51 n. 123
שׁרת
משרת, 42 n. 89 (משר־ < משריתכה תיכה)
שׁשׁ, 42 (שיש), 92
שׁתה
ישתוהו/ישתהו, 36 n. 66
תא, 176 (תו)
תאנה, 26 n. 17 (התנאה), 60 n. 153
תר/תור/תאור/תואר/תֹּאַר, 51 n. 123, 54, 84, 187
תבונה, 27, 168
תהו, 81 n. 63, 102 (תהוו), 103 n. 162 (תוה), 141, 144
תהום, 101 (תומות)
תוך, 26 n. 16, 27
תור, 47
תורה, 32 (תורא)
תזיז, 165
תוחת/תחת, 171
תלשׁ (verb), 188
אתמול/תמול, 151–52
תמם
תיתם/תתם, 31
איתם, 31 n. 49, 42
התמכך, 27 n. 20
תעות, 56 n. 135
תענית, 121 n. 225
תפראת/תפארת, 87
תופלה/תפלה, 172
תפשׂ
יתפושם, 215
תפושם (inf. cstr. + suff.), 204–5
תפתח, 110

Hebrew/Aramaic Proper Nouns

אבדון, 32
אבירם, 180–81 (אבירום)
אברהם, 31 (אברהרם)
אברם, 31
אופיר, 54
אחז, 34 (אכחז)
אליב/אליאב, 125, 129, 141, 229
אמורי, 119
אסר־חדן , 181 (אסרחודן)
אריאל , 181 (ארואל)
ארם, 54
הוררט/ אררט, 105, 174
אשׁאול. *See* שׁאול
אשׁור, 29 n. 38 (אשו)
בית שׁאן, 79 n. 58 (בית שׁן)
בנימין, 67 (בנימים)
דדנים, 181 (דודנים)
דויד/דוד, 38
דיפת, 30 n. 44
דניל/דניאל, 47, 81 n. 63, 102, 129, 141, 229
הוררט. *See* אררט
חופרי/חופר, 172
חוזקיהו/חזקיהו, 173
הנע, 101 (נע)
יאור, 54 n. 131
יהודה, 32, 103 (יאודה)
יון, 44 (יואן)
יעקוב, 92
ישׁעיהו, 92
ישׂחק/יצחק, 28 n. 28, 109 (ישהק)
יורדן/ירדן, 175 n. 80
ירושלים/ירושלם, 31
ישׂראל, 31
אשמעל/ישמעאל, 66
כנעני, 120 n. 222
כתי, 82, 119–20, 127–29, 141, 226, 229
לויאים/לויים/לוים, 120

מדין, 67 (מדים)
מושה, 31
ממוכן, 27 n. 21 (מומכן)
מסה, 69 (משה)
מערב, 98 (מארבא)
מצרי, 120 n. 222
נבאות, 121, 141
נכו, 57 n. 139
סדם, 181 (סודם)
סלע, 96 (סלה)
סמון, 98 (שמון)
עדלמי, 181 (עודולמי)
עיפה, 176 (עיפו)
עמלק, 29 (עמלך)
ערער, 181 (עורערו)
עשׂו, 43 (עישׂאו), 147
עשׂר, 98 (אסר)
פלשׁתי, 120
צער, 95
קיר, 181 (קור)
ראובן, 54, 81 (רובן), 137, 144
ריפת, 30 n. 44
רמליהו, 181 (רומליהו)
שׂראצר, 181 (שראוצר)
שְׁאוֹל and אשאול, 2 n. 3, 32, 81, 152
שָׁאוּל, 54 n. 131
שׁבא, 176 (שבאו)
שׁובנא/שׁבנא, 174
שׁלח, 109 (שילה), 178 n. 89 (שולח), 181
שׁמעון, 98 (שמון)
תרצה, 181 (תורצה)
תרשׁישׁ, 30 n. 38 (תרשישה < תלשישה)
תרתן, 181 (תורתן)

Aramaic

אית, 46
גיף, 47 (גאף)
חוי
  אחוית, 70
חטא
  חטו, 189
טמא
  אטמיו, 189
כוי
  כוייה, 62
נכרי, 119
פותי, 47
קשׁוט/קשׁוט, 185
ריס, 47 (ראס)
שׁעה, 98 (שתא)
שׁרי
  שׁריוא, 126 n. 246, 144 n. 309

Author Index

Abegg, Martin G., 3, 4, 39, 41, 52, 68, 69, 72, 74, 84, 90, 147, 155, 157, 159, 162, 177, 195, 197–200, 202, 204, 208, 220
Alexander, P., 7, 31, 38, 91
Allegro, John M., 66, 71, 91, 93, 164, 190
Andersen, Francis I., 48, 78, 80, 85, 144, 146
Baden, Joel, 193
Baillet, Maurice, 29, 40, 91, 95, 164, 172
Bar-Asher, Moshe, 17, 45, 79, 102, 109, 128, 148, 154, 165, 167, 183, 193
Barr, James, 20, 41, 58
Bauer, Hans, xii, xv, 45, 115, 116, 117–19, 157, 175, 178, 180, 186, 191
Baumgarten, Joseph M., 34, 159
Ben-Ḥayyim, Ze'ev, 15, 29, 47, 60, 83, 114, 135, 146–48, 152, 195, 210, 212, 221
Bergsträsser, G., 16, 19, 66, 82, 87, 115–19, 123, 128, 175
Beyer, Klaus, 70 n. 24
Biber, Douglas, 15 n. 6
Blau, Joshua, 13, 16, 17, 19, 58, 78, 82, 83, 114, 115, 117, 119, 123, 124, 131, 186
Bloomfield, Leonard, 16
Bolozky, Shmuel, 83, 117
Breuer, Yohanan, 17, 114
Brockelmann, C., 115
Brønno, Einar, 70, 210, 212
Carmignac, J., 39
Charlesworth, James H., 14, 25, 28, 31, 34, 91, 94, 98, 108, 109, 159, 176, 180, 183, 208, 223,
Collins, John J., 10
Cross, Frank Moore, 33, 71, 109, 163, 193
Delitzsch, Friedrich, 27, 28, 30, 76, 109
Dimant, Devorah, 26, 49, 122, 125, 162, 165
Doudna, Gregory L., 159
Elizur, Binyamin, 102, 134
Elwolde, John F., 2, 51, 71
Eshel, E., 24, 98, 109
Eshel, H., 98
Farrar, Christopher, 83
Fassberg, Steven E., 158, 163, 194, 204, 210, 233
Fitzmyer, Joseph A., 14, 70
Flint, Peter W., 4, 104, 126
Forbes, A. Dean, 48, 78, 80, 85, 144, 146
García Martínez, Florentino, 2, 24, 25, 28, 31, 40, 50, 55, 62, 66, 91, 93, 95, 108, 159, 164, 172, 176, 180, 191
Gogel, S. L., 41, 137, 146
Gordis, R., 79
Goshen-Gottstein, Moshe H., 71–73, 76, 113, 210
Gumpertz, Y. F., 66, 127
Harrington, Daniel J., 20, 31, 34, 43, 44, 108, 110, 167, 178, 192, 196, 202
Harviainen, Tapani, 138, 139
Hayon, Yehiel, 83
Hurvitz, Avi, 2, 14
Isbell, C. D., 66
Janssens, G., 70, 84, 212
Joüon, P., xv, 66, 68, 80, 88, 115, 117, 118, 206, 208, 209, 212, 216
Kesterson, J. C., 14
Khan, G., 65, 68, 70, 84
Kim, Yoo-Ki, 47
Kister, Menahem, 18, 50, 71, 93, 164, 165, 167, 168

Könnecke, Clemens, 181
Kutscher, E. Y., 1, 3, 13–15, 17, 19, 29, 33, 34, 39, 43–48, 50, 57–62, 67, 68, 72, 73, 75–78, 85–87, 89–93, 95–97, 99, 101–3, 105, 107–11, 113, 125, 129, 132, 133, 135, 139, 140, 146, 148, 152, 155, 157, 159, 160, 164, 171–74, 176–78, 181, 183, 184, 188, 190–92, 194, 195, 197, 201, 206, 210–12, 216, 218, 220, 221
Leander, Pontus., xii, xv, 45 n. 101, 115 n. 202, 115 n. 203, 116, 116 n. 208, 117, 117 n. 212, 118 n. 214, 118 n. 215, 119, 119 n. 217, 157 n. 20, 175 n. 76, 178 n. 88, 180 n. 95, 186 n. 121, 191 n. 137
Licht, Jacob, 208
Martin, Malachi, 3, 4, 91
Mercati, G., 212
Meyer, Rudolf, 13, 20, 139, 140
Milik, J. T., 25–27, 89, 94, 95, 98
Morag, Shelomo, 6, 13, 14, 17, 18, 140, 143, 210, 220
Moreshet, Menahem, 191, 193
Morgenstern, Matthew (Moshe), 47, 86, 102, 163
Muraoka, T., xv, 2, 19, 33, 40, 46, 47, 57, 59, 66–68, 70–72, 75, 79, 80, 86, 88, 98, 105, 115, 117–19, 124, 128, 137, 143, 144, 151, 152, 157, 158, 163, 185, 187, 189, 191, 206, 208, 209, 212, 216, 220, 223, 232
Murtonen, A., 73, 74
Naudé, Jacobus A., 14, 15
Newsom, Carol, 24–26, 29, 30, 35, 40, 43, 44, 80, 88, 91, 93, 94, 101, 106, 108, 138, 149, 164, 180, 182, 184, 200
Nitzan, B., 69
Nöldeke, Theodor, 126
Norton, Jonathan, 82
Novick, Tzvi, 165
O'Connor, M., 76, 191
Ohala, J. J., 15
Pérez Fernández, Miguel, 95, 152
Poirier, John C., 17
Puech, Émile, 88, 89, 92, 93, 98, 103, 132
Qimron, Elisha, 1–4, 6, 13, 16, 18, 27–31, 35, 36, 39–44, 46–50, 53, 55, 57, 60, 63, 66, 67, 69, 70, 72–75, 78, 79, 82, 85, 88, 90–96, 100–4, 106, 108–10, 120–22, 124–30, 132–37, 140, 143, 144, 148–52, 155, 156, 159, 161, 162, 164, 167, 169–72, 175–85, 191–93, 199, 200, 207, 208, 210, 213, 220, 221
Rabin, Chaim, 14
Ravid, Dorit Diskin, 66
Rendsburg, Gary A., 13, 14, 69, 72, 102, 128, 134
Reymond, Eric D., 63, 187
Sáenz-Badillos, Angel, 71
Schniedewind, William M., 13, 14
Schoors, Antoon, 4, 49
Schuller, E., 24–26, 30, 33, 35, 39, 40, 71, 80, 88, 91, 93, 94, 101, 105, 108, 138, 148, 164, 180, 182, 184, 200
Seely, D., 40, 165
Segal, J. B., 149
Segal, M. H., 62
Skehan, Patrick W., 94, 104, 210
Smelik, Willem F., 232
Smith, Mark S., 105
Sperber, Alexander, 104
Stegemann, Hartmut, 24–26, 30, 35, 39, 40, 80, 88, 91, 93, 94, 101, 108, 164, 180, 182, 184, 200
Steiner, Richard C., 68, 70, 156, 161
Strugnell, John, 20, 31, 34, 43, 44, 108, 110, 167, 178, 192, 196, 202
Stuckenbruck, Loren, 25, 28, 180, 208, 223
Sukenik, E. L., 15
Tigchelaar, E., 24, 25, 28, 31, 40, 50, 55, 62, 66, 91, 93, 95, 108, 159, 164, 172, 176, 180, 191, 218, 220
Tov, Emanuel, 6–10, 20, 23, 24, 26, 31, 33–35, 37, 58, 60, 62, 66, 82, 92, 96, 98, 109, 184, 218–20
Uffmann, Christian, 117, 129
Ulrich, Eugene, 4, 26, 27, 29, 31, 33, 61, 76, 89, 90, 94, 96, 97, 104, 107–10, 121, 124, 126, 132, 160, 184, 211, 216

VanderKam, James C., 4, 57, 89, 94, 95
Vegas Montaner, Luis, 163
Vermes, G., 7, 31, 38, 91
Waltke, Bruce K., 76, 191
Watson, Janet C. E., 83
Weinfeld, M., 40, 165
Weitzman, Steve, 18
Wernberg-Møller, P., 107, 183
White, S., 24, 62, 92, 96
Wright, W., 114
Yadin, Yigael, 14, 25, 91, 92
Yalon, Henoch (Hanoch), 183, 191
Yardeni, Ada, 102, 109, 134
Yeivin, Israel, 144, 207, 210–13, 220, 222
Young, Ian, 14, 160
Yuditsky, Alexey (Eliyahu), 71, 72, 84, 102, 121, 134
Zevit, Z., 158

www.ingramcontent.com/pod-product-compliance
Lightning Source LLC
Chambersburg PA
CBHW021819300426
44114CB00009BA/238